10 August 2010

Dear Sylvia and hen,
   It was such fun being
with you both in Marlbao!
   With my warmest best wishes,
Pslema

Shame and Humiliation
Presidential Decision Making on Vietnam

Adopting a psychoanalytical approach to politics, Blema Steinberg examines the impact of personality dynamics on the decision making of Lyndon Johnson, Richard Nixon, and Dwight Eisenhower during the Vietnam War, arguing that these dynamics influenced the critical decisions they made about U.S. intervention in Vietnam.

Steinberg focuses on the narcissistic personality, identifying it as intensely self-involved and preoccupied with success and recognition as a substitute for parental love. She asserts that narcissistic leaders are most likely to use force when they fear being humiliated for failing to act and when they need to restore their diminished sense of self-worth. Providing case studies of Johnson, Nixon, and Eisenhower, Steinberg describes the childhood, maturation, and career of each president, documenting key personality attributes, and then discusses each one's Vietnam policy in light of these traits. She contends that Johnson authorized the bombing of Vietnam in part because he feared the humiliation that would come from inaction, and that Nixon escalated U.S. intervention in Cambodia in part because of his low sense of self-esteem. Steinberg contrasts these two presidents with Eisenhower, who was psychologically secure and was, therefore, able to carry out a careful and thoughtful analysis of the problem he faced in Indochina.

Shame and Humiliation reveals how personality traits affect our perception of reality and offers a powerful demonstration of the impact of psychodynamics on presidential decision making.

BLEMA STEINBERG is associate professor of political science, McGill University, a psychoanalyst in private practice, and an affiliate in the Department of Psychiatry at the Jewish General Hospital, Montreal.

Shame and Humiliation

Presidential Decision Making on Vietnam

BLEMA S. STEINBERG

McGill-Queen's University Press
Montreal & Kingston • London • Buffalo

To Arnold

© McGill-Queen's University Press 1996
ISBN 0-7735-1391-4 (cloth)
ISBN 0-7735-1392-2 (paper)

Legal deposit second quarter 1996
Bibliothèque nationale du Québec

Printed in Canada on acid-free paper

Published simultaneously in the United States by
University of Pittsburgh Press

This book has been published with the help of a grant from
the Social Science Federation of Canada, using funds provided
by the Social Sciences and Humanities Research Council of Canada.

McGill-Queen's University Press is grateful to the Canada Council
for support of its publishing program.

Canadian Cataloguing in Publication Program

Steinberg, Blema S.
    Shame and humiliation: presidential decision making on Vietnam
    Includes bibliographical references and index.
    ISBN 0-7735-1391-4 (bound)
    ISBN 0-7735-1392-2 (pbk.)
    1. Vietnamese Conflict, 1961–1975 – United States. 2. United States –
    Politics and government – 20th century. 3. Eisenhower, Dwight D.
    (Dwight David), 1890–1969 – Psychology. 4. Johnson, Lyndon B.
    (Lyndon Baines), 1908–1973 – Psychology. 5. Nixon, Richard M.
    (Richard Milhous), 1913–1994 – Psychology. I. Title.
    DS558.S74   1996   959.704′3373   C96-900063-4

This book was typeset by Typo Litho Composition Inc.
in 10.5/13 Baskerville.

Contents

Preface

The links between American foreign policy and psychoanalysis are not immediately obvious. I began my academic career as a political scientist and subsequently developed an interest in the dynamics of decision making in foreign policy. Yet I soon became dissatisfied with arguments that ignored psychological factors. I explored the literature on social and cognitive psychology, but after doing so I concluded that even these theories were insufficient to explain certain puzzles.

Then I embarked upon my training as a psychoanalyst. From my own psychoanalysis and my work with patients, I was given first-hand empirical evidence of the power of unconscious needs, fears, and drives and their role in shaping behaviour. Psychoanalytic theorizing, with its emphasis on the role of unconscious determinants in the moulding of character and personality, seemed to offer a valuable way of understanding many of the critical decisions reached by foreign-policy leaders.

As someone whose formative years as a young academic were shaped by the intense debate over the Vietnam War, it seemed to me that that conflict provided a textbook example of the way in which the character and personality of successive presidents had played a significant role in shaping political decisions. I became increasingly persuaded that the type of psychologically informed study that Alexander and Juliet George had written in 1956 about Woodrow Wilson and his inability to compromise over American entry into the League of Nations needed to be done for presidential decision making on Vietnam. And so I came to write this book.

Whereas the Georges focused primarily on Wilson's obsessive-compulsive character, my study looks at narcissism as a central organizing construct and examines the impact of feelings of shame and humiliation and the extent to which these were reflected in major decisions taken during the war. The presidents whose Vietnam decisions I examine are Dwight Eisenhower, Lyndon Johnson, and Richard Nixon. Conspicuously absent from this list is John F. Kennedy. My interest is in comparing decisions to effect a major escalation – those taken by Johnson and Nixon – with a decision to forego intervention – that taken by Eisenhower in 1954 – and to explore the role that feelings of shame and humiliation played in each of them. Although Kennedy gradually increased the number of military advisers in Vietnam, his assassination meant that he never had to confront the issue of whether to escalate the conflict by sending military forces, or to de-escalate it and forego further intervention. Thus, Kennedy's behaviour and the motivations for his decisions on Vietnam lie outside the perimeters of my study.

I owe an enormous debt of gratitude to the many people who facilitated my research. To my analyst, Dr Paul Lefebvre, who helped me to understand the relationship between narcissism and issues of self-esteem and to resolve my writer's block, I offer my deepest appreciation. I am grateful as well to my family and close friends; their warmth and encouragement during the lengthy writing process sustained me over the inevitable humps.

Despite their busy schedules, colleagues read either part or all of the manuscript and offered wise advice and encouragement. In this regard, Michael Brecher and Janice Gross Stein were particularly generous with their time and effort. The constructive suggestions of Alan Alexandroff, Rhoda Cohen, Alexander George, Eva Lester, Peter Loewenberg, Mireille Steinberg, Yaacov Vertzberger, and Vamik Volkan also significantly enhanced the quality of the book. Comments by anonymous reviewers alerted me to areas of ambiguity and offered valuable strategies for improving the manuscript.

A number of research assistants, Keith Bergner, David Carment, Michael Colson, Jason Fox, Grainne Mulvaney, Terry McNamee, and Mark Peranson, worked with me over the years. Their diligent library searches, bibliographic preparation, xeroxing, editing, and genuine interest in the manuscript were enormously helpful. My editor, Curtis Fahey, did an admirable job of eliminating jargon and fixing other stylistic lapses. As a result of his superb skills, the book's readability has been greatly enhanced. I wish to thank, too, Howard Baker for his meticulous work on the index.

The Social Sciences and Humanities Research Council of Canada provided me with generous funding for the research, the Faculty of Graduate Studies at McGill University gave me a grant to help complete the manuscript, and the Social Science Federation of Canada supported publication with its Aid to Scholarly Publications Programme. Without their invaluable assistance, this book might never have seen the light of day. At the secretarial level, Rosalie Hodson provided helpful assistance and kept the project moving; Florian Fullum, my computer guru, was available for every crisis.

And finally, my husband, Arnold, was given a new definition of *ménage à trois*: husband, wife, and her word processor. He demonstrated unfailing support and good humour throughout the many evenings and weekends that I worked; I am deeply grateful for his editorial suggestions, his love, and his belief in me and the manuscript.

Blema S. Steinberg,
Montreal, Quebec
June 1995.

Shame and Humiliation

Introduction

Such is our fascination with the Vietnam War that the literature on the subject, from the descriptions of those who fought there to official memoirs and analyses by historians and political scientists, continues to grow. How did the United States become involved in a war that was to be so politically divisive? In 1954 Dwight Eisenhower refused to escalate American military involvement at Dien Bien Phu; eleven years later, Lyndon Johnson began the bombing of North Vietnam and the commitment of American fighting forces to South Vietnam. And in 1969 and 1970, Richard Nixon stepped up American involvement with his decision to bomb, and then invade, Cambodia.

Was it simply that the American commitment to South Vietnam had increased so dramatically that, by 1965 and 1969–70, Johnson and Nixon had no choice but to act as they did, and that any president faced with the same issues would have made the same decisions? The evidence suggests that both presidents had options that did not demand an expansion in the level of American involvement. Nevertheless, they chose the option that required an increase in the use of force. What explains their behaviour?

Most published accounts addressing the topic fit into three categories. Systemic analyses highlight factors external to the state such as the structure of the international system and Cold War superpower competition.[1] Closely linked are analyses that focus on factors that operate at a level between the international system and the individual. These include the role of ideology, a commitment to the doctrine of containment,[2] domestic political pressures,[3] bureaucratic politics,[4] and group dynamics.[5] Individual-level analyses explore aspects of cognition (beliefs, analogical reasoning)[6] and motivation – the characters and personalities of senior decision makers.[7] At this level of analysis, the emphasis is frequently on the president,[8] and the war in Vietnam is explained either as a function of his beliefs and his use of analogies or of his flawed character and/or the pathological advisory system he created.

This study also situates itself at the individual level of analysis and focuses on the president. It starts from the premise that our understanding of how and why Lyndon Johnson and Richard Nixon chose to escalate the conflict in Vietnam, while Dwight Eisenhower desisted, remains incomplete. Missing is an explicit focus on those dimensions of their emotions, character, and personality, and the factors that shaped them, that can help explain the way they perceived external and internal environmental pressures. I argue that a psychoanalytically focused exploration of feelings and emotions, particularly those involving shame and humiliation, as they operate within the construct of a narcissistic personality structure can expand our understanding of presidential decision making during the Vietnam War.

A psychoanalytic interpretation of decision making in foreign policy runs the risk of two major types of criticism: that it ignores traditional explanations that revolve around environmental constraints and opportunities, thus opening the door to charges of reductionism; or, if it does acknowledge a role for these explanatory factors, it provides few guidelines to assess the importance of a psychoanalytic component. Yet to argue, as I do, that narcissistic political leaders are particularly vulnerable to issues of shame and humiliation and that an actual or potential loss of self-esteem will affect their decisions does not denigrate the critical importance of external reality; rather, it focuses on how wounded narcissism interacts with environmental constraints and opportunities to shape decisions. Thus, my argument is not designed as a substitute for any of the alternative explanations of the Vietnam War; instead, its more modest goal is to complement them through an exploration of the psychodynamic context in which all of these variables may have been operative. The emphasis will be on how concerns relating to issues of shame and humiliation act as a psychological lens through which external reality is perceived.

For the reasons suggested above, this study will not provide answers to the question of the precise weight to be accorded a psychoanalytic as against competing explanations. Rather, it offers a way of looking at reality that underscores the impact of unconscious determinants – needs, drives, emotions, and feelings. It demonstrates both theoretically and empirically the relationship between shame, humiliation, and narcissism, and the conditions under which perceptions of domestic and foreign variables encouraging aggressive behaviour are likely to be fostered.

Sometimes the concepts of character and personality are used interchangeably. More typically, character is used to describe those stable, typical, personality traits and attitudes that tend to cluster together and enable us to recognize a particular person. A psychoanalytic perspective attempts to explain how and why certain clusters of traits occur together with greater than chance frequency[9] and their impact on behaviour. In the early days of psychoanalysis, studies of these clusters initially gave rise to such descriptive labels as the oral, anal, phallic, and genital character; more recent psychoanalytic theory uses such terminology as hysterical, obsessional, schizoid, paranoid, narcissistic, and borderline to identify character types.

Narcissistic personalities are characterized by intense self-involvement and an inordinate preoccupation with success and fame. Achievements often become a substitute for the love they failed to receive, and their interpersonal relations are frequently marked by a lack of empathy for other people. They oscillate between feelings of grandiosity and omnipotence – seeming not to care about or need other people – and feelings of inferiority and low self-esteem. Because of their need to accomplish, to feel superior, and to be acclaimed, they are particularly susceptible to feelings of shame and humiliation when they fail to live up to their often unrealistic ego ideals. In chapter 1, I utilize a psychoanalytic perspective to explore the theoretical links between intense feelings of shame and humiliation and the narcissistic personality, with a view to explaining the behaviour of such individuals. The reader unfamiliar with psychoanalytic ideas should be aware that the concepts developed in the introduction and chapter 1 will become more comprehensible in light of the evidence presented in the succeeding psychobiographical chapters and its relationship to presidential decision making.

As I will argue, Lyndon Johnson and Richard Nixon were two highly narcissistic individuals who suffered from painful feelings of shame and humiliation. It was these feelings, in the overall context of their narcissistic character structures, that played an important role in shaping their presidential decisions on Vietnam. Dwight Eisenhower, in contrast, was not a narcissistic personality. As a confident, psychologically well-adjusted individual, his political decision making in 1954 was less coloured by his psychological needs and fears.

As I began thinking about the similarities and differences between the three presidents,[10] it seemed to me that important clues to the development of their characters and personality traits would be found in their personal histories – relationships with parents, siblings, and peers – and the impact of those factors upon their innate characteristics. Chapters 2 and 4 explore the making of the narcissistic characters of Johnson and Nixon, respectively, with special attention to their experiences of shame and humiliation. In Chapter 6, I document Eisenhower's healthy narcissism and the relative absence of experiences of shame and humiliation in his make-up, and I suggest some reasons for the development of his character profile.

Rather than look at the presidents chronologically, I chose to explore Eisenhower's character development, and his decisions on Dien Bien Phu, last. My primary interest and focus is on the "dog that barked," that is, the two presidents who escalated the war and the role that their narcissistic, shame-prone personalities played in those decisions. Eisenhower, as the one president who, when faced with a crisis, chose not to escalate American military involvement, was the anomaly. An exploration of the linkages between his psychodynamics and his Vietnam decisions offers an interesting counterweight to the linkages between the wounded narcissism of Johnson and Nixon and their decisions to escalate the conflict.

In Chapters 3, 5, and 7, I examine, respectively, the Vietnam decision making of Johnson in 1965, Nixon in 1969 and 1970, and Eisenhower in 1954, with particular emphasis on the role that shame and humiliation (the case of Johnson and Nixon) or the lack of it (the case of Eisenhower) played in the making of their foreign policy.

The concluding chapter offers cross-case comparisons and explores the common elements in the life experiences of Johnson and Nixon that account for their narcissism and their sensitivity to issues of shame and humiliation. It examines the ways in which they differed from each other, and from Eisenhower. It also addresses the issue of ego-strength in explaining how Johnson and Nixon, despite their shame-prone characters, were finally able to tolerate an end to American involvement in the Vietnam War. And finally, it raises the larger implications of the impact that personality variables can play in foreign-policy decision making.

In undertaking this investigation, I am indebted to the myriad of scholars who have done research on presidential decision making during the Vietnam War, to the numerous biographers of Presidents Johnson, Nixon, and Eisenhower, and to the many psychoanalysts, beginning with Freud, who have explored the issues of shame, humiliation, and narcissism. Their findings have provided me with a wealth of information that facilitated my own analysis.

1 Shame, Humiliation, Loss of Self-Esteem, and Aggression

Psychoanalysis has much to say about the importance of shame, humiliation, and reactions to narcissistic injury in the conduct of human affairs. This chapter explores the way in which shame and humiliation are linked to issues of narcissism and how damage to self-esteem and the experience of narcissistic injury can affect an individual's emotional responses. He or she may be influenced in the assessment of external and domestic environmental pressures because of a need to please others. Alternatively, narcissistic issues may colour the choice of an aggressive response as a way of restoring feelings of pride, honor, and dignity and re-establishing psychic equilibrium.

The experience of shame and humiliation is an all-too-human phenomenon, and there is widespread agreement in the psychoanalytic literature as to what this experience entails at the affective level. Shame is generally viewed as an unpleasant emotional experience implying an acute lowering of self-esteem. Arising in response to being slighted, put down, dishonoured, disgraced, humiliated, mortified, and so on, it involves feelings ranging in intensity from shyness and bashfulness to embarrassment. Thus, it is possible to speak of the "shame family of emotions."[1]

A review of the psychoanalytic literature on shame and humiliation reveals that these terms are used virtually interchangeably and that, within the spectrum of affects connoting shame, feelings of humiliation are generally considered one important variant. Feelings of shame and humiliation can be observed typically in response to what might be called a shame-inducing event. Such an event may involve only self-exposure, but it usually includes elements of rejection.[2] In its most intense form, shame can also be understood as a specific form of anxiety evoked by the imminent danger of unexpected exposure, humiliation, and contemptuous rejection.[3]

The shame-filled individual perceives himself/herself as having failed to live up to ideal standards which he/she accepts (an ego ideal). "Shame might be related to 'I cannot see myself as I want to see myself or as I want others to see me.'"[4] Unlike the guilty act for which one can make confession, expiation, penance, or reparation, the shameful act seems an indictment of the individual.[5] In the experience of shame, there is a drop in self-esteem occasioned by the failure to measure up to the ego ideal. Shame is thus a narcissistic reaction evoked by a lapse from the ego ideal.[6] The more ambitious and peremptory (narcissistic) the ego ideal is, the more painful is the wound about failing and the more pervasive is the narcissistic anxiety about yet more mortifications of such nature – in other words, the more shame-prone is that person.[7]

For A.O. Kris, the expression of shame "reflects punitive unconscious self-criticism" which can become part of a vicious cycle of self-deprivation and excessive "demandingness." Feeling deprived, yet narcissistically entitled, and not recognizing that they themselves are the source of criticism and deprivation, shame-prone people make their demands upon a world that usually responds with little sympathy. Because of their characteristic all-or-nothing, black-or-white, either-or attitudes, such individuals assume that if they are in any way culpable then they are totally culpable. To avoid the painful affects of shame and humiliation, they externalize the punitive unconscious self-criticism and believe that it is the outside world that is critical.[8]

Feelings of humiliation, as a variant of shame, seem to necessitate the presence of "another," either an internalized disapproving parental figure or its representation in the external world. When a child is chastised, some aspect of the idealized parent is lost, but in order to maintain a stable – if no longer real – object image, the ego introjects a sense of parental omniscience which is retained in the superego. This representation and the experience of devaluation in its presence contributes to the experience of humiliation.[9] In the experience of humiliation, in contrast to shame, the attack on self-esteem is felt to be less deserved and more unjustified;

therefore, it is more likely to elicit a punitive response directed at an external target, not at oneself.[10]

When shame-prone individuals perceive their own pride, honour, or dignity, or that of a narcissistic extension of themselves (for example, their children or their country), as having been attacked and successfully undermined, the response pattern is frequently one of humiliation coupled with a desire to avenge the insult. As a corollary, individuals whose self-esteem is heavily bound up with notions of pride, honour, and dignity tend to be vulnerable to experiences of humiliation.[11]

PSYCHOANALYTIC EXPLANATIONS OF SHAME AND HUMILIATION

If psychoanalysts are in general agreement on the affects that characterize the shame experience, they offer different hypotheses as to the psychodynamics that produce feelings of shame and humiliation. These can be roughly categorized into three major groupings: those that emphasize drive-defenses, those that explore the role of object-relations and struggles of autonomy and individuation, and those that stress the impact of narcissism. For some individuals, the dynamics elaborated in all three approaches may be equally operative, while for others, one or another may predominate. Because the evidence for drive-defense explanations is more dependent on insights gleaned from a psychoanalytic setting, I have chosen to apply both object-relations concepts and theories of narcissism in the explanation of the shame and humiliation experienced by Presidents Johnson, Nixon, and Eisenhower.

Psychoanalysts initially interpreted shame as a defense against unacceptable sexual drives.[12] Freud stressed the importance of self-exposure in reactions of shame, stating that self-reproach for a sexual act in childhood can easily turn into shame "in case someone else should find out about it."[13] Shame and disgust were mental forces which acted to "impede the course of the sexual instinct and like dams, restrict its flow." They served to inhibit the expression of sexuality in the latency child.[14] In a similar vein, both Freud and Abraham underscored the role of shame as a defense against scoptophilia – essentially the wish to see the genitals of the parents[15] – while Jacobson and Fenichel viewed shame as a reaction to the loss of instinctual control over urethral, anal, and phallic instinctual impulses.[16]

A second approach to understanding the shame experience draws upon object-relations theory and the individual's struggle with separation, identity-formation (individuation), and autonomy. Rather than a consideration of shame as a defense against drive components, it emphasizes the role of internal objects and interpersonal relations in the development of shame. In his study of the eight stages of man, Erik Erikson labels the second stage "autonomy vs. shame and doubt" and relates shame to anal-phase struggles between the child's struggle for autonomy and parental attitudes towards toilet training and faecal products. "From a sense of loss of self-control and foreign over-control comes a lasting propensity for doubt and shame."[17]

Otto Rank suggests that shame is an emotional reaction to the child's realization of differences which is accompanied by a sense of inferiority.[18] In G. Kaufman's view, there is no more humiliating experience than to have one's relative lack of power, in relation to another, continually rubbed in one's face.[19] The intense feelings of shame provoked by such experiences are often exacerbated by memories of earlier feelings of inadequacy, the product of oedipal competition and rivalry.[20] A person may deal with feelings of inferiority by displaying increased aggressiveness, by attempting to deprecate the competitor, or by fantasizing himself or herself as superior, as in megalomania.[21]

A third major approach to the analysis of shame and humiliation links it more directly to issues of narcissism and self-esteem. From this perspective, shame arises when narcissistic wishes are abruptly disappointed and concerns of self-esteem unexpectedly violated. In *Beyond the Pleasure Principle*, Freud writes that infantile sexuality, doomed to inevitable disappointment by the limits on the child's physical development, leaves the child with feelings of loss of love and failure. As he observes, "His own attempt to make a baby himself, fails shamefully. The lessening amount of affection he receives, the increasing demands of education, hard words and an occasional punishment – these show him at last the full extent to which he has been scorned … [The child's] loss of love and failure leave behind them a permanent injury to self regard in the form of a narcissistic scar."[22]

Expanding on this theme, Bela Grunberger describes the infant as an outcast in two worlds: it is unable to satisfy its instinctual urges or achieve narcissistic satisfaction.[23] The result is a humiliating sense of powerlessness, which is frequently referred to as a narcissistic wound or narcissistic injury.[24] For these reasons, Leon Wurmser calls shame "the veiled companion of narcissism,"[25] while R. Bursten observes that "shame is the enemy of the grandiose self and makes the narcissist feel unacceptable to the omnipotent object."[26]

Narcissism, at its most basic level, can be understood simply as self-love. It includes what is known as a "libidinal investment" in oneself that reflects a normal sense of entitlement. Healthy narcissism is a requirement for all humans in order for them to be able to master their environment and the psychological demands they encounter in the course of their development (separation-individuation, oedipal rivalry, and so on). In this context, narcissism can be considered a prerequisite for self-esteem.[27] A leader who possesses a healthy kind of narcissism feels comfortable in his/her role and is able to sustain it without lapsing into grandiosity. But not all narcissism is healthy. At one end of the spectrum there is a normal feeling of entitlement and healthy self-esteem. Farther along, there is an exaggerated libidinal investment in the self, the narcissistic personality.[28] And at the far end, there is the "malignant" or "archaic" narcissism[29] that characterizes the type of person who utilizes aggression in order to support a pathological need for self-esteem.

Individuals and leaders with a narcissistic personality organization – those whose narcissism extends beyond appropriate feelings of entitlement and healthy self-esteem – are preoccupied with their self-importance and fantasies of endless success and lofty rank. Even when they do satisfy their goals, it does not seem to be enough because their ambitions are anchored not in reality but in fantasized helplessness; there is a driven "pleasureless" quality to their ambitions which even high office may fail to satiate because of an unresolved feeling of emptiness and a need to expunge feelings of shame.

There is an apparent paradox in the work life of narcissistic individuals. They may be quite successful professionally and appear to devote their energies to socially productive endeavours. But their efforts are really exhibitionistic, designed to gain recognition, fame, and glory. The search for renown and adulation that animates these individuals springs from their excessive self-preoccupation, intense ambition, and grandiose fantasies.[30] But underlying this quest is an inner emptiness and uncertainty about themselves and their acceptability.

One way of interpreting this behaviour is as a narcissistic reaction against feeling insignificant – the fear of being considered a nobody. Narcissistic leaders seem to be haunted by an inner voice telling them they do not amount to anything. They then become convinced that the world also sees them in the same light. To assuage these feelings, they have a strong urge to prove the world wrong. They are determined to get even, to enjoy a vindictive triumph, and to make it to the top in spite of all the forces arrayed against them. Their need to compensate for the wrongdoing done to them (imagined or not) becomes an overpowering force that explains their incredible drive.

Although narcissists demand admiration, they themselves lack a genuine capacity to share in the good fortune of others. They quickly become envious and begrudging. They are self-centred and their emotional involvement with other people is often shallow. Indeed, others are seen as extensions of the self, who are there only to supply admiration and gratification. Thus, the narcissist surrounds himself/herself with admirers and sycophants and requires a constant stream of adulation from them. But when the follower is no longer useful to the narcissist, he/she can be suddenly dropped without a backward glance. The supporter is valuable only insofar as he/she provides the narcissist with a mirror for his/her own grandiose reflections; he/she is not seen as a separate individual with needs of his/her own.

The narcissist is often extremely charming and delightful to be with, but an aspect of the "special" quality of these individuals is the feeling of entitlement they convey. They expect special treatment from others, anticipate that others will do what they want, and are angered when others fail to live up to their unreasonable demands. They regularly ignore the rights and needs of others in the service of their own self-aggrandizement. Their personal exploitativeness reveals a disregard for the feelings and needs of others, and, not surprisingly, a major inability to sustain loyal relationships over time.[31]

Although the narcissist behaves as though he/she were self-sufficient in a superior way, close scrutiny of his/her behaviour reveals that he/she is vulnerable and goes through complicated manoeuvres to avoid being hurt. One technique he/she adopts is to feign cold indifference and envelop himself/herself in what has been described as the "glass bubble." But this merely underlines the narcissist's intense feelings of inferiority and overdependence on the approving attention of others.[32]

It is true that virtually every individual is concerned with issues of self-esteem. All the character defenses – repression, regression, reaction-formation, projection, introjection, idealization, identification with the aggressor,[33] and so on – have, among other functions, a narcissistic one: they protect self-esteem.[34] But those individuals whose character defenses seem specifically, and almost exclusively, designed to protect or enhance self-esteem are the narcissistic personality types. And within this category are to be found many political leaders whose choice of a career in the public eye is frequently determined by a ceaseless search for mirroring objects to shore up their fragile self-esteem.[35]

The leader with a narcissistic personality who is intelligent, talented, and creative may be able to transform his/her environment (for example, by repeatedly winning elective office) so that the outer world can "feed" the hungry inner world.[36] But he or she will continue to experience an insatiable need to maintain a grandiose self-image and to be vulnerable to criticism and rejection which in turn leads to feelings of shame and humiliation. "Indeed, humiliation is for [him/her] the ultimate degradation – the humiliation of dependency, the humiliation of defeat."[37]

THE PSYCHOGENESIS OF NARCISSISM[38]

In the earliest stage of development, the phase of primary narcissism, the infant does not distinguish itself from others. It experiences the external world (its mother) as part of itself. This is the first stage of psychosexual development in which the infant and young child's libidinal interests are centred on itself and its own body. Then he/she begins to differentiate himself/herself from others and, according to Freud, has two libidinal (love) objects: "himself and the woman who tends him, thus one can postulate a primary narcissism in everyone."[39] Because self-love is so satisfying, Freud says, the individual is reluctant to forego the experience of narcissistic gratification when he was truly "His Majesty the Baby."[40]

As the young child experiences the frustrating reality of the external world's less-than-perfect response to his/her needs, he/she becomes increasingly aware that he/she is no longer the centre of the universe. The inevitable loss of this original state of perfection stimulates the creation of an "ego ideal" (a standard of perfection that later comes to include social and cultural ideals) which serves as a replacement for the lost narcissism of his childhood – the time when he/she was his/her own ideal. The narcissistic aim of being loved and approved by one's self merges with the desire to be loved and approved by the ideal internalized parent, the superego.[41]

Freud states that narcissism is never overcome but only rechanneled, because it represents an especially complete and profound mode of gratification and humans are loath to abandon a pleasure once experienced. If the "ego ideal" is immature, not well integrated with the superego (the "ideal ego"),[42] this rechanneling will be ineffective and will lead to the quest for immediate gratification regardless of the appropriateness of the setting or the object, or to the pursuit of narcissistic perfection.[43] If, on the other hand, the ego is mature, narcissism may serve as a stimulus for the achievement of the highest ideals.[44]

In "normal" child development, the "mirroring" response of the mother, her admiration and loving attention, leads the child to feel special and highly valued. This enviable position is maintained by an important psychological mechanism – "splitting." The very young child is unable to tolerate the bad aspects of itself and its environment and to integrate them with the good ones into a realistic whole. The infant splits the good and the bad into the "me" and the "not me." By rejecting all aspects of itself which do not conform to an ideal self, the infant is able to maintain an idealized self-image. With "good enough" caretaking, the child is able to integrate the good and the bad aspects of itself into a more integrated whole and does not continue to employ "splitting" as a major psychological defense.

If a child is either traumatized and/or disillusioned by his caretakers during this critical period of development, the formation of an appropriate sense of self may be impaired, resulting in a "fusion of ideal self, ideal object and actual self image, as a defense against an intolerable reality in the interpersonal realm."[45] In other words, the normal tension between the actual self on the one hand and the ideal self and ideal object on the other is eliminated by the creation of an inflated self concept within which the actual self, the ideal self, and the ideal object are confused. Such damage can occur in several ways. Children rejected by cold, ungiving, or depressed mothers who manifest covert but intense aggression may be left emotionally hungry, with an exaggerated need for love and admiration and a concealed rage at their parents that is frequently displaced onto others.

Another form of rejection pertains to the cold and hostile mother who values her child only for accomplishing what is important to her; she cannot let her child fashion a separate identity because she sees him/her as an extension of herself. Her own sense of perfection seems to depend on her child's perfection. In this situation, the child quickly learns that it is loved not for itself but for its ability to gratify the parent's need for success and recognition. These children often occupy a pivotal position in their family structure, such as being the only child, the only "brilliant" child, or the one who is supposed to fulfil the family aspirations.[46]

Children who are singled out as "special" may be driven to accomplish as a way of ensuring that the maternal love they crave will not be withdrawn. They are apt to develop a grandiose self as a way of denying both the absence of genuine parental caring and their consequent rage. In their fantasies, these children identify themselves with their own ideal self-images in order to deny normal dependency on external objects.[47] Thus, grandiosity can be understood as a "manic" defense against the depressive anxiety of feeling small, helpless, abjectly dependent, and deeply envious.[48]

Otto Kernberg portrays the narcissistically prone infant as so frustrated and hateful as to be unable to tolerate hope, the possibility of anyone's offering him/her anything pleasurable or sustaining. So little is forthcoming, the child concludes, that it is better to expect nothing, to want nothing, to spoil and devalue everything that may be offered. The resulting "grandiose self" is experienced as complete, perfect, and self-sustaining. "I am/have everything. You are/offer nothing." This position serves as both an expression of and a defense against explosive envy and oral aggression, and the only secure solution in a world experienced as treacherous and sinister. Maintenance and protection of the grandiose self becomes the central psychodynamic motive, resulting in a contemptuous and disdainful manner of relating to others.[49]

Narcissistic illusions of omnipotence and grandiosity protect the narcissistic individual from the dreadful state in which he/she spent much of the first several years of life, depending on others for protection and care yet perpetually dissatisfied, victimized, and enraged. The establishment of the grandiose self removes the psychic pain of this situation, and, once established, the grandiose self perpetuates the devaluing assumptions about others which made its establishment necessary in the first place.[50] It creates a "vicious circle of self-admiration, depreciation of others, and elimination of all actual dependency. The greatest fear of these [individuals] is to be dependent on anybody else, because to depend means to hate, envy, and expose themselves to the danger of being exploited, mistreated and frustrated."[51]

Grandiose "mirror hungry" narcissists, then, hunger for confirming and admiring responses to counteract their inner sense of worthlessness and lack of self-esteem. Yet, no matter how positive the responses they receive, they are insatiable and continue to seek new audiences from whom to elicit the attention and recognition they crave. This type of personality structure is a defensive adaptation to rage and envy. In adapting to its environment in this way, the child can build the foundations of someone who is so superior and self-reliant that he/she is above being injured. Whenever the "grandiose self" is threatened, the child will attempt to replenish its narcissistic supplies in order to maintain its self-esteem. But should that fail, the response to the awareness of vulnerability, neediness, and dependency that originated with unsatisfied oral needs will be envy and narcissistic rage – an urge to lash out and punish.[52]

The child's second mechanism for remedying frustration and incompleteness is to attach itself to an ideal object (Kernberg)[53] or an idealized parental "imago" (Heinz Kohut).[54] This is the fantasized image of the all-powerful, all-knowing, all-giving, all-loving parent. The "ideal hungry" self gains a sense of being complete and worthwhile by experiencing itself as connected to and united with its idealized object. The unconscious fantasy is "if I am not perfect, I will at least be in a relationship with someone perfect." Idealized people on whom the child depends frequently turn out to be projections of their own aggrandized self-concept.[55] For healthy development, the growing child and then the adolescent needs to be gradually and repeatedly exposed to a disillusionment in self and object.[56] If, however, de-idealization occurs suddenly or traumatically, idealization will be reinforced as a refuge from persecutory anxiety and murderous rage towards bad objects,[57] which are, none the less, needed for survival.

These two central psychic mechanisms of the narcissist, "I am perfect" and "You are perfect, but I am part of you," are employed in order to preserve a part of the original infant experience of narcissistic perfection. And in adolescence, these narcissistic formations may intensify as a result of the emotional turbulence of this period.[58] Moreover, the way in which they function leads to difficulties in interpersonal relationships. In their dealings with other people, narcissistic personalities oscillate between two poles. Either they concentrate perfection and power upon their grandiose selves and turn away disdainfully from an outside world to which all imperfections have been assigned, or they idealize important others as a way of partaking in their perceived grandiosity and omnipotence.

Although it is true that the ideal-hungry narcissist tends to be more prevalent among subordinates and followers, it is often part of the psychological make-up of the narcissistic political leader as well. "Ideal-hungry" narcissists experience themselves as worthwhile only so long as they can relate to individuals whom they can admire for their power, prestige, beauty, intelligence, or moral stature. They continue to search for such idealized figures, but they are constantly disappointed as their inner sense of emptiness cannot be satisfied.

NARCISSISM AND AGGRESSION

For the most part, the term aggression is used in psychoanalysis to describe both non-destructive and destructive behaviour. Non-destructive aggression appears to be a ubiquitous finding of the normal infant's strivings toward assimilating and mastering the self and the environment.[59] In contrast, destructive aggression involves enmity, hostility, or hatred, that is, the entire gamut of intentional or purposive harm to the object ranging from the inflicting of pain or humiliation to death or annihilation.[60]

Two distinctive approaches to an understanding of destructive aggression can be discerned. The first begins with the premise that aggression is either an instinct or a drive that arises endogenously and emerges spontaneously. The second strategy analyses aggression as a reaction to exogenous stimuli.

In *Beyond the Pleasure Principle*, Freud described aggression as a special and self-subsisting instinct arising independently from libido and operating "beyond the pleasure principle." He developed his ideas further in *Civilization and Its Discontents*, focusing on aggression in the light of thanatos – the death instinct which carries each of us to the grave. His conclusion was that man's natural aggressive instinct is the derivative and main representative of the death instinct which exists alongside Eros. There is a need to harm and destroy, which often finds frustrations to serve as a rationale; but if there are no causes to be found, no rationales, the need for the discharge of aggression may overrun the defensive controls that normally inhibit its expression and aggression emerges spontaneously.

Melanie Klein also believes that aggression originates in the death instinct. Moreover, because of the persecutory terror she sees as the consequence of the death instinct, Klein maintains that aggression is a central force in the creation of psychic structure, one that comes into play early in life and continues throughout. In her view, primitive aggression is with us always and hostile destructiveness is never far from love and devotion. Klein portrays the infant as beset with terrifying anxieties involving the containment of aggression, and she regards early development as a movement from paranoid and depressive anxieties towards a more integrated and secure sense of reality.[61]

Anna Freud notes that while there are important differences in functioning between sex and aggression, an impression of their sameness remains, derived from the way in which various tools for aggressive discharge are borrowed from one or the other of the libidinal stages; so, for example, the teeth during the later part of the oral stage for the aggressive purpose of biting; excrement during the anal stage for the aggressive purpose of dirtying, polluting; the penis in the phallic phase for aggressive display. In fact, almost any part of the infant's or young child's body can serve the same aggressive purpose: the voice, for expressing anger, rage, fury by screaming and crying; the mouth for aggressive spitting; the feet and legs for kicking; the hands, fists, arms for hitting; indeed the musculature as a whole for aggressive attack.[62]

Kernberg also underscores the role of instinct in the narcissistic expression of aggression while acknowledging that "it is hard to evaluate to what extent this development represents a constitutionally determined strong aggressive drive, a constitutionally determined lack of anxiety tolerance in regard to aggressive impulses, or severe frustration in their first years of life."[63] Later, he laments the excessive importance attached to environmental failures as an explanation for aggression. This leads, in his view, to a neglect of the clinical importance of unconscious conflict. He expresses concern that a focus on the traumatizing conditions which are understood to precede and underlie aggression ends up allowing individuals to rationalize their aggressive reactions as a natural result of the failure of other people in their past.[64] For Kernberg, aggression is not a justifiable response to a situation but an unjustified, distorted, prestructured set of proclivities brought to a situation that are exacerbated by the denial of the existence of aggressive fantasies and wishes.[65] He also observes that inappropriate or excessive expressions of aggression are characteristic of the severely narcissistic personality. "When primitive aggression directly infiltrates the pathological grandiose self, a particularly ominous development occurs, perhaps best described as malignant narcissism." In this category are those narcissistic individuals whose grandiosity and pathological self-idealization are reinforced by the sense that they can triumph over fear and pain through inflicting fear and pain on others.[66]

In contrast, non-drive theorists see aggression as a response to the environment. For Joseph Sandler, the attempt to account for aggressive behaviour by postulating an underlying aggresive drive is tautological. To say we are aggressive because of an aggressive drive is to elevate a descriptive concept into an explanatory one. He introduces the notion of "the capacity to be aggressive" as a given, inherited by the species. This capacity, in his view, is mobilized and used by the ego in relation to its attempts to avoid unpleasure and pain.[67]

Ironically, Freud subsequently came to wonder whether aggression might not be provoked by frustration. A decade after he had conceptualized the death instinct as the source of aggression he wrote: "No, man must be naturally good or at least good-natured. If he occasionally shows himself brutal, violent or cruel, these are only passing disturbances of his emotional life, for the most part provoked, or perhaps only consequences of the inexpedient social regulations which he has hitherto imposed on himself."[68]

His daughter, Anna, comments that as the ego matures and the defenses against psychic conflict and anxiety are developed, the child and then the adolescent may exhibit aggression as a response to "the aggression of the adults in whose eyes he felt guilty." Having exchanged passive for active, through "identification with the aggressor," he/she is then able to direct his/her own aggressive acts against those same people,[69] or against others towards whom the anger has been displaced.

For Harry S. Sullivan, aggression operates largely as a defense against the profound helplessness generated by the experience of anxiety,[70] while, for W.R.D. Fairbairn, aggression is a reaction to deprivation and lack of gratification of the infant's intense dependency and object-seeking.[71] Harry Guntrip characterizes aggression as "a reaction to the working of elementary fear, anxiety, and flight."[72]

If one regards aggression as a response to subjectively perceived endangerment, this allows us, according to Stephen A. Mitchell, to keep what is most helpful about the two polarized traditional approaches to aggression. From the drive-theory side comes the notion that aggresssion is a biologically based, physiologically powerful, and universal force which plays an inevitable and central role in the generation of experience and the shaping of the self. From the non-drive-theory side comes the idea that aggression is not a pre-psychological push looking for a reason but always a response to endangerment within a personally designed subjective world.[73] "A double determination of aggressive behavior – endogenous and cultural – suggests itself as the most likely."[74]

To the extent that environmental stimuli are implicated in destructive aggression, several possible causes have been advanced that stress difficulties in the parent-child relationship: John Bowlby looks to parental absence and issues of separation, Daniel Stern addresses breaks in attunement between parent and child, Harry S. Sullivan examines parental anxiety, Donald W. Winnicott explores the impact of the overly protective parent and the child's sense of impingement, and Jerome Kagan also underlines the aggressive impulses that can be stimulated in the child as a result of its constantly being interrupted or interfered with.[75] Underlying the sense of endangerment that these circumstances arouse is the issue of wounded narcissism that appears to be an important linchpin in the process.

In an effort to reconstruct speculatively the earliest provocation of aggression, Heinz Hartmann invokes Freud's assumption that the neonate tends to project all discomforts and tensions to the outer world and to assign all gratification or pleasure to the self. The self and its acknowledged extensions are seen as, a priori, good and lovable, and others are seen as bad, the objects of suspicion and potentially the natural objects of violent attack, especially if they create tensions or fail to gratify.[76]

The child's primitive feelings of pleasure and unquestioned security are undermined as it comes into contact with a less than gratifying environment. The infantile fantasy of omnipotence, of being able to subject the uncooperative object world, including one's own body, to the wishes of the infantile ego (primary narcissism) diminishes, producing uncontrollable feelings of helplessness, anxiety, and rage. These represent narcissistic injuries that necessitate continuous compensatory measures. In this context, self-esteem plummets and attempts to restore the feelings of infantile bliss can produce defensive narcissistic self-inflation. This state of self-inflation is intensely competitive as a rule. "I am bigger than you, I am better, I am the best." Such a crude type of comparison easily lends itself to being used for purposes of aggressive competition since the very process of self-inflation necessitates devaluation and contempt for the other.[77]

For Robert Waelder, it is withdrawal of love by another, or defeat in competitive striving, that makes it difficult to continue to love oneself and produces extreme and vindictive rage.[78] Failure to achieve and feelings of inadequate gratification can, moreover, create conditions of traumatic helplessness that range from the inner or outer threat of death, or castration, to such complex matters as the experiencing of profound insult or humiliation and the need for vengeance. In a similar vein, Heinz Kohut postulates that destructive aggression emerges out of excessive frustration with an unempathic environment. Under normal circumstances, the child manifests healthy assertiveness, which Kohut likens to fundamental biological units, organic molecules. Only under extreme pathological selfobject failures[79] does healthy assertiveness break down into hostile destructiveness, much as organic molecules may be broken apart into inorganic molecules. Kohut observes that aggression arises from the matrix of archaic narcissism and expresses itself in the phenomenon of narcissistic rage. Ridicule, shame, humiliation, contempt, and conspicuous defeat tend to provoke narcissistic rage; empirically, Kohut argues, the narcissistically vulnerable individual responds to actual (or anticipated) narcissistic injury either with shamefaced withdrawal (flight) or with narcissistic rage (fight).[80]

Addressing the relationship between narcissistic pathology and rage, Kohut notes that such individuals are sensitive to external provocations; they have "rage-and-revenge-prone personalities."[81] In his final work, *The Restoration of the Self*, Kohut concludes: "In essence then, I believe that man's destructiveness ... arises originally as a result of the failure of the selfobject environment to meet the child's need for optimal ... empathic responses ... Destructive rage, in particular, is always motivated by an injury to the self."[82]

Observational data on aggression in children seems to confirm this proposition. It suggests that the human infant is not born with a certain quality of hostility or hostile destructiveness which it must discharge. Henry Parens notes that, while "the normal-enough neonate is born with a capacity to experience and express rage ... born with a ready-to-function apparatus of rage-experience-discharge, which is not acquired," this apparatus does not discharge spontaneously from endogenous pressure. Rather, Parens argues, "a unique condition was required for rage to appear: the intensely-felt experience of excessive, sufficient unpleasure." He comments that, although aggression emerges as a reaction to danger and threat, all babies at times seem to feel endangered and threatened. "It appears even in what seems to be excellent child-endowment and child-object circumstances."[83]

Although virtually everyone tends to respond to shame with some feelings of anger and embarrassment, the most violent forms of narcissistic rage arise in those highly narcissistic individuals for whom a sense of absolute control over their internal and external environment is indispensable. This occurs because the maintenance of self-esteem and indeed of the self depends on the unconditional availability of the approving-mirroring functions of an admiring object, or on the ever-present opportunity for a merger with an idealized one.[84]

For G. Rochlin, when narcissism is threatened, that is, when the approving-mirroring or the idealized object is withdrawn, humiliation ensues and self-esteem is injured. A lowering of self-esteem and the accompanying disappointment, hurt, and rage mobilizes aggression to provide relief from the overpowering sense of diminished worth.[85] Acting on the rage by behaving aggressively converts the sense of helplessness into a sense of mastery and in so doing raises self-esteem.[86]

A study of some of the great classics of literature reveals the understanding their authors had about the relationship between aggression and injured narcissism. The characters of Medea, Achilles, Othello, and Captain Ahab are eloquent testimony to the vulnerability of human self-esteem and the compelling need to repair its injury with acts of vengeance and hostility.[87]

Psychoanalytic approaches that focus on the experience of shame and humiliation offer us a way to understand some of the aggressive foreign-policy decisions of narcissistic leaders. Foreigners, in whom we place little value and to whom we are ordinarily indifferent, provide a convenient repository for the narcissist's rage, as aggression, born of shame and humiliation, is displaced onto outsiders.[88] The evidence suggests that, when faced with conflicting recommendations from their advisers as to the merits of using force, there are two sets of circumstances in which narcissistic shame-prone leaders are more likely to escalate a conflict. Both of these operate partially at an unconconscious level. The first is when decision makers are feeling intensely humiliated and need to act aggressively in order to restore their diminished sense of self-worth.[89] In these situations, aggressive behaviour will be a function of an unconscious need to supplant feelings of impotence with those of power. The second is when leaders are fearful about being humiliated should they fail to act. Here, forceful behaviour may not be a displacement for aggressive feelings that belong elsewhere. Rather, such behaviour may be motivated by a fear of losing face lest inaction be challenged by idealized advisers.

While issues of shame and humiliation and their impact on the perception of the environment do shape behaviour, this does not mean that narcissistic personalities, by definition, always give free rein to these feelings, ignoring any ego or superego constraints. Truly malignant narcissists whose grandiosity and omnipotence is untrammeled by any ego-reality testing may exhibit few restraints on the expression of aggressive impulses. But many narcissistic individuals possess good ego functioning and, in response to changing social and political contexts, may demonstrate the capacity to tolerate their feelings of shame and humiliation rather than displacing them onto the outside world.

2 Lyndon Johnson: The Humiliated Narcissist

The Johnson administration's decisions to escalate American military involvement in Vietnam, beginning with Operation Rolling Thunder in February-March 1965, and then to continue with a substantial increase in American fighting forces in July 1965 have been the subject of countless analyses focusing on a wide variety of explanatory variables. Largely ignored is the contribution that Johnson's personality and character played in shaping those decisions. More specifically, Johnson's narcissistic need to avoid any potential shame or humiliation made it important that he take no action that would subject him to any suggestion of cowardice or raise questions about his competence to manage American foreign policy. To understand the nature of the president's emotional vulnerabilities, an examination of the factors that shaped his character development from childhood into adulthood is essential.

Lyndon Johnson was born on 9 August 1908, the first child of two extraordinarily different parents. His mother, Rebekah Baines, was the daughter of parents who had money, position, and respectability. Rebekah's father, Joseph Wilson Baines, was a lawyer, educator, and lay preacher in the Baptist church in Blanco, Texas, and his daughter regarded him as a paradigm of religious ideals, moral thought, and civic duty. In the late 1870s he had served Texas as secretary of state and afterward as a member of the state legislature, where, as Rebekah told her son, "he thrilled the chambers with eloquent speeches on the rights and duties of mankind, the evil of liquor, the importance of cleanliness in thought and deed, and the iniquity of speculation."[1] With her father's encouragement, Rebekah attended Baylor University – one of a small number of Texas women to attend college at that time – where she majored in literature and planned to write a novel about the Old South before the Civil War.

Shortly before her father's death, Rebekah finished her formal education and returned to Fredericksburg, Texas, where she taught elocution and wrote for some newspapers. At the suggestion of her father, she arranged an interview with Sam Johnson, Jr, who had taken Joseph Baines's seat in the legislature. A "whirlwind court-ship" began in the spring of 1907 when Sam, who "was enchanted to find a girl who really liked politics," began visiting Fredericksburg, some twenty miles away, at every opportunity. His crude and often vulgar language, hard drinking, and lack of formal education troubled her, but he was "dashing and dynamic" and, like her father, a man of "principles" who seemed destined for better things.[2]

Eight months after her father's death, Rebekah Baines married Sam Johnson and moved to the small shack on the long shallow slope leading up from the muddy little river that was to be her home. The college graduate, lover of poetry, and soft-spoken, gently dreamy-eyed young woman found herself transplanted to a world in which, like the other farm wives of the Pedernales valley, she would be forced to endure back-breaking labour. To her eldest son, Lyndon, Rebekah expressed her profound discontent, describing in painful detail the ordeal of her life on the Pedernales with Sam Johnson. "To her mind," Johnson said, "his life was vulgar and ignorant. His idea of pleasure was to sit up half the night with his friends, drinking beer, telling stories, and playing dominoes. She felt very much alone. The first year of her marriage was the worst year of her life. Then I came along and suddenly everything was all right again. I could do all the things she never did."[3]

Condensed into those reminiscences are the memories that Johnson had of his mother's undoubted unhappiness and deprivation. But the contrast that he portrays between his mother's feelings before and after his birth is striking. It suggests some of the unresolved oedipal longings for his mother and the concomitant jealousy that Lyndon harboured for his father, as well as his grandiosity in thinking that his birth was so momentous an event in his mother's life as to make "everything all right again." As for Rebekah, her joy at the birth of her son Lyndon is incontestable. She seems to have viewed him as so special that she could never acknowledge his delivery by a midwife, the local physician arriving several hours later.[4]

Lyndon Johnson was named to fulfil his father's ambition. His mother had wanted to name him for some heroic character in a book; his father, who had so desperately wished to be a lawyer, wanted him named for a lawyer. After squabbling over the matter for three months, during which time young Lyndon was simply called "the baby," Sam finally got his wish. He suggested the names of three of his close friends who were lawyers: Clarence Martin, Dayton Moses, and W.C. Linden. When Rebekah rejected the first two, Sam asked, "Would you call him Linden?" Rebekah wrote that, following a long pause, she replied: " 'Yes, if I may spell it as I please, for L-y-n-d-o-n Johnson would be far more euphonious than L-i-n-d-e-n Johnson.' 'Spell it as you please,' said Sam. 'I am naming him for a good smart man … We will call the baby for him and for your father.' 'All right,' I responded, 'he is named Lyndon Baines Johnson.' "[5]

When he was nearly six months old, Rebekah wrote to her sister-in-law in Lyndon's name. "I can sit alone now and perform many amusing capers. My father says that I am quite an orator and translates my speech into political axioms. Mother thinks I have the studious look of a professor and is always wondering what problems I am struggling to solve."[6] In this letter we have an early, but often repeated, expression of the divergent wishes of Sam and Rebekah for their son's future: for his father, it was the active life of the politician; for his mother, it was the more contemplative, intellectual life of the mind.

When Rebekah and Sam attended a picnic near Stonewall in the spring of 1909, Lyndon greeted each neighbour with a smile and tried to scramble out of his father's arms to reach them. According to his mother, one of them exclaimed, "Sam, you've got a politician there. I've never seen such a friendly baby. He's a chip off the old block. I can just see him running for office twenty-odd years from now." And neighbors remembered how Sam beamed as his boy was praised.

Encouraged by the affection and praise, and blessed with a prodigious intellect, Lyndon became the prototype of the gifted child. He learned the alphabet from blocks before he was two; he knew

the Mother Goose rhymes and poems from Longfellow and Tenny-
son by the age of three; and he could read and "spell most anything
that he could hear" by the time he was four.[7] "I'll never forget how
much my mother loved me when I recited those poems," Lyndon
said later. "The minute I finished she'd take me in her arms and
hug me so hard I sometimes thought I'd be strangled to death."[8]
The intensity of Rebekah's pleasure at her son's prowess would be
matched in later years by the depth of her disapproval when he
failed to achieve what she had mapped out for him.

The birth of a sibling is an inevitably dislocating experience for a
child, especially an only child who has been on the receiving end of
his parents' undivided attention. When Lyndon was two, Rebekah
gave birth to a namesake daughter. In the next six years, she was
followed by three other siblings, Josefa, in 1912, Sam Houston in
1914, and Lucia in 1916. While most children adjust to the birth of
rivals for parental love, Lyndon's experience of being "a household
idol"[9] seems to have instilled in him a determination to maintain
his close ties with his mother.

From the age of eighteen months, Lyndon had begun wandering
away from home, and, as he grew older, the pattern intensified.
Scoldings and spankings from his parents did little to deter him. In
Lyndon's recollection of one of these episodes, he recalled that his
mother "became very frightened when she … couldn't find me.
She had two smaller children in the house and couldn't locate me."
He also remembered that, while his father searched the field for
him, his "mother stood and held the baby in her arms."[10] It is very
likely that this constituted a memory condensation of a number of
similar incidents (a "screen memory") in which Lyndon perceived
his mother's preference for the babies over him. This could have
stimulated his determination to get his mother's attention back in
any way he could, and to punish her for his fall from grace.

For the child that had been displaced by two younger siblings,
seeing his mother's anguish and tears at his repeated disappear-
ances served to undo the anxiety that he was no longer central to
her existence; it was a way for Lyndon to deny the reality of his siblings' impingment on his life. In his fantasy, Rebekah's behaviour
indicated that he was still the most important person in her life.
Running away may also have bolstered his sense of "specialness":
he could force his parents to suspend their activities and make
him the centre of their undivided attention. The very repetitive-
ness of the behaviour suggests that, at a deeper level, Lyndon felt

unsure of his special position and had to keep testing his parents' love.

Lyndon's constant need to be the centre of attention expressed itself in a variety of ways. His mother dressed him in red Buster Brown or white sailor suits, or in a cowboy outfit, complete to a stetson hat. Lyndon not only did not object to being dressed differently from the other boys who wore farm clothes, he insisted on it. His cousin, Ava Johnson Cox, explained: "He wanted to stand out." When Kate Deadrich, his teacher, excused one of her students to use the privy out back, the student had to write his or her name on one of the two blackboards that flanked the back door. The other students would write their names in small print; whenever Lyndon left the room, he would reach up as high as he could and scrawl his name in capital letters so huge that they took up not one but both blackboards. His schoolmates could still remember – seventy years later – that huge LYNDON B. on the left blackboard and JOHNSON on the right.[11] Although young Lyndon took great pains to distinguish himself in the classroom, he later recalled that he preferred to be at home with his mother than in school.[12]

Remembering his early years, Johnson spoke almost exclusively of his mother. When he mentioned his father, it was to enumerate his liabilities as a husband and explain what he did to Rebekah. In particular, Johnson remembered the fights provoked by his father's drinking. According to Johnson,

there was nothing Mother hated more than seeing my daddy drink. When he had too much to drink, he'd lose control of himself. He used bad language. He squandered the little money we had on the cotton and real estate markets. Sometimes he'd be lucky and make a lot of money. But more often he lost out … These ups and downs were hard on my Mother … When she got upset, she blamed our money problems on my father's drinking. And then she cried a lot. Especially when he stayed out all night. I remember one bad night. I woke up and heard her in the parlour crying her eyes out. I knew she needed me. With me there, she seemed less afraid. She stopped crying and told me over and over how important it was that I never lose control of myself and disappoint her that way. I promised that I would be there to protect her always. Finally she calmed down and we both fell asleep.[13]

This memory condensed Johnson's sense of importance and specialness to his mother and confirmed him in the justice of his contempt for his out-of-control father who could not be relied upon to protect his mother. Johnson's own oedipal wishes to replace his father and have his mother to himself seem to have received an important stimulus from his mother's disappointment with his father and her use of Lyndon as a narcissistic object who would repair the wounds she suffered at the hands of her husband. Lyndon appears to have seen himself, the eldest child, as a vehicle whereby his mother's difficult marriage and their oscillating economic fortunes could be remedied. The son would fulfil the dreams she had never carried out and become the important person she and her husband had failed to be.

Lyndon also recalled that his mother would play games with him that only the two of them could play "and she always let me win even if to do so we had to change the rules."[14] This suggests that Lyndon learned early on that if you were special enough you were entitled to have the rules changed so you could win. Johnson then went on to say: "I knew how much she needed me, that she needed me to take care of her. I liked that. It made me feel big and important. It made me believe I could do anything in the whole world."[15]

Freud has described this state of mind as "the feeling of a conqueror, that confidence of success that often induces real success."[16] That such feelings were instrumental in instilling Johnson with the drive, determination, and confidence that later became so evident in his life is only one side of the picture. Lyndon's memories of his mother's need of him reflected, in part, a projection of his own cravings for her, as evidenced in his frequent running-away episodes. To cope with feeling small, unloved, and needy, Johnson reversed his psychic reality so that he became big and important with a mother who needed him.

Johnson's memories of his closeness to his mother make it is easy to imagine him an only child, when in fact he had four siblings. He had, moreover, little memory of his relations with his brothers and sisters, except for one very vivid event that occurred when he was five – an event that may have been either a screen memory, a dream, or a powerful aggressive fantasy. He recalled:

I was throwing a baseball to my oldest sister, Rebekah. We were playing in the yard in front of our house. Mother was watching. My younger sister, Josefa, was sitting in her crib behind us crying. I threw the ball straight and fast, but just as it left my hands, Mother moved toward Josefa and stepped right in the path of the ball. She was very pregnant with Sam then. The ball hit her hard, right in the middle of her stomach, and she lost her balance and fell down. I was terrified at the thought of what I'd done. I was certain that her belly would pop just like a balloon. Later, I found out that she had been even more frightened than me. She was, she told me much later, certain that the baby had been damaged. But at the time she said nothing of her fear; she immediately gathered me up into her arms and held me until I finally stopped crying.[17]

This "memory" suggests that Lyndon may not have been as confident of his special relationship to his mother as he suggests. The story indicates an aggressive wish to get rid of two of his siblings – Josefa and the unborn Sam – both rivals for Mother's affections, as well as a wish to punish his mother for her plan to bring home yet another hated rival. In an attempt to disavow his rage, Johnson, the author of the memory, makes his mother responsible for the accident. She is the one who steps in front of the ball in order to protect his little sister Josefa. Frightened perhaps by the intensity of his angry feelings, the little boy then designs a happy ending for himself with a forgiving mother who sweeps him up in her arms.

However much Lyndon attempted to persuade himself and others of his special, almost symbiotic, relationship with his mother, the impression remains that Rebekah's love was neither steady nor reliable but conditional on Lyndon's behaviour. When he failed to do as she wished and complete the dancing and violin lessons she had arranged for him, he experienced not only criticism but a complete withdrawal of affection. He told Doris Kearns many years later: "For days after I quit those lessons she walked around the house pretending I was dead. And then to make it worse, I had to watch her being especially warm and nice to my father and sisters." As Lyndon recalled it, if Rebekah was unhappy with him she would speak to him in "a terrible knifelike voice" or greet him with an impassive stare and entirely close him off, "refusing to speak or even look at him."[18]

In response to his mother's deep-freeze, Lyndon often misbehaved and acted against her wishes. One of the sharpest conflicts arose in the area of education. When Lyndon refused to go to college, his mother simply shut him out and refused to speak to or even look at him.[19] He was devastated; his mother's behaviour reinforced his fear that he was loved not for himself but only inasmuch as he satisfied her need for an accomplished son who could compensate for the drabness of her own life. He recalled, "We'd been such close companions, and boom, she'd abandoned me. I wanted to please her, but something told me I'd go to pieces if I went to college. I'd just finished ten years of sitting inside a school; the prospect of another four years was awful."[20]

For the most part, Lyndon denied ambivalent feelings towards his mother. When he was a grown man, he described his mother to friends as the finest, the most intelligent woman he had ever met, and he also told them that anyone who reminded him of her would be given favoured treatment in professional postings. It was hard for Lyndon to be critical of his mother; after all, Rebekah Johnson had always believed in Lyndon – all her hopes, which had not been realized in her own life, would be attained through him. When he was elected to Congress, she wrote him:

My darling boy:

Beyond "Congratulations Congressman" what can I say to my dear son in this hour of triumphant success? In this as in all the many letters I have written you there is the same theme: I love you; I believe in you; I expect great things of you. Your election compensates for the heartache and disappointment I experienced as a child when my dear father lost the race you have just won.[21]

Rebekah's letter is a classic expression of the way in which the narcissistic mother perceives her child; his designated role is to reconstitute her damaged sense of self through superior accomplishments.

For all Lyndon's difficulties with his "smothering," narcissistic mother, he undoubtedly felt closer to her than to his father. Slapped and spanked repeatedly by Sam, Lyndon was clearly afraid of him. "My father, he'd take a razor strap and just whip the hell out of us," Lyndon later told an interviewer. And there was also the verbal rage to contend with. Lyndon's siblings and friends remember the constant struggle to get him to do his school work and his father's angry shouts: " 'That boy of yours isn't worth a damn, Rebekah! He'll never amount to anything. He'll never amount to a God-damned thing.' "[22]

A boyhood friend of Lyndon's recalled the time someone put oil of mustard in the barbershop chair Lyndon liked to sit in while reading the newspaper. "Lyndon began to run and squirm ... He was on fire and he began to cry and holler ... He got his pants down, but he didn't take them completely off and he ran out on the sidewalk ... His daddy heard him hollering out there. He came up out of there and ... he took his belt off and he grabbed Lyndon by the hand and every so often he'd pop him one across the rear ... I thought he was the meanest man in the world." When the barbers explained what had happened, Sam "just said ... there wasn't any kid of his that was going to run up and down the streets with his bare butt hanging out."[23]

The father was to test his son's manhood in a variety of ways. Lyndon recalled hunting squirrels and rabbits with his friends. Although he carried a gun and every now and then would point it at the animals, he "never wanted to kill any of them. I wanted only to know that I could kill if I had to. Then one day my daddy asked me how did it happen that I was the only boy in the neighborhood who had never shot an animal. Was I a coward? The next day I went back into the hills and killed a rabbit. It jumped out at me from behind a bush and I shot it in between the eyes. Then I went to the bathroom and threw up."[24]

By the time Lyndon reached grade nine, he had to attend school in the town of Albert, four miles away from home. There he was mocked because, at twelve years old, he still rode a donkey instead of a horse to school. After a while, Sam relented and gave him a pony, but Lyndon would always remember the humiliation. "It helped a little when my mother told me that Jesus rode into Jerusalem on an ass," he would recall.[25] In the story that Lyndon told there is both humiliation at the hands of his father and redemption at the hands of his mother; he might have to ride a donkey, but his mother had compared him to Christ.

When he wrecked his father's car, at age fifteen, Lyndon was "too frightened to know what to do. 'I knew only that I could not face my father.'" He took a bus to visit an uncle in a nearby town. When his father telephoned, Lyndon felt like he "was going to the guillotine. I tried to keep my legs and my voice from shaking." Though he was relieved to learn that Sam had traded in the wrecked car for a brand-new automobile, he quickly realized that his father would exact his pound of flesh in the process. As Lyndon later recalled the episode:

My daddy said: "Lyndon, I traded in that old car of ours this morning for a brand-new one, and it's in the store right now needing someone to pick it up. I can't get away from here and I was wondering if you could come back, pick it up, and drive it home for me. And there's one other thing I want you to do for me. I want you to drive it around the courthouse square, five times, ten times, fifty times, nice and slow. You see there's some talk around town this morning that my son's a coward, that he couldn't face up to what he'd done, and that he ran away from home. Now I don't want anyone thinking I produced a yellow son. So I want you to show up here in that car and show everyone how much courage you've really got. Do you hear me?"[26]

In telling the story, Johnson saw it as a lesson in courage; in returning home he had proven that he could "stick it out." Yet what Johnson chose to gloss over was the carefully crafted humiliation that was meted out in his father's instructions. Such experiences must have impressed upon Lyndon that, in his father's view, acting like a sissy, a crybaby, and a coward were crimes of the tallest order that deserved to be punished with private or public humiliation. In later life, Johnson would be extremely sensitive to such an image and would try to avoid placing himself in situations where the potential to be shamed in this way could arise.

From the age of six or seven, Lyndon's identification with his father and his interest in politics were apparent. After his father re-entered politics in 1917, politicians – state and local – began dropping by the Johnson home for chats and strategy discussions. Usually, these were held on the porch adjacent to a bedroom where the nine-year-old Lyndon would hide, sitting on the floor, craning upward so that his ear was almost against the window listening. In 1918 Governor William P. Hobby came to Johnson City for a Fourth of July speech and had dinner at the Johnsons'. The children were sent off to the kitchen to leave room for the many invited local politicians. But Lyndon hid under the dining-room table all through the meal to listen to the talk.[27]

It was probably in 1918 that Sam Johnson first took Lyndon to a legislative session in Austin; thereafter, he took him frequently. Doris Kearns recalls Johnson telling her:

I loved going with my father to the legislature. I would sit in the gallery for hours watching all the activity on the floor and then would wander around the halls trying to figure out what was going on. The only thing I loved more was going with him on the trail during his campaigns for re-election.

We drove in the Model T Ford from farm to farm, up and down the valley, stopping at every door. My father would do most of the talking. He would bring the neighbors up to date on local gossip, talk about the crops and about the bills he'd introduced in the legislature.[28]

Sam made a strong impression on Lyndon and, despite the harsh punishments he administered, he was someone his son admired and wished to emulate, certainly in the years between 1913 and 1920, when Lyndon was ages five to twelve. At that time, the family lived in Johnson City, where Sam was a successful and prominent member of the community. He earned a good living by buying and selling real estate and cattle, investing in cotton futures, and holding a small interest in the local bank. Sam provided maids for Rebekah, drove "the biggest and most expensive car in the whole Hill Country," and made the Johnsons the best-dressed family in town. According to Lyndon, "Sam was, financially and socially, among the top three men in the area."[29]

An interesting dichotomy emerges between the picture of Lyndon as the admiring son who did everything possible to emulate his adored father, and that of the insolent, disobedient, and disrespectful son. Robert Caro finds the explanation in events of 1920–21, when a catastrophic drop in the Johnson family fortunes occurred. From a son that adored his father and was prepared to suffer the humiliations meted out by him, he was transformed into an arrogant and cruel young man who came to despise his father for the demeaning circumstances into which he had brought the family.[30]

In November 1919 Sam had sold or mortgaged everything he owned to buy the 433-acre family farm in Stonewall from his brothers and sisters. In the aftermath of the First World War, cotton prices had soared to forty cents a pound. Remembering that the farm had yielded a fair cotton crop six years before, Sam hoped to make a financial killing. However, instead of a financial bonanza, floods, searing heat, and an international cotton surplus left Sam with some $40,000 in debts, forcing him to sell the farm in 1922 and impoverishing him until his death in 1937.

Unable to earn an income – the legislature paid only two dollars a day when it sat – Sam was forced to give up his seat in 1924 at the age of forty-six and take the only job he could get: a two-dollar-a-day, part-time game warden. He was unable to pay off his back bills at Johnson City stores, and store owners began writing "Please!" on their monthly statements. Afraid of antagonizing and losing the business of his brother and the rest of the large Johnson clan, they hesitated to cut off his credit, but he kept falling farther and farther behind. "After a while he owed everyone in town," according to Truman Fawcett, and "they just cut him off."[31]

As finances got tighter and tighter, it sometimes seemed as if the Johnsons did not have enough to eat. Children in Johnson City often ate at each other's houses; those who ate at the Johnsons remember very small meals. Clayton Stribling recalled: "We were poor, but we always had enough to eat. But once I ate over at the Johnsons, and there was just bread and a little bit of bacon, and the bacon was rancid, too." Other children vividly remember the younger Johnson children, Josefa, Sam, and Lucia, eating meagrely – "a little dab of chili for the whole bunch." One Christmas, there was nothing to eat in the house until Sam's brother Tom arrived with a turkey and a sack of potatoes.[32]

That Lyndon was aware of what had happened is clear. His parents had become the laughing-stock of the town.[33] Once he had been able to charge more in stores than other children, but now he could charge nothing at all and had to stand watching while his friends charged purchases to their parents' accounts. He recalled the transformation this way: "in a scale of A to F being up there with the A's and then two years later losing it all and dropping to the bottom of the heap."[34] It must have been both embarrassing and anxiety-provoking to have been yanked from security into an insecurity that included continual worry about whether the very house in which he and his family lived was going to be taken away from them. His family, moreover, had been catapulted not just out of public respect but into something close to contempt.[35]

The shame and humiliation that such experiences must have engendered were particularly intense for someone such as Lyndon. Even before his parents' fall from grace, he desperately needed to lead and dominate others with the force of his personality and to be recognized as special. His family's declining fortunes added a powerful dose of insecurity and humiliation to Johnson's developing character structure. They also intensified his need to dominate others and to be in a position where he would never again be humiliated.

That he was regarded as damaged merchandise was poignantly brought home to him shortly after his graduation from high school. During the spring of 1924, Lyndon and his classmate Kitty

Clyde Ross were, their friends said, "in love." In class, they passed notes arranging to meet after school, and at parties they tried to kiss only each other. Their classmates wondered if they would get married someday – although Lyndon would not be sixteen until August. Kitty Clyde was a year older and Johnson City girls married young.[36]

Kitty Clyde's father was E.P. Ross, the "richest man in town." He was a merchant – one of the merchants who was writing "Please!" on the bills he sent to Sam Johnson every month. Twenty years earlier, his wife's family had forbidden her to marry Sam Johnson, and he was to behave similarly with his daughter. Shortly after graduation, the principal of Johnson City High School, Arthur K. Krause, asked Ross's permission to court Kitty Clyde. Ross gave it and encouraged the courtship even though Krause was almost thirty. Kitty's parents, in fact, ordered her not to spend time with Lyndon and took exceptional measures to ensure that their wishes were carried out. Krause was frequently invited for dinner at the Ross home and, after dinner, Kitty and Krause would go for a drive in the Ross's fancy new car with the Rosses as chaperons. Lyndon would be talking or playing with friends and would see the Ross car pass by.[37]

Ava Johnson Cox recalled that he told her that he "was working up his nerve" to ask Kitty Clyde for a date despite her parents' disapproval of him. He guessed, he said, that he would ask her to go with him to the annual Johnson City-Fredericksburg baseball game and picnic. He did, and Kitty said that she would have to ask her parents. Then she came back and told him that she would not be able to go; her parents would not allow her. After that Lyndon never asked her again.

As Ava described it: "It was so unfair. It [the Ross's attitude] didn't have anything to do with Lyndon. He had never done anything wrong. It was because they thought Lyndon was going to be just like Sam. I was a Johnson, and it was very unfair to the Johnsons, and it was very unfair to Lyndon. And I saw how it made Lyndon feel when that big car drove by with Kitty Clyde in it with another man. And I cried for him."[38] But Lyndon Johnson never forgot Kitty Clyde and the humiliation he suffered at her parents' hands. When he became president, he invited Kitty Clyde and her husband to Washington and took them for a flight on Air Force One. It was his way of showing her what she and her parents had thrown away in their cavalier and dismissive treatment of him.

The Kitty Clyde episode, however, would only be the first of several damaging blows to Johnson's self-esteem in the period following his high school graduation. His initial decision to forgo college underlines his intense fear of humiliation. Although Lyndon had the brains, he had little else; at college not only would he not be special, but he would run the serious risk of failing academically and being reminded daily of the poverty into which his family had sunk.[39] Although academic standards were much lower at Southwest Texas State Teachers College, in San Marcos, Lyndon was afraid that they were still too high for him. Subsequent events were to prove him right. Lyndon's cousin Elizabeth Romer Clemens said: "He didn't have a full education and he knew it." Lyndon also knew, according to Clemens, that although tuition at Southwest Texas was low, he would have to work while at school and "going to school as just another poor boy – well, that wasn't something Lyndon wanted to do."

The only work available in the Texas hill country at the time of Lyndon's graduation in the summer of 1924 was gravel-topping six miles of the highway between Johnson City and Austin. The work was hard and Lyndon hated every minute of it. More and more frequently he would not get up on time. Coming into his room, his father would say harshly: "C'mon Lyndon, get up – every boy in town's got an hour's start on you and you never will catch up." Although Lyndon felt there had to be a better way to earn a living – he had detested physical labour since childhood – he persisted at his gravel-topping job rather than do what his parents wanted, which was to go to college. And he continued to stay out late at night, drinking and driving recklessly.[40]

On the day that four of his former classmates went to San Marcos to enter college, Lyndon went, too, in response to a direct order from his parents. As graduates of an unaccredited high school, all five had to pass entrance exams in three "nonaffiliated" courses including mathematics. These exams usually followed at least six weeks of intensive subcollegiate instruction. Lyndon enrolled in the college preparatory courses, possibly in August 1924. When he filled out registration forms at Southwest Texas in 1927, he listed this earlier attendance. But the remedial work was never successfully completed; Lyndon either dropped out or was forced out of these courses because of poor performance. In later years, he ruefully referred to being "kicked out" of Southwest Texas. In any event, Johnson was unable to matriculate with his classmates.[41]

After this galling failure, Lyndon returned home to Johnson City to face his parents' criticism. He could have repeated his work in the subcollegiate courses during the next quarter. Instead, however, he chose to retreat and avoid the additional humiliation of failing again. Rebekah seems to have been bitterly disappointed at Lyndon's academic failure. It threatened her romantic hopes for a great career for her first-born – her narcissistic extension. Thus, she struggled for more than two years to get Lyndon back to San Marcos. With the cooperation of his family, particularly his brother Sam Houston, Johnson eliminated this frustrating interlude from a carefully cultivated LBJ legend.[42]

A week or two after abandoning college, he left home with four older boys, and without the permission of his parents, to look for work in California. During the trip Johnson walked around carrying his suitcase as though it were incredibly heavy and contained enough clothes for an entire family for several years. His companions could not imagine why Johnson, with so much luggage, wore the same clothes day after day. One afternoon, the baling wire that Johnson had used to tie up the suitcase came loose, and it opened on the street. Out rolled the sum of Johnson's worldly possessions – a straw hat![43] He obviously could not bear the thought of being perceived by his friends as the poor boy he really was.

In California, Johnson lived for a time with his cousin, Martin. He was a lawyer who, prior to coming to California, had destroyed a brilliant career in Texas through his drunk and disorderly behaviour. Martin held out the hope to Lyndon that he could take the bar exams in Nevada – there were no written examinations and the oral examinations were very informal, especially when the candidate came recommended by a prominent attorney, and Martin had several such friends. Once accepted by the Nevada bar, Johnson could be admitted to the California bar under a provision which made it virtually automatic. And as soon as he was admitted, Martin promised to take him into his own profitable practice.[44]

In assuring him that he would be able to obtain a Nevada licence after a few months' preparation, Martin had overlooked the fact that a Nevada lawyer had to be at least twenty-one. In the summer of 1925, Lyndon was only seventeen; he would have had to wait four more years! As for the reciprocal California licence that was available to Nevada attorneys, California law required that such reciprocal licences would go only to attorneys who had been practising in another state for at least three years. And finally Lyndon learned that Nevada was in the process of tightening up its previously slack requirements for obtaining a licence to practise law; it was going to be much more difficult to obtain one without a college degree, and virtually impossible with only a Johnson City High School education.[45] The entire experience was humiliating. Martin had proved to be as unreliable as his father and Lyndon's aspirations to become a successful lawyer had been shattered.

Johnson returned to Texas in September 1925, having decided how to achieve the security and respect he wanted without needing to accept his parents' insistence that he attend college. A political career would satisfy many of his conscious and unconscious goals. It would enable him to identify with the manly side of his father and suppress his fears of being weak and dependent like his mother. Not only would he succeed where his maternal grandfather and father had failed, but in doing so he would also experience the oedipal triumph of surpassing his father at his own game of politics.

In later years, he told Doris Kearns that it was on the trip back to Texas that he found his vocation of politics. As he recounted it, he thought a great deal about his parents during the trip.

I still believed my mother the most beautiful, sexy, intelligent woman I'd ever met and I was determined to recapture her wonderful love, but not at the price of my daddy's respect. Finally, I saw it all before me. I would become a political figure. Daddy would like that. He would consider it a manly thing to be. But that would be just the beginning. I was going to reach beyond my father. I would finish college; I would build great power and gain high office. Mother would like that. I would succeed where her own father had failed; I would go to the Capitol and talk about big ideas. She would never be disappointed in me again.[46]

But Lyndon did not embark on his future career immediately upon his return from California. He still seemed determined not to continue his education, yet he remained desperate to stand out, to be somebody. For a time he worked on a road gang and made a habit of showing off, bragging about his lineage, swaggering, and strutting. His "big talk" grew bigger; he frequently predicted that he would be "the President of the United States" one day.[47] Then, at a dance hall in Fredericksburg in February 1927, Lyndon met his Waterloo. His overbearing manner provoked a fight with a German farm boy who beat him unmercifully until Lyndon was forced to give up. Lyndon was known for losing fights; he hated physical encounters and this one seemed to have left him depressed and subdued. Perhaps the beating before his friends was the last straw in the humiliations he had endured since he had returned from California. It forced him to recognize that remaining in Johnson City would involve more of the same. Even at a rustic dance hall he could not be somebody. The next morning he told his parents that he would go to college.[48]

Southwest Texas State Teachers College was the choice of poor students in the Texas hill country. It cost only about $40 a month, but even that seemed almost prohibitive for Lyndon. His parents arranged with Cecil Evans, the school's president, for Lyndon to have an eight-dollar-a-month job on the campus clean-up squad collecting trash, removing weeds, and picking up rocks. Lyndon then persuaded Percy T. Brigham, who once worked as a law clerk for Rebekah's father and was the president of the Blanco bank, to lend him $475. Supplemented by another $25 from home, he had enough cash to meet the expenses of one term. He scraped through the subcollege course, recalling later how his mother "came to San Marcos and stayed up with me the entire night before the math exam, drilling me over and over until it finally got into my head." Even then, he attained only a seventy, the lowest passing grade.[49]

On 21 March 1927, the start of the spring term, Lyndon became a regularly enrolled student. Even though he had struggled to gain admission, his pleasure was tempered at the recognition that San Marcos, as most students called the college, was a small provincial school with a humble reputation in the world of higher education. It had become an accredited four-year college only in 1925, and even then it barely met the standard. A library of 21,000 volumes and a single holder of a doctorate among its fifty-six faculty members, some of whom had no degree at all, gave it official standing in Texas merely as a "third-class" college. Academic standards were lax and course requirements were closer to those of a high school than a college.[50]

Even though Johnson was able to earn his BS degree in education and history, he retained a palpable sense of his inferior background and education. As Clark Clifford later wrote, "He [Johnson] alternated between embarrassment and defensiveness about the fact that he had attended an obscure college in Texas … instead of one of the prestigious institutions of higher learning in the East which he associated with the Kennedys. I was always struck by his attitude toward his poor origins – his combination of pride, shame, and sensitivity."[51]

Throughout his life Lyndon remained intensely ambivalent about men of culture, particularly those educated at Ivy League schools. He admired their background and intellectual formation, but he also envied and hated them for it and expressed a lasting distrust and fear of ideas, intellectuals, books, and eloquence. He believed that it was the intellectuals who hated him: "The men of ideas think little of me, they despise me," he was to say later in life.[52] Such attitudes reflected, in part, a projection of his own contempt of intellectuals, as well as an identification with his father's values. But there was also some truth to his claim – given the prejudices of the academic, literary, and publishing world towards the boisterous style of Lyndon Johnson.

As a student at San Marcos, Johnson displayed the same tendency to "talk big" that he had demonstrated in Johnson City. He would introduce himself as "Lyndon Johnson from Johnson City," thereby intimating that he was a member of the town's founding family. If he was asked directly whether he was, he would answer in the affirmative, saying that Johnson City had been founded by his grandfather, a statement that was an outright lie.[53] He told fellow students at Mrs Gates's boarding-house that he had an IQ of 145 and created the impression that he was a "brilliant student." His actual intelligence quotient has been lost in time, but the two faculty members in charge of administering the tests during the time he was at San Marcos both say it was not outstanding. As for his grades, his overall average was B-. In later years, he frequently remarked that he had taken forty courses and obtained thirty-five A's. He actually took fifty-six regular classroom courses and received eight A's.[54]

The need to exaggerate his background and his accomplishments carried over into his social life as well. His brother, Sam Houston, recalled that more than once, when he visited his brother at San Marcos, Lyndon, coming back into the room naked after a shower, would take his penis in his hand, and say: "Well, I've gotta take ol' Jumbo here and give him some exercise. I wonder who I'll fuck tonight."[55] The evidence suggests that Lyndon's braggadocio was not well founded; while he was sought after for double-dating since he had permission to drive to Austin, it was often difficult to find a date for him. His unpopularity with women students would not have aroused particular comment on campus had it not been for the way in which he boasted about his sexual prowess. "I mean we all boasted and bragged about girls," said one classmate, "but Lyndon's boasting and bragging were to an extent that was ridiculous. Nobody believed him."[56]

Lyndon's need to be seen as special even led him to lie about where he bought his clothes. "Once I was sitting next to him in class, and I saw him wearing a new tie and socks," Horace Richards recalled.

I knew where he had bought them, but I asked him where he had bought them. He said, "I got them over at Scarborough's in Austin. I paid a dollar for the socks and a dollar for the tie." Scarborough's was the fanciest store in Austin, and a dollar was a whole lot of money in those days. I said, "Lyndon, you're just lying. You were never in Scarborough's yesterday. Besides, I saw them in Woolworth's window yesterday. The socks were ten cents and the tie was twenty cents." But Lyndon just had to lie and say he was wearing a dollar tie. It just seemed like he had to lie about everything.[57]

What classmates found remarkable was Lyndon's apparent lack of embarrassment when caught out in an exaggeration or an outright falsehood. "You could catch him in a lie about something, and it was like he did not care," Richards said. "The next day he'd be back lying about the same thing again."[58]

There was a driven quality and an essential consistency in Lyndon's lying. His lying was directed not at hurting others but at elevating his own reputation. His lies were designed to make himself appear better than he was: richer, smarter, and more attractive to women. Lyndon seems to have lied in order to eradicate painful feelings of low self-worth and the shame of feeling loved for his accomplishments or his acquisitions rather than for who he was. The lesson he had learned from his mother was that her love was contingent on his "being somebody," and so, for the rest of his life, he would be driven to prove that he was "somebody."

That he was perceived as unlovable, at least by the crowd that counted in his eyes, was amply demonstrated when the college athletes who had formed a "secret" organization called the Black Stars refused to make him a member. Even the determined efforts of Boody Johnson (no relation), Lyndon's room-mate and a popular athlete on campus, could not secure him a place in the club. In later years, Lyndon would maintain that a single blackball – cast by a student whose girlfriend Lyndon had stolen – had kept him out of the organization, but the truth was otherwise. The Black Stars were virtually unanimous in their opposition to Lyndon joining their ranks.

A classmate, Ella So Relle, commented on how hurt he was. "He wanted so badly to belong to the 'in' crowd," she said. "He would have loved to be part of that crowd, to be accepted by them. But they wouldn't let him in. He was just not accepted. You had the feeling of climbing and climbing – and then he didn't make it. You see, he was just one of the mass. And he so badly wanted to be more."[59] The need to be accepted, to be part of the "in crowd," was an expression of Lyndon's unconscious fear that he was unacceptable to his parents and thus of his tendency to seek constant reassurance of their love. Rejection by the Black Stars must have been a humiliating experience for someone as narcissistically vulnerable and as ambitious as Lyndon.

While a student at San Marcos in 1927–28, Lyndon met Carol Davis, whose father, A.L. Davis, was the richest man in town. Lyndon made no secret of his desire to find a rich girl and often boasted about their relationship. However, her father objected to his daughter's involvement with the son of an impoverished, "no-account" hill country family, whom he supposedly characterized as a "bunch … of shiftless dirt farmers and grubby politicians. Always sticking together and leeching onto one another so the minute one starts to make it the others drag him down. None of them will ever amount to a damn."[60]

Lyndon worked hard to overcome this prejudice. "Lyndon was pretty determined to get on his good side," recalled Carol's eldest sister, Ethel. He tried to chat with Davis on his porch, but the latter, after one or two conversations, would leave the porch when his daughter's suitor arrived. "My father always sat on the porch and talked to people," Carol said. "But he wouldn't talk to Lyndon."[61]

The romance flowered, none the less, for a short time. Although Carol was very much taken with Lyndon, she also had her doubts. They seemed to centre less on Lyndon's social standing than on his sharply different interests. She loved music and "picture shows," but politics, which consumed Lyndon, bored her.[62] Her reservations about his suitability were undoubtedly enhanced by her father's continued antipathy to Lyndon. "I knew I couldn't go against my father's wishes," she said. She told Lyndon how strongly "my father felt about him," and "it was always hanging over us. All the time we were going together, it was hanging over us. The whole time."[63]

Lyndon's attraction to Carol rested partly on his ambition to marry well; such a marriage would advance his social standing and financial security. Thus, in spite of his recognition of how ill-matched they were, he aggressively pursued the relationship. While teaching in Pearsall, Carol met a young postal clerk named Harold Smith who shared her interests, and of whom her father approved. She was torn between the two men, and so her father sent her to California with Ethel to think things through. Waiting for her upon her return were two letters proposing marriage, one from Cotulla (where Lyndon was teaching) and one from Pearsall. "She sat down in the back room, where Daddy used to sit when he thought," Ethel recalled. When she emerged she had made her decision. While he was still down in Cotulla, Lyndon Johnson was notified in the spring of 1929 that Carol Davis was engaged to Harold Smith.[64]

So painful was the rejection that Johnson was to reverse the sequence of events so that it was he who rejected Carol. Lyndon claimed that he had known from the outset that the relationship would be difficult since Davis was an extreme conservative in politics and a member of the Ku Klux Klan. In fact, however, Davis opposed the Klan. At a Klan parade held in San Marcos when the organization was at the height of its power – a parade in which virtually every prominent local family, except the Davises, participated – he had defiantly announced that "no member of my family will be with them."[65]

Johnson later claimed that what had really tipped the scales was the way Davis had assailed his father's politics and then disparaged his grandfather, saying that everyone in Blanco County knew that Sam Ealy Johnson had been "nothing but an old cattle rustler." As far as Lyndon was concerned, that was it. " 'To hell with the whole family,' I said to myself. 'I'll never marry Carol or anyone in the whole damn family ...' I left the Davis home that night determined never to see Carol again."[66] In a bravado effort to inflate his badly damaged self-esteem, Lyndon reputedly told Carol: "You can tell your Daddy that someday I'll be president of this country. You watch and see."[67]

Johnson described how Carol came into his room the next morning and, red-faced from crying, told him that notwithstanding how much she loved her father, and how much pain it would cause her to go against him on this issue, "she decided that she had to do it. She loved me and she wanted to marry me. All the while she was talking I thought of the many nights we had dreamed of our future together. But all this had to be put in the past, forgotten. It could never work for us. I told her that, I was very firm and after a long moment of silence, she went away."[68]

In Johnson's reconstructed memory of his rejection by Carol, he becomes the one who, even in the face of Carol's tears and protestations of love, walks away from her. It is he who administers rather than suffers the humiliation of rejection. Distorting reality in this way allowed Lyndon to deny the shame he must have felt and permitted a re-inflation of his damaged self-esteem.

Issues of self-esteem and the drive to achieve were what made Lyndon run so hard. Although he had decided after graduating from college in August 1930 that he wanted to make a career in politics rather than teaching, there were no state jobs available. He spent a very brief period teaching in Pearsall and that October a position opened in the speech department at the Sam Houston High School in Houston. Lyndon was hired and devoted himself to the job and to his students in a way never before seen at the school. He insisted on perfection, giving his hand-picked debating team training that would last for endless hours. His team faced every team in Houston that would debate them, and he then arranged a tour far more ambitious than any ever scheduled by a Texas high-school debating team.[69]

After sixty-seven consecutive victories, one more would have given them the state championship. As it happened, the team lost the last debate by one vote, three to two. Although Johnson told the team they had done well and comforted them, he went behind the stage and vomited.[70] So intense was his need to win, to make something of himself, that the psychological boundaries between the coach and his students had been virtually eradicated. In its place, a fusion had occurred in which the team had become a narcissistic extension of Lyndon Johnson.

In November of his second year in Houston, Lyndon was offered a job as private secretary to Richard Kleberg, whom Johnson had never met but who had just won a special election to fill a vacancy in Texas's Fourteenth Congressional District. As Kleberg's secretary, Lyndon worked himself to the bone with a frenzied, driven, almost desperate energy for four years. He worked as hard as he did, putting in fourteen- and sixteen-hour days, according to his assistant Estelle Harbin, because "he couldn't stand not being somebody – just could not stand it. So he was trying to meet everyone, to learn everything."[71] But there were the constant small humiliations – having to step back when his congressman stepped into the MEMBERS ONLY elevator, having to wait outside the congressional cloakrooms because he was not allowed inside – all of which served as daily reminders that, "after almost four years, he was only an assistant; he was not a somebody, but a nobody – just one of the crowd of low-paid, powerless congressional secretaries."[72]

If Johnson worked and played hard to further his ambition to make something of himself, his aides were expected to do no less for him. He expected their total loyalty and subservience and permitted them virtually no free time. Encountering an aide whose preparedness to work endless hours for Johnson did not include a willingness to surrender his personality for him, Johnson determined to bend the man by intimidation and finally humiliation. L.E. Jones seems to have been the first of Johnson's entourage to have been subjected to his penchant for forcing subordinates to watch him defecating. Those who observed it knew it was done to humiliate Jones and to prove to him who was boss.[73] The shaming of Johnson's subordinates in such fashion suggests an historical analogue in Lyndon's own childhood toilet training. In response to what he seems to have experienced as helplessness and loss of control, Johnson, as an adult, would demonstrate his dominance and control, deciding how, when, and in front of whom he would defecate. His delight in talking to visitors while on the toilet, in using crude and scatological language, and in exhibiting his sexual organs was especially pronounced when he dealt with "gentlemen of culture."[74] The more important they were, the better he seemed to like it. In this way Johnson was able to transform passivity into activity by identifying with his powerful parents who had shamed him as a child.

He continued that pattern throughout his political career. His ability to ingratiate himself with series of powerful benefactors, such as Sam Rayburn, the speaker of the House, was legendary. But Edward A. Clark, then the Texan secretary of state, also saw the flip side of Lyndon's ability to appear confident and poised. Accompanying Johnson to cocktail parties, Clark observed his nervousness up close. "He didn't want to be standing there by himself," Clark would recall. "If I started to walk away, he would say, 'Stand with me, Ed, stand with me.' Insecurity. There was a lot of insecurity in Lyndon. He had some kind of inferiority complex. You could see that right away."[75]

The insecurity and ambition fused in a way that made Johnson a formidable political campaigner. Although he had powerful financial backers, his most prodigal expenditure in every campaign he ran was not money but himself. In his first campaign for the special election for congressman in the Tenth Congressional District of Texas in 1937, he ran extraordinarily hard, covering large sections of the district in a single day – speaking each day in as many as a dozen little communities and, between speeches, visiting scores of farms and ranches.

Even though he complained about stomach cramps and doubled over in pain, he kept working harder. He lost his voice almost completely, but instead of cancelling speeches he scheduled still more. Despite an acute attack of appendicitis, in which the pain was so great that he had to sit down in the middle of a speech, he insisted on finishing it. Then and only then was he driven to hospital where the doctors found that "his appendix was on the point of rupturing" and they operated immediately. Against five major candidates, Lyndon won with 8,280 votes, 3,000 votes more than his nearest opponent. But even this represented less than 28 per cent of the votes cast and only slightly more than 3 per cent of the district's population. Johnson had been elected with by far the fewest votes of any of the nation's 435 congressmen.[76]

The extraordinary drive which brought Lyndon electoral success did not diminish once he entered office; in fact, it intensified.[77] During his first term, Johnson displayed both energy and ingenuity in obtaining considerable benefits for his constituents from the federal bureaucracy. But his standing on Capitol Hill – outside the Texas delegation – was more problematic. Although he was recognized as someone who had the ability to lead, it was clear that his pragmatism and caution – he would never speak on the floor in support of any congressional bills – created scorn and enmity among his colleagues. It seemed as though Lyndon could not endure being a follower, a mere one of a crowd; he needed to lead and even to dominate. His behaviour was reminiscent of his boyhood on the vacant lots of Johnson City, where, if he could not pitch, he would take his ball and go home – the quality that led one Johnson City companion to say, "If he couldn't lead, he didn't care much about playing."[78]

During President Franklin Roosevelt's trip to Texas in July 1938, Johnson's lack of White House entrée was brought home to him forcibly; he was not on the initial list of Texas congressmen invited aboard the president's train. Only a last-minute invitation secured for him en route got him aboard. Once there, his name was added to the list of congressmen on whom Roosevelt bestowed public praise, but not to the list of those allowed a few private minutes with FDR.[79]

If others would not give him the recognition he craved, Johnson, who still needed to be the best, have the most, and impress himself on everyone he met, would take what he could. He was the first congressman to choose the fifth or attic floor in the old House office building, where he had nearly double the space of other congressmen. He stayed there long after he had enough seniority to move out, because it gave him something other representatives did not have. Later in his career, he "was thrilled when he was the first in Washington to have a car phone." Senator Everett Dirksen of Illinois, a friendly competitor, then got one too. When he called Johnson's limousine to say that he was calling from his new car phone, Johnson replied, "Hold on a minute, Ev, my other phone is ringing."[80]

The need for attention and the need to feel special was not confined to his relations with his male colleagues. It was also reflected in his choice of a wife. The two previous women he had courted, Carol Davis of San Marcos and Kitty Clyde Ross of Johnson City, had been the daughters of the richest men in town. In 1934 he began courting a third young woman. She was Claudia Alta Taylor (nicknamed Lady Bird) of Karnack, Texas – her father was also Karnack's richest man. However, unlike the other two men, Lady Bird's father liked and admired Lyndon.

Although Lyndon finally realized his ambition to marry a rich girl, it soon became clear that it would be impossible for one woman to satisfy Johnson's narcissism. He quickly developed a reputation as a womanizer. According to one journalist who knew him beginning in 1937, Johnson had what amounted to a harem: "One way you could visualize Lady Bird is as the queen in Anna and the King of Siam. It worked that way; you know the scene where she sits at the table and all the babes – Lady Bird was the head wife." Johnson seems to have had a compulsive need for conquests. In his late fifties, for example, when he was president, a White House secretary, who was described as "a very pretty young woman," claimed that a flirtation between them had led to casual sex on an office desk. Mention of John Kennedy's womanizing would lead Johnson to pound on a table and shout that he "had more women by accident than Kennedy had on purpose."[81]

In this boastful statement we see Johnson's strong competitive drive and his need to be perceived as superior to his rival. His behaviour offers a classic illustration of the phallic narcissist who engages in frequent sexual encounters in order to reassure himself of his potency and his maleness in the face of unconscious, passive yearnings.

There was at least one long-term relationship that seems to have given Johnson a measure of the self-worth that he so desperately sought. It began sometime in the late 1930s with Alice Glass, the strikingly beautiful mistress and later wife of Charles Marsh, the wealthy Austin newspaper publisher. Excited by his dynamism, and captivated by his relentless ambition, Alice fell in love with Lyndon and began an affair with him that lasted several years and remained a secret from even her closest friends. The love and admiration of Alice Glass, considered "the most beautiful woman in Washington," must have given Johnson's ego an enormous boost. It certainly fostered his inclination to humiliate his perceived inferiors; at Longlea, Marsh's exquisite country estate, he seems to have had no compunction about humiliating Lady Bird with his studious disregard for her. Harold Young, who was Henry Wallace's assistant, remembers that "Lyndon would be sittin' out there flirtin' with her [Alice] a little and Lady Bird would be out there very distressed about her husband."[82]

Yet Johnson's involvement with Alice Glass was not enough to cause him to lose sight of his political goals. Johnson may have considered leaving Lady Bird, but he never acted on that impulse. He was undoubtedly aware that a divorce would have been disastrous for his political career. In the 1930s and 1940s, a divorced man had little chance of winning high political office. And Lyndon Johnson's political ambitions had not begun to be satiated.[83]

In the spring and early summer of 1941, he ran for a Senate seat after Morris Sheppard, the senior senator from Texas, died after a brief illness. A special election to complete Sheppard's term meant that Lyndon could run without giving up his House seat; he leapt at the opportunity. By 21 June, Johnson, after trailing badly for most of the race, was in a virtual deadlock with the incumbent governor, "Pappy" O'Daniel, and Gerald C. Mann, the Texas attorney general.

Twenty-four hours after the polls closed on Saturday, 28 June, with 96 per cent of the vote counted, Johnson led O'Daniel by

5,150 votes. The next day, the Texas Election Bureau and newspapers around the state declared Johnson the unofficial winner. Johnson campaign workers were jubilant, parading around the Stephen F. Austin hotel with Lyndon on their shoulders. Lyndon was so confident of victory that he "practically hired a staff."[84]

But Johnson underestimated the resourcefulness of a coalition of political forces determined to put O'Daniel in the Senate, or, more precisely, to get him out of the governor's chair. On Sunday, 29 June, with some 18,000 rural east Texas votes still to be counted, the O'Daniel beer and liquor interests conspired with fifteen state senators to put enough of these ballots in O'Daniel's column to give him the election. What made defeat so painful for Johnson was not only the fact that he had lost, but that he had allowed victory to be stolen from him. It was humiliating, and it must have tapped a fear that perhaps he was destined to be like his Daddy, who had no common sense, realism, or pragmatism and ended up a drunken, impoverished nobody.[85]

The Johnson camp appealed to Roosevelt for help. He agreed to send some FBI men to scrutinize the returns and ask the county judges to explain the great reversal in the delayed vote returns. To be sure, the investigators found that many people without poll-tax receipts were permitted to vote and that in rural communities election officials counted "incomplete" and "mutilated" ballots. The FBI concluded, however, that "no evidence of any unlawful intent" had been disclosed.[86] Having failed to prevent altered returns for O'Daniel by this preliminary investigation, Johnson opposed the suggestion of doing more. One of his advisers, Professor Howard M. Greene, told Johnson that they should challenge the returns and Greene remembers that "he just laughed and shook his head." Worried that an even-handed inquiry would reveal the many violations of campaign finance and election laws by his supporters, Lyndon told his brother, who had asked him if he was going to have the election results investigated, "Hell no, I hope they don't investigate me."[87]

Although he tried to appear jaunty in defeat, in fact he was "in a very black mood" and even Roosevelt could not cheer him up. The president may well have added to Johnson's humiliation by "kidding the hell out of him": " 'Lyndon, up in New York the first thing they taught us was to sit on the ballot boxes.' "[88] What seems to have sustained Johnson was the thought of revenge – that he would turn victory into defeat the next time around – which was a way of restoring his self-esteem. "Did you ever see a shooting gallery with its circular, rotating discs with lots of pipes and rabbits on the circuit?" he asked Tommy Corcoran. "Well, when you miss one the first time, you get a second chance. And the sonofabitch who trimmed you will always come up again. And then you can get him."[89]

Still, the defeat rankled. Johnson described the months after his defeat as "the most miserable in my life." Although he considered leaving politics altogether, Lyndon acknowledged that "in the end, I just couldn't bear to leave Washington. Besides, with all those war clouds hanging over Europe I felt that someone with all my training and preparedness was bound to be an important figure."[90] Johnson's determination to be recognized as a "somebody" was still alive and well.

During the course of the war, Johnson obtained a commission as a U.S. Naval Reserve officer. But he was determined to see action, since he felt that he might be able to parlay battle experience into votes in future election campaigns. Johnson managed to convince General Douglas MacArthur and his staff to let him participate in an air-combat mission in the Pacific; his task was to report back on the conditions facing pilots attacking Japanese installations in the conquered portion of New Guinea. Having trained near Melbourne, Australia, American pilots were required to fly more than a thousand miles north to the bases from which the air raids were launched. The missions were extremely dangerous – American raiders sometimes lost a quarter of their planes and crews on a sortie – and the one Johnson participated in was no different. One of the three planes was shot down; the pilot of the plane in which Lyndon was flying managed to keep from being shot down, but not without absorbing hits on the wings and fuselage from the attacking Japanese fighter planes.[91]

Upon his return to Melbourne, Johnson once again met with MacArthur. After listening to an hour-long report, MacArthur concluded the meeting by announcing that Colonel Francis R. Stevens, who had been shot down, was being awarded a Distinguished Service Cross and that Stevens, Lieutenant-Colonel Samuel Anderson from the operations and plans division of the War Department general staff in Washington, and Johnson would each receive a Silver Star. The crew members who died on the *Wabash Cannonball* received Purple Hearts; Johnson was the only one on the *Heckling Hare* who got a medal for the 9 June mission.

Johnson did exhibit some self-consciousness about getting a medal, implying to Harold Ickes in July 1942 that he had refused it. But the temptation to inflate his self-esteem and play the hero was too great. Johnson not only kept the medal, he also made more of it in future political campaigns than the facts warranted, repeatedly exaggerating what had actually happened. As one journalist later wrote, Johnson's medal was "one of the least deserved but most often displayed Silver Stars in American military history."[92]

During the years before the war, Lyndon Johnson had felt an intense need to accumulate money to ensure that he would not end up like his father, who had died penniless in the humiliating job of a state bus inspector, or like some former congressmen who were forced to work in poorly paid and demeaning jobs after their political careers had ended. He would hark back to a conversation he had struck up with an elevator operator in the Capitol, who told him that he had once been a congressman.[93]

By 1943 a business opportunity presented itself – the purchase of radio station KTBC in Austin. Because KTBC was bought in his wife's name – she became president of the company and was active in its affairs – Lyndon Johnson maintained the fiction that the company, which would eventually consist of a galaxy of radio and television stations, was all hers and that no conflict existed between his role in government and his interest in a government-regulated industry.[94] This was a deliberate distortion of the truth. The full measure of his on-going involvement and use of political influence to obtain favourable rulings for the station have been documented at great length.[95]

At the station's staff meetings – held frequently during his stays in Austin – Johnson would combine appeals to naked self-interest with sermons on higher ideals such as loyalty. He would tell the employees, "We are building this station. It's going to be big. Work hard and be loyal and you'll be rewarded." In public, he talked about "loyalty"; in private, he gave staff members his definition of that quality. "I want real loyalty," he told one young staffer. "I want someone who will kiss my ass in Macy's window, and say it smells like roses. I want his pecker in my pocket."[96]

Rumours that several staff members were attending a meeting of a union attempting to organize employees of radio stations infuriated Johnson. He indicated that he thought they were one big family and that he would take care of them. He would alternate between being paternalistic and abusive, surrounding himself with people who would tolerate the abuse he meted out and the humiliation he inflicted on them. In the repeated acts of dominating and humiliating his subordinates – he liked to use the term "son" in addressing them even when the person in question was many years his senior – Johnson was driven to attempt to master the humiliating trauma of his own childhood and adult life.

As abusive and humiliating as Johnson could be with subordinates, he could be as deferential – an obsequious "brown noser" – with his superiors. Stories of his ability to ingratiate himself with superiors, beginning with his teachers and the president of his college and continuing in his relationships with powerful businessmen and politicians such as the speaker of the House, Sam Rayburn, abound in all the Johnson biographies. For twenty-five years he cultivated Rayburn. Their relationship was cemented by the particular closeness that developed between Lady Bird and the crotchety old bachelor, who came for dinner several times a week. Johnson knew that he needed Rayburn for the realization of his great ambition. If you want to be president, he told William O. Douglas during the 1940s, "you've got to do it through Sam Rayburn."[97]

But the resentment at being forced to defer to Mr Sam occasionally surfaced. When he was in the Senate, he would sometimes say to Jim Rowe, "Oh Rayburn's so goddamned difficult – I've got to go over there to the Board of Education and kiss his ass, and I don't want to do it." But he went over, and did it – day after day, year after year. In 1957, when he was Senate majority leader, he attended the dedication of the Sam Rayburn Library in Texas. While talking with several prominent Texans, one of Rayburn's aides, House doorkeeper "Fishbait" Miller, came up and told him that the speaker would like to see him. He ignored Miller's request, and when Miller persisted he exploded: "Goddammit, I have to kiss his ass all the time in Washington, I don't have to do it in Texas, too, do I? I'm not coming!" But then he ran after Miller to make sure the message wasn't delivered, and hurried off to see the speaker.[98]

Being forced to fawn before a series of wealthy or politically powerful men must have been humiliating to someone with Lyndon's narcissism and ambition to become somebody before whom others would have to grovel. After Johnson retired from politics, the governor of Texas asked to visit him at his ranch in 1971. "What did the governor want?" an aide asked Johnson. "Damned if I know," Johnson replied. "He came with his wife and daughter and sat around my living room all afternoon but never said what

he wanted. Maybe he wanted me to kiss his ass. After all, that's the
business I've been in for the last forty years."[99] To cope with the
daily humiliations he felt forced to endure as a child, and then as
an adult politician, it is not surprising that Johnson turned passive
into active and exploited every opportunity to treat his subordinates in an equivalent fashion.

In the period following Roosevelt's death in 1945, Lyndon Johnson
seemed to lose much of the political power he had worked so hard
to attain. The new president, who had watched Johnson's fawning
treatment of Rayburn – the "professional son" act, as it was scorn-
fully referred to – "never quite trusted him," according to Truman's
daughter Margaret. Hence, Johnson never became part of Truman's
inner circle and no longer possessed even a trace of the aura of an
administration insider. He was only a congressman, one of many.[100]
  There were other humiliations in Washington and back in his
own district. Following a disagreement between Lyndon Johnson
and Bryce Harlow, a young staff member on the naval affairs committee who threatened to resign, Chairman Carl Vinson virtually
forced Johnson to apologize. In his own district, Lyndon was prohibited from acquiring space in the United States courthouse. He
was forced to ask Attorney General Tom Clark to intervene, but the
bureaucratic delays humiliated Johnson and he reacted with rage.
The incident became widely known and a source of amusement in
Austin.[101]
  Johnson's re-election campaign in 1946 also showed a decrease
in popular support. Although he won by a large margin, political
observers were startled by the size of the anti-Johnson vote and the
bitterness against the congressman that surfaced during the campaign. He was attacked as "an errand boy for war-rich contractors."
On one occasion, he asked Ed Clark the reason that he was not
more "loved" in the district for which he had done so much. "That's
simple," Clark said, "you got rich in office." Johnson leapt to his
feet without a word and strode from Clark's office. The fact that one
out of every three voters had opposed him, in a district to which he
had brought such great economic benefits, preyed upon his mind
so incessantly that he could not stop talking about it. He desperately
craved support and affection from his constituents, and he was
never again able to believe that he had it.[102]
  Even his social life offered reminders of his lack of political
power. While he remained stuck for more than a decade on the

same rung of the Washington ladder, other members of the little circle of ambitious young men with whom he associated had been climbing. Tom Clark, whom he had helped get his first job, was now attorney general of the United States. Abe Fortas had been only a staffer at the Securities and Exchange Commission when they met; he became under-secretary of the interior. In 1946 Fortas formed a law firm, Thurman Arnold and Paul Porter, and it became a power-house in Washington. Previously Johnson had monopolized the conversation in his social set; now the centre of gravity in the group was shifting and Fortas held forth at length. Johnson's parties were still well attended, but many came only because they knew that Sam Rayburn would be there.[103]

By 1948 Lyndon had spent eleven years in the House of Representatives. His early rise had been fast, but his career had stalled. He worried that his one mistake in the 1941 Senate race had doomed him to political obscurity. A severe eczema-like rash on his hands, which had bothered him intermittently for years, worsened and "made him suffer with each signature."[104] However, since substantial power was not possible for him in the House, he decided to try for the Senate again, even though he would have to sacrifice his House seat to enter the race. Johnson genuinely feared losing and had substantial reservations about making the physical and emotional sacrifices tied to a Senate race.[105] Yet, as he later told Doris Kearns, he felt that "something was missing from [his] life" and he wanted, as one friend remembered, "to be Senator more than anything else in the world right then."[106]

Despite his concern that his decision might signal the end of his political career, Johnson exuded confidence as he formally announced his candidacy at an afternoon press conference on 12 May 1948. Although he faced an uphill battle in trying to defeat "Coke" Stevenson, the popular governor, his decision to run for the Senate triggered an explosion of energy. With less than eleven weeks to go before the 24 July election, Johnson launched a heli-copter blitz of Texas that carried him to 118 cities and towns in 17 days. During his time on the road, Lyndon usually worked a twenty-hour day. Aides remembered that he "even worked in the bathtub!" He never stopped. The cost of the campaign was enormous, and both Johnson and Stevenson ignored the legal limitations dealing with campaign contributions.[107]

Although the election on 24 July gave Stevenson only 40 per cent of the votes cast and thus ensured a run-off campaign, it was a grave disappointment for Johnson. He had received a mere 34 per cent of the vote, while George Peddy, a third candidate, increased his share from the 11 per cent polled in early July to 20 per cent. In the run-off campaign, Johnson would have to capture 200,000 votes or nearly two out of three of the 320,000 votes cast for Peddy and the eight other minor candidates. "We thought we were going to come out of it winning or be real close to the top," Lady Bird said, "and we were overwhelmingly, vastly, horribly behind … It looked hopeless."[108]

Despite Lady Bird's fears of flying and speaking in public, Johnson decided that they had to get out the women's vote and so Lady Bird would have to meet local clubwomen and give interviews to local reporters. When aides mentioned that this would mean that Lady Bird would have to fly, Johnson said: "She'll fly." And fly she did – "perhaps as much out of concern about what the humiliation of overwhelming defeat would do to her husband."[109] Lady Bird knew only too well how much Johnson needed to win and, ever the loyal wife, she told Lyndon that "I'd rather put in our whole stack, borrow anything we could, work 18 hours a day, and lose by 60,000 than to lose by 70, or maybe we could hew it down to 50, or maybe we could even conceivably win."[110]

The overall result of the run-off, as one opinion poll earlier in the week had forecast, was so close that no one could be sure who won. The initial returns on election day, Saturday, 28 August, favoured Stevenson; by midnight he led by 2,119 votes out of the 939,468 counted. But then the see-saw battle began. By 9:00 p.m. on Sunday, Johnson held a 693-vote edge out of the 979,877 ballots cast, with an estimated 11,000 votes yet to be counted. By Monday evening, Stevenson had swung back into the lead by 119 votes, but 400 ballots were still uncounted. The following day, 31 August, the lead increased to 349 votes. When the Texas Election Bureau gave its final unofficial return on 2 September, Stevenson's lead was 262 votes.[111]

During the five days after the election, both sides had jockeyed to ensure a favourable outcome. Remembering that early reporting of pro-Johnson counties in 1941 had told O'Daniel's men how many votes they needed to win, and how a failure to watch east Texas counties closely had turned Johnson's victory into a defeat, Johnson backers now withheld final official tallies in several of his counties for as long as possible. Although both sides clearly engaged in vote manipulation, Johnson was better organized than his opponent. "Every time the Stevenson forces would come through with some votes," a Johnson insider later said, "Connally [his campaign manager] would top it." Having instructed Johnson supporters in various counties to under-count his vote and hold back final official returns, Connally now had Johnson backers send in higher tallies.[112]

The "corrected" returns on 3 September reduced Stevenson's total by 205 votes and increased Johnson's by 174, giving him a 17-vote lead. The biggest single shift had come from the town of Alice in Jim Wells County in south Texas where Johnson received an additional 202 votes and Stevenson one. Other "corrections" from around the state the next day increased Johnson's lead to 162. The altered results, particularly in Jim Wells, generated charges of fraud, and the evidence is persuasive. Following a lengthy controversy Johnson's name went on the ballot.[113]

After he had won the election in November and his title to the seat was confirmed in the Senate, Johnson developed a kind of gallows humour about the controversy. Although he told Harold Ickes that he wished he had won by 87,000 votes instead of 87, he could laugh at being dubbed "Landslide Lyndon." He also loved to tell a joke about a little Mexican boy in Alice sitting on the curb crying. A passer-by asked him, "Son, are you hurt?" He said, "No, I no hurt" ... "Are you sick?" ... "No, I no sick" ... "Are you hungry?" ... "No, I no hungry." The passer-by asked: "What's the matter? What are you crying for?" He said, "Well, yesterday, my papa, he been dead four years, yesterday, he come back and voted for Lyndon Johnson, and he didn't come by to say hello to me."[114] People hearing Johnson reminisce about the campaign or watching the smirks and winks with which he joked could hardly escape getting the impression that the election had been stolen and that he was not ashamed of the fact but rather proud of it. In 1967 a Texas journalist and long-time critic, Ronnie Dugger, who was writing a biography of Johnson, interviewed the president in his bedroom in the White House. According to Dugger, Johnson suddenly excused himself and returned "beaming" from Lady Bird's adjoining bedroom with a photograph of five smiling men gathered around the front hood of an automobile with a "Texas-1948 license plate." Balanced on the hood of the car was a ballot box marked "precinct 13." The men were all Jim Wells County political operatives. Dugger wrote that Johnson "held it [the photograph] forward to me with a kind of pride ... The President watched my face as I searched the photograph for its meaning," and "as I got it … he grinned at me with a vast inner enjoyment." A few years later, Dugger mentioned the photograph in conversation with Luis Salas, a Mexican barroom brawler who had been employed as a precinct enforcer by George Parr, the corrupt judge in Duval County, Texas. Salas said, "Yes, I know the one you mean!" and he showed Dugger his own copy of the photograph. Salas told him that it had been taken on the day of the second primary in 1948 – before the polls had closed.[115]

As Robert Caro has noted, "For a president to preserve as a personal memento a photograph showing the notorious Box 13 in the possession of his political allies – a photograph which by implication proves that someone was indeed in a position to stuff it – is startling in itself. For him to display the photograph to a hostile journalist is evidence of a psychological need so deep that its demands could not be resisted."[116]

But what motivated Johnson to boast implicitly about his manipulation and his wheeler-dealer abilities? Again, Caro astutely observes that Johnson's need to be known as calculating, shrewd, ruthless, and practical had its roots in the circumstances of Lyndon's youth. He was a member of a family that was a laughing-stock because it did not possess "common sense," the quality that mattered most in hill country. He was pained that he had been the son of a man whose honesty, idealism, and lack of pragmatism had led the family into ruin. His brother Sam knew that "it was most important to Lyndon not to be like Daddy." To prove that he was not, he needed to show that he possessed the "common sense" his father lacked even if it meant portraying himself as a wheeler-dealer.[117]

Almost no one disputed the fact that the additional votes in south Texas gave Johnson his narrow last-minute victory and that these votes were obtained by tainted means. The ballot manipulation was obvious; it called into question his legitimate claim to a Senate seat and drove him to justify his presence in that body by becoming one of its leading figures. Yet, even if there had been no question of his use of fraudulent means to secure his seat, Johnson's consuming ambition and his need to assert his power and authority would have required him to be the best senator Texas ever had. The public humiliation he had suffered, and even invited, made it imperative that he alleviate the damage to his self-esteem by proving that his detractors were wrong. He was determined to be remembered as one of the greatest members of the upper house in

American history. And he succeeded, thus satisfying some of his narcissistic needs.

Although Johnson's election in 1948 placed him among an exceptionally strong group of freshman senators, he quickly grasped the political possibilities that working quietly within the institution of the Senate could offer to a man of ambition. He was elected party whip and two years afterwards became the leader of the Democratic Party in the Senate. His success was attributable to his sophisticated understanding of the power of the coalition of conservative Republicans and southern Democrats which ran the Senate, and he soon became an important confidant of the senior senator from Georgia, Richard Russell. That he relished his growing reputation as "just about the hottest young senator in the Capitol," as many magazines were calling him, is hardly surprising. What is significant is the way in which his position as a freshman senator stimulated his grandiosity and ambition – the belief that it was he who ran both houses of Congress and deserved to be president one day.

In the spring of 1951, journalist and later Johnson biographer Alfred Steinberg interviewed Johnson. Steinberg later remembered how Johnson had tried to persuade him to write not an article on congressional leaders but "a whole big article on just me alone." Steinberg queried him as to "what would the pitch of an article on you be? That you might be a vice-presidential candidate for 1952?" Johnson was quick to reply, "Vice-President hell! Who wants that? ... President! That's the angle you want to write about me ... You can build it up by saying how I run both houses of Congress right now." Steinberg then asked Johnson for more details and received the following reply: "Well, right here in the Senate I have to do all of Boob McFarland's work because he can't do any of it ... And then every afternoon I go over to Sam Rayburn's place. He tells me all about the problems he's facing in the House, and I tell him how to handle them. So that's how come I'm running everything here in the Capitol."[118]

In 1955, when the Democrats gained control of the Senate, Lyndon Johnson became majority leader and won acceptance for his proposed reforms in the committee system. These reforms guaranteed each new senator at least one good committee assignment and reduced senior senators' major committee assignments from three to two. Freshmen senators would usually consult Johnson as to what committee assignments to apply for, and his advice and assistance enhanced his power. As Senate majority leader,

Johnson also became chairman of the Democratic policy committee in the Senate; under his chairmanship the policy committee
was confined largely to the task of scheduling legislation on the
floor. Whenever a senator wished either to expedite or to delay a
bill, he would have to request Johnson's assistance. Johnson used
the power with great skill, and the decisions of the policy committee came to express his will so much that he began to refer to it as
"my cabinet."[119]

As someone who was personally starved for recognition and lived
with the constant memories of his humiliating childhood and
youth, Johnson recognized that need in others. He built his net-
work of political alliances in the Senate, not only through the use
of his institutional prerogatives, but through the personal attention
he devoted to his colleagues. No courtesies were too small, or too
difficult, for Johnson to dispense. He attended funerals of mothers
and nieces of senators, even though he hated all funerals and was
apt to become physically ill in the presence of death. He was also
the purveyor of hundreds of cards and flowers dispatched on special occasions as well as hundreds of boxes of candy for all the men
and women who worked for the Senate.[120]

Recognizing that the older men in the Senate were often troubled by a growing awareness that their performance was deteriorating with age, Johnson made a special point of helping them with
their committee work, briefing them on the issues and assisting
them on the floor. These men, who had once been at the centre of
power, "now," as Johnson put it, "feared humiliation, they craved attention. And when they found it, it was like a spring in the desert;
their gratitude couldn't adequately express itself with anything less
than total support and dependence on me."[121] Johnson may well
have been right in his estimation of the impact that the desire for
recognition and the fear of humiliation had on his older fellow senators. Perhaps more important, his observations were extremely
suggestive of Johnson's own needs and fears.

Johnson's capacities for control and domination found their con-
summate manifestation during his private meetings with individual
senators. Face to face, behind office doors, Johnson would try to
persuade each senator that his support in some particular matter
was absolutely essential to the country, the Senate, the party leader,
and, last but not least, the senator himself. Having studied each
man carefully, he used that knowledge to supplement his own intu-
itive sense of what made that person tick. He would choose the

arguments, words, and rhythms that persuaded each listener best – and in this effort he had no peer.

In spite of his successes during his twelve-year career in the Senate, Johnson never felt as though he had "made it." It is of the essence of the narcissistic character that he (or she) is only as good as his last performance; he has difficulty deriving sustained pleasure from his past accomplishments and must have continuous external reinforcement as to his value. In later years, it rankled Johnson that his prodigious feats in the Senate failed to earn him the recognition and admiration of many in the media and academe. To Doris Kearns, he lamented:

A lot of people have written a lot of nonsense about my private meetings with Senators, that's because most of the writing is done by the intellectuals, who can never imagine me, a graduate from poor little San Marcos, engaged in an actual debate with words and with arguments, yet debating is what those sessions were all about.

But the Harvards, they picture it, instead, as a back-alley job with me holding the guy by the collar, twisting his arm behind his back, dangling a carrot in front of his nose, and holding a club over his head. It's a pretty amazing sight when you think about it. I'd have to be some sort of acrobatic genius to carry it off, and the Senator in question, well, he'd have to be pretty weak and pretty meek to be simply standing there like a paralyzed idiot.[122]

In his observations, one hears Johnson's frustration that he will never be accepted by the self-styled intellectuals whom he imagines as looking down on him and caricaturing his behaviour. We also see Johnson's deep-seated feelings of inferiority about his humble background and inferior education. Feeling misunderstood and humiliated by his perception of the intellectuals' contempt for him, Johnson proceeds to restore his damaged self-esteem by lashing out at the Harvard "types" and, in his fantasy, punishing them by denigrating their manhood.

From the autumn of 1958 to the Democratic convention in July 1960, Johnson was intimately involved in the struggle for the party's presidential nomination. By the beginning of 1959, political pundits agreed that senators Hubert Humphrey, Lyndon Johnson, John Kennedy, and Stuart Symington, New York Governor Averell Harriman, and former Illinois governor and presidential candidate

Adlai Stevenson were the front runners. Johnson, however, was torn between his tremendous desire to be president and his fear of failure. He believed that an open bid for the nomination would lead to his defeat. He worried that an aggressive campaign would strengthen the image of him as power-hungry, and he felt that his best chance for the nomination would be if he were publicly sought after rather than the reverse.[123]

Although Johnson was puzzled at the emergence of John Kennedy as the leading candidate,[124] he seemed ready to help Kennedy add to his lustre, but only up to a point. He had been prepared to support Kennedy's 1958 bill on labour reform, because he felt that would create a rapport between him and Joe Kennedy, Jack's father, that could be turned to good advantage if and when Jack's campaign faltered. Johnson had already supported Kennedy for the vice-presidency in 1956 and he had elevated him to the foreign relations committee in 1957. After he gave foreign relations to Kennedy instead of to Estes Kefauver, who was four years his senior, Lyndon "kept picturing old Joe Kennedy sitting there with all that power and wealth feeling indebted to me for the rest of his life, and I sure liked that picture."[125] In Johnson's fantasy, he could reverse previous experiences of humiliation at the hands of other rich and powerful men by turning the tables and making Joe Kennedy beholden to him.

The need to avenge previous experiences of humiliation by humiliating opponents or their surrogates was evident in an encounter that took place between Bobby Kennedy and Lyndon Johnson just after the close of the congressional session in September 1959. Uncertain about what Johnson's presidential intentions were, Jack Kennedy sent Bobby, his campaign manager, to Johnson's ranch to ask him directly. Johnson said he was not running and would neither oppose nor assist Jack. During the course of the visit, Johnson insisted that they hunt deer. Bobby was knocked to the ground and cut above the eye by the recoil of a powerful shotgun that Johnson had given him to use. Reaching down to help the thirty-four-year-old Bobby to his feet, Johnson, savouring the humiliation he had just inflicted, commented: "Son, you've got to learn to handle a gun like a man."[126] The message was clear, if only implicit: you're no man, and your brother is also a boy, unfit to be president.

Johnson told Bobby Baker that he knew ten times more about running the country than Jack did. "The kid needs a little gray in his hair," Lyndon said. He refused to take him seriously, referring to him as a "playboy" and a "lightweight" who was "smart enough" but had shown little capacity for the sort of hard work required of an effective president. What Johnson failed to appreciate was that his own success in the Senate had failed to endear him to many Americans, who saw only his crudeness and his wheeling and dealing. Such was his grandiosity that, convinced that he had earned the nomination and would make the best Democratic candidate, he assumed that the party would come to him without an all-out public effort on his part.[127]

But Lyndon's reluctance to campaign aggressively for the nomination may also have been a function of his fear of rejection and humiliation. To have openly tested his popularity in the primaries, and to have lost against any other candidate – all of whom he perceived to be far less qualified than himself – would have been a major blow to Johnson's ambitions and to his narcissistic personality structure. He carefully defended himself against that possibility by waiting to be chosen. If he were selected by his party, the chances of public humiliation would be considerably reduced; he would have behind him both a united party and an electorate that was tired of the politics of the Eisenhower administration.

Hubert Humphrey's defeat in the West Virginia primary convinced Johnson that Kennedy was probably unstoppable and that only some new aggressive strategy might deadlock the convention and make possible his own selection. He seized every opportunity to undercut Kennedy and question his suitability for the White House, and he stepped up the campaign to win delegate support. On 5 July, to no one's surprise, Johnson formally announced his candidacy, predicting that he would win on the third ballot. He attributed his late entry to his role as majority leader and his need to be present for all the Senate votes. As for the nomination, the issue before the convention was experience and capacity to lead.

On 13 July Kennedy won the nomination on the first ballot with 806 to Lyndon's 409 votes. Kennedy's first task as leader was to select a running-mate and Johnson's name appeared high on a number of lists prepared by his campaign advisers. In conversation with congressman Tip O'Neill, Kennedy said that, of course, he wanted Lyndon Johnson. "The only thing is, I would never want to offer it and have him turn me down; I would be terrifically embarrassed. He's the natural. If I can ever get him on the ticket, no way we can lose. We'd carry Texas. Certainly I want him. I'll call Sam Rayburn."[128]

There were good reasons for Johnson to want the vice-presidential nomination. Among them was Johnson's concern about the potential political alienation of the south. As Arthur Schlesinger, Jr, observed, he may well have seen in the vice-presidency "a means of leading the South back into the Democratic party and the national consensus."[129] Johnson also recognized that his power base was shrinking and that he could no longer control the Senate as he had in 1955–58. In 1959–60 party liberals and Eisenhower's assertiveness had undermined Johnson's leadership. He recognized that his best days as majority leader had passed. "Power is where power goes," he explained to a friend who was counselling him to reject Kennedy's offer.[130]

Ignoring the historical evidence that the vice-presidency had never constituted a power base, Johnson believed that he could turn it to his advantage. Repeatedly, as assistant to president Cecil Evans at San Marcos, as speaker of the Little Congress (a body formed by congressional secretaries in 1919), as party whip and leader, Johnson had taken positions with no apparent power base and recast and expanded their functions in a unprecedented fashion. He simply assumed that the vice-presidency would be no different.[131]

Therefore, Johnson accepted his party's nomination. The events leading to his selection as the vice-presidential nominee are virtually impossible to reconstruct since there are almost as many versions as there were participants in the unfolding drama. What is certain is that Johnson emerged from the process feeling humiliated and enraged, particularly with Bobby Kennedy but also with Jack Kennedy, whom he never completely exonerated.

At about 8 a.m. on the morning of 14 July, Jack called Johnson; at around ten o'clock, he met with him and invited him to join the ticket. According to Robert Kennedy, Jack had no expectation that Johnson would accept, and when he did Jack and Bobby spent the rest of the day "alternating between thinking it was good, and thinking that it wasn't good that he'd offered him the vice presidency – and how could he get out of it."[132]

Although it is difficult to believe that Jack was surprised that Johnson was interested in the nomination, there can be little doubt that the Kennedy camp was thrown into disarray once Johnson accepted the offer. When the principal campaign advisers were informed, a raging debate erupted. Kenneth O'Donnell later said that he was "so furious" that he "could hardly talk. I thought of the

promises we had made to the labor leaders and civil rights groups
… I felt that we had been doublecrossed." Meetings with labour
leaders Walter Reuther, Arthur Goldberg, Jack Conway, and Alex
Rose elicited the same reaction.[133]

According to Robert Kennedy's recollection, shortly after offering Johnson the vice-presidential nomination, the Kennedys tried
to get him to withdraw. Between two and four in the afternoon,
Bobby Kennedy remembered seeing Johnson twice: first to feel him
out, and then to propose his withdrawal. At the second meeting, as
Bobby remembered it, Johnson, after receiving the news, turned on
a sad look, shook, and, with tears in his eyes, said, "I want to be Vice
President, and if the president will have me, I'll join with him in
making a fight for it." Kennedy then said, "Well, then that's fine.
He wants you to be Vice President if you want to be Vice President."[134]

Others such as Phil Graham remembered the Bobby Kennedy
visits differently. Rather than seeing Lyndon the first time, Bobby
saw Sam Rayburn. Bobby suggested to Sam that Lyndon be Democratic national chairman instead of vice-president. "Rayburn is reported to have given Bobby a long look and answered 'Shit.'" Lady
Bird and Graham persuaded Johnson not to see Bobby. Graham
called Jack to tell him that Johnson would take the nomination
only if Jack were to draft him. Jack asked Graham to call back a few
minutes later since he was tied up in meetings. When Graham got
back to him, Kennedy said, "It's all set … Tell Lyndon I want
him."[135]

Graham did precisely as he was told, only to receive a call from
Johnson shortly thereafter to say that "Bobby Kennedy had been
back down to see Rayburn some twenty minutes before and had
said Jack would phone directly." No call had come and Johnson was
very anxious. Finally, Graham telephoned Kennedy. When told
what Bobby had said to Rayburn, he promised to call Johnson at
once, but he also talked about the opposition to Johnson and asked
Graham for his advice. Graham attempted to reassure Jack and advised him that southern gains to be achieved through Johnson's
nomination would more than offset losses among liberals.[136]

Shortly afterwards, Kennedy called Johnson and read him a press
release about the vice-presidency. Johnson's only response was: "Do
you really want me?" Kennedy said, "Yes," and Lyndon said, "Well,
if you really want me, I'll do it."[137] In this brief, poignant exchange,
we can see Johnson's need to deny the evidence that he is not

wanted. To further his ambitions, he was prepared to accept Kennedy's minimalist response. But what followed was a further humiliation that left its mark on Johnson's psyche and made him into an implacable opponent of brother Bobby.

Just after 4:00 in the afternoon, while he was trying to reach Bobby Kennedy about seconding speeches for Johnson, Graham received another summons from Johnson. He found him "in a high state of nerves ... about to jump out of his skin. He shouted at me that Bobby Kennedy had just come in and told Rayburn and him that there was much opposition and that Lyndon should withdraw for the sake of the Party." Prodded by Rayburn, Graham called Kennedy again. "'Jack,' I said, 'Bobby is down here and is telling the Speaker and Lyndon that there is opposition and Lyndon should withdraw.' 'Oh,' said Jack, as calmly as though we were discussing the weather, 'that's all right; Bobby's been out of touch and doesn't know what's been happening.'" Kennedy then asked that Lyndon make a statement right away, adding that he had just finished making his. Jack then asked to speak to Bobby who said "Well, it's too late now," and Graham saw Bobby "half slam down the phone."[138]

Phil Graham believed that Bobby Kennedy had acted on his own in trying to keep Johnson off the ticket. But Bobby later disputed Graham's conclusion, arguing that, given the close relationship between him and his brother, he would not have acted on his own initiative.[139] Johnson staffer Jim Rowe later told biographer Merle Miller: "My own theory is that Bobby had left Jack Kennedy's suite to tell Johnson that there was a hell of a lot of pressure against him. While he was gone, Graham called Jack and then Jack called Lyndon. But Bobby didn't know that Jack had just called and made the final commitment. It was just a matter of bad timing, but Johnson thought that Bobby was out to get him, to do him in."[140]

Whether Rowe or Graham was right is a matter of interest to historians and political scientists; from a psychological perspective, what is important is that Johnson believed Graham's thesis – it was less devastating to accept it than to believe that Jack was trying to weasel out of his offer. He never forgave Bobby, and in his dealings with the Kennedys and their circle he never really overcame this attack on his always vulnerable self-esteem.

At the end of July, Johnson went to the Kennedy compound at Cape Cod to discuss campaign strategy. Of principal concern was the need for Johnson to do a selling job for the ticket in the south without alienating northern liberals. It was decided that Johnson would emulate former president Harry Truman, who had used the back platform of a train so effectively. Starting in Virginia, Johnson's train trip covered 3,500 miles across eight states and included sixty speeches.[141]

It soon became apparent that Johnson's influence in the south might be limited. Hecklers with signs declaring "LBJ is a Friend of Socialism" and "The *Yellow* Rose of Texas" showed up in the crowds that gathered to meet the train. Lyndon was especially worried about Texas, where the race was close. In mid-October, he told John Connally that he was "deeply disturbed about Texas ... We just must not win the nation and lose Texas. Imagine when we win how the new Administration will look upon us."[142] Jim Rowe remembered that Johnson "was wound up tight like a top and I think the ever haunting fear of losing Texas never left him for a second."[143] Johnson knew that the thinly veiled contempt of the Kennedy advisers prior to the election would only escalate should Kennedy win without Texas; he would suffer even more slights and humiliations and his dreams of an expanded role for the vice-presidency would be reduced to ashes.

Johnson's prayers were at least partially answered on 8 November, when Kennedy won the presidency by 112,881 votes out of the 66,832,818 cast and the Democratic Party captured the Electoral College votes of Texas with a slim margin of 46,233 votes out of a total of 2,311,670. It had been a tight race. Johnson won his own Senate seat by a larger but closer than expected margin, obtaining 56.5 per cent of the votes compared to 43.5 per cent for his Republican rival, John Tower.

But Johnson's hope that he might remain an effective and powerful political figure in the vice-presidency was doomed to disappointment. When the Senate Democrats convened in caucus on 3 January 1961, Mike Mansfield of Montana, the new majority leader, proposed to change the rules so as to elect the new vice-president the chairman of the Democratic conference, which would make him the presiding officer at formal meetings of the Senate's Democratic members. Mansfield's proposal, which he had failed to clear with his colleagues, was strongly attacked. Liberals and conservatives joined in arguing that such a move would surely violate the spirit of the separation of powers. Unspoken was the fear that it might also violate their autonomy and independence; Democratic senators were reluctant to give Johnson the opportunity to control their deliberations.

When the motion came up for discussion, seventeen senators voted nay, a number large enough to persuade Mansfield and Johnson to let the motion die.[144]

Johnson was deeply wounded by the vote and interpreted it as a profoundly personal rejection. All the hopes he had entertained of leading the Congress from the vice-president's chair were dashed. His loss of power was clear for all to see; he had been separated from the institution to which he believed he had given the best part of his life.[145] Although he seldom mentioned the humiliation of that caucus vote, he never forgot it. He responded in one of the two ways that deeply humiliated people frequently do. Rather than lashing out aggressively and restoring his self-esteem, he was so hurt and angry over the seventeen negative votes that he simply withdrew from exercising any significant leadership role in the Senate. It may be that his behaviour, rather than being a bitter disappointment to the president, as Kearns has suggested,[146] was preferable to the alternative – Johnson as a powerful rival.

Indeed, Kennedy relied on his own congressional liaison staff and called on the vice-president only on occasion. Johnson himself was incredulous that he was not consulted more about administration bills and tactics in Congress.[147] His being ignored in this way undoubtedly contributed to his feelings of rejection and powerlessness which, in turn, manifested themselves as silence at the president's weekly White House breakfasts for legislative leaders. Johnson rarely said a word at these meetings. When asked directly by Kennedy for his opinion on a bill, he answered in monosyllables so low he could scarcely be heard.[148]

Nor was Johnson more successful in his dealings with the executive branch. Shortly after the inauguration he sent an unusual executive order to the Oval Office for President Kennedy's signature. It outlined a wide range of issues over which the new vice-president would have "general supervision" and effectively placed every department and agency on notice that Lyndon Johnson was to receive all reports, information, and policy plans that were generally sent to the president himself. The document led to remarks in the White House comparing Johnson to William Seward, Abraham Lincoln's secretary of state, who had sent his president an equally grandiose memo on how the government should be conducted and how he, Seward, should be the lead conductor. Kennedy's response was similar to Lincoln's; in both cases, the memos were diplomatically shelved.[149]

Having been, in his view, rejected from playing a significant role in the new administration, Johnson was loath to assert himself. His gloomy silence at cabinet and National Security Council (NSC) meetings was misinterpreted by Robert Kennedy as a sign of inability to cope with the great problems of the day, and Bobby's views were widely circulated throughout the administration. Johnson's golden days as majority leader were forgotten. He began to be marked down as a lightweight – a back-room politician ill-equipped to meet the challenges of the 1960s.[150]

From there, it was an easy step for Lyndon Johnson to become the butt of jokes throughout Washington. "Whatever happened to Lyndon?" became the often asked question of the day. Since he was deeply sensitive to any hint of criticism, such abuse hurt Johnson and some of his friends promptly blamed the Kennedys for starting it. The criticism also raised Johnson's guard and increased his caution, which in turn further lowered the administration's regard for him.[151]

Johnson found it particularly difficult to accept the cultural critique implicit in the comparison between him, the western cowboy, and Kennedy, the urbane aristocrat. The more praise Kennedy received for his oratorical ability, for his skill in debating, and for his brilliant parries at press conferences, the more uneasy the vice-president felt in front of even the most friendly audience. Nor was he comfortable with what he described as "all the fuss and excitement" about Kennedy's transforming Washington into a cultural centre.[152]

Apprehensive at being judged culturally inferior, Johnson groaned at every announcement of another luncheon for writers and scholars and loathed each new invitation to a formal dinner. He would read the lists of the invited guests, who included such luminaries as Thornton Wilder, Tennessee Williams, Arthur Miller, Paddy Chayefsky, Edmund Wilson, Elia Kazan, Leonard Bernstein, Fredric March, and Sir Ralph Richardson. At most, he knew the names of two or three and could never think of more than ten words to say to any of them. In the hush of these formal settings, when, as Johnson later described it to Doris Kearns, the White House smelled like a musty museum or a university lecture room, he felt called upon to speak on music, literature, or art, about which he knew little and cared less. Repeated exposures to Kennedy's guests made him feel more and more like an outsider, and he became embarrassed and resentful at what he viewed as his inability to perform as well as others expected.[153]

Johnson's attempts to eradicate his sense of social and cultural inferiority had their amusing side. In an effort to acquire the sophistication of the Kennedys and their associates, he tried emulating them. Reading that President Kennedy loved soups, Johnson insisted that his plane be stocked with dozens of soups. Once in a restaurant he watched Secretary of Defense Robert McNamara order shrimp salad with precisely three shrimps. For weeks after that, Johnson ordered exactly the same thing.[154]

For Johnson, the loss of a leadership position was like a political death. There were times, Johnson later admitted, when he felt that he would simply shrivel up.[155] His brother Sam believed that Johnson's stay in the vice-presidency was the most miserable three years of his life. "I know him well enough," he wrote, "to know he felt humiliated time and time again, that he was openly snubbed by second echelon White House staffers who snickered at him behind his back and called him 'Uncle Cornpone.'"[156] Johnson's responses to his reduced importance during his tenure as vice-president demonstrated his vulnerable self-esteem. Lacking adequate endogenous sources of esteem and heavily dependent on external refuelling, Johnson was devastated by the destruction of the world that had so rewarded him as majority leader.[157] He thought about becoming a one-term vice-president, and he talked vaguely about leaving politics altogether in 1964 and returning to Texas. He mentioned the possibility of becoming president of his alma mater, Southwest Texas State Teachers College in San Marcos.[158] Returning from one of his last trips abroad as vice-president in the autumn of 1963, Johnson was gloomy and morose about his future. "His friends felt," write journalists Rowland Evans and Robert Novak, that "he was concerned more about being dumped from the ticket in 1964 than in dropping off it voluntarily. In early October, he complained to a Texas congressman that he had lost the president's confidence. 'Why does the White House have it in for me?' he asked, and he became preoccupied with fears that Kennedy would pick someone else for his running-mate in 1964."[159]

The fateful events of 22 November 1963 dramatically altered the political agenda. With the assassination of President Kennedy, Lyndon Johnson, the outsider, suddenly became the quintessential insider – but only in title. He continued to feel vulnerable to comparisons with his predecessor, John Kennedy. As Johnson was later to describe his situation to Doris Kearns: "I took the oath, I became President. But for millions of Americans I was still illegitimate, a naked man with no presidential covering, a pretender to the throne, an illegal usurper. And then there was Texas, my home, the home of both the murder and the murder of the murderer. And then there were the bigots and the dividers and the Eastern intellectuals, who were waiting to knock me down before I could even begin to stand up. The whole thing was almost unbearable."[160]

But notwithstanding Johnson's palpable sense of shame – references to his lack of a legitimate claim on the presidency, his nakedness, and his fear of humiliation at the hands of his enemies – he was able to effect a smooth transfer of governmental authority and assure his own nomination for the presidency. Nowhere was his skilful handling of the transition better illustrated than in his treatment of the members of the cabinet and the White House staff. Recognizing the immense popularity of the late president among Democratic supporters, Johnson was determined to inherit his mantle by executing his will and "this meant his people as well as his programs. They were part of his legacy. I simply couldn't let the country think that I was all alone."[161] The Kennedy team would cover his "nakedness," make him legitimate, and protect him from the humiliating barbs of the eastern establishment.

Johnson met personally with all of the Kennedy men, and, through a powerful mixture of rational argument and emotional appeals, convinced them to stay on. Although he approached each of these men differently, depending on their particular relationship to the late president, his appeals ended in the same way: "I know how much he needed you. But it must make sense to you that, if he needed you, I need you that much more. And so does our country."[162] In atypical fashion, Johnson requested rather than ordered; he spoke of his shortcomings and shared his doubts. And he was successful. With the exception of Theodore Sorensen, who resigned, and Robert Kennedy, who rarely showed up for work, the large majority stayed on – Robert McNamara, McGeorge Bundy, Kenneth O'Donnell, Dean Rusk, Richard Goodwin, Lawrence O'Brien, among others. Gradually, Johnson added his own people to the White House staff – Walter Jenkins, George Reedy, Jack Valenti, Bill Moyers, and Horace Busby – but they, too, were expected to show deference to the Kennedy men.

Even after Johnson won an overwhelming electoral victory eleven months later, he kept a number of the Kennedy people, such as McNamara, Rusk, and McGeorge Bundy, in the cabinet. Partly he admired their talents and ability, but his approach also reflected his idealization of Kennedy and the eastern intellectuals and his desperate craving for their respect. As he himself admitted to Doris Kearns in response to her question of why Johnson kept the Kennedy men: "I needed that White House staff. Without them I would have lost my link to John Kennedy, and without that I would have had absolutely no chance of gaining the support of the media or the Easterners or the intellectuals. And without that support I would have had absolutely no chance of governing the country."[163] Johnson's brief period as vice-president had so shamed and humiliated him that he was convinced that, if left to their own devices, the Kennedy men and their allies in the media and the eastern intellectual establishment would undermine and destroy his presidency.

Publicly, Johnson was forced to woo Kennedy's advisers and then ask for their help to maintain a continuity of authority. And the more he tried to do so, the less could he be his own uninhibited self. His salty style had to be toned down, and he assumed an alien dignity that came across on television as acute discomfort. His insecurities were exposed by this situation as by no other. George Ball rightly observed that Johnson, ringed by Kennedy's Rhodes scholars, did not suffer from the lack of a good education but from his *sense* of lacking a good education.[164]

The Kennedys, Johnson complained, would never let him rule in his own right. The more he deferred to them, the more they tried to make his White House theirs, even before he had left it.[165] But why did he continue to tolerate their condescension and backbiting in the face of the massive electoral mandate that he had received from the American people? Johnson, like many narcissistic characters, was a prisoner of his need for constant reassurance and approval from those individuals whom he had unconsciously designated as "ideal objects" and whose support was essential to shore up his fragile sense of self.

Privately, Johnson's behaviour on relatively minor issues revealed a need to respond vindictively to the shame of feeling like an usurper to the throne. When an intimate of the late President Kennedy went to the White House to talk to Johnson alone for the first time, he brought up two items of unfinished business. Kennedy, he said, had planned to name two distinguished Harvard professors to high office. Economist Seymour Harris was to be a member of the Federal Reserve Board; Samuel Beer, a professor of government, was to be ambassador to Uruguay. The appointments had been cleared by the White House shortly before Kennedy left for Texas. Kennedy's friend told Johnson that Arthur Schlesinger, Jr, was confident that Beer was an excellent choice for Uruguay. Johnson replied, "Arthur Schlesinger isn't running Latin American policy anymore." In 1960, as national chairman of the ADA (Americans for Democratic Action), Beer had prepared an attack on Johnson's presidential candidacy. Neither Beer nor Harris was appointed.[166] In this covert fashion, Johnson could allow himself the luxury of "sticking it" to the "Harvards" and the late President Kennedy – as compensation for the need to maintain his legitimacy by retaining virtually all of Kennedy's senior advisers.

But there was one senior adviser whom Johnson could not abide – Bobby Kennedy – and he was determined to cut his nemesis down to size. He saw Bobby as the symbol of the emotion and sentimentality that swept the country after Dallas, as the custodian of the Kennedy dream. He was also, in Johnson's view, the architect of that humiliating moment in 1960 when Johnson had been told that Jack Kennedy did not want him on the ticket.

In the early months of 1964, close Johnson advisers spent countless hours discussing the "Bobby problem." The president told intimates that he had devoted three years' service to John Kennedy and the time now had come for total independence from the Kennedys. If he took Bobby Kennedy on the presidential ticket with him, he feared that his presidency would become a transitory episode between two Kennedys. "If Bobby became Vice-President," Johnson told close friend and prominent Democrat Clark Clifford, he "would forever be sandwiched between the two Kennedy brothers, unable to govern or command public support for his programs."[167] He rejected that possibility out of hand.

When Robert Kennedy refused to help Johnson by declaring that he was not a candidate, Johnson, in order to ensure that Bobby Kennedy was excluded from consideration for the post of vice-president, announced: "It would be inadvisable for me to recommend to the convention any member of my Cabinet or any of those who meet regularly with the Cabinet." The Bobby problem had been dealt with by a mass execution of the entire cabinet as well as two vice-presidential dark horses who met regularly with the cabinet, Adlai Stevenson and Sargent Shriver.[168]

Prior to the announcement, Johnson called in three White House correspondents for a leisurely lunch. During this lunch he described a meeting with Kennedy in which he informed him that he would not be on the ticket. Mimicking Bobby, Johnson demonstrated how Kennedy had gulped when the news was broken.[169] Having been treated with humiliating disdain by Robert Kennedy, Johnson could not resist the temptation to retaliate.

Even when there was no external stimulus, Johnson's need to humiliate his associates kept resurfacing. In the case of his eventual choice as vice-president, Hubert Humphrey, he seized opportunities to remind him of his total dependence, forcing him to behave with a demeaning servility. The indignities Humphrey was subjected to ranged from the petty – not being permitted to take out the presidential yacht or use one of the many available private planes without an inordinate amount of red tape – to the more serious – being excluded from the significant decisions on the Vietnam War because of his expressed opposition to escalation.[170]

In November 1964, two months before taking office, Humphrey had given a speech in New York on education. Carried away by his enthusiasm, he departed from his text and in so doing incurred the president's wrath. Johnson was furious at Humphrey for giving the impression that perhaps he would be the architect of the administration's education policies; this was Johnson's terrain and Humphrey was given that message in no uncertain terms. To ensure that there would be no mistake about it, Johnson called in the White House reporters who were with him on the ranch and told them, "Boys, I've just reminded Hubert that I've got his balls in my pocket."[171]

One month after Humphrey became vice-president, Johnson humiliated him again. When Winston Churchill died after a long illness that first January of Humphrey's term, Johnson withheld the privilege from his vice-president of attending the funeral to represent the United States and, instead, sent Chief Justice Earl Warren.[172]

It became clear that Johnson had no intention of protecting Humphrey from that special misery he, himself, had suffered as vice-president; on the contrary, he intended to pass it on in even greater doses. George Ball commented that Johnson "treated him [Humphrey] pretty much in the way the Kennedys treated him [Johnson] when he was vice president. I would have thought that Johnson, having been through this miserable experience himself and being excluded from most things, would have leaned overback-wards to treat Humphrey differently, but he didn't."[173]

From a psychoanalytical perspective, Johnson's behaviour can be understood as an unconscious re-enactment of the experiences of shame and humiliation he had endured as vice-president. In his efforts to master these and earlier shame-filled ordeals, he turned passive into active. Rather than continuing to see himself as a vic-tim, he identified with the aggressive behaviour of his tormentors. Johnson humiliated Humphrey the way he, in turn, had been hu-miliated by Kennedy.

Publicly, Johnson was determined to avoid situations that would demonstrate his vulnerability to being shamed. Nowhere was his awareness of the potential for being humiliated more apparent than in the field of foreign policy. His interests and achievements as a senator had been in the realm of domestic affairs. And while he had learned the language of international conflict, he was not an abstract, deductive thinker. He thought in terms of personalities, power, and good works. Thus, for example, Johnson had visited South Vietnam once for three days and had met Ngo Dinh Diem, but now Diem was dead and he knew almost nothing about his successor. Without the ability to personalize American-South Viet-namese relationships, Johnson was at a loss.[174]

Sceptical of his own ability to sort out the complicated strands of religion, political parties, and culture in the Vietnam conflict, Johnson became increasingly dependent on John Kennedy's men – Robert McNamara, McGeorge Bundy, Dean Rusk, and Maxwell Tay-lor – and reluctant to challenge their perspectives lest his igno-rance and naïvety be questioned. Johnson believed, author Tom Wicker has suggested, that "there was a close relationship between the Kennedy family and 'claque' and political columnists like Joseph Alsop; he was exceptionally eager to avoid action that would cause these columnists to write that he was ignoring or going against the advice of McNamara, Bundy, Taylor, Lodge and others who had been appointed by Kennedy."[175] As we shall see, Johnson became a virtual hostage to the "best and the brightest" and, despite serious misgivings, accepted their recommendations for escalating the Vietnam War rather than lose face.

3 Johnson and Vietnam

An almost undisputed consensus exists that Lyndon Johnson's decision to begin the systematic bombing of North Vietnam and commit hundreds of thousands of American combat troops to South Vietnam was a mistake of gigantic proportions. But why did Johnson commit America's power and prestige in a risky land war in Asia? Part of the explanation lies in the nature of his world-view. Like Truman, Eisenhower, Kennedy, and most of America's foreign-policy leaders after the Second World War, Johnson subscribed to sharply etched stereotypes of communism and democracy and firmly believed that communism had to be contained or it would destroy democratic regimes. Like his predecessors, too, Johnson was convinced that communism threatened the American way of life and that any communist gains anywhere weakened the long-term American effort to contain and defeat the world-wide communist menace.

Acceptance of the containment philosophy, however, did not mean that the United States would invariably take decisive action to counter the extension of communist power everywhere. Three major Vietnam decisions taken prior to 1965 reveal that the United States was prepared to accept the defeat of the French at Dien Bien Phu (1954), to live with a negotiated settlement in Laos (1961), and to avoid direct military confrontation with the National Liberation Front (NLF) (1961). In each of these cases, senior policy makers, including the president, believed that if communist advances were not stopped vital American interests would be adversely affected. But the responses varied. As Yen Foong Khong has argued: "Containment, therefore, cannot tell us whether U.S. concerns will result in action or not: neither can it tell us the form of the action if it is taken."[1]

Given that containment seems consistent with a variety of outcomes – from refusing to intervene militarily (1954) to military intervention (1965) – the question arises as to what other factors might be useful in discriminating between outcomes. Cognitive psychologists point to the important role that the use of historical analogies play in shaping decision makers' preferences.[2] They explain the acceptance of particular historical analogies with reference to formative generational experiences, while tending to ignore the deeper psychological factors that may influence the choice of analogies. But this focus fails to explain the differences in the Vietnam policies of Eisenhower and Johnson. Both men belonged to the same generational cohort; both used Korea as their principal historical analogy; and yet each man drew very different lessons from that analogy and chose very different policies.

The choice of an analogy may, in and of itself, be insufficient to explain the broad decisions of refusing to intervene militarily or escalating significantly. If, as I will argue, personality variables, and more particularly the feelings of shame and humiliation to which the narcissistic political leader is most vulnerable, are neglected explanatory factors, then this may explain both the choice of analogy and the particular meaning ascribed to it.

Lyndon Johnson's resolve to escalate the Vietnam War was the product, not merely of the political context in which he found himself, but of the impact of his psychological needs on that environment. Those needs created a prism through which strategic, bureaucratic, cognitive, and domestic factors were filtered. His decisions were, in significant measure, the responses of a president whose primary concerns were, first, to avoid both the private and the public humiliation that would stem from abandoning South Vietnam, and, second, to resist those military options that might involve the United States in a war with China.[3] On a personal level, Johnson was anxious to retain the loyalty and support of the Kennedy team of advisers and to avoid taking decisions that could expose him to charges of naïvety and ignorance about foreign affairs. At the public level, Johnson was concerned not to be the first American president to lose Vietnam and not to make himself and the Democratic Party vulnerable to charges of treason or softness on communism.

The psychological meaning underlying those priorities was Johnson's need to prove that he was not a "sissy" or a coward, that he was brave enough to stand the heat, and that, even though the going was tough, he was not going "to cut and run." As well, Johnson was determined to be perceived as in control and competent – a worthy successor to John F. Kennedy. What had to be avoided at all costs was the threat to his self-esteem that any private or public humiliation might entail.

To argue that Johnson was particularly susceptible to a small coterie of advisers who urged escalation is not to argue, as does Irving Janis, that Johnson was a victim of "groupthink" since his advisers failed "to canvas the full range of alternative courses of action."4 There is ample evidence to suggest that close advisers who opposed escalating the war included not only George Ball, the under-secretary of state, but at least five other important political figures, Vice-President Hubert Humphrey, Senator Richard Russell, Clark Clifford (then head of the Foreign Intelligence Advisory Board), Senator J. William Fulbright, and Senator Mike Mansfield – all of whom had continuing access to Johnson in the period under consideration and communicated their strong reservations to him.5 What emerges is the picture of a president who wrestled with the different courses of action open to him in dealing with the Vietnam problem, but who ultimately resolved in favour of escalation. His decision was strongly influenced by his fear of losing the support of Kennedy's senior advisers and exposing himself to public assaults on his courage and commitment.

Ball and Russell (and to a lesser degree, Humphrey and Mansfield) voiced their own personal theories about why Johnson chose to go to war in Vietnam.6 While differing somewhat on the details, there was (and is) widespread agreement that, in matters of foreign policy, Lyndon Johnson was unusually susceptible to the influence of the so-called intellectuals in the Johnson administration who were hold-overs from the preceding presidency of John Kennedy.7 They included McGeorge Bundy, Dean Rusk, and, most especially, Robert McNamara.

Bundy had served Kennedy as special assistant for national security affairs before working for Johnson. A graduate of Yale with Phi Beta Kappa honours, Bundy had gone on to be a Harvard professor and dean. A reserved, somewhat cold man, he none the less enjoyed Johnson's considerable respect. Dean Rusk was another Phi Beta Kappa man, a Rhodes scholar and former president of the Rockefeller Foundation. He and Johnson shared a personal bond as southerners. But far and away the most influential member of the Johnson cabinet during the early war years was McNamara. Johnson respected his intelligence and his Johnson-like capacity for work and was impressed by his success in business and his rise to the presidency of the Ford Motor Company. He was, said Johnson, the "smartest man" he had ever known,[8] a man in whose presence you could "almost hear the computers clicking."[9] As Johnson's aide Harry McPherson observed: "Johnson promoted McNamara everywhere ... No doubt he was trying to win over" the Kennedy people "as his personal friends and supporters."[10]

Ball, Russell, Mansfield, and Humphrey were aware of the powerful hold Johnson's inner circle of foreign-policy advisers had upon him, and they believed that his dependency upon these advisers explained his decisions to escalate the war. Humphrey saw Lyndon Johnson trying "desperately and sincerely" to continue the Kennedy mandate, to "assuage the Kennedy people," and to be the heir to the affections of the Kennedy insiders as well as the nation.[11] George Ball remarked that "President Johnson was overawed by these people around him," and "the fact that Johnson never went to a high-class school meant that he took them more seriously than he should."[12]

According to Ball, "the impetus toward escalation never came from Lyndon Johnson." Johnson was "dragged into Vietnam" by men like Bundy, who saw the Vietnam situation as a "fascinating set of operational problems," and McNamara, who "was analyzing this thing as a man who was trained in quantification, who believed in systems analysis, who believed in application of games theory to strategy, who was enormously persuaded by the disparity in military power."[13]

Richard Russell lamented to a friend at the end of 1965 that, although McNamara had "made many mistakes" in the area of international relations, he nevertheless exercised a "hypnotic" influence over the president.[14] Like Russell, Mike Mansfield saw in the secretary of defense a man who was pushing a somewhat reluctant Lyndon Johnson into Vietnam.[15] He pleaded with the president: "I think it is about time you got an accounting from those who have pressured you in the past to embark on this course and continue to pressure you to stay on it. It is time to ask, not only what immediate advantages it has in a narrow military sense, but where does it lead in the end."[16] Johnson responded: "I consider Bob McNamara to be the best Secretary of Defense in the history of this country."[17] Criticism of McNamara would not be entertained.[18]

The views expressed by Ball, Russell, Mansfield, and Humphrey all underscored the insecurity vis-à-vis the "intellectuals" that led Johnson towards a policy of escalation.[19] And, as will be demonstrated in greater detail, what lay behind Johnson's insecurity was a fear of being humiliated and scorned should he become the first president to lose a war.

Since so many of Johnson's advisers favoured military intervention in 1964 and 1965, does that imply that they, too, were motivated by the same narcissistic problems as Johnson? Although that possibility cannot be ruled out a priori, an analysis of the factors motivating the senior American bureaucratic establishment in the area of national-security policy goes beyond the scope of this inquiry. Here the focus is on Johnson's behaviour and motivations. And the critical issue is not that Johnson ultimately came to favour escalation, but that his tortured assessment of options suggests internal psychic conflicts that highlight issues of shame and humiliation. Even if Johnson's decisions had produced "victory" in Vietnam, his narcissistic traits would still have been an integral part of that process. The same personality characteristics that under certain conditions may contribute to policy failures can also be at work in contributing to a leader's skilful behaviour and successes.

In November 1963 it would not have been especially difficult to disengage from Vietnam. There were only a few thousand American troops there and all of them were professional soldiers. Furthermore, the vast majority of Americans knew little or nothing about the conflict in Vietnam. Johnson himself, notwithstanding his strong anti-communist beliefs and his acceptance of the fundamental precepts of the domino theory, was concerned about the widening scope of American involvement in Vietnam. He had opposed any American intervention in 1954 to rescue the French at Dien Bien Phu, and he was sensitive to the classic American military doctrine which opposed fighting a land war in Asia. Why then, George Reedy, his press secretary, has asked, did he not pull out when the pulling was good?

Reedy argues that psychological factors played an important role. He recalls that, from the first White House meeting after the assassination of President Kennedy, it was clear that in the realm of foreign policy the new president was not really prepared to lead. Instead, he looked to Kennedy's people for cues as to what the former president would have done. Without their support, Johnson seemed unable to reach a decision. Eventually, he would follow the Kennedy people into the quagmire of a land war in Vietnam rather than challenge their views and risk losing their support.[20]

Aside from the influence of the Kennedy advisers, two other factors linked to narcissistic issues and the attempt to avoid shame played their part in Johnson's continuing escalation of the war. First, he felt a deep responsibility for the wounded and the dead, and this was translated into a determination that their suffering would not be in vain. To Johnson, the United States had to "win" in order to vindicate its casualties[21] and, by implication, presidential decisions that had led to those injuries and deaths. To abandon the battlefield in the light of American casualties was seen as a shameful act. Secondly, as vice-president, Johnson had visited Vietnam and used extravagant language in promising American support against North Vietnam. He felt that he had an obligation not to go back on his word[22]; reneging on his commitment would have been shame-inducing.

Johnson's first direct exposure to South Vietnam came in May 1961 when he visited President Ngo Dinh Diem in Saigon as part of the Kennedy strategy to allay Diem's anxiety over the administration's willingness to negotiate a settlement in Laos. Johnson was also charged with asking Diem whether he wanted American troops and a bilateral defense treaty with the United States, both of which Diem refused.[23] After talks with Diem, Johnson likened him to the "Winston Churchill of Southeast Asia" and issued a joint statement signed by himself and the South Vietnamese leader which read: "The United States recognizes that the President of Vietnam, Ngo Dinh Diem, who was recently re-elected to office by an overwhelming majority of his countrymen despite bitter Communist opposition, is in the vanguard of those leaders who stand for freedom on the periphery of the Communist empire in Asia."

In the two months before his death, Kennedy's public utterances expressed his determination that the United States had to remain in Vietnam. On 2 September 1963, in a well-publicized television interview with Walter Cronkite, the president expressed disagreement with those who urged withdrawal from Vietnam, although he acknowledged that he did not think the Diem regime would be able to regain popular support without "changes in policy and perhaps with personnel." In another television interview a week later, this time with Chet Huntley and David Brinkley, he underscored his insistence that there would be no withdrawal by attesting to his belief in the "domino theory." "If South Vietnam went," the way would be open for "a guerrilla assault on Malaya," and it would "give the impression that the wave of the future in Southeast Asia was China and the Communists."[24]

In response to Diem's failure to consolidate support for his regime or effectively prosecute the war against the Viet Cong, the Kennedy administration gave the green light to a junta of military leaders headed by General Duong Van Minh for the assassination of the South Vietnamese president. The United States formally extended diplomatic recognition to the new government on 8 November 1963. Fourteen days later, Kennedy was dead.

This was the Vietnam backdrop that Johnson inherited: a martyred president whose public utterances suggested an unwavering determination to stay the course in Vietnam even if it meant tacitly encouraging political assassination. President Johnson's associates recall him as always believing that his predecessor's complicity in the overthrow of President Diem had been the worst error made by the United States during its involvement in Vietnam; in effect, the United States had become responsible for the fate of successive governments in South Vietnam.[25] General William Westmoreland also expressed the view that "this action [the assassination] morally locked us in Vietnam ... Were it not for our interference in political affairs of South Vietnam ... we could in my opinion have justifiably withdrawn our support at that time in view of a demonstrated lack of leadership and unity in South Vietnam."[26]

Despite his deep reservations about the wisdom of assassinating Diem, Johnson recounted that, as Air Force One carried him back to Washington after the tragedy in Dallas, he made a solemn private vow that he would devote every hour of every day during the remainder of JFK's unfulfilled term to achieving the goals he had set. "This meant seeing things through in Vietnam ..." Certainly Kennedy's public pronouncements and behaviour up to the time of his death would have given Johnson no indication that he was in any way rethinking the extent of American involvement in the war.[27] Two days after President Kennedy's assassination, Johnson told Henry Cabot Lodge, the American ambassador to Saigon, "I am not going to lose Vietnam. I am not going to be the President who saw South East Asia go the way China went."[28]

The period following Diem's death in November 1963 and President Johnson's November 1964 election victory was one of political chaos in Saigon and doubt in Washington. Reporting from Saigon on 21 December 1963, Secretary McNamara noted that "the situation is very disturbing. Current trends, unless reversed in the next 2–3 months, will lead to neutralization at best and more likely to a communist-controlled state. The new government [headed by General Duong Van Minh] is the greatest source of concern."[29] The Minh government was overthrown with American support in another coup on 30 January 1964. But, despite substantially increased military and economic backing from the United States, Nguyen Khanh, Minh's successor, was never able to establish anything like a viable political base. Nor was he able to maintain what little cohesion his regime had initially enjoyed. He leaned ever more heavily upon the United States and American officials could see no option but to continue giving him full support.

In response to McNamara's report, the Joint Chiefs of Staff (JCS) immediately recommended punitive bombing against the North as a means of controlling the insurgency in the South. South Vietnam was described as occupying "the pivotal position ... in our worldwide confrontation with the communists,"[30] and bolder military action was viewed as a prerequisite for obtaining stability in the South. Bombing the North had advocates within the administration, and so did blockading Haiphong harbour.

As Johnson began his full term in office, his theme was still continuity; it seemed good politics, and he sincerely admired most of the cabinet members he had inherited from Kennedy. He knew, moreover, that he was unlikely to "trade up" in replacing them. Thus Johnson planned no real transition from a quasi-Kennedy administration to a Johnson-picked administration.

But more was at stake than mere continuity. Underlying that desire was a profound need to be loved and admired; he was determined to retain his popularity by not upsetting the apple cart with any new initiatives. Departures from the cabinet based on disagreement over Vietnam policy (as a result of Johnson's advocacy of disengagement and negotiations) would run the risk of exposing the president to criticism for his ignorance in foreign affairs and his lack of courage in dealing with communist aggression. On both scores Johnson felt exceedingly vulnerable. His self-esteem had always suffered from his inferior educational accomplishments and he bent over backwards to assert his machismo as a compensation for a pervasive sense of weakness and inadequacy. Thus, to challenge seriously his senior advisers – men who had staked their reputations on the success of the war – and if need be replace them, was an intolerable prospect for a man whose fear of being shamed and humiliated was so all-encompassing.

By early spring 1964, pressures on Johnson to escalate American military intervention in Vietnam were mounting. These stemmed not only from the JCS and internal Pentagon innuendos that the administration was dragging its feet on the bombing because of considerations of domestic political expediency; impinging with increasing force were the hawkish views of Senator Barry Goldwater, the Republican Party's candidate for president. While his views were ultimately to frighten many voters who feared that as president he might either risk a nuclear conflict with the Soviet Union or involve the United States in a full-fledged war in Vietnam, his early campaign attacks on Vietnam policy weakened any inclination within the administration to compromise for fear of exposing itself to charges of insufficient zeal in the struggle against world communism.[31]

Acting upon the recommendation of Secretary of Defense McNamara, President Johnson instructed the JCS to prepare a contingency program of graduated military pressure against the North. The president also approved covert operations along the North Vietnamese coast. Operation Plan 34-A was part of the "progressively escalating pressure" against the North. These 34-A operations included American patrol boat missions against North Vietnamese coastal installations. The navy also began DeSoto patrols (involving electronic espionage that stimulated enemy radar installations so that their locations could be pin-pointed). As part of its overall strategy, the administration secretly prepared contingent drafts for a congressional resolution (the Gulf of Tonkin Resolution, enacted on 7 August 1964) authorizing the president to take vigorous measures to protect American forces.[32]

On 2 August 1964 the destroyer *Maddox* was returning from an electronic espionage mission when it came under fire from North Vietnamese torpedo boats. The North Vietnamese attack came directly after a South Vietnamese naval bombardment of two offshore islands carried out as part of the clandestine Operation Plan 34-A. Rather than withdrawing American ships from this danger zone, the president ordered another destroyer, the *C. Turner Joy*, to join the *Maddox* in the Gulf of Tonkin. Unbeknownst to the Senate, which was to give Johnson a blank cheque to conduct offensive operations against the North Vietnamese with the passage of the Gulf of Tonkin Resolution, "the *Maddox* sent a message to the commander of the 7th Fleet stating that evaluation of information from various sources indicated that the North Vietnamese considered the patrol [of the two American destroyers] directly involved with the South Vietnam attacks on North Vietnam."[33]

On 4 August both the *Maddox* and the *C. Turner Joy* reportedly came under attack.[34] While there is little doubt that North Vietnamese gunboats were operating in the area, the intelligence information was extremely ambiguous. Nevertheless, the president, under pressure from his senior advisers, authorized a one-day, sixty-four-sortie retaliatory air attack against North Vietnamese naval bases and oil-storage facilities. Until more of the classified government documents are released, it is impossible to determine whether Johnson's advisers deliberately kept pertinent information from him, but the suspicion is there. Within the next two or three days, doubts about the evidence that an attack had occurred began to surface in Johnson's mind. He said to Bundy at one point "with disgust," "Hell, those dumb, stupid sailors were just shooting at flying fish."[35]

The president's misgivings and hesitation surfaced again at a meeting held on 9 September with Maxwell Taylor, the new ambassador to South Vietnam, and some of his advisers. The principal item of business was a two-fold recommendation: for a resumption of U.S. naval patrols in the Gulf of Tonkin, which had been suspended after the August incident: and for retaliation against North Vietnam in case of an attack on American units. Concern was voiced that any drastic action could produce such a strong reaction from the communists that the still-weak government in Saigon, and its armed forces, might not be able to meet the challenge successfully. "As one gloomy opinion followed another," Johnson recounted, "I suddenly asked whether anyone at the table doubted that Vietnam was worth all this effort."[36]

In giving voice to his own doubts, Johnson may have hoped for other voices to support him. Instead, the president reported that Ambassador Taylor answered quickly: "We could not afford to let

Hanoi win in the interests of our overall position in Asia and in the world." He was strongly supported by General Earle Wheeler, chairman of the JCS, who argued that if South Vietnam was lost the United States would inevitably lose Southeast Asia. CIA Director John McCone agreed, as did Secretary of State Rusk "with considerable emphasis."[37]

Johnson refused to respond to a subsequent effort by the JCS to get him to order reprisal air strikes in retaliation for what they insisted had been another Gulf of Tonkin attack against a U.S. navy vessel on 18 September. His decision suggests two things: first, that his earlier decision to order the August reprisal raids was not simply a pretext to execute a bombing policy; and secondly, that he distrusted the evidence of the 4 August reports. Sceptical from the outset, he "made it clear that he was not interested in rapid escalation on so frail evidence and with a very fragile government in South Vietnam." On the advice of Rusk and McNamara, he was initially willing to go so far as to authorize "preparatory orders" for a strike. But then, resentful at "having his hand forced" by provocative leaks from the military, and finally discovering that "evidence of actual hostile attack [was] thin to non-existent," he cancelled even these orders.[38]

Evidently wishing to avoid further incidents of this nature, Johnson suspended the provocative DeSoto patrols by U.S. destroyers, and he did not resume them for almost five months. Further, notwithstanding a major attack on 1 November against the large U.S. air base at Bien Hoa in which four Americans were killed, the president refused an urgent request from the JCS and Taylor that he order retaliatory bombing of the North.[39] The picture of Johnson that emerges is not that of a hawk looking for a justification to escalate the war but of a man struggling to avoid escalation against the advice of his senior military advisers. Confronting the military, however, was far less difficult than overruling civilian advisers with whom he was clearly enthralled.

Johnson's overwhelming victory at the polls in November 1964 meant that his scope for taking major new initiatives in Vietnam was much greater than either he or Kennedy had previously enjoyed. James Thomson, a member of McGeorge Bundy's staff, saw the election as providing the "last and most important opportunity that was lost" for disengaging the United States from Vietnam on acceptable terms. He concluded that, had Johnson been "more confident in foreign affairs, had he been more deeply informed on Vietnam and Southeast Asia, had he raised some hard questions that unanimity [on the part of his advisers] had submerged, this President could have used the largest electoral mandate in history to de-escalate in Vietnam, in the clear expectation that at the worst a neutralist government would come to power in Saigon and politely invite us out."[40] What Thomson failed to appreciate was the nature of Johnson's narcissism which fostered his idealization of his advisers as a way of participating in their perceived grandiosity and omnipotence.

Insofar as Johnson's advisers did discuss the question of negotiations with him, they did so critically, admonishing him that these were not to be considered for the present and could not realistically even be explored until after the ratio of military power in South Vietnam had been drastically altered in favour of the Saigon government. Given the balance at the time, negotiations were regarded as tantamount to capitulation, and it was thought that even discussion of the matter was likely to be disastrous to the morale of the Saigon government.[41]

By the early fall of 1964, George Ball, who as under-secretary of state had previously been involved in European matters, had become concerned at the increasingly interventionist stance of the president's advisers and their constant denigration of negotiations. He felt that the United States should be prepared for a compromise solution, even if the prospect of negotiations ran the risk of leading to the collapse of the Saigon regime.

To warn Johnson of the danger and fruitlessness of an escalation in U.S. military involvement, Ball prepared an extensive memorandum for Bundy, McNamara, and Rusk, assuming that after they had discussed it Bundy would pass it on to Johnson. Ball recognized that these three were adamantly opposed to his ideas on negotiations, but he regarded the president as more open-minded on matters pertaining to Vietnam. He hoped, therefore, that the views contained in his 5 October memorandum would at least persuade Johnson that there were options to explore beyond the narrow range being presented by his senior advisers.[42]

Of several possible frameworks for achieving a negotiated settlement, Ball favoured "a localized negotiation between a neutralist South Viet-Nam government and the National Liberation Front." The United States would not immediately press for negotiations and would encourage "a period of ambiguity" and delay that "would permit the various sectors of Vietnamese opinion to adjust to the possibility of a political solution." A cease-fire would be a prerequisite to negotiations between Saigon and the NLF and as part of the settlement U.S. forces would have to be withdrawn, perhaps in phases. An ultimate communist take-over was not ruled out, but Ball hoped that a solution more palatable to the United States might be achieved if other powers could be brought in to guarantee South Vietnam's continued neutralization.[43]

Hearing that George Ball had launched a serious attack on the administration's Vietnam policy, Washington columnist Joseph Alsop wrote on 23 November that Ball's "knowledge of Asia could be comfortably contained in a fairly small thimble."[44] It was the first of a series of articles in which Alsop tried to dissuade the president from "bailing out" of Vietnam by focusing on the distinction between those who were weak and wanted "out" and those who were courageous and were prepared to escalate American involvement.

Although Bundy, McNamara, and Rusk all read Ball's brief, none chose to send it on to Johnson. It was only with the help of Bill Moyers that the memorandum finally reached the president, more than a month later.[45] This delay is not surprising given the attitude of Johnson's senior advisers, who believed that the United States "could not withdraw from Vietnam without humiliation ... They still tenaciously believed that we did not dare negotiate until we had so battered the North that any settlement talks would concern only the terms of Hanoi's capitulation – which was out of the question."[46] Thus, Johnson had no negotiating option to consider, and his advisers continued to warn against any consideration of one – at least until such time as the military balance had shifted decisively in favour of Saigon, a development that in their view could come about only as a result of a large injection of additional U.S. power.[47]

None of the policy options Johnson received for his 1 December review of Vietnam policy focused on a negotiated settlement. Instead, each of the alternatives presented to the president were variations on the same theme of escalating the conflict. For Johnson's senior policy advisers, it was out of the question even to contemplate negotiations before Hanoi had brought the insurgency in the South to a halt and accepted a secure non-communist South Vietnamese state. The president's long meeting with his top advisers reduced the working group's options to two. One possible course "was to continue present policies indefinitely," including intensifying existing covert forms of action against North Vietnam and in Laos but with the outside possibility of U.S. reprisal actions against North Vietnam. The second option set out a slow-paced and cautious, but still substantial, escalation. It provided for "graduated military moves against infiltration targets, first in Laos and then in the DRV, and then against other targets in North Vietnam."[48]

From then on, these options were referred to respectively as Phase I and Phase II of a potentially two-stage program. But Johnson remained preoccupied with the weakness of the Saigon government. At this critical juncture in the evolution of U.S. policy, Johnson's overwhelming concerns were with the creation of a stable government in Saigon as a prerequisite to any additional American involvement. While stipulating that he would endorse Phase I, provided that there was clear provocation, he accepted Phase II only in principle; its implementation would require the fulfillment of certain strict conditions by the Saigon government.[49] In his 3 December instructions to Ambassador Taylor, Johnson made it clear that there would be no sustained U.S. military escalation until Saigon demonstrated that it possessed political cohesion, governmental stability, and effectiveness in its own campaign against the Viet Cong. But Johnson was unable to adhere to his own stipulations.

Johnson's belief that the United States needed an effective government in Saigon before proceeding farther was attacked by Taylor, Bundy, and McNamara, all of whom argued that it would be sufficient to have a military base made up of the South Vietnamese armed forces alone; an actual political base would come about only as the consequence of the favourable psychological atmosphere that bombing the North would induce among the South Vietnamese.[50]

December 1964 was not a happy month for the president. He would complain to those who came to see him, mostly liberals, that all the chiefs did was come in every morning and tell him "bomb, bomb, bomb" and then they would come back in the afternoon and tell him again "bomb, bomb, bomb." But he was unable to make a decision one way or the other.[51] Uneasy about the lack of decision and fearing that a change in direction might be in the offing, Joseph Alsop again impugned the president's courage in his 23 December column: "There are plenty of discouraged Americans in Saigon who think the President is consciously prepared to accept defeat here. They believe that he cannot bring himself to take the measures needed to avert defeat, and they therefore suspect that he is simply planning to wait until the end comes and then to disclaim responsibility."[52]

The following evening, Christmas Eve, 1964, the U.S. officers' billet at the Brinks Hotel, located in the heart of the most heavily guarded section of Saigon, was bombed. Two Americans were killed and thirty-eight were injured. Ambassador Taylor and the U.S. military requested that Johnson order a reprisal bombing strike against the North. They argued that this was a flagrant example of the sort of provocation that was supposed to justify Phase I retaliatory air attacks. But the president, revealing his dissatisfaction with the continued deterioration of the political climate in Saigon, refused to order the bombing of the North. Suspicious of the information he received from Saigon, he observed that neither the American public nor international opinion was likely to believe that the NLF, rather than one of the Saigon factions, was actually responsible for the Brinks incident; indeed, it was several days before the administration itself concluded that the NLF was actually behind it.

"In view of the overall confusion in Saigon," the State Department cabled Taylor, reprisal bombing against the North would be certain to elicit a strong feeling in "U.S. opinion and internationally" that the administration was "trying to shoot its way out of an internal [South Vietnamese] political crisis."[53] Johnson also revealed his scepticism about the value of bombing the North. In a cable to Taylor he remonstrated: "Every time I get a military recommendation it seems to me that it calls for large-scale bombing. I have never felt that this war will be won from the air." [54] Although the bureaucracy had obviously reached a consensus about bombing the North, Johnson clearly had not yet joined it and was still sympathetic to George Ball's position that "the bombing would not provide any great answer."[55]

Pressure from Joe Alsop for Johnson to take a harder line continued with an uncanny sense of Johnson's particular raw nerve: "The unpleasantness of making the required effort does not need underlining. But it must certainly be underlined that the catastrophe now being invited will also be remarkably unpleasant. For Lyndon Johnson, Vietnam is what the second Cuban crisis was for John F. Kennedy. If Mr. Johnson ducks the challenge we shall learn by experience about what it would have been like if Kennedy had ducked the challenge in October, 1962."[56]

And so the question had been posed again: Did Johnson have as much manhood as Jack Kennedy? David Halberstam reports that Walter Lippmann read those columns with a sick feeling and told friends that, if Johnson went to war in Vietnam, at least 50 per cent of the responsibility would be Alsop's. The columns clearly attacked Johnson's narcissistic vulnerabilities. They posed the question as he knew it might be posed out in the hinterland, as he, Lyndon Johnson, might pose it himself against a political adversary.[57]

Following his inauguration, Johnson told congressional leaders on 22 January 1965 that the "war must be fought by the South Vietnamese."[58] With nearly all of his senior advisers advocating a pro-escalation position almost as ardently as the joint chiefs, Johnson was left with only Dean Rusk to support his stipulation that any such program remain conditional on political improvement in Saigon. However, as the political situation in Vietnam worsened, Rusk joined Johnson's other senior advisers in supporting escalation. All feared that Buddhist leaders would channel the mounting tide of anti-war sentiment in South Vietnam into the creation of a government that would demand a negotiated settlement with the NLF and the departure of the Americans.[59]

On 26 January Taylor cabled Bundy that another coup was under way and that its leaders might form a government "which will eventually lead the country into negotiations with Hanoi and the National Liberation Front." In light of these developments, Secretary of Defense McNamara and National Security Adviser Bundy decided to advocate altering basic U.S. policy directives toward Vietnam. Bundy prepared a long memorandum that was approved by McNamara for his meeting with Johnson the following day. The memorandum argued against the president's continuing restraint and prerequisites for escalation. In forceful terms he wrote, "Both of us are now pretty well convinced that our current policy can lead only to disastrous defeat ... Bob [McNamara] and I believe that the worst course of action is to continue in this essentially passive role which can only lead to eventual defeat and an invitation to get out in humiliating circumstances."[60]

Speaking for himself and McNamara, Bundy proceeded to tell Johnson that he had just two alternatives: to use military power to force a change of communist policy or to deploy all resources along a track of negotiation in order to salvage what little could be preserved. He made it clear that they both favoured the first option, but he called upon Johnson to study both alternatives carefully. In emphasizing the prospect of "eventual defeat and an invitation to get out in humiliating circumstances," Bundy and McNamara illustrated their keen understanding of the president's psyche and how unattractive this second option would appear to a man like him.[61]

Still, according to Bundy staffer James Thomson (and the accuracy of his recollection has been attested to by William Bundy, McGeorge's brother and assistant secretary of state for Far Eastern affairs), "the sense in the White House was that the President did not want to do this, and this was one reason for the McGeorge Bundy mission – his felt need for a final determination shows his reluctance."[62] Chester Cooper, Bundy's aide who accompanied him on this mission to South Vietnam, later wrote that the president wanted a fresh look at the situation. "Out of such an examination, he felt, would come recommendations either to move ahead in new and more vigorous ways to gain the initiative against the Viet Cong, or to proceed down a path of disengagement."[63] Prior to the Bundy mission, Cooper concluded, "the option of disengagement, or at least the possibility of a serious consideration of disengagement or a scaling down was a live one."[64]

With the bombing decision still hanging in the balance, an attack on Qui Nhon took place on 7 February, the fourth and last day of Bundy's stay in Vietnam. A company of Viet Cong soldiers launched an attack against a poorly guarded U.S. helicopter base and advisers' barracks at Pleiku in the central highlands. Eight Americans were killed, 126 wounded; ten U.S. planes were destroyed and numerous others damaged. This was by no means the largest of ten Viet Cong attacks launched that day, but it involved the greatest number of Americans killed and wounded in the conflict thus far. In contrast to the Brinks attack of 24 December, there was no doubt that this time the Viet Cong were responsible.[65] After visiting the wounded, Bundy promptly joined other advocates of bombing in insisting that the Pleiku assault constituted the type of credible, clear-cut provocation cited by the president as a possible trigger for a one-shot American retaliatory air strike against the North.[66]

Johnson then presided over a meeting of the National Security Council in Washington, attended by all his advisers save Rusk, who was ill. Except for the Senate majority leader Mike Mansfield, the entire group[67] supported a retaliatory air strike. Johnson articulated his support for the bombing reprisal as follows: "We have kept our gun over the mantel and our shells in the cupboard for a long time now. And what was the result? They are killing our men while they sleep in the night. I can't ask our American soldiers out there to continue to fight with one hand tied behind their backs."[68] "What would happen to me," he asked, "if I didn't defend our boys; what would the American people think of me, with those boys out there dying in their sleep?"[69] The unspoken answer in Johnson's mind was that they would think him a coward, and that Alsop, and others like him, would have a field-day at his expense. A failure to respond would invite public humiliation.

Less than fourteen hours after the Pleiku attack, 132 carrier-based U.S. jets bombed four different barrack complexes inside North Vietnam. Phase I (code-named "Flaming Dart"), the retaliatory bombing campaign, had begun.[70] The Pleiku attack not only precipitated the almost immediate launching of the Phase I bombing of North Vietnam, but was well timed for strengthening the efforts of those who argued that it should be promptly succeeded by Phase II. Prior to Bundy's departure for Saigon, he and Taylor had agreed to include the topic "Extension of the War Beyond SVN" on the agenda for their talks in Saigon. In the aftermath of the Pleiku attack, and before the psychological climate induced by the incident and the bombing reprisal could dissipate, Bundy moved to persuade the president to commit the United States to a Phase II escalation.[71] The arguments Bundy put forward strongly influenced Johnson in his decision to take this action three weeks after having finally authorized the retaliatory bombing triggered by Pleiku.[72]

In his report, Bundy struck a note of crisis:

The situation in Vietnam is deteriorating and without new U.S. action defeat appears inevitable – probably not in a matter of weeks or perhaps even months, but within the next year or so. There is still time to turn it around, but not much. The stakes in Vietnam are extremely high ... The international prestige of the United States, and a substantial part of our influence are directly at risk in Vietnam. There is no way of unloading the burden on the Vietnamese themselves, and there is no way of negotiating ourselves out of Vietnam which offers any serious promise at present. It is possible that at some future time a neutral non-Communist force may emerge, perhaps under Buddhist leadership, but no such force currently exists, and any negotiated U.S. withdrawal today would mean surrender on the installment plan.[73]

This assessment of the possibilities for a negotiated settlement was, in fact, extremely misleading. Contrary to what Bundy told the president, a "neutral non-Communist force" had already emerged and it was "under Buddhist leadership."[74] Lest Johnson possibly be attracted to explore this route, the end of Bundy's memorandum was designed to discourage this option. It read: "We should not now accept the idea of negotiations of any sort except on the basis of a stand down of Viet Cong violence ... The best way of increasing our chances of success in Vietnam ... [is a policy of] sustained reprisal ... [that was] justified by and related to the whole Viet Cong campaign of violence and terror in the south ... Episodic responses geared on a one-for-one basis to 'spectacular' outrages would lack the persuasive force of sustained pressure."[75]

In his rationale for escalating, Bundy directly confronted Johnson's conviction that some political and military improvement of the Saigon regime was a necessary precondition for carrying the war to the North. Assuring the president that the members of his group had made it their "particular business" to examine "whether and to what degree a stable government" was necessary, he contended that this was an unrealistic prerequisite. "We emphasize," he said, "that our primary target in advocating a reprisal policy is the improvement of the situation in South Vietnam." As a consequence of reprisal bombing, he assured Johnson, "it seems very clear that ... there will be a sharp immediate increase in optimism in the south among nearly all articulate groups."

Bundy continued that the United States would also benefit from the likely "substantial depressing effect" that sustained reprisals, "even in a low key," would have upon the morale of Viet Cong cadres in South Vietnam. Bundy then chose words calculated to engage the president's pride. He said that his judgment was based, among other things, "upon the solid general assessment that the determination of Hanoi and the apparent timidity of the mighty United States are both major items in Viet Cong confidence."

Finally, Bundy tried to relate this policy to the domestic and global reputation of the administration and the United States. Though acknowledging that the policy of sustained reprisal bombing might not succeed, he asserted: "What we can say is that even if it fails, the policy will be worth it. At a minimum it will damp down the charge that we did not do all that we could have done, and this charge will be important in many countries, including our own."[76]

Clearly, Bundy was addressing the fear that the adminstration could be accused of having been "too soft" on communism and "too cowardly" to stay the course.

But it would still take five days after the meeting of 8 February for Johnson to endorse formally the proposal for the sustained bombing program, and twenty days to announce it publicly. In the interim, he was to hear dissenting opinions from James Thomson, George Ball, Adlai Stevenson, and Hubert Humphrey.[77] Ball later recounted:

My colleagues interpreted the crumbling of the South Vietnamese government, the increasing success of the Viet Cong guerrillas, and a series of defeats of South Vietnamese units in the field not as one might expect – persuasive evidence that we should cut our losses and get out – but rather as proving that we must promptly begin bombing to stiffen the resolve of the South Vietnamese government ... Thus, it was argued, we must engage our power and prestige even more intensely since otherwise the South Vietnamese might fall apart, negotiate covertly with the Liberation Front of Hanoi, and ultimately ask us to leave.[78]

But those who counselled negotiation and withdrawal were neither as senior nor as influential with Johnson as his senior Kennedy advisers (particularly Bundy, McNamara, and Rusk), Ambassador Taylor, and the JCS. Their combined pressure as well as pressures from outside the administration were to prove decisive.

Adamant calls for escalation came from all corners. Former vice-president Richard Nixon insisted that the United States must now attack North Vietnam hard and consistently "day by day" and "night by night." He exhorted Johnson that, even though the average American probably favoured disengagement, this was "no time for consensus government ... It's a time for leadership."[79] Wesley Fishel, chairman of the American Friends of Vietnam, phoned the State Department to inform it and the White House staff that the lobby's executive committee urged retaliation against North Vietnam. If such advice was not acted upon, his group, "all of whom he described as experts and prolific writers on South Vietnamese affairs, would proceed to publish highly critical articles on U.S. policy in South Vietnam" and, within a week or two, would run a full-page advertisement in the *New York Times*.[80] And former president Eisenhower argued that air strikes "could discourage the North Vietnamese and make them pay a price for continuing their aggression. He said that, in his opinion, our retaliatory strikes had helped the situation greatly, especially in terms of raising morale in the south, but that he felt the time had now come to shift from retaliation to a 'campaign of pressure.'" Eisenhower then proceeded to assure Johnson of "his full and complete support for any course of action I decided was necessary."[81]

Johnson was also aware of a Gallup poll which showed that his overall approval rating had gone from 66 per cent positive on 1 February to 69 per cent just after the two reprisal bombings, with approval of his "handling the situation in Vietnam" rising from 41 per cent to 60 per cent in the same period. Released on 15 February, the poll found that, out of 91 per cent of Americans who had heard or read about the reprisal bombings of North Vietnam during the previous week, 67 per cent approved and only 15 per cent disapproved. Sixty-four per cent favoured the United States continuing its efforts in Vietnam, as against 18 per cent wanting a "pull out."[82]

Although the president had reason to believe that a substantial majority of Americans supported the retaliatory bombing program on which he had just embarked and that a sizeable number would favour more hawkish policies, he still held back from authorizing implementation of Phase II. This reluctance stemmed partly from indications that the reprisal bombing had neither reduced Viet Cong military morale nor strengthened the dedication of the South Vietnamese government to prosecute the war, and partly from the impact that George Ball's critical analysis (prepared in October 1964 but only given to the president on 24 February 1965) had had on him.

Ball gave the memorandum to Bill Moyers at lunch on 24 February, and he, in turn, gave it to the president that afternoon. The following morning, Moyers called Ball to say that Johnson had read and re-read his memorandum, had "found it fascinating and wanted to know why he had not read it before." The following Friday, 26 February, the president called a meeting to discuss Ball's memorandum. "That he had studied it was clear; he challenged specific points I had made and even remembered the page numbers where those arguments occurred."[83] Such attentiveness indicated that Johnson was not dismissing Ball's opposition to further escalation of the war in Vietnam out of hand. As Ball recounted, after he had finished outlining his position, Secretary McNamara "responded with a pyrotechnic display of facts and statistics to prove that I had overstated the difficulties we were now encountering, suggesting at least by nuance, that I was not only prejudiced but ill-informed. Secretary Rusk made a passionate argument about the dangers of not going forward."[84]

The pressures on Johnson were enormous both ways; there was going to be no easy way out. He was deeply concerned about what greater American involvement in Vietnam would mean for his Great Society, the program of legislative reforms designed to eradicate poverty and provide equal opportunities for all Americans. Yet he worried that "if I don't go in now and they show later I should have gone, then they'll be all over me in Congress. They won't be talking about my civil rights bill, or education or beautification. No sir, they'll push Vietnam up my ass every time. Vietnam. Vietnam. Vietnam. Right up my ass."[85]

To Doris Kearns in 1970, Johnson described the early weeks of 1965 as agony. He felt that, if communist aggression succeeded in South Vietnam, the "mean and destructive debate" would

shatter my presidency, kill my administration, and damage our democracy. I knew that Harry Truman and Dean Acheson had lost their effectiveness from the day that the Communists took over in China ... And I knew that all these problems taken together, were chickenshit compared with what might happen if we lost Vietnam. For this time there would be Robert Kennedy out in front leading the fight against me, telling everyone that I had betrayed John Kennedy's commitment to South Vietnam. That I had let a democracy fall into the hands of the Communists. That I was a coward. An unmanly man, a man without a spine. Oh, I could see it coming all right.[86]

Johnson's account of his dreams during this period offers a sharply etched picture of the intensity of his fears. "Every night," he recalled, "when I fell asleep I would see myself tied to the ground in the middle of a long, open space. In the distance, I could hear the voices of thousands of people. They were all shouting at me and running toward me: 'Coward! Traitor! Weakling!' They kept coming closer. They began throwing stones. At exactly that moment I would generally wake up ... terribly shaken."[87] If Lyndon's deepest anxieties could not be repressed during sleep, in waking life he would do what he could to avoid any recrudescence of his childhood fears of weakness, inferiority, and the loss of self-worth.

As Johnson weighed the advice he was getting on Vietnam, it was the "boys" who were most sceptical (including his vice-president, Hubert Humphrey) and the "men" (Bundy, McNamara, and Rusk) who were the most convinced and hawkish and who had Johnson's respect. Hearing that one member of his administration was becoming a dove on Vietnam, Johnson said, "Hell, he has to squat to piss."[88] Doubt itself, he thought, was an almost feminine quality; doubts were for women and weak men.

Psychologically, Johnson seemed determined to distance himself as far as possible from any identification both with his intellectual but weak mother, who could barely care for her family, and with his father, whose failure as a farmer-businessman had earned him the contempt of his peers and made him the laughing-stock of the Pedernales valley. Anything that smacked of the appearance of weakness had to be avoided like the plague.

Of the doves, only Ball really had his respect. Ball might be a dove, but there was nothing soft about him. He had made it in the tough and savage world of the big law firms and his approach was hard-nosed and sceptical. He was a "do-er," an activist, and Johnson would tell him again and again, even as Ball dissented, "You're one of these 'can-do' fellows too, George."[89] In contrast, Johnson thought that Hubert Humphrey, even as vice-president, was too prone to talk, instead of act, and not a person that other men in a room would respect when it got down to the difficult decisions. Real men didn't look up to Humphrey; Johnson felt that he didn't have the weight.[90] So, when Humphrey voiced his doubts on Vietnam, he was simply excluded from the action for over a year until he muffled his dissent.[91]

Thus were the scales weighted; given Johnson's psychological make-up, the advocates of force were taken more seriously while the doubters, by virtue of having doubts, were seen as lesser men. The latter were the cowards, the traitors, and the weaklings – projections of Johnson's own self-doubts that had to be disavowed.

Events in Saigon were to tip the already precarious balance between the hawks and the doves. The head of the Saigon government, General Khanh, had been openly flirting with the NLF and the Buddhists. Talk of a negotiated settlement frightened Ambassador Taylor into mounting a major effort to oust Khanh. He was successful and the new military leaders who assumed power, generals Ky, Thi, and Thieu, gave their strong support to the sustained bombing campaign, Operation Rolling Thunder. The incumbent prime minister, Pham Huy Quat, recognizing where power lay in Saigon, declared that there could be no peace until "the communists end the war they have provoked and stop infiltration." The day after Quat's announcement, 2 March 1965, American planes launched their first attack in the sustained bombing of the North.[92]

Once the decision was made to launch sustained air strikes, the argument was put forward that American air bases in South Vietnam would become increasingly vulnerable to enemy attacks. General Westmoreland requested that two battalion landing teams of marines, 3,500 men in all, be assigned to guard the key base at Danang. Despite Ambassador Taylor's fears that this would be the "thin edge of the wedge," the Joint Chiefs of Staff supported Westmoreland's request for the two battalions, and President Johnson approved it on 26 February without general discussion with his advisers. This allowed him to deny to himself, his associates, and the public that there had been any significant change in policy.[93]

At a 10 March retreat at Camp David, Johnson's desire for a negotiated settlement confronted his determination that it be "on honorable terms" so that he would not be "the first American President to lose a war." At that gathering, Rusk observed that "at some stage" the administration would face a choice between "escalation or negotiation." "Can you buy this?" he asked Johnson. Johnson replied that he was interested in "any honorable basis" for negotiations, but he doubted that North Vietnam was ready because "we've not done anything yet." In effect, Johnson was saying that unless the United States proved it had the stomach for a real fight, it would never earn the respect of the North Vietnamese. He was clearly under the illusion that he would be able to negotiate an effective outcome of the war, one that maintained the security and integrity of South Vietnam, once he had turned around the military situation.

Noting the joint chiefs' recommendation of "continuous activity in SVN on an accelerated scale," Johnson commented that the United States had to be "prepared to pay some price ourselves." If there was continuous military pressure against the communists, "maybe by May 1, they'd grab it." If the United States were to "give in," he continued, there would be "another Munich." Johnson concluded with an idiomatic outburst rendered phonetically by Bundy: "Come hell or high water, we're gonna stay there. We [will] beg, borra, or steal to get a government. You gotta get some Indians under your scalp."[94]

On 20 March the JCS formally recommended the introduction of ground units into combat, calling for at least two – and if necessary three – U.S. divisions (eighteen to twenty-seven battalions). Taylor's strenuous opposition restrained the administration somewhat: two additional Marine combat battalions were authorized in early April, rounding out the Marine force to four battalions. Johnson also ordered 18,000 to 20,000 non-combat support troops as a precaution against unforeseen military deterioration. But, succumbing to pressure from the military and the JCS, Johnson allowed for a change in the mission of the Marines in Vietnam to permit them to be used more aggressively. The Marines were authorized to expand the area they patrolled in stages – first to ten miles, then to thirty miles, and, as of 1 June, to fifty miles.[95]

During the period 10–24 March 1965, John McNaughton, the assistant secretary of defense, prepared a draft memorandum for McNamara that began with a discussion of U.S. aims. He listed them as follows:

70% – To avoid a humiliating U.S. defeat (to our reputation as a guarantor).
20% – To keep SVN (and the adjacent) territory from Chinese hands.
10% – To permit the people of SVN to enjoy a better, freer way of life.

What is striking is the size of the percentage – 70 – attached to the goal of avoiding a humiliating defeat. Concerns about U.S. security and the precepts of the domino theory accounted for only 20 per cent of American aims.

McNaughton described the "deteriorating situation" in South Vietnam, noting that there was a 50 per cent chance of a coup within three weeks. He posited three possible alternative courses of action: "progressively squeeze North Vietnam; or add massive U.S. ground effort in South Vietnam; or downgrade the apparent stakes." The first was already under way and the second would be approved shortly, but the third option, that of lowering the stakes in Vietnam, was not given a serious hearing.

In the initial draft, McNaughton did not append any mention of the risks that this third option might entail. However, two weeks later, presumably after feedback from McNamara and others, the new version did contain such a caveat, which read in its entirety: "Risks. With the physical situation and the trends as they are the fear is overwhelming that an exit negotiated now would result in humiliation for the US."[96]

"This fear of national humiliation," writes George Kahin, "and the attendant damage to their own prestige remained at the forefront of the minds of the president's advisers and of the president himself."[97] Moreover, the majority of the president's advisers remained confident that a massive injection of U.S. power could engineer the survival of a separate state in the southern half of Vietnam, even in the absence of indigenous support. They clearly hoped that the results would vindicate them and the advice they had already given the president, while saving him and the country – and themselves – from the disgrace they believed would ensue from switching to a negotiations track at a time when the Saigon regime was so weak.[98]

Partly because the administration had publicly endowed the struggle in Vietnam with such importance through its apocalyptic rhetoric as well as its actions – the American role had become the focus of world-wide attention – Johnson's advisers now placed heavy emphasis on how the United States looked in its efforts to manage the conflict. In this context, both Johnson and his advisers had difficulty in distinguishing between their personal prestige and that of the United States.

If McNaughton's internal memorandum underlined the importance of avoiding a humiliating defeat as the overwhelming priority of American policy in Vietnam, the official rationale the administration presented for its Vietnam policy was very different. For the public, the relative importance of McNaughton's three objectives was reversed; the need to avoid a "humiliating defeat" was deemed, in and of itself, too humiliating to acknowledge. Thus the major emphasis in Lyndon Johnson's speech, at Johns Hopkins University on 7 April, was the goal of self-determination, premised, however, on there being an "independent nation of South Vietnam." "The first reality," the president asserted, was aggression against "the independent nation of South Vietnam." Invoking the domino theory, he stated that, if the United States retreated from Vietnam, "the battle would be renewed in one country and then another" for "the appetite of aggression is never satisfied."[99]

Yet it was becoming increasingly evident that bombing the North was insufficient to alter the military or political equation. Morale in the South did not improve nor did the government's internal cohesion or willingness to fight. As the political and military fabric of the Saigon regime unravelled even more rapidly than before, almost all of Johnson's advisers pressed for a second dimension of escalation – the introduction of significant numbers of U.S. combat forces. Only if this level of U.S. military intervention was added, they now contended, would the bombing sorties against the North yield successful results in the South.

In order to assess more accurately what was happening in South Vietnam on the ground, Johnson scheduled a meeting at Honolulu for 19–20 April between Taylor and other senior foreign-policy figures in the administration.[100] The result of that meeting was a unanimous recommendation calling for a major escalation that McNamara gave to the president on 21 April. Thirteen U.S. combat battalions, numbering 82,000 men, were to be added to the 33,500 U.S. troops already in Vietnam (this included the four marine battalions stationed at Danang and Chu Lai).[101]

The proposal was presented to the president as a prescription not for winning the war but rather for denying victory to the Viet Cong. The "victory" envisaged for the United States, McNamara explained, was "to break the will of the DRV\VC by depriving them of victory," or, as Taylor put it, "a demonstration of communist impotence, which will lead to a political solution." What McNamara and his supporters were proposing to Lyndon Johnson was in effect a holding action – a recommendation for a sufficient increment of combat soldiers to hold the Viet Cong at bay.[102] There was also the hope that, with additional external support, the Saigon regime might in time become strong enough and the Viet Cong sufficiently stymied for the United States to risk negotiations that would preserve the South as a separate, non-communist state.

When confronted with McNamara's proposal, Ball responded with an emotional plea that the president not take such a hazardous leap into space without further exploring the possibilities of a settlement. Johnson replied, "All right, George, I'll give you until tomorrow morning to get me a settlement plan. If you can pull a rabbit out of the hat, I'm all for it!"[103]

In a long memorandum which he sent to the president later that night, Ball pointed out that Operation Rolling Thunder had not achieved its declared purposes and that they dared no longer postpone a settlement. Ball's point of departure was that, if the Vietnam situation was to be settled without a major war, the United States would have to prepare itself for a settlement that fell short of its publicly stated goals. The United States, he argued, should "try to find some common ground that would save face for Hanoi, and permit it to pull back even though that action were only tactical, and Hanoi hoped to prevail at some later date. In my view such a tactical withdrawal is probably the most we can realistically try to achieve short of totally destroying North Vietnam."[104]

Ball's solution called for the creation of a coalition government followed by an election, monitored by an international commission. This, in his view, could yield a government that would be reasonably representative even though pro-American elements might not come out on top. In addition, "the Saigon regime would declare a general amnesty permitting all Viet Cong wishing to return to the North" to do so. The International Control Commission would undertake to police the cease-fire. "Once the new government was installed, the United States would withdraw."[105]

Johnson read the memorandum overnight and the following morning Bill Moyers called to tell Ball that the president was very interested in his ideas. The following day Moyers called Ball again to say that, in the light of his memorandum, the president had talked about the need to get people together to do nothing for three or four days but ponder the political and peaceful alternatives in Southeast Asia.[106]

Yet, for a president whose major preoccupation was the Great Society, a holding action in Vietnam seemed preferable to the risks involved in deciding to withdraw. The loss of prestige, the enormous political backlash in the United States which Johnson expected would follow the collapse of South Vietnam, the shame and humiliation that he would be subjected to – all this was too high a price to pay. In comparison, the investment of men and treasure advocated by McNamara and other advisers seemed at least tolerable, and he gave their recommendations partial approval on 21 April and the balance on 15 May.[107]

Despite the troop increases that had been ordered, Johnson soon realized that such American forces alone could not even sustain a holding action in South Vietnam. Although the United States embarked on a major effort to secure additional support from its allies, by June 1965 there was no more than five thousand third-country forces in Vietnam. Even the considerable increase scheduled for the next few months would not come close to providing the needed reinforcement of U.S. forces. The Army of the Republic of Vietnam (ARVN) was disintegrating more rapidly than ever and had suffered a further series of defeats even though most of the Viet Cong main-force regiments and battalions had not yet been committed.[108]

Given the steady erosion in the Saigon regime's support, a familiar question again arose: "What is to be done?" Essentially, Johnson was left with just two alternatives. He could lower his sights and settle for more modest political goals via negotiation; or, if he insisted on striving for his original objectives, he could send in a much larger number of U.S. ground-combat units. The JCS, Taylor, Westmoreland, Ambassador-designate Lodge, and all of the president's top-level Washington advisers, except George Ball and Clark Clifford, supported the second course.

Their support for a greater U.S. ground-force commitment was sharply enhanced by the cable traffic of 7 June in which General Westmoreland reported that the Viet Cong were on the offensive and the South Vietnamese army had suffered serious losses and was in immediate danger of disintegration. Even with only two out of its nine regiments and a similar proportion of separate battalions heavily engaged, NLF troops were inflicting heavy defeats on the ARVN. A week later, Westmoreland cabled that during the previous three weeks the Viet Cong had mauled five ARVN battalions so badly they were "inoperative," ARVN desertion rates had become "inordinately high," and the fighting strength of many of its battalions "unacceptably low."[109]

To cope with the danger, Westmoreland requested an increase of about 41,000 troops, to bring the total of U.S. forces to about 125,000. He added that more troops might be needed in the future. If authorized, the latter would bring the total of American forces to approximately 175,000, including thirty-four combat battalions, plus ten battalions from other nations – a total of 200,000. This became known as the forty-four-battalion request. Just to prolong the holding action until the end of the year would now require more than double the 82,000 men the president had authorized on 21 April.[110]

Johnson was clearly reluctant to approve this recommendation. He was privy to considerable opposition to the idea of a vastly increased force, principally from Senator Mike Mansfield and George Ball. Nevertheless, after five weeks of debate, the president was prevailed upon to take a step that locked the country into a major ground war. Unlike his predecessor, Eisenhower, who was able to reject the advice of his senior advisers to escalate the American role at Dien Bien Phu in 1954, Johnson capitulated. Fearful of the humiliating fall-out that would accompany withdrawal from Vietnam, and determined to avoid any criticism of his stewardship of Vietnam foreign policy by his senior Kennedy advisers should he reject their counsel, Johnson persuaded himself that escalating the war was the lesser of two evils.

Two important phases in the process of shaping the decision concerning the JCS/Westmoreland recommendations can be observed. The first ran from 7 June to 20 July, when Robert McNamara offered his final recommendation and laid much of the groundwork for the second and more critical phase, which began on 21 July and involved intense discussions lasting for an additional week.[111]

During the first phase of decision making, the sceptics desperately tried to dissuade the president from escalating the war. Senator Mansfield, recognizing that the United States was no longer supporting even the semblance of a government in South Vietnam, but merely the Saigon military, asked the president what the American purpose was in Vietnam. In his view, the administration had failed to indicate what specific goals the United States had in remaining there. If the administration was planning to stay in Vietnam "until we or our Vietnamese military allies prevail everywhere south of the 17th parallel down to the smallest hamlet," then "we are talking in terms of years or decades, and upwards of a million American soldiers on the ground in South Vietnam, assuming that the Chinese do not become involved with men." If, instead, the administration had lowered its sights to "holding the military situation about where it is now," he contended that the estimate of 300,000 men ascribed to McNamara was too low.

Aware that McNamara was supporting the JCS/Westmoreland request for substantial troop increases, George Ball made another effort to forestall escalation. Because of his concerns about Mansfield's questions, Johnson appeared to be unusually attentive to Ball's memorandum, which was headed "Keeping the Power of Decision in the Vietnam Crisis." Rather than routing it through Rusk, Bundy, or McNamara, Ball sent it directly to presidential assistant Bill Moyers on 18 June. Moyers called him three days later to tell him that Johnson had read it over the weekend and agreed in substance "with most of the memorandum – one or two slight changes possibly."[112]

Ball's central argument was that "the best formula for maintaining freedom of decision is (a) to limit our commitments in time

and magnitude and (b) to establish specific time schedules for selection of optimal courses of action on the basis of preestablished
criteria." In raising its commitment from 50,000 to 100,000 or
more men, and deploying most of the increment in combat roles,
the administration, he warned, was beginning a "new war – the
United States *directly* against the Viet Cong." Even 500,000 American soldiers would not necessarily secure existing objectives: "Before we commit an endless flow of forces to South Vietnam we must
have more evidence than we now have that our troops will not bog
down in the jungles and the rice paddies – while we slowly blow the
country to pieces."[113]

Ever since 1961, Ball continued, "we have tended to under-
estimate the strength and staying power of the enemy. We have
tended to overestimate the effectiveness of our sophisticated weapons under jungle conditions ... We have been unable to bring
about the creation of a stable political base in Saigon." Moreover,
there was still insufficient evidence "that the South Vietnamese
will stand up under the heightening pressure – or, in fact, that the
Vietnamese people really have a strong will to fight after twenty
years of struggle." And the more forces the United States deployed
in South Vietnam, "the harder we shall find it to extricate without
unacceptable cost if the war goes badly. With large forces committed, the failure to turn the tide will generate pressures to escalate."[114]

Johnson read Ball's memo at Camp David and "was deeply
affected" by his analysis. He "seemed to question whether or not
he could go ahead with the major commitment,"[115] while recognizing that South Vietnam would fall to the communists within a
matter of weeks unless the United States authorized a substantial
ground commitment. To resolve this dilemma, the president directed McNamara and Ball, with one or two staff men each, to produce studies covering military and political moves over the next
three months and beyond. They were to come back in a week.[116]

Ball's paper, dated 28 June 1965, was entitled "Cutting Our Losses
in South Vietnam." It announced at the outset that it was "written on
the premise that we are losing the war." In it, Ball repeated his well-
worn arguments for disengaging American interests from Saigon's,
once more stressing Eisenhower's conditions for American aid.
Unless a government of national union under civilian leadership was
put together in a month, he argued that the United States should
reconsider the extent of its commitment. If the South Vietnamese

government (now headed by General Nguyen Cao Ky) refused to comply and the United States

withdrew after having demonstrated that Saigon was unprepared to perform its part of the bargain, most friendly nations would recognize that we had kept our commitments ... The position taken in this memorandum does not suggest that the United States should abdicate leadership in the cold war. But any prudent military commander carefully selects the terrain on which to stand and fight, and no great captain has ever been blamed for a successful tactical withdrawal ... Even if we were to commit five hundred thousand men to South Vietnam we would still lose ... In my view, a deep commitment of United States forces in a land war in South Vietnam would be a catastrophic error. If ever there was an occasion for a tactical withdrawal, this is it.[117]

On 1 July McGeorge Bundy forwarded four position papers to Johnson – there were now papers by William Bundy and Dean Rusk in addition to the studies Johnson had requested from Ball and McNamara. The meeting, Bundy advised, would not actually make decisions but would be for "sharpening any issues you want studied."[118] The McNamara memo, which William Bundy was later to describe as the "lead paper," was a strong brief for Westmoreland's forty-four-battalion request, including a call-up of the reserves. It was to be a clear precursor to the one he would submit three weeks later following another visit to South Vietnam. For McNamara, the central U.S. political objective remained unchanged – maintenance of a separate non-communist southern state. He urged a major increase in air and naval action against the North, including the mining of major ports. Recommending increased political initiatives as well, McNamara noted that these were "likely to be successful in the early stages only to demonstrate U.S. good faith." He foresaw little chance of movement toward "an actual settlement" until "the tide begins to turn (unless we lower our sights substantially)." Overall, McNamara foresaw the prospect of a demanding war: "The tide almost certainly cannot begin to turn in less than a few months, and may not for a year or more; the war is one of attrition and will be a long one."[119]

Dean Rusk, who rarely wrote position papers, was brief and avoided identifying himself with any particular military proposal, contenting himself with warning against targets in the Hanoi-Haiphong area "for the present." But he insisted that the United

States must "insure that North Viet-Nam not succeed in taking over or determining the future of South Viet-Nam by force," adding that "the integrity of the U.S. commitment is the principal pillar of peace throughout the world."[120]

Ball's 1 July memorandum was a toned-down version of his stronger 28 June submission; at a 29 June meeting that Johnson did not attend, the president's advisers (in William Bundy's words) "ridiculed" Ball's earlier memorandum as too extreme.[121] Ball shifted his emphasis from withdrawal to negotiation and titled his new, less alarming memorandum "A Compromise Solution."[122] It called for maintaining force levels only at their present level, which he put at 72,000 men. Fundamental emphasis was placed on a series of possible steps that could secure a negotiated settlement. Ball favoured a phased negotiating sequence with Hanoi, beginning with secret feelers and moving towards a multinational peace conference. He argued that "in any political approaches so far, we have been the prisoners of whatever South Vietnamese government was momentarily in power." Ball also stipulated that Saigon should not be consulted "until after a substantial feeling out of Hanoi."[123]

Ball's preference for a negotiated settlement was premised on the fact that the United States was embroiled in a losing war and that "no one can assure you [Johnson] that we can beat the Viet Cong or even force them to the conference table on our terms no matter how many hundred thousand white foreign (US) troops we can deploy." He continued to underline that the decision facing the president was crucial. "Once large number of U.S. troops are committed to direct combat they will begin to take heavy casualties in a war they are ill-equipped to fight in a non-co-operative if not downright hostile countryside. Once we suffer large casualties we will started a well-nigh irreversible process. Our involvement will be so great that we cannot – without national humiliation – stop short of achieving our complete objectives. *Of the two possibilities, I think humiliation would be more likely than the achievement of our objectives – even after we had paid terrible costs.*"[124]

In an effort to persuade the president to change course, Ball also appealed to Johnson's fear of personal humiliation. He argued that, for the president, there was a greater risk of humiliation in committing American land forces in substantial numbers than in negotiating a way out. His memorandum recognized as well that, once involved, Americans would have great difficulty in accepting that a technologically primitive, small third-world country could

defeat the powerful United States. Such an admission would acti-
vate feelings of powerlessness and shame at being reduced to an
inferior, helpless state. And the stage would then be set for even
greater commitments of American forces.

William Bundy's "middle course" memorandum criticized Ball's
approach as an abandonment of the South Vietnamese at a time
when the fight was not going all that badly. But Bundy's approach
was also aimed at avoiding a troop increase of the magnitude that
McNamara was advocating. He favoured permitting a modest increment that would keep the troop level no higher than 100,000
men, and an exploratory effort that would continue only through
the summer to establish whether the South Vietnamese government and military could perform better and whether U.S. combat
forces could function effectively in South Vietnam.[125]

Immediately before meeting with the memorandum writers,
Johnson spoke to former president Eisenhower. In the notes on
their seven-minute telephone conversation, recorded by Lilian
Brown, Eisenhower's confidential secretary, President Johnson
reported that McNamara, Westmoreland, and Wheeler recommended expansion of U.S. military forces. He noted that this
would stir up such people as House Republican Leader Gerald
Ford, "who is for continuing the bombing but no ground troops,
and also Bobby Kennedy[126] and Mansfield who oppose further involvement." Eisenhower noted that merely pursuing an enclave
policy meant paying a price and not winning.

"President Johnson then asked, 'Do you really think we can beat
the Viet Cong?' – this rather plaintively"[127] – an indication of his
own growing doubts and perhaps of a wish to be reassured. Eisenhower's reply was that of the professional military man. It would
depend on Viet Cong force levels and North Vietnamese infiltration rates, he replied. Although Johnson can scarcely have found
Eisenhower's explanation reassuring, it appeared as though Eisenhower's concluding advice pressed Johnson to accept the forty-
four-battalion recommendation. As the notes indicated: "When you
once appeal to force in an international situation involving military
help for a nation, you have to go all out! This is a war, and as long
as they [the enemy] are putting men down there, my advice is 'do
what you have to do!' It was his [Eisenhower's] feeling that we
should go ahead with the plan as quickly as we can. 'We are not going to be run out of a free country that we helped to establish.' "
When Johnson expressed concern that "we will lose the British and

the Canadians and will be alone in the world," Eisenhower replied, "We would still have the Australians and the Koreans – and our own convictions."[128]

Although Eisenhower's position and advice seemed at odds with his handling of the Dien Bien Phu crisis, the variance was not as great as appeared. The former president's advice to Johnson reflected his adherence to the "all-or-nothing" approach of the "never again" school. The lesson he derived from the Korean War was that the United States should "never again" allow itself to be dragged into an Asian land war in defense of less than vital national interests. Where the protection of American interests was not absolutely essential to its security, the United States should do "nothing." But having once intervened to defend its vital interests, the United States should never fight a limited inconclusive war with one arm tied behind its back. At the time of Dien Bien Phu, the United States had not as yet intervened in the French war and Eisenhower had to consider whether to do so. In his view, becoming involved again in an Asian land war for less than compelling reasons ran the risk of repeating the Korean debacle. Therefore, he had decided to do "nothing" in the service of "never again."

In the Vietnam crisis that Johnson faced, the United States had committed itself to the defense of South Vietnam and had already intervened in a limited military way. Eisenhower had taken the lead in this respect in the aftermath of Dien Bien Phu, when the United States set up South Vietnam and supported it financially after the Geneva conference in 1961. And given the steadily increasing commitment of the United States to South Vietnam under the Kennedy and Johnson administrations, and the repeated pronouncements that the loss of South Vietnam would cause irreparable harm to American interests, Eisenhower believed that the other lesson of the Korean War was that, having once intervened, force levels had to be sufficient – the "all" approach – to win a decisive military victory.[129]

On the surface, this suggests that Eisenhower was no different from Johnson and Nixon in his willingness to use force. But what distinguishes Johnson and Nixon from Eisenhower was the way in which the former arrived at their decisions to escalate – by means of a process strongly influenced by psychological needs and fears. In contrast, Eisenhower demonstrated the ability to arrive at difficult decisions based on a more objective assessment of the facts.

Worried by the considerable range of conflicting advice from his regular advisers, Johnson looked to fresh counsel from people such as General Omar Bradley, former chairman of the JCS, Roswell Gilpatric, former deputy secretary of defense, Dr George Kistiakowsky, former presidential science adviser, Arthur Larson, former director of the United States Information Agency, and John J. McCloy, former high commissioner to Germany and assistant secretary of war during the Second World War, all of whom met separately in three panels and then assembled for a joint afternoon session.

The panel's reaction, according to William Bundy, was "clear and unmistakeable." It accepted both the argument that Vietnam was a test case of "wars of national liberation" and the argument that a U.S. defeat would lead to widespread questioning whether American commitments could be relied on. "What was important," he recalled, was that "the panel thought that standing firm in Vietnam was of very great importance to American interests and to the independence of many nations and areas" and "felt that there should be no question of making whatever combat force increases were required."[130]

Although the president "probably expected that most of the panel would be generally in favor of a firm policy," Bundy postulated that "this must have had a distinct impact on his personal and private deliberations." As he observed, "There can be no doubt that a large strand in the President's make-up was he should not fall short of the standards set by those who had played leading parts in World War II, and throughout the period of American successes in the Cold War. Now a fair sample of these men ... had advised him to see this one through."[131] For someone such as Johnson who needed to be mirrored and accepted by his advisers, particularly those whose respect and admiration was so important to him, extricating himself from Vietnam was becoming more and more psychologically impossible.

Notwithstanding this new advice, Johnson still held back from any final decision on major new ground-force deployment. On 10 July he agreed to the dispatch of 10,400 logistic and support troops (due to arrive 15 August) "to support current force levels and to receive the airmobile division, if deployed." But he refused to commit himself further until McNamara returned to Vietnam to confer with Taylor and Westmoreland concerning the condition of the Saigon government and U.S. military requirements, and until he had an opportunity for extensive discussion of these findings with his other senior advisers. As Johnson recalled, "I was not about to send additional men without the most detailed analysis ... I knew we faced a crucial question, one that was at the heart of our treaty commitment to Southeast Asia. If necessary, would we use substantial U.S. forces on the ground to prevent the loss of that region to aggressive forces moving illegally across international frontiers?"[132]

McNamara's findings were communicated to the president in a memorandum on 20 July. In it, he painted a stark but accurate picture of Saigon's political and military deterioration – a picture designed to win support for the dispatch of additional U.S. ground forces to Vietnam. "The situation in South Vietnam is worse than a year ago (when it was worse than a year before that)," he reported. "Nor have our air attacks in North Vietnam produced tangible evidence of willingness on the part of Hanoi to come to the conference table in a reasonable mood."

McNamara offered the president the same three options of three weeks before, once again couched in language that could lead to only one conclusion. As for the first option – "cut our losses and withdraw under best conditions that can be arranged" – he described it as "humiliating" to the United States and "very damaging to our future effectiveness on the world scene." For Johnson, preoccupied with image and status, McNamara's analysis undoubtedly engendered anxiety about the potential humiliation that might befall the president "who lost Vietnam."

The second option – continuing at the present level – was also deemed unacceptable. The third option – "substantially" expanding U.S. military involvement – was what McNamara had recommended three weeks earlier, except that he now stipulated that it was something to be undertaken "promptly." He also added a new sentence. It read: "This alternative would stave off defeat in the short run and offer a good chance of producing a favorable settlement in the longer run; at the same time, it would imply a commitment to see a fighting war clear through at considerable cost in casualties and material, and would make any later decision to withdraw even more difficult and even more costly than would be the case today." He recommended the third alternative "as the course of action involving the best odds of the best outcome with the most acceptable cost to the U.S." The message of this submission was clearly that no settlement acceptable to the Johnson administration could be negotiated until after the United States had applied the additional military force McNamara was proposing.

With McNamara's advice before him, the president then embarked upon a week of the most intensive discussions with his advisers he had ever conducted. The first and apparently most crucial meeting occurred on 21 July.[133] Prior to Johnson's arrival that morning, McNamara began by reviewing his recommendations, which included the call-up of large numbers of reserves. After three-quarters of an hour, Johnson arrived and asked a series of questions. "What I would like to know is what has happened in recent months that requires this kind of decision on my part? What are the alternatives? Have we wrung every single soldier out of every country that we can? Who else can help us here? Are we the sole defender in the world? What are the compelling reasons for this call up? What results can we expect? Again, I ask you what are the alternatives? I don't want us to make snap judgments. I want us to consider all our options."[134]

The participants understood the gravity of the decisions that would be made. As George Ball recalled: "This meeting was special only in that once the decision under consideration was accepted, the United States would commit thousands of its young men not just to passive defense missions but to aggressive combat roles ... There would be no turning back for months, perhaps years – and that would not occur until we had suffered horrible casualties, killed thousands of Vietnamese and raised the level of national anxiety and frustration above the threshold of hysteria."[135]

The picture that emerges is of a deeply troubled Johnson. Obviously unhappy with the implications of McNamara's advice to increase significantly the number of U.S. forces in Vietnam, he queried General Wheeler at one point: "Tell me this. What will happen if we put in 100,000 more men and then two, three years later you tell me you need 500,000 more? How would you expect me to respond to that? And what makes you think if we put in 100,000 men, Ho Chi Minh won't put in another 100,000 and match us every bit of the way?"[136] In these and similar exchanges, one gets a sense of Johnson's prescient scepticism about the hawkish advice he was receiving.

But, in the end, the dovish advice of George Ball fared even less well. Ball told the president that "there is no course that will allow us to cut our losses. If we get bogged down, our cost might be substantially greater." To which Johnson replied, "Tell me then, what other road can I go?" Ball then replied, "Take what precautions we can, Mr. President. Take our losses, let the government fall apart, negotiate, discuss, knowing full well there will be a probable take-over by the Communists. This is disagreeable, I know." Johnson re-torted: "I can take disagreeable decisions. But I want to know can we make a case for your thoughts? Can you discuss it fully?" Ball replied: "We have discussed it. I have had my day in court." The president then resumed: "I don't think we have made any full com-mitment, George. You have pointed out the danger, but you ha-ven't really proposed an alternative course."[137]

Notwithstanding Johnson's insistence that he could take dis-agreeable decisions, his response was one of denial. His reaction to Ball's program, which anticipated the collapse of the South Viet-namese government and a probable communist takeover, was to argue that Ball had not proposed an alternative course of action, when in fact he had – albeit a psychologically unacceptable one.

As Larry Berman observes, the morning meeting highlighted just how far from logic American decision makers had travelled. To achieve military victory against the North, Ambassador Lodge rec-ommended that the government of South Vietnam be ignored. The United States had an obligation to fight communist aggression re-gardless of the governmental structure in the South. But it was Ball, not the military and their supporters, who had to bear the burden of proof for his suggestion that the "least bad" scenario would be to let the government fall and negotiate an agreement – a course that, as Ball well recognized, would ultimately lead to a communist take-over. When Ball noted that 175,000 Americans could not fight effec-tively in the jungle terrain, General Wheeler's sharp retort was that "search and destroy" would achieve the necessary end.[138]

During subsequent exchanges between Ball and the president, on the afternoon of 21 July, Ball began by telling Johnson: "We can-not win, Mr. President. This war will be long and protracted. The most we can hope for is a messy conclusion." He then said: "I think we all have underestimated the seriousness of this situation. It is like giving cobalt treatment to a terminal cancer case. I think a long protracted war will disclose our weakness, not our strength." He ob-served that "the least harmful way to cut losses" in Vietnam was to let the South Vietnamese government "decide it doesn't want us to stay there. Therefore, we should put such proposals to the GVN [Government of South Vietnam] they can't accept. Then it would move to a neutralist position. I have no illusion that after we were asked to leave South Vietnam that country would soon come under Hanoi's control."[139]

At this juncture, Johnson's discomfiture at the thought of an American withdrawal became more sharply drawn. He responded to Ball: "But George, wouldn't all these countries say that Uncle Sam was a paper tiger, wouldn't we lose all credibility breaking the word of three presidents, if we did as you have proposed? It would seem to be an irreparable blow. But I gather you don't think so." Ball's rejoinder was: "No sir. The worst blow would be that the mightiest power on earth is unable to defeat a handful of guerrillas."[140]

Ball then attempted to describe when "remaining in" was an appropriate strategy and when it was inappropriate. "If we were actively helping a country with a stable viable government, it would be a vastly different story. But we're dealing with a revolving junta." He asked rhetorically: "How much support do we really have in South Vietnam? ... Western Europeans look upon us as if we got ourselves into an imprudent situation." At this point Johnson interjected: "But I believe that these Vietnamese are trying to fight." Ball replied: "Thieu spoke the other day and said the Communists would win the election." Since such an outcome would clearly call into question South Vietnamese opposition to the communists and raise fundamental questions as to the justification for American involvement in Vietnam, Johnson quickly replied, "I don't believe that. Does anyone believe that?"[141] McNamara, Lodge, Bill Bundy, Leonard Unger all indicated their disbelief, expressing views contrary to Ball's. (In fact, several Saigon government leaders had told McNamara, Lodge, and Unger, in meetings with them in Saigon a few days before, that in a political competition the NLF would win.[142])

McNamara allowed that "Ky will fall soon. He is weak. We can't have elections there until there is physical security, and even then there will be no elections because as Cabot [Lodge] said, there is no democratic tradition." The president then hunched against the edge of the table and said: "There are two basic troublings within me. First, that westerners can ever win a war in Asia. Second, I don't see how you can fight a war under direction of other people whose government changes every month."[143]

At noon the following day, 22 July, the president met with the country's military leadership and a few of his civilian aides.[144] Once again, the transcripts of the conversation reveal Johnson's anxiety about the nature of the military analysis and advice that he was receiving. Jack Valenti recounted how he and Johnson had been alone in his office for some minutes before the meeting began. The president noted that "all these recommendations seem to be built on a pretty soft bottom. Everything blurs when you get almost to the gate." In Valenti's opinion, "LBJ felt bound by President Kennedy's actions and the prospect of unhinging the linchpin of the Kennedy commitment was dismally disturbing to him. And yet there was that queasy tremor of doubt that kept skittering through his thoughts." In the meeting that followed "with the military brass the president was unleashing those skeptical ruminations which he had kept under wraps."[145]

In response to Admiral David L. McDonald's statement that "by putting more men in, it will turn the tide and let us know what further we need to do," Johnson, "his face grim and somber," asked: "But you don't know if 100,000 will be enough. What makes you conclude that if you don't know where we are going – and what will happen – we shouldn't pause and find this out?" McDonald: "Sooner or later we will force them to the conference table." Johnson: "But if we put in 100,000 men, won't they put in an equal number and then where will we be?" McDonald: "No, if we step up our bombing." Johnson: "Is this a chance we want to take?" McDonald: "Yes sir, when I view the alternatives. Get out now or pour in more men." Johnson: "Is that all?" McDonald: "Well, I think our allies will lose faith in us." Johnson: "We have few allies really helping us now."[146]

The president then asked: "If we come in with hundreds of thousands of men and billions of dollars, won't this cause China and Russia to come in? No one has given me a satisfactory answer to that." General Harold K. Johnson replied: "No, sir. I don't think they will." The president: "MacArthur didn't think they would come in either." General Johnson: "Yes sir, but this is not comparable to Korea." The president continued: "But China has plenty of divisions to move in, don't they?" General Johnson: "Yes, they do." The president: "Then what would we do?" There was a long silence in which the room was absolutely still. General Johnson finally said, "If so, we have another ball game." "But I have to take into account they will," said the president. General Johnson: "I would increase the buildup near North Vietnam, and increase action in Korea." The president: "If they move in thirty-one divisions, what does it take on our part?" McNamara: "Under favorable conditions they could sustain thirty-one divisions and assuming the Thais contributed forces, it would take 300,000 plus what we need to combat the VC."[147]

Johnson then revealed the source of his disquiet: "But remember they are going to write stories about this like they did in the Bay of Pigs. Stories about me and my advisers. That is why I want you to think carefully, very, very, carefully about alternatives and plans."[148] Implicit in his admonition to his advisers was a thinly veiled plea that they not leave him with policy recommendations that would expose him to the type of shame and humiliation that the Kennedy administration (of which he was a part) had been forced to endure as a result of the Bay of Pigs foul-up.

In reading the verbatim files of this meeting, one observes Johnson asking penetrating and sceptical questions but unwilling, in the final analysis, to draw the obvious inferences from their replies. As soon as the president gets close to the uncomfortable truth of an endless war whose outcome was uncertain at best, he stops the questioning. Moreover, one should not regard Johnson's seemingly zealous pursuit of alternatives in the same vein as Eisenhower's similar efforts during the 1954 Dien Bien Phu crisis. Eisenhower engaged in a thorough canvassing of alternatives in order to weigh the costs and benefits of a given policy, and he then decided on a course of action based on those calculations. By contrast, in Johnson's intensive questioning there was more than a hint of desperation. Further, his search for options could not disguise the fact that, in the end, Johnson was incapable of breaking with his senior advisers over Vietnam and exposing himself to any potential humiliation that ignoring their advice might have entailed.

On the afternoon of that same day, 22 July, Johnson met with his regular senior aides and several prominent ad hoc civilian advisers – Clark Clifford, John J. McCloy, and Arthur Dean – to report to them on his morning meetings with the military. Although no full record of this meeting is available, Ball recalled that for the first time he found support from an unexpected quarter – Clark Clifford, an old friend of the president. Clifford voiced strong opposition to the commitment of combat forces, proffering the same arguments that Ball had made the day before.[149] In addition, he gave the president a more authoritative assessment of the probable domestic consequences.[150]

After the 22 July meetings, Johnson journeyed to Camp David to reflect on the conflicting advice he had just received. In an effort to assuage Johnson's anxiety regarding the possible incompatibility of increased military spending with his Great Society programs, McGeorge Bundy sent him memoranda arguing against the necessity of a large fiscal appropriation to meet the costs of McNamara's package. At the same time, he indicated his support for the McNamara/JCS/Westmoreland recommendation. With Bundy now backing the proposal, the president appears to have agreed to approve some measure of increase in ground-combat forces. But he had not yet decided on how much of an increase or on how he would raise these troops.[151]

On the afternoon of 25 July, Johnson invited three people to Camp David for what would be the last and most critical meeting: Clark Clifford, Arthur Goldberg, ambassador to the United Nations, and Robert McNamara. During the discussions the only others present were Johnson's two aides, Horace Busby and Jack Valenti.

Goldberg joined Clifford in strongly opposing McNamara's recommendation that the president call up the reserves. McNamara, no doubt anticipating the possibility of having to retreat on this issue, had come to Camp David prepared to advise Johnson that an overall expansion of American armed forces by 600,000 men could be managed without calling up the reserves and that "his senior military advisers thought that the drawbacks of the draft method – confusion, slower rate of build-up, less experienced men – were acceptable."[152]

Sometime between 21 and 26 July, President Johnson decided that he would not fight a major war at the troop levels recommended by either McNamara or the JCS. Nor would he accept the consequences of what he perceived to be George Ball's negotiated surrender. "Johnson would not lose Vietnam by running away."[153] On 26 July, the day after his Camp David discussions, the president held final meetings on Vietnam with McNamara and his other top advisers (Clifford and Goldberg were also present). At this meeting he announced his decision on the McNamara/JCS/Westmoreland recommendation. With respect to troop deployment, the president decided to meet their recommendation about half-way – an immediate increase of 50,000 U.S. troops for a total 125,000, rather than the proposed 104,000 increase for a total 179,000 – but with the expectation that the latter figure might be required by the end of the year and that more men would be needed in 1966. He refused to call up the reserves, although he agreed to a substantial increase in the draft and an extension of tours of duty. By not calling up the reserves, Johnson avoided the necessity of requesting a new mandate from Congress and the intense debate that this would have precipitated.[154]

When Senator Mansfield was informed of this decision, he met with five of the Senate's most influential leaders – two Republicans (George Aiken of Vermont and John Sherman Cooper of Kentucky) and three Democrats (J. William Fulbright of Arkansas, Richard Russell of Georgia, and John Sparkman of Alabama) – and told them of Johnson's decision. In a detailed memorandum to the president, they noted that "even if you win, totally, you still do not come out well. What have you achieved? It is by no means a 'vital' area of U.S. concern."[155] The senators can perhaps be forgiven for their sense of puzzlement; their reputations and their egos were not on the line as a function of American policy in Vietnam. For Johnson and his advisers to acknowledge, even to themselves, that they were pursuing a quixotic victory in order to avoid the humiliation of coming to terms with a costly and intensifying quagmire was simply not in the cards. Such analysis and introspection would have been too painful to contemplate.

At a late afternoon meeting on 27 July, the president outlined the five available options, one involving a negotiated withdrawal, the four others maintaining or escalating the conflict. Johnson explained that he favoured the option of doing what was necessary to meet the situation but avoiding a call-up of reserves. He also noted later that he had asked the assembled group, "Did anyone object to this course of action? I questioned each one in turn. Did he agree? Each nodded his approval – said yes."[156] As for the one option that involved withdrawal, Johnson had this to say: "We could get out on the ground that we don't belong there. Not very many people feel this way about Vietnam. Most feel that our national honor is at stake and that we must keep our commitments there." In articulating "most" people's concern about national honour and commitments, Johnson was also projecting his and his advisers' fears about their own honour. To insist that the United States did belong in Vietnam, notwithstanding the instability of the South Vietnamese regime, the lack of support for the GVN among its own population, and the costs of escalation, was psychologically conceived to defend against the anxiety of withdrawal with its potential for shame and humiliation.

The president communicated his decision to the country at a televised news conference on 28 July. His address and responses to questions were couched in language emphasizing that continuity with past policy and objectives was being maintained. He announced that there would be an almost immediate increase of U.S. fighting strength in Vietnam from an existing 75,000 to 125,000 men, but additional forces would be required later and would be sent "as requested" by General Westmoreland.

Exactly when the president made this decision continues to be a topic of controversy. Berman argues that Johnson had decided on the forty-four-battalion request upon the receipt of McNamara's 20 July memorandum, and the ten days it took before he announced his decision reflected his uncertainty about how to implement it.[157] Kahin disagrees with this perspective; he maintains that the record available for this crucial week challenges the view that the president had already made up his mind in favour of a substantial increase in U.S. ground forces. Although William Bundy initially claimed that Johnson's questions to his advisers were "a bit of a set piece,"[158] he was later to state in conversation with Kahin that "this was no charade" and that as late as 24 July the president "was still framing his decision and retaining the option to reverse" the gathering consensus for McNamara's position.[159]

George Ball concluded that the substance and flavour of the many long discussions that took place on 21 July provides "some sense of the president's agonizing reluctance to go forward, his desire to explore every possible alternative, and finally, his inability to reconcile his vaunted Texas 'can-do' spirit with the shocking reality that America had painted itself into a corner with no way out except at substantial costs in terms of pride and prestige."[160]

And so, in the end, Johnson chose to escalate the war. His honour and dignity were too intimately tied to avoiding the appearance of failure or cowardice. A withdrawal would have seriously eroded his always fragile self-esteem and stimulated childhood fears that he was indeed a chip off the old block, a failure like his father. His narcissism had to be defended from an intellectual awareness of the folly and short-sightedness of his Vietnam foreign policy. As James Thomson notes: "No discussion of the factors and forces at work on Vietnam policy-makers can ignore the central fact of human ego investment."[161] In an effort to avoid losing face, and thus damaging his self-esteem, Johnson was driven to try to prove himself right. To have admitted error and attempted to extricate himself would have been too shameful. Pressure on Johnson to escalate stemming from concerns about shame and humiliation also led to his psychological entrapment. An individual who finds himself in a prolonged conflict in which one or both sides have invested much is apt to get "locked into a self-perpetuating cycle of attempts to regain or

justify ... past losses."[162] In some instances, the concern about the
loss of face becomes so critical that it "swamps" the importance of
the tangible issues at stake.[163] That, in part, is what happened to
Johnson.

At the same time, Johnson was unable to divorce himself emotionally from the crisis. That he personalized his predicament is
evident from his references to "my boys" and "my planes" and from
the siege of sleeplessness that afflicted him on the nights of air
strikes. He would telephone the Pentagon situation-room two or
three times during the course of a raid to find out whether all the
American planes had made it back to base. He felt personally responsible and suffered with every reported casualty.[164]

But Johnson's ego was not only caught up in avoiding the epithet
of "coward"; it also craved accolades. Johnson needed to be perceived as a truly great president – one who would bury the Kennedy
legend forever. And the instrument whereby he expected to accomplish that goal was the domestic legislation of the Great Society. Yet,
in his view, that could be accomplished only insofar as no major
shifts in Vietnam policy occurred. Johnson later said: "I knew the
Congress as well as I know Lady Bird, and I knew that the day it exploded into a major debate on the war, that day would be the beginning of the end of the Great Society."[165]

Negotiating a withdrawal would destabilize the political equilibrium. Congress, Johnson believed, would turn on the president and
the right-wing backlash would be devastating. It would deflect public attention away from domestic issues to attacks on Johnson and
his administration for failing to keep South Vietnam from going
communist. Television screens would report the "communist car-
nage" in all its gory details. Hanoi's propaganda would focus on the
United States as a paper tiger, while China and the Soviet Union
would mock American "commitments." Allies would never again
trust the promises of the United States.[166]

Just after leaving office Johnson spoke with particular fervour to
an oral historian about his desperate need to be perceived as courageous:

From November 1963 really until July 1965 ... I did everything I could to
avoid taking steps that would escalate our commitment. But I finally came
to the conclusion that all of my advisers reached, namely that we either
had to run or to put extra men in ... Either way I went it was a terrible situation. I knew that if I ran out ... I'd be the first American President to

ignore our commitments, turn tail and run, and leave our allies in a lurch after all the commitments Eisenhower had made, and all that SEATO had made, and all that the Congress had made, and all that the Tonkin Gulf [Resolution] said, and all the statements that Kennedy had made, and Bobby Kennedy had made ... I'd be the first American President to put my tail between my legs and run out because I didn't have the courage to stand up and support a treaty and support the policy of two other Presidents.[167]

Psychologically, Johnson could not tolerate the prospect of being found lacking in courage in comparison with his predecessors. Once his advisers, and particularly those whom he had inherited from Kennedy, indicated their opposition to withdrawal and demanded greater numbers of troops as the only way to avoid the collapse of South Vietnam, it was game over. As George Ball observed, "A determined President might at any point have overruled those advisers, accepted the costs of withdrawal and broken the momentum, but only a leader supremely sure of himself could make that decision, and Lyndon Johnson, out of his element in the Vietnam War, felt no such certainty."[168] That factor, in conjunction with his narcissistic idealization of his Kennedy advisers, also militated against any dramatic policy change.

The Johnson administration's fateful decision in July 1965 locked the United States on course for more than seven years – until the bankruptcy and hopelessness of the policy had become so widely understood by Congress and the American people as to force him to acknowledge its failure and withdraw from the 1968 presidential race. It would take Johnson's successor almost as long to yield to reality and withdraw from Vietnam. But this would occur only after Nixon's own issues of shame and humiliation had helped to precipitate the bombing and invasion of Cambodia.

4 Richard Nixon: The Angry Narcissist

A focus on the psychological underpinnings of Richard Nixon's behaviour vis à vis Cambodia, and, more particularly, on the specific role played by Nixon's feelings of shame and humiliation, must begin with his character development. Nixon's personal history was one of repeated humiliations that occurred from infancy and persisted until his ultimate humiliation – being forced to relinquish the presidency.

Nixon was born on 9 January 1913 in Yorba Linda, California, the second son in a family that would ultimately consist of five sons. The first Nixon son, Harold, had been born on 1 June 1909, and Nixon's younger brothers Francis Donald (Don), Arthur, and Edward would be born twenty-two months, four years, and seventeen years later respectively. On his father Frank's side, Nixon's forbears were generally loud, boisterous, emotional, and Methodist. On his mother Hannah's side, they were generally quiet, restrained, unemotional, and Quaker.

Frank Nixon's mother had died of tuberculosis when he was a child of eight; three years later, his father remarried to a harsh and demanding stepmother. Frank detested her and ran away from home at age thirteen, taking his first job as a farm-hand earning twenty-five cents a day. The experience of the poverty of his family and the cruelty of his stepmother left its mark on Frank. He became a strident, argumentative young man who was extremely aggressive and had difficulty in getting along with people. He drifted from one menial job to another and eventually ended up in California where he again became a farm-hand at a ranch, east of Whittier. In that Quaker environment, he met Hannah, his wife-to-be, at a church social.[1]

Hannah's parents were leaders of the community. Her father, Franklin, planted orange groves and operated a nursery while her mother, Almira, made their home into a centre for social and religious activities. Almira and Franklin Milhous's emphasis on religion, family, and duty dominated Hannah's youth and left her a very serious, religious, and duty-bound young woman.

Observers who have studied the Nixon family background generally agree that Hannah married far beneath her station.[2] Into this union of opposites, Richard Nixon was born. He was a large, eleven-pound boy with a "powerful, ringing" cry. Unlike Harold, who had been a smaller, quiet baby, the new son would be known in the family as a "screamer."[3] That pattern would persist; Nixon later referred to himself as the "biggest crybaby in Yorba Linda."[4]

Following Richard's birth, Hannah took weeks to recover from the long labour. Despite her weakness, she managed to breast-feed the new baby. Six months later, Richard was forced to share his mother's breast when she began to nurse the new-born son of her sister Elizabeth, who lived nearby.[5] Sometime late in that first year of Richard's life, Hannah had mastoid surgery at a Whittier hospital and went back briefly to her parents' house. Shortly after, when Richard was only fourteen months, Hannah found herself pregnant again, and for the birth of her third son she moved back once more into her family's home.[6]

The picture of Nixon's early childhood presented by his biographers is of a succession of rivals for his mother's time and attention coupled with her absence from home. His persistent screaming and crying could indicate that he was either uncomfortable and needed attention or felt lonely and wanted company. He was in the first year of his life, the oral phase, during which all a baby's feelings centre on food and nursing. Until it is taken care of, it cries and whines, as this is its only way of making its wants known.

To an infant, love is felt mainly through receiving food. The infant starts its contact with the world through its skin or mouth, both of which are fundamental sources of pleasure. It unconsciously associates the oral sensations of taking in food with love and security. When children are fed and at the same time fondled, they learn to enjoy these pleasurable feelings. Their sense of being secure and loved grows. The quicker their needs are gratified, the happier they are. But if they are not taken care of at once, they experience rejection or pain. If an infant is denied emotional gratification via the mouth, it feels rejected and unloved; and this may lead to oral aggression.[7]

In the case of Nixon, we note his early screaming. An infant's crying may be caused at times by physiological difficulties such as colic, and the mother may not be able to quiet it. But crying can also be the baby's way of responding to not being able to find a "fit" between its needs and the corresponding satisfaction it receives from the mother. The infant may internalize this frustrating experience with the mother and feel unloved; then, in later life, he/she may try to acquire the love and attention that had been denied in infancy. By all accounts, Nixon seems to have held on to his crying behaviour for some years. Afterwards, his crying would be sublimated: he turned instead to developmentally related oral substitutes such as public speaking that would enable him to influence and control others. He became a fierce debater at school and then a politician. Throughout Nixon's life, he would be ceaselessly driven to seek public office, acclaim, and applause as a substitute for the oral satisfaction and love he was deprived of as a child.

Both Nixon's mother and grandmother attempted to rationalize his early behaviour with the prediction that his crying foretold a future at the bar or in the pulpit. Instead of having empathy with his discomfort, they said: "He'll be a preacher. He'll be an orator." They considered him to be a "special" child instead of a distressed one.[8]

Unquestionably, Nixon, both as a child and later as an adult, was a person who felt cheated out of love. Hannah observed that, of all her children, Richard seemed to "need" her the most, and this suggests that he felt dissatisfied with what he was receiving and consequently wanted more. That sense of deprivation may partially explain his profound inability to trust anyone and his feeling that "in my job [vice-president] you can't enjoy the luxury of intimate personal friendships. You can't confide absolutely in anyone."[9] His deep-seated inability to trust indicated, according to Bryce Harlow, Nixon's presidential aide, that "he was hurt very deeply by somebody … someone he deeply trusted. Hurt so badly he never got over it and never trusted anybody again." Harlow speculates that as a result of this experience Nixon never learned how to trust and thus people never really trusted him.[10] In the last traumatic days of

Watergate, sitting in the White House with journalist Hugh Sidey, Henry Kissinger commented, "Can you imagine what this man would have been like had somebody loved him?" Kissinger then went on to explain that "I don't think anybody ever did, not his parents, not his peers. There may have been a teacher but nobody knows, it's not recorded." Finally, Kissinger said, "He would have been a great, great man had somebody loved him."[11]

That Nixon felt abandoned, bereft of love, and profoundly sad at a very early age is suggested in a letter he wrote at the age of eleven to his mother during one of her periodic retreats to the Milhous family home.

November 12, 1923.

My Dear Master:

The two dogs that you left with me are very bad to me. Thier dog, Jim, is very old and he will never talk or play with me. One Saturday the boys went hunting. Jim and myself went with him. While going through the woods one of the boys triped and fell on me. I lost my temper and hit him. He kiked me in the side and we started on. While were walking I saw a black round thing in a tree. I hit it with my paw. A swarm of black thing came out of it. I felt a pain all over. I started to run and as both of my eyes were swelled shut I fell into a pond. When I got hom I was very sore. i wish you would come home right now.

Your good dog,
Richard.[12]

Central to this letter are the themes of the two invading "dogs" (perhaps his cousin and his brother Donald), the "very old" dog "Jim" (his father, Frank), and Nixon's desire for Hannah to return home to take care of him.[13] The letter can be understood as a fantasy full of symbols, "a tale of hurt, panic and depression"[14] with the imagery portraying "a high level of confusion and despair."[15] According to Nixon's neighbour and cousin, Jessamyn West, it was not unusual for Hannah to go home briefly to her mother "tired to death with her boys."[16] This may have been one of those times and it suggests that Nixon felt very frightened and sad at being left in the care of his father.

The anxieties in this letter are markedly different from Richard's fantasies at age three when he imagined himself as a hunter, killing elephants and tigers. Here, he is the hunted, kicked, stung in many places, blinded, and threatened with drowning, although he is also biting and striking out at a "black round thing." If nothing else, the letter demonstrates how early he had begun to exaggerate the wrongs inflicted on him by others.

In later years, friends would recall Harold or Don Nixon with warmth, affection, closeness, Richard with a description of his "seriousness." Richard "wasn't a boy you wanted to hug" was the way townspeople described him, although they were impressed by his powers of memory and by his intelligent and active interest in politics at a young age.[17] To a reporter in 1968, Nixon indicated that Harold was "kind of a favorite as you can imagine with my mother and father."[18]

If Harold was a favourite because of his easy-going disposition and open personality, Nixon was special to his mother for his intellectual precociousness. As Fawn Brodie observes, in the making of the narcissistic personality there is frequently a recognition of special gifts for which the child then feels loved. In Nixon's case, his mother recognized early that he was a gifted child, and she took pains to teach him how to read before he entered kindergarten. While it is difficult to construct the nature of Hannah's love during Richard's childhood, as well as Richard's own feelings about it, he may have believed that she loved him only for his obedience, his deference, his quickness at learning, his cleanliness (about which she was fanatical), and his skill at appeasing his father.[19]

Not only did Hannah expand Richard's curiosity and capabilities far beyond the horizons of the average five-year-old, she drilled into him the importance of working hard in order to grow up to be somebody so that he might avoid the humiliations of his childhood. After Frank's lemon grove failed, his mother went to work at the Sunkist lemon packing house in Yorba Linda, taking Richard, aged six, and Donald, aged four and a half, with her both to be watched and to work as sweepers. Richard frequently became nauseated at the noise of the packing-house machinery.[20] A year later, Richard and Donald went to work as child labourers picking beans and lemons; "We would work twelve long hard hours to earn that one dollar," Richard would recall.[21] Equally painful was the shame of seeing their mother forced to work alongside the largely Mexican and poor immigrant labourers.[22]

A small clue to Hannah's aspirations for her second son was her attempt to stop the use of the nickname Dick, which she thought too frivolous for a future man of importance.[23] She later remembered that, although her four sons shared a room in Yorba Linda, this changed when they moved to Whittier: Harold, Donald, and Arthur bunked together while Richard, then aged nine, "had a small room of his own. He was studious, and he needed privacy for study."[24] One might expect the eldest, youngest, or opposite-sex child to be treated in such fashion, but to be singled out as the second son for this type of special treatment carried with it a subtext: you are special; we expect you to succeed and we are counting upon you. It would be imperative for Nixon to achieve in order to ensure his mother's continued regard and interest in him.

As a youngster, Richard was given piano lessons. Since his progress seemed slow to his mother, she talked about more advanced work with her younger sister, Jane Beeson, who was an accomplished teacher. Jane convinced her sister Hannah that Richard should live with the Beesons for a time to take daily lessons from her. At the age of twelve and a half, he spent five unhappy, homesick months away from his family at the Beeson ranch two hundred miles away. Richard's success as a pianist was deemed more important than his ongoing presence in the Nixon household.

Almost immediately upon his return from his Aunt Jane's home in the summer of 1925, his younger brother Arthur, with whom he had a special affinity – he was intelligent, quiet, and somewhat of a loner like Richard – fell ill, suffering headaches and indigestion. He died one week later, at the age of seven, of what was generally assumed to be tubercular meningitis. His death had a deep impact on the entire family. The mood at home became even heavier as both Hannah and Frank dealt with their grief and their guilt. With the resumption of school, Richard was soon back at the old routine of work and study and he threw himself into both with still more noticeable resolution. "From that time on," Hannah said, "it seemed that Richard was trying to be three sons in one, striving even harder than before to make up to his father and me for our loss."[25]

Friends and relatives of Nixon's frequently commented on his drive to excel and his need to win. His cousin Floyd Wildermuth described how he and Nixon's older brother Harold were able to use this character trait to their advantage.

One of the interesting things, Harold and I, we'd be out in the grove and tired, wanting to get some cookies or something. We'd often try to get

Richard to go run our errands for us. Although he'd be reluctant, we found how we could always get him to do it because he was quite a competitive boy. He was very competitive in fact ... This is one of the things I can remember particularly about Richard Nixon as a boy, his strong competitive spirit. We used it to his detriment, I guess, and worked him to run our errands.[26]

Shortly after Arthur's death, Nixon's parents decided to send Harold, whose headstrong ways and indifference to learning had caused them considerable anxiety, to the Mount Hermon School for boys in Northfield, Massachusetts. The decision was to have momentous consequences for the Nixon family. In April 1927 Harold Nixon returned suddenly from Mount Hermon sick with a cough and sore throat that signalled the onset of tuberculosis. For the next six years, until his death in 1933, Hannah Nixon would be required to leave her family to care for Harold more than four hundred miles away in Prescott, Arizona, a small mountain resort then known as a haven for tubercular patients.

This was Hannah's third departure from Richard. Unconsciously, the message that Richard internalized was that he was in fact unlovable. As a defense against such feelings, he strove to become president of every organization he was involved in as a way of convincing himself that he was loved – more loved than his opponents (unconsciously, his siblings) in elections for such positions.

Wildermuth recalled that, when he and Richard were in high school, Nixon said to him, "Anybody can become President." He added that he "never did believe it myself, but he [Nixon] believed it ... And I swear, from that, I believe that Richard Nixon was dedicated to becoming President."[27] In a far more critical vein, another high school class-mate, Forrest Randall, saw Richard's ambition early on: "I mean I'm sure the minute he had his first thought, he was going to be President of the United States. And this is the way he worked everything. He was going to be president of the student body and that's the way he worked it."[28]

Two years after the Nixons' move to Whittier, Frank had opened a gasoline station. In 1925 he expanded the business by buying an old church, moving the building to his gasoline station lot, and opening a general store. With their mother nursing Harold in Prescott, the burden of running the store fell on the remaining Nixon sons. Without Hannah, the father and sons took turns preparing meals, though none could cook or apparently bothered to learn.

Richard recalled eating canned chili and soup, spaghetti, pork and beans, frequent fried eggs, and hamburgers. "There were many mornings," he said, "when I had nothing for breakfast but a candy bar."[29] Alone with their father, the brothers fought frequently with Frank and one another.

Later in life, Richard would describe these years as having had their redeeming aspects: "It was a rather difficult time actually, from the standpoint of the family being pulled apart, but looking back, I don't think that we were any the worse for it, because we learned to share the diversity and you grew stronger for having to take care of yourself ... not having your mother to lean on." But he ended his recollection with a passage that more than hinted at the distress he felt regarding his mother's absorption with Harold. "We all grew up rather fast in those years," he remarked, then adding the pointed qualification, "those of us who remained home."[30] In that comment, we glimpse Nixon's envy of his older brother, who, through his illness, could prolong his childhood and enjoy his mother's undivided attention.

Even though Nixon's mother was an excellent cook whose pies were sold daily in the Nixon grocery store, he would give away her carefully prepared desserts and sandwiches to his friends in college.[31] It was as though he needed to demonstrate that he could live without his mother's supply of food or its symbolic equivalent, love, since both had been erratic and unpredictable. To the narcissistically vulnerable individual, the pretense of self-reliance and autonomy is crucial. In the case of Richard Nixon, even after he became president he continued to prefer such foods as hamburgers and spaghetti – items he and his brothers had prepared themselves – a practice which suggests that he never quite overcame his concerns about unpredictable supplies of food and love.[32]

Harold's subsequent death in 1933 intensified Nixon's yearning to be loved in the one way that still seemed open: successful accomplishments. As his mother observed: "With the death of Harold his determination to make us proud of him seemed greatly intensified."[33] In 1960 Nixon admitted privately to Buff Chandler, the wife of the publisher of the *Los Angeles Times*, that the reason he would run against Kennedy, despite his wife's opposition, was that he'd "never been in the center stage, in the leading role ... And I'll never be satisfied until I'm in that role."[34]

Nixon's drive to succeed in the face of innumerable obstacles seems to have been the product both of Hannah Nixon's early expectations and explicit demands that her son Richard excel as the price of her love, and of Nixon's guilt that, having survived two of his brothers, he would have to pay for this triumph by bringing his parents the successes that would lessen their painful feelings of loss. That Nixon never really succeeded in getting his mother's unconditional love and support is suggested in her remarks to one of Nixon's biographers, Bela Kornitzer. A Hungarian refugee who hated the Soviets and thought that Nixon's trip to Moscow and his debate with Nikita Khrushchev had been an enormous triumph, he was discomfited by Hannah's refusal "to admit that he had done a remarkable job in Russia. The most she would say was, 'I just didn't think it could be a flop.' "[35]

Later, during the election campaign of 1960, Kornitzer interviewed both Hannah Nixon and Rose Kennedy, asking them the same questions. The difference between the measured answers of the Quaker mother and the enthusiastic outpourings of Rose Kennedy is striking. When Mrs Kennedy was asked if she thought her son would make a good president, she answered, "I think he would make a wonderful president." Hannah Nixon answered by saying that he would make a good president "if God is on his side."[36] Hannah Nixon's carefully controlled manner of expressing her feelings must have been characteristic of the way in which she communicated her affection for her son as he was growing up. It was to be reflected in Nixon's own difficulties in expressing loving feelings. Failing to elicit the love that he had missed, he would substitute electoral success for love and, in his interpersonal relationships, settle for people's respect and admiration.

Even Nixon's success in winning the presidency failed to produce much maternal pride in her son's accomplishment. After Hannah heard Andre Watts play at the Nixon inaugural, she was overheard to say to Richard as he got up to go out at the intermission, "Now Richard, if thee had practised more on the piano, thee could been down there instead of up here."[37] On the day that should have seen Nixon savouring his triumph, his mother was reminding him, in none too subtle fashion, of the way in which he had failed her.

If Nixon's mother tended to be undemonstrative, Nixon's father was even more constrained in the expression of loving feelings for his children. He appears to have been very punitive, gruff, bad-tempered, and tight-fisted. Jessamyn West recounted one famous story of Frank Nixon's capacity for punitive behaviour. In Yorba Linda, there was an irrigation canal running between West's house and that of the Nixons that brought water through the town to citrus ranches south and west of the town. Frank Nixon forbade his sons to swim in the canal even though it was only dangerous for children under the age of three, and everyone older swam in it. Jessamyn West and her aunt Elizabeth were watching once when Frank caught Richard and one of his brothers in the canal. He hauled them out and then flung them back in again, shouting, "Do you like water? Have some more of it." The aunt, fearing that he was drowning the boys, began screaming, "You'll kill them, Frank! You'll kill them."[38]

Although Richard Nixon was to tell this story as an adult and laugh about it, he may have felt at the age of six or seven that his father was indeed trying to drown him and his brothers like unwanted puppies. But Nixon did not readily acknowledge the anger and rage in his father's character. The worst thing he would say about Nixon senior was that his father had a hot temper and was "sometimes impatient and – well – rather grouchy with most people," that he had "tempestuous arguments with my brother Harold and Don and their shouting could be heard all through the neighborhood."[39] Hannah Nixon noted that her husband "would not hesitate using the strap or rod on the boys when they did wrong," but she did not remember "that he ever spanked Richard."[40] Yet Nixon himself told Thomas Bewley, a partner in the law firm Wingert and Bewley who gave him his first job after graduation from law school, that "I got the strap."[41] Similarly, he revealed to journalist Kenneth Harris that his father spanked them sometimes.[42]

Nixon, however, learned to avoid most punishments from his father: "I used to tell my brothers not to argue with him ... Dad was very strict and expected to be obeyed under all circumstances. He had a hot temper, and I learned very early that the only way to deal with him was to abide by the rules he laid down. Otherwise I would probably have felt the touch of the ruler or the strap as my brothers did."[43]

Whatever the actual reality of the spankings, their "psychic" reality had an impact on Nixon. It fostered an identification with his aggressive father as a way of coping with this feared authority figure. It also led to a deep-seated wish to avenge himself on his authoritarian father by administering equivalent humiliations to a succession of perceived tormentors and surrogate fathers – opposition politicians, the press, college students, and so on. In later life, the control over his emotions which Nixon tried so hard to maintain would shatter when his self-esteem was attacked, and he would lash out in a manner similar to that which he had experienced at the hands of his father.

As Nixon and his brothers matured, Frank Nixon still yelled at them but they retaliated with a vengeance. Visiting the grocery in the early 1930s, neighbour and cousin Eldo West was astounded that the Nixon boys "could be so cruel, so loud-mouthed, so outspoken, so critical of their father there in the store before everyone else." His daughter, Jessamyn, could not understand the anger "unless they felt they got it when they were young and now they are paying their father back."[44]

In adulthood, Nixon would pride himself on trying to be cool and not exploding in public displays of anger. For the most part, he was able to manage his rage; experiences of shame and humiliation, however, triggered either passionate outbursts or a more calculated determination to exact revenge. If he could not always get as mad at his tormentors as he would have liked, he could displace his anger elsewhere, as in his decisions to bomb and then invade Cambodia.

Illustrative, perhaps, of the sense of shame and humiliation that Frank Nixon's unruly and ungovernable temper engendered in Nixon was the effort Richard took to disavow it. He castigated some of the media who portrayed his father as a "crude, uneducated oaf who did not have the respect of his sons and was disliked by most who knew him. If they had been privileged to know him as I did, they would have painted a very different picture." Nixon proceeded to describe his father as someone who worked harder and longer than anyone else he knew. Acknowledging that Nixon senior was a fighter, he defensively observed that he fought "always verbally, never physically." What occupied the greater part of Nixon's defense of his father was "his driving ambition, not for himself but for his sons." He recalled that, because of illness in his father's family, Nixon senior "had to leave school after only six years of formal education. Never a day went by when he did not tell me and my four brothers how fortunate we were able to go to school. I was determined not to let him down. My biggest thrill in those years was to see the light in his eyes when I brought home a good report card." Nixon also recounted that his father "wanted [him] to become the best orator and debater in the country."[45]

There are, however, no references to bonds of love or affection between father and son. Rather, the picture that is presented is of a relationship in which it was the son's responsibility to satisfy all of the pent-up frustrations and ambitions of his uneducated father. Richard would be valued and would come to value himself in terms of his successes – as an excellent student, debater, and politician.

That Frank Nixon may not have been averse to kicking his sons – a particularly humiliating form of physical punishment – is suggested, albeit indirectly, by Nixon's behaviour and his comments. The theme of kicking and of being kicked appears early in Nixon's life and surfaces repeatedly.[46] In a letter written at age ten, he complained about being kicked.[47] In Peru, when he was spat upon, he kicked the hostile demonstrator in the shin and he would later report his satisfaction with the incident in his book *Six Crises*. His statement to the press in 1962 after his failed bid for the California governorship became famous: "You won't have Dick Nixon to kick around any more." Less well known were private comments such as "we'll kick their toes off in 1968" and "kick the weirdos and beardos on the college campuses."[48] Presidential tapes reveal Nixon saying to Presidential Counsel John Dean on 13 March 1973, "Have you kicked a few butts around?" When Dean turned against him on Watergate, Nixon said to Mitchell, "Kick him straight."[49] In retirement he confessed to David Frost: "People blow off steam in different ways. Some of them kick the cat. I don't like cats, but my daughters do. I should not have said that. But nevertheless, if there were one around I would probably kick the cat."[50] While Frank Nixon may never have kicked his son, Richard certainly felt abused, and he identified with the brutal side of his father's character as a way of turning passive into active and mastering the mistreatment.

Hannah Nixon also played a role in administering punishment. Her way was not to yell or spank but to give her children "quietly eviscerating little talks."[51] Nixon spoke critically of his mother only once in public, shortly after her death, when he described with distaste her method of punishment. In his 1968 campaign film, when she was questioned about spanking, Hannah had said that she believed in "silent punishment – in making a child sit quietly while he thinks through what he has done. That makes it punishment enough. It gets better results."[52] In the same film, Nixon also referred to his mother's statement that she never gave them a spanking. "I'm not so sure. She might have. But I do know that we dreaded far more than my father's hand, her tongue. It was never sharp, but she would just sit you down and she would talk very quietly and then when you got through you had been through an emotional experience."[53] Unspoken, but clearly evident, was the sense of shame that Hannah induced in her sons for their misconduct.

Richard Nixon, then, grew up in a family where he felt obliged to achieve in order to earn his parents' love and admiration. Such a matrix often provides the makings of a narcissistic character with a fragile sense of self-worth who is driven to accomplish in order to replenish his emptiness as a result of the failures of early parenting. Even if the child is highly valued for his accomplishments, he has the uneasy feeling that the love is conditional upon his successes. This produces a profound sense of shame, which in turn acts as a spur to continued striving for success as a way of shoring up self-esteem. When that success is not forthcoming, or when other people fail to respond to, or frustrate, the narcissistic individual's need for external validation and support, the end result is the expression of rage and vindictiveness.

Nixon's wish to earn his father's approbation explains, in part, his continued efforts to make the Whittier high school and college football teams. Nixon senior, eager to make a man out of his poorly coordinated, unathletic second son, frequently came to watch and instruct his son in football practice. It was to be of no avail. Nixon never made the starting team in high school, and in college the highest spot he achieved was third-string guard on a thirty-three-man team.[54] On the rare occasions that Nixon actually played in a game, the coach would put him in only during the last minutes, by which point it was already won or lost. None the less, Nixon was extremely eager to distinguish himself. A class-mate who was a lineman said, "When Dick went in I always got out the five-yard penalty marker ... I knew he'd be offside just about every play."[55]

Although Nixon physically "wasn't cut out to play the sport," according to Clint Harris, who played tackle across the line from Nixon, his tenacity and spirit during practice sessions amazed his coaches and fellow team-mates. Gail Jobe, also on the third team, recalled, "Nixon and I were cannon fodder."[56] Coach Wallace Newman agreed. "We used Nixon as a punching bag. If he'd had the physical ability he'd have been a terror." Harris remembers thinking, "Dick Nixon, I don't know why you do this, but I admire your red-blooded intestinal fortitude."[57] For Nixon, being physically abused in this way held out the hope that if he could endure the punishment he would succeed in earning his coach's (and father's) love and respect.

That he was preoccupied with his parents' approval is suggested in the surprising ways that Nixon's fear of their displeasure surfaced. He would defy their admonitions in countless ways, such as drinking and card-playing, but to their faces he would try to present himself as the "good boy." The evening Nixon was elected to Congress in 1946, he was invited to the home of Norman Chandler, publisher of the *Los Angeles Times*. He was accompanied by his wife, Pat, his parents, and his brother Donald and his wife. As Mrs Chandler recalls the incident, she asked them all what they would like to drink. Everyone wanted milk, and "so I went around to go into the kitchen to tell the cook everybody wanted milk ... when Nixon came out in the hall and said, 'Buff, could you get me a double bourbon? I don't want Mother and Father to see me take a drink.' "[58] This suggests the degree to which Nixon had remained hostage to parental approval. To reveal the truth about himself was dangerous lest it lead to the withdrawal of his parents' love and admiration.

In his senior year of high school, Nixon met Ola Florence Welch, his first girlfriend, whom he would date for the next seven years. She was bright, pretty, vivacious, and well liked. Richard was the first boy Ola had dated, and she thought him "really quite handsome ... tall and good-looking" and admired his intelligence. Their relationship was fairly tempestuous. Whatever the subject, they argued and fought often during their college years. "We had a very stormy relationship, more stormy than most," Ola remembered.[59] To many who watched them together, Nixon appeared flinty and sharp. "He was combative rather than conciliatory. He had a nasty temper," said a fellow student.[60] From time to time, they each dated others at Whittier, usually with Nixon making the break and leaving Ola to discover it afterward in hurt or jealousy. The urge to punish and to be vindictive was evident throughout their relationship.

Of their last two years at Whittier, Ola would say that "there was a tacit agreement that we would be married some day."[61] Nixon had asked her to marry him, and they had begun to make plans, though no date was set. However, during his senior year, Nixon's relationship with Ola became increasingly problematic. Ola felt that after his election as president of the student body "she wasn't good enough for him."[62]

But once at Duke University law school, Nixon began to write Ola long moody, often despondent accounts of the homesickness he was encountering. In his letters from Duke, he seemed to take their renewed romance and eventual marriage for granted. In June, when he returned home, he called Ola to tell her he was coming over. She informed him that Gail Jobe, Nixon's former team-mate, was at that moment sitting in her living-room and they were seeing each other. Nixon recoiled in hurt and anger and they quarrelled angrily. One of their mutual friends from college, recalling the clash, said that "Richard was furious. With that temper of his, he went through the roof."[63] "If I never see you again," Nixon lashed out at her, "it will be too soon."[64]

But the following day he went to the Welch house and acted as if the quarrel and the entire conversation had never occurred. More than once over that summer he asked her to marry him, and each time he promptly ignored the awkward vagueness of her response. It was as though Nixon's sense of entitlement coupled with an inability to countenance rejection blinded him to Ola's cooling ardour. For her part, Ola did not pursue the subject of her deepening relationship with Jobe. "Well, she was dating Gail Jobe," a friend would say later, "and still keeping Richard on the string."[65]

Nixon returned to Duke in September 1935, and over the first months of the new term he faithfully sent letters to Ola each week. "He still wrote until the middle of his second year as if we would get married," she recalled.[66] Meanwhile, Ola accepted Gail Jobe's marriage proposal. Before Christmas, she wrote Nixon to end their relationship. "Once again, he was pained, indignant, unbelieving."[67] For a long time, his letters to her continued; when she did not answer, he wrote a final plaintive note.

Friends were generally surprised and puzzled that their relationship had ended. Few knew the extent to which Ola had rejected him. Nixon, himself, gave Edith Nunes, who knew them both well, an explanation so implausible that she was too embarrassed to repeat it even decades later. His humiliation had to be kept secret; he never admitted the seriousness of his involvement with Ola, nor confided to anyone his anguish at her rejection of him. Friends at Duke heard him talk about his family, the grocery, Whittier, but never about the girl to whom he wrote love letters for more than a year and a half at law school and her decision to marry another man.[68]

In his relationship to the woman who was to become his wife, Thelma Catherine "Pat" Ryan, Nixon's conduct shifted over time.

During his pursuit of her, he adopted a humble, self-deprecatory stance, evidently prepared to accept mere crumbs from his beloved's table; then, after their marriage, he became the chief architect of her humiliation. Once again, Nixon, unconsciously, needed to take revenge on his wife; it would alleviate the sense of humiliation he had previously suffered from Ola's rejection and the early embarrassments he experienced at the hands of Pat.

Richard met Pat Ryan during the fall of 1937 in Whittier, where she had just been hired to teach secretarial courses. They both had joined a small theatre group and were cast opposite each other. For Richard, it was love at first sight. He was to engage in a "cloying, undaunted, often unrequited pursuit of Patricia Ryan over the next two years."[69] She was pretty and worldly with a strong sense of independence. Weekends were spent at her sister Neva's apartment in Los Angeles where her dates would pick her up and drop her off. She led an active social life with former boyfriends from the University of Southern California and elsewhere.

Throughout the spring of 1938, Nixon asked her repeatedly for dates. Turned down always on weekends and often during the week, he began showing up at her rooms unannounced in the evening to take her on drives or walks through the hillside blocks around the college. Pat thought him "a bit unusual" and continued to put him off. When she tactfully excused her own indifference by remarking lightly that she was a vagabond or gypsy, Nixon wrote her affectionate little notes addressed to "Miss Vagabond" or "My Irish Gypsy." When she pointedly arranged a date for him with her room-mate, he agreed readily to go, and during the evening he talked only about Pat.[70]

Eventually, she bolted her door from the inside against his weeknight visits and did not answer his knocking, though he obviously knew she was at home. Undeterred, he went off to write notes and returned the same night to slip them under her locked door. After much persistence, he won the privilege of driving her on Friday nights to her sister's apartment and then picking her up there Sunday evenings, usually after she had been brought back from a date with another man. If she were late, or out with a boyfriend unexpectedly, he methodically killed time in the city by going to a movie, walking aimlessly, or sitting in hotel lobbies reading.[71]

Pat became increasingly uneasy at his attachment to her. One night late that spring, when he dropped by once again without calling, she confronted the issue squarely and threw him out. Rebuffed so openly, Nixon finally reacted with an angry, petulant show of unconcern. But within days he had written another plaintive note in which, among other things, he commented:

But I can honestly say that Patricia is one fine girl, that I like her immensely, and that though she isn't going to give me a chance to propose to her for fear of hurting me! and though she insulted my ego just a bit by not being quite frank at times, I still remember her as combining the best traits of the Irish and the square-heads –

Yours,
Dick

In this note, we feel Nixon's barely suppressed anger at Pat when he uses the word "honestly" before his statement that she is one fine girl. In fact, what the word suggests is that she had hurt him and was not "one fine girl." There is also an acknowledgment of the damage to his self-esteem that her behaviour has caused – "insulted my ego just a bit" – and he sounds a note of recrimination when he remarks that it is she who has not played fair with him, "not being quite frank at times."

Pat, however, found the note sufficiently moving to relent; she agreed to see him again and to allow the weekend chauffeuring into Los Angeles to continue. Yet this was accompanied by an explicit understanding that there would be, as she later told her daughter, "no declarations of love or proposals of marriage."[72] Nixon's persistence and his flattering prediction that she was destined to achieve "great things," coupled with her own ambition to move beyond the stifling confines of Whittier, eventually paid off. A year later she finally accepted his proposal – though with misgivings. "Even as she consented," her daughter was to write, "she was not sure she wanted to marry. She was twenty-eight years old and had been independent for a long time."[73]

Close friends and observers of the Nixon marriage have commented on the unusual quality of their relationship and the obvious lack of warmth between them. Tom Dixon, his radio coordinator in 1948 and 1950, said, "I never saw him touch Pat's hand ... She was farther away from him than I was ... I never have seen quite as cold an arrangement."[74] Evlyn Dorn, Nixon's secretary in the Whittier law firm and a long-time family friend, said that in all her years of knowing the Nixons she never saw him reach out to touch his wife except once; they were standing together in the back of a car in an election rally, and he put out his hand to steady her.

On Pat's sixty-first birthday, Nixon was helping to celebrate the opening of the Grand Old Opry in Nashville, Tennessee. She joined him on her way home from a Latin American trip. "There was a huge celebration," Helen McCain Smith remembered: "Pat, seated at the back of the stage, was surprised and delighted when an upright piano was wheeled out and the President played Happy Birthday for her with everyone joining in the singing. At the last chord, her face glowing, Pat rose from her chair and moved toward her husband. He apparently wanted to get on with the program. He turned, stepped brusquely to the center stage – and ignored Pat's outstretched arms. I shall never forget the expression on her face."[75]

Georgia Sherwood remembered that Nixon treated Pat with almost routine incivility. "He would always hold the door for me," she said, "but would walk through in front of Pat as if she wasn't there at all."[76] Once when the two women were sitting on uncomfortable chairs in a tiny anteroom, and Pat got up and walked into the radio office, "Nixon flared at her like a prima donna." He ordered her out "with as little ceremony as he would have a dog," saying, "You know I never want to be interrupted when I'm working!" Tom Dixon was nettled by the outburst. "It gave me an insight into the man. If he had been doing a brand new speech, I could have understood it, but this speech he knew by heart."[77] Days later in Fresno, Mac St Johns saw much the same scene re-enacted. Pat had come in to say that it was time to leave, and Nixon shot back testily, "I'll go when I'm damned well ready."[78]

Nixon's beliefs regarding the proper role for a president's wife were made strikingly clear during an interview with the Washington press corps about Pat's birthday celebration in 1971. In commenting on his surprise at seeing Eleanor Roosevelt visiting the troops in New Caledonia during the Second World War, he said, "It made an enormous impression on me. Not negative. An enormous impression."[79] Nixon's need to underscore that the impression was "not negative" betrayed his true feelings. In discussing Lady Bird Johnson's beautification program, he said most people would dismiss it as "planting a few pansies on the freeways," but he conceded that "it helped."[80] Again, there was the grudging, dismissive attitude towards women who play an independent role in political life and who could be seen as competitors for public admiration.

At a meeting on 11 March 1971 with the White House women's press corps, Nixon's warmest words were reserved for the non-political First Ladies, Grace Coolidge, Mamie Eisenhower, and Bess Truman. When Harry Truman was in trouble, he speculated, "I'm sure Bess stood there like a rock." What really mattered to him, he said, was to have around him when faced with a tough decision "people who are standing with him, people that are strong, people who aren't panicking, people who aren't throwing up their hands about what they heard on television that night, the lousy column or the terrible cartoon or this or that or the other thing; somebody who brings serenity, calmness and strength into the room. That makes a great difference. That is why, for example – did you meet Mrs. de Gaulle, a marvellous woman."[81] Nixon left some of the women reporters wondering whether Pat brought serenity, calmness, and strength, like Mrs de Gaulle, or threw up her hands about the awful television reportage, the lousy column, or the terrible cartoon.[82]

Although Nixon insisted on Pat's campaigning with him, it was understood that she would never speak but simply greet the crowds pleasantly, smile, even at hecklers, and hand out campaign literature. Tom Dixon, who saw the Nixons almost every day through the 1950 campaign, was questioned about Pat's always remaining silent. "I think he would have made it very miserable for her if she hadn't."[83]

After 1970 Pat Nixon was finally permitted to make trips on her own; she was always well briefed and accompanied by experts. Reporters were charmed to discover that away from her husband she dropped her mask and came alive, a shy but nevertheless independent woman. In his memoirs, Nixon explained: "Pat is one of those rare individuals whose ego does not depend on public attention."[84]

Over the years Nixon praised Pat as a campaigner, often noting with envy her popularity. Shortly before his resignation he called her "the best ambassador the United States has."[85] But, as we have seen, he could slight her outrageously on public platforms, and in private, in the presence of friends, he could be caustic and boorish. Pat Nixon's White House aide, Helen McCain Smith, who told several stories of Nixon's public humiliations of his wife, was especially angered when on the night before the resignation he said to a group of congressmen, "I have a wonderful family and a pretty good wife." In his last tearful speech in the White House, the morning of his departure, he mentioned his cabinet, his staff, his parents, and his dead brothers, but never his wife.[86]

For Nixon, "a wife complements her husband by shoring him up,"[87] something he felt Pat had failed to do. He wanted her to mirror him, reassure him, and do nothing which would suggest that she might have her own desires or needs independent of his. Again, Nixon's view of the ideal helpmate reveals that he had failed to obtain the "shoring up" and reassurance by his parents that would have strengthened his self-esteem and made it less imperative for him to receive constant stroking as an adult.

As someone who grew up feeling shamed and humiliated, Nixon utilized a classic psychological defense mechanism; rather than identifying with the victim of the humiliation, he attempted to master the early traumas by identifying with the aggressor and behaving aggressively. Humiliating his wife on repeated occasions served to augment Nixon's own sense of self and was, in part, a displacement for a wish to revenge himself on his earlier childhood tormentors, his parents, and particularly his mother, whose acknowledged "goodness" had made him feel quietly enraged.

Nixon's experiences of humiliation were not confined only to his relationships with his family, his girlfriend, and his wife. The legal, financial, and political realms were to provide more than their fair share of disappointments and shame for Nixon as he matured into manhood. Particularly noteworthy in the earlier years was Nixon's inability to get a job with an eastern law firm or the FBI, his bungled first law case, and his business failure with Citra-Frost.

Graduating third in his Duke law class of twenty-six, Nixon found it difficult to secure a job in New York. Duke was then a new law school and its graduates were treated with some contempt by the city's best law firms. Nixon made the dreary round at Christmas, several months before graduation, with two of his friends. Bill Perdue, who had graduated top of the class, got a job with a distinguished law firm, while his other friend found work with a large oil corporation. Nixon did not receive any offers from the firms to which he had applied.[88]

Discouraged, Nixon went to the dean, Claude Horack, and asked him to write a letter of recommendation to the FBI. The dean was surprised, thinking him "too good a man for that," but Nixon announced that "he was attracted to it." The FBI responded favourably to Nixon's application, but a budget cut prevented his appointment and Nixon never learned until he was vice-president why he had not received an answer to his application.[89] In June 1937 he had to

suffer the humiliation of telling his parents and grandmother Milhous, who at eighty-eight had journeyed east to celebrate his graduation, that he had failed to get a job either with a New York firm or
with the FBI. It is not surprising that his resentment against the east
– against Ivy league colleges and New York City in particular – would
fester for many years.

Nixon's humiliation at not getting a job would be compounded
by his handling of his first law case for Thomas Bewley. Nixon had
not wanted to join the firm of Wingert and Bewley in Whittier. He
had been so confident of a job in New York, or with the FBI, and so
reluctant to return to Whittier, that he had not even applied for
permission to take the California bar examination. At the last moment, with no job at hand, he asked Duke University's Dean
Horack to intercede on his behalf, begging that he be granted special permission to take the examination in the summer and his
request was granted.[90]

Nixon passed the bar exam, the hardest test in his life before en-
tering politics, he said, and was sworn in before the California Supreme Court at Sacramento on 9 November 1937. Six days later he
was acting for Bewley in the Los Angeles Municipal Court on behalf
of a young woman named Marie Schee. Schee was suing her uncle,
Otto Steur, to pay back a $2,000 loan. Nixon got a court order in
November 1937 to pay Schee back by selling a house the uncle
owned in an execution sale. The house was said to be worth $6,500.
The execution sale took place on 29 June 1938 and Nixon, waiting
for the proceedings to begin, and feeling unsure of himself, asked
the opposition lawyer for his assistance. He advised Nixon to bid
the entire sum due Schee, which Nixon did, without consulting his
client. Nixon should have checked to determine if there were any
liens or mortgages on the house affecting its value. Failing that, he
could still have bid a nominal sum for the property to protect
Schee against any such unknown claims allowing her a "deficiency
judgment" from the sale, thus leaving her uncle still liable for the
debt while she took deed to the house. Nixon did neither. It then
emerged that there were two liens on the house. Nixon's error set
off nearly five years of suits and countersuits hinging on his own
"misconduct" and the "malpractice" of the firm.

Bewley intervened to remedy Nixon's mistake and advised Schee's
parents, his old clients Charles and Emilie Force, to buy out the
other claimants and then force foreclosure themselves in order to
resell the property and retrieve both their costs and their daughter's

money. They took Bewley's advice and this time Bewley attended the sale late in December 1938, having advised the Forces to bid, as Nixon should have back in June, only a nominal sum. But what was professional and prudent in June was an even worse blunder in December. Another buyer came to the sale, bid more than the Forces, though still less than $3,000, and thereby wiped out Schee's repayment while taking the property. Enraged, Marie Schee instituted a malpractice suit against Wingert and Bewley, who settled out of court in March 1939 for $4,800.

The case would drag on in various forms until the end of 1942; the Steurs moved for satisfaction of judgment after the sale of their house to end Marie Schee's tangled claim on them, while Schee contested their action, losing, appealing, and losing again. In those lawsuits, Nixon personally was called to defend himself by affidavit or to testify under hostile cross-examination by Schee's new attorney. Each time his work was put on trial, there were overtones of seediness. Although Schee was defeated on two appeals, and Nixon's lack of skill or authority in the original case ruled beside the point by the higher court, Nixon's "alleged misconduct" would be inscribed in the California appellate records.[91] The case was a bitter reminder of the tenor and quality of his Whittier career – the malfeasance of both him and Bewley – and of his distance from the carpeted suites of prestigous New York law firms.[92]

By the close of 1939, a little more than two years after he joined them, Wingert and Bewley invited Nixon to become a full partner. He accepted without pause. "Now for the first time I was no longer Frank and Hannah Nixon's son," he wrote about the promotion, "I was Mr. Nixon, the new partner in Wingert and Bewley."[93] But it was not that simple. While Hannah's intercession to get him the job was known only to Bewley, Paul Smith (a young Quaker history professor at Whittier), and a handful of Milhous relatives, Nixon had so few clients that he was forced to live at home and even to work part time for the store. Dr I.N. Kraushaar later remembered Dick, by then a lawyer, making a grocery delivery to a home in the wealthier section of town where Kraushaar was on a house call. Dick had to telephone his father and return for another trip when the customer objected to the cut of meat. He reacted to the episode, the physician noted, in his usual "serious" and polite manner.[94] But to a proud young man, sensitive about his enforced return to his parents' home, and conscious of his standing as a lawyer, the humiliation must have been great indeed.

Perhaps in an effort to distance himself from the grocery store, Nixon became involved in a business scheme proffered by one of Wingert and Bewley's clients. A costly surplus in oranges had led local growers to try to overcome the glut in whole fruit by freezing the juice of the oranges. They found in Dick Nixon an eager young lawyer willing to become the front man. After "some discussion," as Bewley recalled, they christened their new company Citra-Frost and made Nixon both counsel and president.

Over the next several weeks, Nixon hurried after hours and on weekends to enlist investors and to get the process started. The money came easily, much of it in large sums from a few Whittier businessmen, but portions, too, in hundred-dollar increments from the meagre savings of teachers and clerks. Nearly all of it was an investment in Richard Nixon and his reputation, as well as in the company.

But the project was badly conceived from the outset. Instead of freezing just the concentrate, Nixon and his partners tried to freeze the juice in its natural state. The error in the basic concept led in turn to a series of failures in the packaging process. With increasing frustration, they tried cans, glass jars, paper cartons, primitive cellophane bags. Nixon would rush out after office hours and in shirtsleeves tirelessly pour juice into the various containers, but nothing worked.[95]

As the money dwindled, Richard became more desperate. Bewley remembered that "he worked like a dog. He was out there cutting oranges and squeezing oranges day and night after he'd worked here."[96] After a year and a half, in a last gamble, they froze the natural juice in small plastic bags and loaded a full refrigerated boxcar. With the car still on the siding, the bags soon exploded, leaving the interior a "sticky mess" and Citra-Frost in bankruptcy.[97]

Later, Bewley would remember that Dick "was more upset about the orange juice thing"[98] than about the embarrassing Schee case. He was also broke. Nixon lost all his own savings from his first year in practice, though the losses and bitterness were even greater among the people who had trusted him to make them wealthy. Nearly forty years later, the firm of Wingert and Bewley still carried some of the costs of the venture on its books. This failure, added to Richard Nixon's share of responsibility for the out-of-court settlement in the Schee case, meant that their new young attorney had cost the Wingert and Bewley firm thousands of dollars in his first two years.[99] For Nixon, the experience was deeply humiliating, no doubt reminiscent of his father's repeated failures to become a successful businessman. To buttress his ego, he quickly dismissed Citra-Frost as a youthful fling and denied altogether his burning desire to achieve financial success. "Public service has always appealed to me more than making money," he would say.[100]

It was, however, in the realm of politics that Nixon experienced his greatest successes and his most painful humiliations. Early in his memoirs, Nixon mentioned, almost in passing, that he suffered his first political defeat in his junior year at Whittier high school when he lost the election for president of the student body. To some students he appeared withdrawn and painfully shy, stand-offish to the point of unfriendliness; to others he appeared aggressive, wanting the position too much. "When he was in Whittier High he was going to be student president and didn't care whose feet he trampled on," Mildred Jackson Johns, an old Milhous family friend, said later when recalling the race. "The students hated him. He didn't care how he went after it ... kids in the school would tell me how he would elbow his way right through [to] anything he wanted."[101] When the student votes were counted, Nixon had been beaten decisively, though the rest of the senior ticket won office. Of his opponent, Nixon observed: "He had something new. He deserved to win," adding "there were no hard feelings."[102] But losing badly in his first foray into politics undoubtedly wounded young Nixon and left scars that would never completely heal.

During the winter of 1939–40 Nixon's first attempt at a political career failed when the popular incumbent, Gerald Kepple, decided to run again as a California assemblyman in Orange County. Nixon was deeply disappointed. For weeks he had been criss-crossing the large, sparsely settled old assembly district, speaking wherever he could arrange an invitation and paying his own mounting expenses. He was careful to keep his real intentions half-hidden to avoid arousing the wrath of Kepple and his associates, but everyone at Wingert and Bewley knew how much "speech making" Nixon was doing. Looking back on his first, thwarted effort in local politics, Nixon took pains to deny how keenly he had wanted an assembly seat, as though to have acknowledged this early failure would have been embarrassing. In a conversation with journalist Stewart Alsop he said, "They talked about running me for the Assembly," but he did not elaborate further. In fact, it was Nixon who seemed to have talked to himself about running for the assembly. To an inquiring publicist who had raised the question about his political interests and activities prior to 1945, Nixon responded: "I would sum them up this way: Interests – a bit above average for a fledgling lawyer, but certainly no conscious plans for a political career, activities ... almost none." Nixon's memoirs are also conspicuous for the absence of any mention of his avid political occupations of 1939–40: the politicking at a convention of businessmen known as the 20–30 club, the jockeying at the Whittier and La Habra city halls, the zeal to succeed Kepple.[103]

Nixon's first failure in politics was followed by two conspicuous successes; in 1946, in a bitter and hotly contested campaign, he defeated Jerry Voorhis in the Republican primary for the California Twelfth Congressional District seat and then won the seat in the congressional elections.[104] He followed this four years later with a successful run for the Senate in which he destroyed his Democratic rival, Helen Gahagan Douglas, in a bare-knuckles, no-holds-barred campaign.[105]

In the mud-slinging that characterized the contest, Douglas fired a number of shots that Nixon found extremely wounding. In a speech outside a Convair plant in San Diego, she lashed out: "I have utter scorn for such pipsqueaks as Nixon and [Senator Joseph] McCarthy ... trying to get us so afraid of communism that we'll be afraid to turn out the lights at night, and will run to Papa Taft for protection."[106] Again, in public, she referred to Nixon as a "peewee who is trying to scare people into voting for him" and customarily described him as a "pipsqueak." The epithets obviously stung. In his memoirs nearly three decades later, Nixon would quote them as proof of her "viciously personal" attacks and cite his own comparative forbearance.[107] At the time, however, he was furious.

Nixon and Douglas once spoke the same day to different audiences in a northern railroad town, and one of his aides came back from monitoring Douglas's speech to report to Nixon her "unflattering" remarks. "Did she say that? Why, I'll castrate her!" he replied to the aide. When he was reminded that such retaliation was "impossible" for a woman, Nixon shot back testily, "I don't care, I'll do it anyway."[108] For Nixon, Douglas was emblematic of the powerful mother he unconsciously feared and hated; he would castrate her in retaliation for what he unconsciouly fantasized she had already done to his father and to him.[109]

Nixon was to have yet another reminder of his "castrated" position two years later on the eve of the 1952 Republican national convention. In the clash between Robert Taft and Eisenhower, Governor Earl Warren had attempted to retain his favourite-son status among the California delegates. Nixon's conservative supporters were pressing him to lead an open break with Warren and to support Eisenhower on the first ballot. But Nixon preferred to await developments. At one point Nixon's backers reminded him just how much they and their views and their friends represented his essential constituency, southern California money. He responded in an indignant, wounded fashion. "Well, after all, I am a United States senator," Nixon told them. "We don't give a damn what you are," they answered brutally. "You wouldn't be anybody if it wasn't for us."[110]

If being attacked by Helen Douglas and demeaned by his conservative supporters stung Nixon's sensibilities, these experiences would pale in comparison to the humiliation he was to suffer at the hands of Dwight Eisenhower. Their relationship was problematic from the outset. In greeting Eisenhower, after being selected as his vice-presidential candidate in July 1952, Nixon's first words were "Congratulations, Chief." The general bristled visibly, obviously "displeased" at being addressed in the manner that had been reserved for the last Republican president, Herbert Hoover.[111] Eisenhower's coolness and "formality"[112] was a harbinger that he would do little to close the gulf in age and different life experiences that separated the two men.

That time did not heal the bitterness Nixon felt is suggested in his reminiscences of a conversation that he had while he was vice-president with his neighbour, General Walter Bedell Smith, Eisenhower's chief-of-staff during the Second World War. Smith complained that he had been forced to handle unpopular chores for Eisenhower and that during the war he "was only Ike's prat boy." Nixon then remarked: "Beneath that sunny, warm Eisenhower exterior was a cold and when necessary even ruthless executive who often used others to carry out unpleasant assignments."[113] That Nixon felt used and abused by his boss throughout their relationship is abundantly clear.

Following Eisenhower's designation of Nixon as the vice-presidential candidate, the two men met at Eisenhower's fishing camp in Fraser, Colorado. Nixon was nattily dressed in a light grey business suit, having just arrived by plane from Denver. Eisenhower, laughing, pointed to his clothes and ordered him off to change into borrowed khaki fishing gear. A casting lesson from the general followed. The shivering young senator was then sent to stand knee-deep in a frigid Colorado stream, and later to peel potatoes with Senator Frank Carlson while Eisenhower and his friends cooked up roast beef. The press and newsreels were to catch Nixon's strained smile when the general flicked back his fishing rod to demonstrate what all the rest of them seemed to know. "The general and I discussed campaign organization and strategy," he assured reporters afterward, though Ike, in fact, had waved aside most political talk around the table in the cabin. He at least learned how to cast, Nixon told the Associated Press as he left, adding ruefully, "But I caught no fish."[114]

In *Six Crises* Nixon commented on his discussions with Eisenhower on 15 September in Denver concerning campaign strategy, again underlining his lack of comfort with his senior running-mate: "Despite his great capacity for friendliness, he also had a quality of reserve which, at least subconsciously, tended to make a visitor feel like a junior officer coming in to see the commanding General."[115] That feeling of inferior status would never be absent in Nixon's dealings with Eisenhower; in fact, it would be exacerbated by Eisenhower's treatment of him throughout the subsequent decade.

Shortly after that Eisenhower-Nixon meeting, the media disclosed the existence of a Nixon private fund. The fund was designed to supplement Nixon's senatorial salary by enabling him to use contributions to pay for speaking engagements, mailings to his constituents, and so on. Its disclosure raised a series of questions about the ethics and legality of a senator or a congressman having a "slush" fund. Nixon, persuaded by close advisers Murray Chotiner and William Rogers that "there is nothing illegal, unethical, or embarrassing about this fund," was inclined to dismiss the attacks as part of Democratic political manoeuvring.

Two days later, a *New York Herald Tribune* editorial demanding Nixon's resignation as Eisenhower's running-mate shattered his composure. "This one really hit me," he acknowledged. That the *Washington Post* had come out with the same demand was, in his view, to be expected, "but the *New York Herald Tribune* was something else again. It was the most influential Republican newspaper in the East." What was even more disturbing to Nixon was that Bert Andrews, the *Tribune*'s chief Washington correspondent who had worked with Nixon on the Alger Hiss case and had become one of his closest personal friends, was on the Eisenhower campaign train. Nixon also knew that "the publishers and other top officials of the *Tribune* had very close relations with Eisenhower and with some of his most influential supporters. I assumed that the *Tribune* would not have taken this position editorially unless it also represented the thinking of the people around Eisenhower. And as I thought more about it, it occurred to me that this might well be the view of Eisenhower himself, for I had not heard from him since the trouble began, two days before."

Nixon's worst suspicions gained credence when he read the last line of the editorial: "The proper course of Senator Nixon is to make a formal offer of withdrawal from the ticket. How this offer is acted on will be determined by an appraisal of all the facts in the light of General Eisenhower's unsurpassed fairness of mind." To Nixon, that "sounded like the official word from Eisenhower himself."

Nixon's first reaction was anger. What he could not understand "was how any of those around Eisenhower could in fairness reach a judgment before they knew the facts." He instructed Chotiner to indicate to Fred Seat, who was acting at that time as the unofficial liasion between the two trains, that he "would not talk to Sherman Adams or anyone else on the Eisenhower train except Eisenhower himself, since this was a matter in which he alone had the authority to make the decision."[116]

But there was to be no call from Eisenhower to Nixon. Reports from the Eisenhower train indicated that, while his advisers were divided, they were all worried and angry that the controversy might cost the Republicans the election and that "it was all my fault." In the meanwhile, Eisenhower had called reporters to his car for an informal, off-the-record talk. There he repeated his personal conviction that, although he did not know Nixon well, he believed he was honest and would not do anything unethical. However, and this was the "kicker," Nixon would have to prove it and convince "fair-minded" people. Then he said: "Of what avail is it for us to carry on this crusade against this business of what has been going on in Washington if we, ourselves, aren't clean as a hound's tooth?"[117]

Jim Bassett, Nixon's press secretary, reported that the press was reading into Eisenhower's statement the implication that Nixon would have to prove himself "clean as a hound's tooth" if he hoped to stay on the ticket. In a classic example of understatement, Nixon observed: "Our little group was somewhat dismayed by reports of Eisenhower's attitude."[118] In fact, they were "enraged."[119] Illustrative of the humiliation Nixon felt at Eisenhower's lack of support was his observation ten years later in *Six Crises*: "I must admit that it made me feel like the little boy caught with jam on his face."[120]

Further reports suggested that 90 per cent of the press on the Eisenhower train believed that Nixon was a liability to the ticket and that if he did not resign of his own accord he would be forced to do so. This left the Nixon camp feeling that some dramatic action was essential. Eventually, they decided that their candidate would talk directly to the people by means of a national television broadcast. Throughout the on-going discussions, it was evident that Nixon was totally demoralized by what was happening to his candidacy. A telegram from his mother telling him that they were thinking of him and knew that everything would be fine reduced him to tears. Pat Hillings and others who left Nixon alone to compose himself returned to see "Dick ... sitting in a huge leather chair, his arms stretched out, his hand dangling in that characteristic way of his ... I knew I was in the presence of total despair."[121]

Later that afternoon, Governor Thomas Dewey of New York called and bluntly told Nixon that the men around Eisenhower were almost unanimously "a hanging jury" on the issue of the fund. While Eisenhower had made no final decision, he said that there seemed to be a consensus among the advisers that the senator should discreetly offer his resignation from the ticket. Nixon's only alternative was to take his case to the American people and let them decide. But then Dewey added his own twist: "At the conclusion of the program ask people to wire their verdict in to you in Los Angeles. You will probably get over a million replies, and that will give you three or four days to think it over. At the end of that time, if it's 60 percent for you and 40 percent against ... say you are getting out ... If it is 90 to 10, stay on."

Dewey proceeded to spell out the underlying rationale for the strategy. "If you stay in, it isn't blamed on Ike and if you get off, it isn't blamed on Ike."[122] "Even the calculus of Richard Nixon's own career survival would be couched in terms of the inescapable priority of the campaign," Roger Morris writes, "the hard, sometimes humiliating political truth of his candidacy and would-be vice presidency – the overriding interest of Dwight Eisenhower."[123]

Later that evening, Nixon's secretary, Rose Mary Woods, came into the room to tell him that "General Eisenhower is on the phone."

Eisenhower's tone was warm and friendly; his message was much less so. "You've been taking a lot of heat the last couple of days. I imagine it has been pretty rough." Nixon acknowledged that it had not been easy. Eisenhower commented that it was "an awfully hard thing for me to decide. I have come to the conclusion that you are the one who has to decide what to do. After all, you've got a pretty big following in this country, and if the impression got around that you got off the ticket because I forced you off, it is going to be very bad. On the other hand, if I issue a statement now backing you up, in effect people will accuse me of condoning wrongdoing."[124] Again, here was humiliating evidence that what mattered was the preservation of Eisenhower's reputation; Nixon's feelings and reputation were deemed irrelevant.

Eisenhower then paused, "as if waiting for me to fill the gap," remembered Nixon. But the younger politician simply waited. After a moment, Eisenhower said that he had been out to dinner with some of his friends and they were all agreed that the senator should have a chance to speak to the country. "I don't want to be in the position of condemning an innocent man," Ike said. "I think you ought to go on a nationwide television program and tell them everything there is to tell, everything you can remember since the day you entered public life. Tell them about any money you have ever received."[125] It was an unprecedented request in the annals of American politics; it was also a humiliating order from a war hero and presidential candidate to his beleaguered running-mate. The public self-revelation for which Nixon would be blamed in later years was being forced on him, against all his own inclinations, personal and political.[126]

As Nixon absorbed the painful reality, he asked almost plaintively, "General, do you think after the television program that an announcement could then be made one way or another?" Eisenhower hesitated and replied, "I am hoping that no announcement would be necessary at all, but maybe after the program we could tell what ought to be done."[127] At that juncture, Nixon, humiliated almost beyond endurance, responded viscerally. "General," Nixon answered heatedly, "I just want you to know that I don't want you to give any consideration to my personal feelings." But that was precisely what Nixon so desperately wanted – to have Ike consider his feelings and treat him as more than an object whose value was contingent on its impact on his boss's election prospects. "I know how difficult this is for you," Nixon continued. "But there comes a time

in matters like this when you've either got to shit or get off the
pot."[128]

To have instructed the former supreme commander in this way is
indicative of the bottled-up rage that Nixon was feeling and his inability to contain it. To deal with the attacks on his self-esteem and
the order from Eisenhower that he virtually disrobe financially, in
public, Nixon lashed back. He administered his own humiliation by
accusing Eisenhower of indecision – a cardinal sin for a political
leader – and ordering him, in graphic, scatological terms, to make
up his mind. But Eisenhower remained, seemingly, unprovoked.
"We will have to wait three or four days after the television show to
see what the effect of the program is," he responded. Then he
ended the conversation almost lightly: "Well, Dick, go on the television show. Good luck and keep your chin up."[129]

The call from Eisenhower produced a kind of release; Nixon's
angry response had given him a sense of mastery and alleviated
some of his feelings of low self-worth; that night he reached a decision that he would stay on the ticket and fight. Now it was up to him
"to assume the responsibility completely and without any compromise." He added pointedly and with new belligerence: "If I considered the broadcast a success, I would stay on the ticket. If I thought
it was a failure, I would get off." He concluded, "Now everything
was up to me."[130]

Just prior to his departure for the television studio, Governor
Dewey telephoned Nixon to deliver a message. He told him that all
of Eisenhower's top advisers felt that at the conclusion of the
broadcast that night he should submit his resignation. Nixon was
"stunned." "What does Eisenhower want me to do?" he asked in as
even a voice as he could summon. Dewey hedged, saying that he
did not want to give the impression that he had spoken directly to
Eisenhower or that the decision had been approved by Eisenhower,
but Nixon felt that they would not have asked Dewey to call him unless his suggestion reflected Eisenhower's views as well. Nixon indicated that to change his remarks would be difficult at this late
stage. At that point Dewey thought he should go ahead as planned
but, at the end, he should say that "although I felt that I had done
no wrong, I did not want my presence on the ticket to be in any way
a liability to the Eisenhower crusade. Therefore, I should submit
my resignation to Eisenhower and insist that he accept it." As if that
were not enough, Dewey then offered the bizarre suggestion that
Nixon could appear "the hero rather than the goat" by announcing

"not only that you are resigning from the ticket, but that you're resigning from the Senate as well. Then in the special election which will have to be called for the Senate, you can run again and vindicate yourself by winning the biggest plurality in history."[131]

"The conversation," Nixon wrote, "was becoming unreal. Silence was the only possible response to this mind-boggling suggestion." To Nixon, it appeared that he was being manipulated into suffering a double humiliation: being forced off the ticket and being forced out of the Senate. Dewey finally said, "Well, what shall I tell them you are going to do?" Nixon exploded in bitterness: "Just tell them that I haven't the slightest idea what I am going to do, and if they want to find out they'd better listen to the broadcast. And tell them that I know something about politics too." And he slammed the receiver back into its cradle.[132] For all his seeming truculence, Pat Hillings said, "Dick looked like someone had smashed him."[133]

In his television address Nixon listed the points that showed the accusations of dishonesty and lack of integrity to be unfounded. The fund, he claimed, was not secret; every penny had been spent for purely political purposes, thereby making his actions both legally and morally legitimate. He detailed all of his personal finances and his net worth, what he and Pat had inherited, what they owed on their mortgage, his earnings from non-political speaking engagements. It did not come to very much. "Pat doesn't have a mink coat," he said – a poke at Democratic scandals. "But she does have a respectable Republican cloth coat." At the end of the speech, Nixon pulled out all the stops when he harkened back to Franklin D. Roosevelt's speech about his dog, Fala, and told his audience about Checkers, the little cocker spaniel, "black and white, spotted," sent by a man down in Texas who had heard Pat say that the children would like to have a dog. "And you know, the kids, like all kids, love the dog, and I just want to say this, right now, that regardless of what they say about it, we are going to keep it." Nixon's voice was charged with emotion, leading his critics to call the performance nauseating, mawkish, a soap opera, a deliberate attempt to manipulate the public. At the close of his speech, Nixon told his television viewers that he was submitting the decision to the Republican National Committee, which he claimed was theirs to make, as to whether he should stay or get off the ticket. He urged listeners to wire or write their opinions to the committee. Three years later, Nixon, the veteran of amateur theatrics, told the Radio and Television Executives Society that he had "staged" the whole show.

Nearly five million Americans sent in wires and letters expressing confidence in Nixon and the press coverage was overwhelmingly positive. But further humiliation was in the offing. Despite the popular success of his television performance, Nixon did not receive an instant and positive reaction from the one man from whom he so desperately wanted it, his presidential running-mate. Angered by Nixon's attempt to rob him of the right of decision by turning it over to the Republican National Committee, and annoyed at the embarrassment of the whole episode, Eisenhower refused to congratulate him by telephone.[134] Instead, he sent him a wire, just as millions of ordinary Americans had done. Eisenhower's and Nixon's aides were in communication by phone, but Nixon insisted on speaking only to Ike, and Ike refused to call him. For Nixon, the general's attitude was humiliating beyond belief and dampened his euphoria over the triumph of his "Checkers" broadcast.

In a speech to a crowd in Cleveland chanting "we want Nixon," Eisenhower praised the vice-presidential candidate as courageous and honest but did not commit himself to keeping him on the ticket, a fact instantly recognized by newsmen when he read aloud the wire he had sent: "Your presentation was magnificent. While technically no decision rests with me, you and I know the realities of the situation require a pronouncement which the public considers decisive. My personal decision is going to be based on personal conclusions. I would most appreciate it if you can fly to see me at once. Tomorrow I will be at Wheeling, W.Va. Whatever personal affection and admiration I had for you – and they are very great – are undiminished."[135]

For Nixon, reading a somewhat garbled wire-service announcement of the telegram, Eisenhower was still "on the pot." Furious, he dictated a telegram of resignation to Rose Mary Woods. She showed it to Chotiner, who tore it up. "What more could he possibly want from me?" Nixon raged. He now thought Eisenhower "completely unreasonable" and his own situation beyond endurance. To his supporters he announced that "if the broadcast has not satisfied the general, there was nothing more I could or would do." He would, he told them, "simply resign rather than go through the stress of explaining the whole thing again."[136] Calling Woods into an adjoining room, he dictated a telegram of resignation, addressing it not to Eisenhower but to the Republican National Committee, in a last act of defiance.[137]

As his secretary left the room, Chotiner intercepted her and tore up the telegram. He then went in and soothed his seething candidate by agreeing that he must not allow himself "to be put in the position of going to Eisenhower like a little boy to be taken to the woodshed, properly punished, and then restored to a place of dignity." Even when the full text of Eisenhower's wire was read to him, with its warm praise and words of personal affection, Nixon still refused to go to Wheeling. Instead, in an action he reported neither in *Six Crises* nor in his memoirs, he sent a wire to Eisenhower saying that he intended to resume his campaign tour which would end on Saturday, 27 September. "Will be in Washington Sunday," he concluded,"and will be delighted to confer with you at your convenience any time thereafter."[138] And he began preparations to take off for Missoula, Montana. Having been humiliated by Eisenhower's continued refusal to give him a clean bill of health, Nixon responded in a psychologically predictable fashion: he would not capitulate but would aggressively dictate the place of their meeting as a way of redressing the balance between the two men.

To Eisenhower's aides, the wire seemed an act of incredible insolence, and, had it been published, the acrimonious private duel would have damaged both men and their party. Arthur Summerfield, a prominent Michigan Republican and strong Eisenhower supporter, called Chotiner and was told that "Dick is not going to be placed in the position of a little boy coming somewhere to beg forgiveness." Bert Andrews, his reporter-friend on the *New York Herald Tribune*, caught Nixon by phone just as he was about to leave for Montana and talked to him, Nixon said, "like a Dutch uncle." Andrews reminded him that Eisenhower had led the allied armies to victory, that he was the "boss of the outfit," and that he had a right to make the decision in his own way.[139] It was an effective scolding.

Nixon agreed to fly to Wheeling from Montana the following day. After the plane landed, Nixon, somewhat delayed in leaving it, was flabbergasted to see Eisenhower coming down the aisle, his hand outstretched. "General, you didn't need to come out to the airport," he said. "Why not," came the reply, "you're my boy."[140] But even that was only a semi-endearment. It drove home, once again, the fact that, at best, Nixon would be forgiven like the prodigal son. A relationship between equals, something he craved, was out of the question.

Nixon's ordeal seemed over, but there was an unexpected and souring aftermath which the memory of five million favourable telegrams and letters never really erased. Eisenhower invited Nixon and his wife to see his private car on the campaign train. What had seemed the friendliest of gestures turned out to be an excuse, they discovered, for Ike to question them about "rumors of several other scandals involving my personal finances." Nixon described only one such rumour, that he "had spent $10,000 with an interior decorator in furnishing our home in Washington." Nixon wrote that "there was not a shred of truth to the charge and a very routine inquiry could have knocked it down before it was passed on to him."[141]

Public-relations director Robert Humphreys had already emphatically assured Eisenhower that the rumour was a canard. He had seen the "decorations" in the Nixon home, he said; they consisted of draperies and a circular couch from Nixon's home in Whittier. Eisenhower chose, nevertheless, to ask the Nixons about the rumour in its full ugliness – specifically, the claim that Mrs Nixon had paid the ten thousand dollars in cash. Pat, the most frugal of women who had made her own draperies and slip-covers for years, was devastated.[142] Although Eisenhower's motivation in raising this issue can only be guessed at, it had the effect of further humiliating his running-mate and reminding him of the subordinate position he would occupy in the new administration.

In his first year in office, Eisenhower sent Nixon on a trip to the Far East. It was his first taste of international diplomacy. Upon his return to Washington, he was met at the plane by all the ambassadors from the countries he had visited, seven Republican senators, and a delegation from the State Department. Eisenhower's welcome, in marked contrast, was at best perfunctory. When Nixon and his wife were driven from the airport to the White House, the president greeted him at the entrance. As reported by the *New York Times*, Ike walked forward, grasped Nixon's hand, and snapped: "It looks like we have a little interest in you, Dick."[143] Explaining that Mamie had a cold, Eisenhower invited them upstairs only for coffee. The meeting lasted a mere half-hour.[144]

The next day Eisenhower sent him a handwritten letter saying that he was glad to have him home and that he had missed his "wise counsel," "energetic support," and "exemplary dedication," adding, "I look forward to some quiet opportunity when I can hear a real recital of your adventures and accomplishments." Nixon said he thought this to be "an extraordinarily warm and personal gesture" coming from "one who meted out praise in very small doses."[145] If Eisenhower ever called him back for that "real recital" of his adventures, Nixon did not mention it in his memoirs; and one has the impression in reading this account that his only reward from the president was a cup of coffee and a thank-you note.[146]

Six months later, Churchill was at the White House with thirty other guests. After dinner, Eisenhower, who had been chatting with Churchill, beckoned Nixon to join them. "This is one of the young men I have been telling you about and I want you to get acquainted with him," he said. Nixon recorded it all in his diary that night, concluding with a comment about how enjoyable an occasion it had been. It was, none the less, an odd introduction. Eisenhower seemed unaware that Nixon had formally met Churchill and Foreign Secretary Anthony Eden at the airport and escorted them to the White House. But more important, he did not say, "This is my vice-president," but rather, "This is one of the young men I have been telling you about." Thus Nixon was reminded, as he would be increasingly in the following months, that he was only one among several "sons," and not necessarily the favourite.[147]

In the aftermath of Eisenhower's coronary in 1955, Nixon conducted himself in exemplary fashion, being careful not to assume even a shred of presidential power. However, the president never acknowledged either Nixon's special responsibilities during this period or the care with which he had carried them out. Nixon noted in *Six Crises* that Eisenhower had spoken or written to him personally of his appreciation after each of his trips abroad. "But after this most difficult assignment of all – treading the tightrope during his convalescence from the heart attack – there was no personal thank you."[148] As if it were too painful to deal with the feelings that such treatment seems to have engendered, Nixon immediately went on to add, somewhat defensively: "Nor was one needed or expected. After all, we both recognized that I had only done what a Vice President should do when the President is ill."[149]

That Eisenhower's gratitude to Nixon was indeed limited became more apparent in the efforts he made to have him removed from the ticket. Eisenhower told Nixon that he had expected only to serve for four years and that by that time the Republican Party would be strong enough to elect another candidate. "It was 'most disappointing' to him [Eisenhower]," he said, "to see that my popularity had not risen as high as he had hoped it would. For that reason, he said, it might be better for me in a new Administration not to be Vice President but to be a Cabinet officer."[150]

Eisenhower clearly hoped that Nixon would resolve the administration's political problem by seeking an important cabinet post. Nixon recounted that the subject came up at five or six of their private conversations, and each time he gave his stock answer. "If you believe your own candidacy and your Administration would be better served with me off the ticket, you tell me what you want me to do and I'll do it. I want to do what is best for you. He [Eisenhower] always answered somewhat obliquely, praising my service to his Administration and saying, 'No, I think we've got to do what's best for you.' "[151]

Nixon acknowledged that he felt it would be improper for him to say, "Look, Mr. President I want to run," and that Eisenhower "never put the question to me in quite the right way for that response. If he had said, 'Dick, I want you to be the (vice presidential) candidate, if you want to be,' I would have accepted, thanked him, and that would have been that."[152]

Although Eisenhower's behaviour indicated that he hoped that Nixon would remove himself from the ticket, Nixon refused to allow himself to internalize the full implications of such a humiliating message. Instead, Nixon defended himself emotionally by partially disavowing its content: "I could not be certain whether the President really preferred me off the ticket or sincerely believed a Cabinet post could better further my career. It probably was a little of both." When Nixon did consider the idea of removing himself from the ticket, his humiliation took a back seat to his political ambition. He acknowledged that, having done "some private agonizing about what President Eisenhower had in mind, I soon reached the practical conclusion that I could not switch jobs without the disastrous appearance that 'Nixon had been dumped.' "[153]

Once Eisenhower announced his candidacy for a second term on 29 February 1956, he was asked if Richard Nixon would be his running-mate. The president did not make a direct reply, saying that he could not properly speak out on the choice of a running-mate until after the Republican national convention itself picked its presidential candidate. Nixon acknowledged that "this ... caused embarrassment to me because I still could say nothing before the President spoke." At the next weekly press conference, on 7 March, the president bluntly declared: "I told him [Nixon] he would have to chart his own course and tell me what he would like to do." At this juncture, Nixon could no longer deny to himself that Eisenhower "was really trying to tell me that he wanted me off the ticket."[154] For Nixon, it "felt as if the clock had been turned back to the fund crisis."[155]

This time, Nixon's response was to contemplate withdrawal. However, a write-in vote of 22,936 in New Hampshire for Nixon as the vice-presidential candidate bolstered him psychologically and politically. Thoughts of flight were replaced by the determination to stay and fight.[156] He went to see Eisenhower and told him that he would be honoured to continue as his vice-president, and that the only reason he had waited so long was that he did not wish to force his way onto the ticket. Although Nixon reported that Eisenhower was delighted with his decision, he was left to tell the reporters himself about the news and to have Jim Hagerty communicate the president's "delight." It must have been an extremely painful and humiliating act for Nixon, who had hoped to be invited to join the ticket.

A re-elected Eisenhower continued to ignore his vice-president. According to James Reston of the *New York Times*, during Nixon's last year in office with Eisenhower, the vice-president watched football games while the president was making his decisions on a summit meeting with Khrushchev. Eisenhower told Arthur Larson, director of the United States Information Agency, that he thought Nixon was good at summarizing alternatives and condensing other men's opinions, but that he did not supply anything original himself.[157]

Nixon's famous trip to Russia revealed Ike's lack of interest in the views of his subordinate. Nixon had not been asked to make the trip; he volunteered for it indirectly through the United States Information Agency, which was conducting an active cultural exchange program at the time. Once he had obtained permission to go, Nixon prepared for months, reading reports and recommendations from the State Department, the CIA, the Joint Chiefs of Staff, and the White House staff, as well as conducting interviews with men who had studied Soviet affairs and others who had met Khrushchev.[158]

Throughout this course of preparation, Nixon was never told that important summit negotiations were under way. Despite all his intensive study for the Russian trip, the vice-president's advice was not sought, nor was he told of the matter until the eve of his take-off. He was then informed only to prevent his stumbling on the plan and botching it. At a later press conference, Eisenhower commented: "I told him and I said, 'So that you will not be astonished or surprised and feel let down by your government should [the subject of Khrushchev's trip] be opened by the other side, you are not yourself, and of course will not open this subject.'"[159]

Ignorant of the proposed summit meeting, the nation hoped for diplomatic gains from Nixon's meeting and discussions with Khrushchev. But Eisenhower threw cold water on this possibility, too, when asked about Nixon's role in Russia. He noted that the vice-president "is not a part of the diplomatic processes and machinery of this government." That fact was underlined by the timing of the announcement of Khrushchev's visit. On 3 August, while Nixon was still abroad, the White House completed its diplomatic exchanges and announced the pending summit. Eisenhower could have waited until 5 August, the date of Nixon's scheduled return, to make the plan public. This would have given the appearance that Nixon had played some role in the project and that his views on the Soviet Union and its ruler had been sought. To add insult to injury, when Eisenhower announced Khrushchev's upcoming visit, he was asked whether the vice-president had known of the future visit when he left for Russia. That is when Ike explained that Nixon had been told lest he inadvertently "open" the matter.[160]

And then, the crowning slight. Nixon had methodically drawn up a set of recommendations on how Khrushchev should be treated in the United States. In essence, they were a restatement of the way Nixon had treated him in Russia – argumentatively and on the offensive. Eisenhower ignored the advice himself and, where it was being heeded, countermanded it. Thus he arranged to stop the mission of Henry Cabot Lodge, who had been chosen to follow Khrushchev around correcting him as a one-man "truth squad."[161]

Immediately after the 1960 Republican national convention, Nixon met with Eisenhower to discuss the latter's role in Nixon's campaign for the presidency. According to Nixon's account in *Six Crises*, Eisenhower "thought he [Eisenhower] should avoid taking so active a part early in the campaign as to overshadow my own appearances." The president offered to make a non-political swing around the country in October and save his partisan speeches until the first week in November.[162] According to Eisenhower, Nixon suggested that he stay out of the active campaign until the last few days.[163] Eisenhower's friends thought that Nixon's decision to keep his distance from the president was a costly mistake and Eisenhower himself complained that "Dick never asked me how I thought the campaign should be run." Nevertheless, he offered advice – for example, not to debate Kennedy – only to have it disregarded.[164]

When Eisenhower learned of Nixon's decision to debate Kennedy, he offered the vice-president the services of television producer Robert Montgomery, who was an expert in lighting, make-up, and other aspects of television and who had stage-managed Eisenhower's TV appearances. Nixon turned down the offer.[165] After eight years of having to endure the humiliation of being treated as an unappreciated inferior, Nixon was determined to distance himself from his boss and make his own decisions. The word went out to the Nixon staff that the vice-president would campaign as a man in his own right, not as Eisenhower's little boy.[166]

Although admittedly unsympathetic to psychological explanations of political phenomena,[167] Stephen Ambrose notes: "Whether or not Nixon's rejections of Eisenhower's advice had a subconscious effect on the President can only be speculated upon, but what is certain is that in his press conferences in August, when he had innumerable opportunities to give Nixon a boost, Eisenhower did serious damage to Nixon's campaign."[168] No matter what he was asked about Nixon, or what he intended to say, Eisenhower's answers always revealed his ambivalence and never constituted that clear-cut total endorsement that Nixon so desperately needed and wanted. The most famous example occurred in a mid-August press conference. Three times Eisenhower was asked about Nixon's role in the decision-making process, since Nixon himself had been stressing his experience. Each time the president replied that he alone made the decisions, although of course he listened to Nixon's advice. Charles Mohr of *Time* persisted. "What major decisions of your administration has the vice president participated in?" Eisenhower replied: "If you give me a week, I might think of one. I don't remember."[169]

It is difficult to contemplate a reply that could have been more dismissive, contemptuous, and humiliating. Although Eisenhower later called Nixon to express chagrin at the way that the press was handling his statement, the damage was done. As Nixon commented, "This question had been most effective in raising a doubt ... with regard to one of my strongest campaign themes and assets – my experience as Vice President."[170]

Although Eisenhower finally gave Nixon his blessing as the presidential candidate, it must have been a source of some humiliation that it did not come without indirect Nixon pressure. Lewis Strauss, chairman of the Atomic Energy Commission, told Barry Goldwater that Nixon had asked his help in persuading Ike to endorse his candidacy: "Nixon said it was an urgent matter because he believed the President was in very poor health and he was afraid Ike might die before he got round to making a supportive statement." Strauss, who was close to the president, got a strong endorsement for Nixon.[171]

By October 1960, stung by Kennedy's description of his administration as eight Rip Van Winkle years, Eisenhower was eager to go on the hustings, and he agreed to the plan suggested by Leonard Hall, Republican Party chairman, for an expanded program of speech-making in the final week. According to Hall, "Nixon wanted to do everything, he wanted no other voice and no other partner." Hall finally arranged a meeting between the two men and extracted from Nixon a promise that he would ask the president to add to his campaign schedule. When the meeting occurred, however, Hall was astonished to hear Nixon say, almost at once, "Mr. President, I think you've done enough already." Ike turned red, Hall said, and the meeting broke up quickly. In a rage, Eisenhower demanded an explanation from Hall and said: "Did you see that? When I had a front-line officer like that in World War II, I relieved him."[172]

In his *Memoirs* Nixon offered an explanation for this incident. Pat, he claimed, had received a distraught phone call from Mamie Eisenhower, who said that her husband was not up to the strain that campaigning might put on his heart. She begged her to have Nixon make him change his mind without letting him know that Mamie had intervened. That call was reinforced the following morning by White House physician Major-General Howard Snyder, who also reiterated that a heavy campaign schedule might be too much for Eisenhower's health. Notwithstanding Eisenhower's enthusiasm for carrying out an expanded itinerary, Nixon stood his ground and insisted that Ike limit himself to the original schedule and the election-eve telecast with Lodge and Nixon. Although Eisenhower finally acquiesced, Nixon was aware of his puzzlement and frustration.[173]

Nixon's memoirs appeared in 1978, eight years after Dr Snyder had died and just prior to Mamie Eisenhower's death in 1979. But he never explained why he chose not to tell Hall about the telephone calls he had received from Snyder and Mamie Eisenhower. This suggests that Nixon's rejection of Eisenhower's offer to campaign actively was the product more of his determination to distance himself from the president than of his concern about Ike's health. The prospect of winning the presidency on Eisenhower's coat-tails may unconsciously have been regarded as one more humiliation, and, as such, it was too high a price to pay.[174]

In retrospect, a more vigorous campaign by Eisenhower might have made the difference between winning and losing the 1960 presidential election. Nixon himself acknowledged that Ike's appearance in southern Illinois, which would have received extensive coverage in eastern Missouri as well, might have tipped the balance in two states that Kennedy won by razor-thin margins.[175]

As it was, Nixon was left to deal with the pain of losing. Not surprisingly, he preferred to focus on other people's responsibility for his defeat. Among those singled out for blame were Democrats who had allegedly committed vote fraud, particularly in Texas and Illinois; and the media, which had been seduced by Kennedy's charisma and sense of personal mission. Nixon also denounced the repeated use of religion as an issue and described Kennedy's team as "the most ruthless group of political operators ever mobilized for a presidential campaign."[176]

Political analysts of the 1960 campaign have their preferred theories about why Nixon lost the presidency. Undoubtedly, Nixon's decision to debate Kennedy on television and his insistence on visiting all fifty states during the campaign – a tour that left him exhausted before the first debate – were significant factors in his defeat.[177] Yet such decisions were not made in a vacuum; an analysis of them reveals the way in which they were shaped by issues of self-esteem and concerns about shame and humiliation. Certainly, Nixon's decision to debate his lesser-known rival stemmed in large measure from his somewhat inflated notion of his forensic abilities and his innate conviction that this was an arena for combat in which he held the advantage. To have rejected Kennedy's request would have exposed Nixon to charges that he had been unwilling to fight. Considerations of shame also played a role in Nixon's campaign strategy. Having promised to visit all fifty states during his campaign, Nixon, despite a badly infected knee, felt compelled to honour his pledge.

The presidential power that had always obsessed Richard Nixon had been snatched away by the kind of privileged and advantaged

man who represented his "worst nightmares of his own inadequacy."[178] To Nixon, Kennedy was a figure to be admired; he was
naturally elegant, rich, and Harvard-bred, with a father who was a
companion of presidents, bankers, ambassadors. Nixon was the son
of an unsuccessful grocer. And Kennedy's much quoted private
judgment on his opponent – the man, he said, had "no class" –
could not have failed to reach Nixon's ears.[179]

To add insult to injury, Nixon even had to put the official stamp
on his own defeat. The American constitution requires that the
vice-president of the United States preside over the joint congressional session at which the electoral votes for president are counted
officially. Thus it was that Nixon became the first vice-president
since John C. Breckinridge in 1860 to be forced to confirm and
announce the victory of an opponent.[180]

Nixon then withdrew to lick his wounds in private, retreating not
only from politics but also from his family. After a vacation with Pat
and close friend Charles "Bebe" Rebozo in the Bahamas, he flew
alone to Los Angeles, where he joined the law firm of Adams,
Duque, and Hazeltine. Earl Adams, who had been one of the do-
nors to the "Checkers fund," had given him the job. Nixon lived
alone for six months in a small bachelor apartment on Wilshire
Boulevard. "I preferred to be alone ... the last thing I wanted to do
was to talk to people about the election ... virtually everything I did
seemed unexciting and unimportant ... It was not an easy time."[181]

Although the loss of the presidency in 1960 was a painful and
humiliating defeat, the loss of the governorship of California in
1962 was even more so. The state governorship was a significant
step down in the hierarchy of political office; losing to a mediocre
and colourless politician such as Pat Brown was devastating. Nixon's
campaign was never able to overcome voters' attention on two issues that were not political but personal – a Howard Hughes loan to
his brother Don and Brown's charge that Nixon regarded the California governorship only as a stepping-stone to the presidency.[182]

Although it had become increasingly clear to Nixon during the
campaign that he could not win, the worst was confirmed when he
learned that he had lost to Brown by 297,000 out of the nearly
6 million votes cast. Herb Klein, Nixon's press secretary, read Nixon's
concession statement to the reporters; he then communicated their
insistence to Nixon that he come down from his hotel suite and
make a personal appearance, only to be met with the reply, "Screw

them. I'm not going to do it. I don't have to and I'm not going to." Hearing the insulting tone of the reporters, who were still asking "Where's Nixon?" he changed his mind and went down to address the press.

It was a remarkable speech for its revelation of Nixon's loss of control and the rage he felt at what he perceived to be the constant humiliation and denigration to which he had been subjected. He began by saying that he believed that a reporter had a right to write things as he felt them. But sometimes "I wish you'd give my opponent the same going over that you give me. And as I leave the press, all I can say is this: for sixteen years, ever since the Hiss case, you've had a lot of – a lot of fun – that you've had an opportunity to attack me, and I think I've given as good as I've taken ... You won't have Nixon to kick around anymore, because, gentlemen, this is my last press conference."[183]

Jules Witcover writes that, for the political community, listening to Nixon's performance before the press that morning was "like stumbling unannounced into a man's monologue to his analyst. It revealed a capacity for deep bitterness in Nixon that through his long public career and long sparring match with the nation's press he nearly always had managed to control or to cover up."[184]

In dictating notes for his memoirs, Nixon recorded, "After the loss in 1962, Pat never once said, I told you so,"[185] a reference to her strong opposition to his wish to run for the governorship.[186] She didn't have to since "the humiliating defeat, coming so soon after the narrow presidential loss, left scars."[187] Once, Tricia Nixon, in talking about the gubernatorial race to her sister Julie, wondered whether their parents made too much of losing. When Julie asked her what she meant, since their parents had rarely had discussed the election with their daughters, Tricia replied, "There was a sadness and the sadness went on for years."[188]

Over the next six years, Nixon engaged in a number of activities designed to bolster his self-esteem. He published a best-selling book, *Six Crises*, which earned him $250,000 and re-established him as a figure to be reckoned with in the Republican Party. Between the royalties for *Six Crises* and the $100,000 annual salary from his law firm, Nixon, for the first time in his life, enjoyed a substantial income. In the 1964 congressional elections, he campaigned actively for Republican candidates and his stint on the hustings was generally conceded to have had a positive impact for a number of successful candidates. Then, in 1968, Nixon staged a comeback, winning his party's nomination for the presidency and afterwards defeating Walter Mondale decisively for the presidency.

But the earlier traumas of his childhood and the repeated experiences of humiliation in the political realm had left their mark. Nixon remained a narcissistically vulnerable individual whose capacity to feel shamed, humiliated, and insulted persisted. This was to have profound repercussions, particularly in his handling of the Vietnam War and most specifically in his decision to begin the secret bombing and eventual invasion of Cambodia.

5 Nixon and Cambodia

Why Richard Nixon decided to begin the bombing of North Vietnamese sanctuaries in Cambodia on 18 March 1969 and subsequently to commit American forces to that country on 30 April 1970 are questions that continue to fascinate scholars. As we shall see, purely military and strategic rationales were less than compelling for expanding the war. And, while domestic political factors played some role, they, too, cannot satisfactorily explain the nature of Nixon's responses. The fact is that Nixon's strategic and domestic perceptions were animated by an underlying psychological dimension. His need to be perceived as invincible, in conjunction with his vulnerable self-esteem, led him to perceive any challenge to his policies, domestic or foreign, as a function of his opponents' desire to humiliate him personally. Both his decision to bomb Cambodia in March 1969 and his subsequent decision to invade it in April 1970 followed on the heels of foreign and domestic attacks that he deemed insulting and hurtful. Nixon chose Cambodia as the arena in which he could displace his rage.

Paradoxically, a good deal of Nixon's emotional energy throughout his life was absorbed with resisting the "temptation" to lash out at his enemies. Innumerable observers from his mother, Hannah, to Thomas Dewey have commented on his self-control. He was described as "introverted," "self-contained," "orderly," "cautious," "patient," "unruffled," "reserved." There were many occasions on which, as at Caracas in May 1958, "anger boiled inside the vice-president but he was outwardly unruffled and composed."[1]

Nixon himself commented on his own determination not to respond to attacks upon himself with anger. In describing the scuffle in Caracas, Nixon referred again and again to the lure of aggression and the need to resist it. Hit in the face with a rubber noisemaker, "I was tempted to give it back to the guy." But "this was an emotional crowd and they might have thought I was being unfriendly."[2] Nevertheless, as the rocks flew, Nixon said that he "could not resist the temptation to get in one other good lick" and experienced "an almost uncontrollable urge to tear the face in front of me to pieces."[3] Restraint, however, won out. Similarly, his experience debating Khrushchev was for Nixon "a situation into which I had become somewhat accustomed – walking on eggs." Whatever Khrushchev did, "under no circumstances could I run the risk of 'rocking the boat.'" Instead, he would have to "avoid the temptation to answer threat with threat and boast with boast," all the while staying "on guard for almost anything," in "full and complete control of my temper." He restrained himself "time and time again from expressing views I deeply felt and wanted to get across."[4]

In all these passages in which Nixon discussed his temptation to lash out and the necessity for tight control, his desire for retaliation is revealed. As is typical of the obsessional, controlled character, the effort is experienced as painful: "There is nothing more wearing than to suppress the natural impulse to meet a crisis head-on, using every possible resource to achieve victory."[5]

Aggression and its control were central themes in Nixon's life. Three features of his struggle in this regard are worth noting. First, there were those occasions when Nixon channelled his aggressiveness into politics, especially campaigning; his speeches and writing were full of the imagery of combat. He saw himself as forever engaged in battles, hit by "terrible attacks," in "virtual hand-to-hand combat" with Khrushchev, for example. By far the most frequent channel for Nixon's aggression were the words spoken to large audiences in some "fighting, rocking, socking campaign," blasting "the whining, whimpering, grovelling attitude of our diplomatic representatives," shouting "don't try anything on me or we'll take care of you" at hecklers and the like. In more formal addresses, Nixon very often moved from defense to attack, larding his rhetoric with aggressiveness.[6]

Second, there were those times when Nixon was more consciously aware of feeling combative, when he saw himself "blowing off steam" – directly and overtly pouring out the surplus aggression he had been accumulating. But it was characteristic of Nixon that he never reflected in any introspective sense on why he was angry. The stimulus was "out there" somewhere; he simply found the resultant anger in himself and accepted its existence as an "instinct."[7] And, finally, there were those occasions when Nixon behaved aggressively, for example, vis à vis Cambodia. Like many people, at such times he seemed to be unaware that his behaviour was a displacement of unacknowledged rage that had its sources elsewhere than in the target of his wrath.

Given Nixon's obsessional anxiety about maintaining self-control, it is hardly surprising that there were periodic breaks in the dike. When he felt himself to have been shamed or humiliated, these breaks would have disastrous consequences. Frequently, the choice of target against whom Nixon directed his fury was unrelated or only tangentially related to the actual source of his narcissistic wounding – a clear example of displacement. Nixon's decision to begin the secret bombing raids against the communist sanctuaries in Cambodia and subsequently to invade that country provide us with classic cases in point.

During the 1968 campaign Nixon benefitted from the divisions within the Democratic Party over the war in Vietnam. He told the American people that he had a plan to end the war "with honor." While no formal "plan" existed, Richard Nixon and Henry Kissinger, his national security adviser, envisaged using the threat of overwhelming force against North Vietnam as a way of forcing it to end the war on terms the U.S. deemed honourable. For the next four years, until Nixon was forced to abandon the policy, honour demanded an insistence upon "mutual withdrawal" and opposition to a cease-fire until that goal was achieved.

Nixon's model for ending the war "with honor" was Eisenhower's threat to use extreme force, including tactical nuclear weapons, when the Korean negotiations were stalemated in 1953. Nixon referred to it as "the madman theory," according to his chief of staff, Bob Haldeman: "I want the North Vietnamese to believe I've reached the point where I might do anything to stop the war."[8]

Early in January 1969 a special task force prepared an "options" paper on Vietnam for the president. The secret "A to Z" options ranged from an open-ended and gradual beginning of the withdrawal of American forces to their indefinite presence in Vietnam. At Nixon's direction, the option for an immediate commitment to a complete U.S. withdrawal within a year or two was deleted from the paper. For Nixon, a total, unilateral withdrawal from Vietnam "would have meant capitulation, a 'bug out,' something Nixon could not tolerate viscerally or intellectually."[9] Nixon's sensitivity to feelings of shame and humiliation did not allow him to give serious consideration to an option that would have propelled those feelings to the forefront and left him feeling powerless and impotent, his self-esteem in tatters.[10]

At the same time that the special task force was drafting its "options" paper on Vietnam, Daniel Ellsberg prepared a list of twenty-eight questions to be asked of the Pentagon, the State Department, and the CIA. When the answers to these questions were received by Kissinger on 21 February, the resulting document (NSSM–1) made it evident that the kind of military pressure applied in Vietnam by the Johnson administration, particularly the bombings, simply had not worked in the past and would not work in the future. The CIA reported that, although air strikes had destroyed transport facilities, equipment, and supplies, they had not successfully interdicted the flow of supplies; much of the damage was frequently repaired within hours. The offices of the secretaries of state and defense also believed that the bombing had not significantly raised the costs of the war to North Vietnam.

Nixon and Kissinger challenged NSSM–1's conclusions. In their view, the way to win the war was "to defy criticism and the risk of escalation" through bombing of unprecedented intensity throughout Indochina. The point was not that bombing should be ruled out because it had proved ineffective, but that it should be increased to maximal levels in order to become effective. From the outset, the White House held the view that the key to a diplomatic solution lay in decisive military action.[11] Nixon's preference for strong military action was dictated only partly by his conception of appropriate strategy and tactics; it was largely activated by his sense of outrage. Nixon was determined that the United States would not be "humbled by Vietnamese Communists." If that were to happen, he feared that "American credibility in Moscow and Peking would be undermined – thus weakening Washington's hand in all future dealings with its 'adversaries.'" Morton Halperin, who was then senior adviser to Kissinger, commented that, for Nixon, Vietnam was important not in and of itself but rather as part of the worldwide struggle between the United States and the Soviet Union, and that he saw himself as being tested in the process.[12] In order to win that struggle and convince the North Vietnamese that the United

States was serious about the possible escalation of the war, Nixon ordered the secret bombing of Cambodia with B-52 aircraft in mid-March 1969.

The genesis of that decision went back two months earlier; on his first day in office Nixon asked the Pentagon how the United States could "quarantine" Cambodia. In the Pentagon's view, there was a legitimate military reason to assault Cambodia directly. Tens of thousands of North Vietnamese soldiers had established bases and supply depots there and were using the sanctuaries as jumping-off points for ground battles in South Vietnam, just across the border. Cambodia also allegedly housed the communist headquarters for the guerilla war in South Vietnam, known as the Central Office for South Vietnam (COSVN).

The joint chiefs of staff had long urged the Johnson White House to divert some of the B-52 missions from South Vietnam to the Cambodian sanctuaries, but without success. The political arguments against such bombings were obvious. The United States was not at war with Cambodia, whose government was headed by Prince Norodom Sihanouk. The official American position, which it shared with North Vietnam, was one of respect for Sihanouk's neutrality. Prince Sihanouk had long been engaged in a diplomatic balancing act to insulate his nation of seven million from the Vietnam War. And, of course, the anti-war movement at home also militated against overt U.S. challenges to Cambodian neutrality.[13]

In the Nixon administration, the joint chiefs were to have more success in their advocacy of attacks on Cambodia. They forwarded the president's quarantine request to Saigon for General Creighton Abrams's[14] advice. It was at that point that the general cabled his own proposal for a single B-52 raid against COSVN headquarters in the North Vietnamese sanctuary of Cambodia known as Base Area 353. The joint chiefs favoured bombing the sanctuaries as well as blockading all Cambodian ports and airports, while recognizing that it would have to be sustained over a long period of time and would be widely criticized abroad.[15] Their position was strongly supported by Colonel Alexander Haig, Kissinger's military aide.

In contrast, the advice Kissinger received from his National Security Council aide for East Asia, Richard L. Sneider, was not encouraging. According to Sneider, Kissinger recalled, raids on Cambodia "didn't make military sense." Earlier, Sneider had studied a proposal to use B-52 aircraft against the North Vietnamese sanctuaries in Cambodia, and he had concluded then that the bombing would disperse the North Vietnamese soldiers from border areas farther west into Cambodia, thus putting more of Cambodia under communist control.[16] Nixon initially waffled. But in late February he ordered the bombing of Cambodia in retaliation for the renewed communist spring offensive in South Vietnam which began on 22 February 1969.[17]

In his memoirs, Nixon wrote that "the savage offensive into South Vietnam ... was a deliberate test, clearly designed to take the measure of me and my administration at the outset. My immediate instinct was to retaliate."[18] He believed that the timing of the offensive, beginning one day prior to his scheduled ten-day ceremonial visit to Europe and before the new administration had had any substantive meetings with the North Vietnamese delegation in Paris, was deliberately intended to humiliate him.[19] Kissinger's perspective was slightly more nuanced. He later noted: "Whether by accident or design, the offensive began the day before a scheduled Presidential trip overseas, thus both paralyzing our response and humiliating the new President."[20] Although Nixon's instincts were to respond viscerally to Hanoi's moves, he was eager that his first foreign trip as president be a success, and he feared that American retaliation might spark riots in Europe.[21]

Kissinger reports that on 23 February 1969, while in the air en route from Washington to Brussels, "Nixon made up his mind; he suddenly ordered the bombing of the Cambodian sanctuaries."[22] Indicative of the absence of any thorough discussion of the issue was Kissinger's consternation: "It seemed to me that a decision of this magnitude could not be simply communicated to Washington and to Saigon by cable from Air Force One without consulting relevant officials or in the absence of a detailed plan for dealing with the consequences."[23]

Nixon agreed to Kissinger's suggestion that he postpone the final "execute" order for forty-eight hours; a meeting between Haig, Haldeman, Kissinger, and the Pentagon planning officer took place on board Air Force One at the Brussels airport on the morning of 24 February. Guidelines were worked out for the bombing of the enemy's sanctuaries and Haig and the Pentagon expert left immediately for Washington to brief Secretary of Defense Melvyn Laird.[24]

Before the day was out, Laird cabled his reservations about the bombings. He thought that it would be impossible to keep the bombing secret; the press would be difficult to handle and public support could not be guaranteed. Kissinger agreed with Laird's conclusions, if not his reasoning. He was concerned that failure to react to "so cynical a move by Hanoi could doom our hopes for negotiations; it could only be read by Hanoi as a sign of Nixon's helplessness in the face of domestic pressures."[25] Nevertheless, Kissinger was bothered by the timing; launching a new military operation while the president was travelling in Europe seemed to him unwise and he counselled Nixon against it. The following day, Nixon cancelled the bombing plan.[26]

It was clear, however, that Nixon was still "champing at the bit in private."[27] He ordered a strike against the Cambodian sanctuaries for 9 March, only to rescind it for a second time after Secretary of State William Rogers objected because of prospects for private talks in Paris between the Americans and the North Vietnamese. "With each time he marched up the hill and down again, Nixon's resentments and impatience increased. Like Laird, he kept saying that he did not want to hit the North, but he wanted to do 'something.' "[28] When asked at a news conference on 14 March 1969 whether his patience was wearing thin, Nixon replied: "We have issued a warning. I will not warn again. And if we conclude that the level of casualties is higher than we should tolerate, action will take place."[29]

The following day, 15 March, the North Vietnamese fired five rockets into Saigon. At 3:35 p.m., that same day, Kissinger reports that the president phoned him to say that he was ordering an immediate secret B-52 attack on the Cambodian sanctuaries: "Capping a month of frustration, the President was emphatic: 'State is to be notified only after the point of no return ... The order is not appealable.' "[30]

Once again, Kissinger moved to stay Nixon's impetuosity, at least until his senior advisers had an opportunity to express their views – if only to protect their boss from the potential public uproar that might follow from the decision. The meeting that took place on Sunday afternoon, 16 March, was attended by Rogers, Laird, General Earle Wheeler,[31] and Kissinger. Kissinger recounts that what went on at the meeting was vintage Nixon tactics. "On the one hand, he had made his decision and was not about to change it; indeed, he had instructed me to advise the Defense Department to that effect twenty-four hours before the meeting. On the other hand, he felt it necessary to pretend that the decision was still open."[32]

The secret B-52 attack took place on 18 March against North Vietnamese Base Area 353, three miles inside the Cambodian border; it was code-named "Breakfast." Although the attack on Base Area 353 was conceived as a single raid, Nixon ordered another strike in mid-April, partly because there had been no reaction from either Hanoi or Phnom Penh to the first, partly because the results exceeded the administration's expectations, but above all because of an event far away in North Korea – the shooting down of an unarmed American reconnaissance plane, an EC-121, by North Korean MIG aircraft over the Sea of Japan on the evening of 14 April 1969.[33] Nixon had been extremely critical of President Johnson for his failure to take forceful measures in response to the capture by North Korea of the electronic ship *Pueblo*, and he initially wanted to react to the shooting down of the EC-121 by bombing North Korea. When he heard about the downing of the American plane, Nixon observed, "I reacted in the same way and with the same instincts that I had felt when the North Vietnamese offensive began: we were being tested, and therefore force must be met by force."[34]

Nixon refrained, however, from attacking North Korea, primarily because of the strong opposition of Rogers and Laird and an urgent cable from Ambassador William Porter in Seoul warning that any major military action that the United States might take would end up playing into the hands of North Korea's extremist movement.[35] "But as always when suppressing his instinct for a jugular response, Nixon looked for some other place to demonstrate his mettle. There was nothing he feared more than to be thought weak."[36]

Even though Nixon held off striking North Korea, the compulsion to retaliate remained. On a news-summary item given him at the end of March, which reported ABC-TV's claim that "the administration 'at the highest levels' is considering an air strike on North Vietnam," Nixon wrote: "Good!! K[issinger] – tell them RN is for this."[37]

Actually, Nixon had no intention of bombing North Vietnam at this juncture. Such a step would have disrupted the discussions in Paris and given the communists an excuse to denounce him.[38] Thus, both North Korea and North Vietnam were eliminated as appropriate targets for Nixon's wrath. This left the Cambodian sanctuaries as the target of choice once again. So, in response to North Korea's shooting down of the EC-121, Nixon ordered a second secret bombing raid at the end of April against yet another Cambodian base area. The strikes against Cambodia were essentially oblique threats, intended to signal to the North Vietnamese Nixon's readiness to resort to tougher measures unless they let up – just as Eisenhower had tamed the Chinese by rattling atomic weapons.[39]

Yet the timing of this particular raid and the choice of Cambodia as a target were more closely related to Nixon's frustration over the behaviour of North Korea than to his exasperation with North Vietnam. What the raid signalled at a personal level was that Nixon was incapable of tolerating weak and impotent feelings in the face of what he perceived to be a deliberate North Korean enemy action. His narcissistic need to be invulnerable and to identify with a powerful United States necessitated a forceful response somewhere, against someone. If the obvious target of a strike, North Korea, was deemed to be unsuitable, then another target would have to be found. Attacking Cambodian sanctuaries ostensibly enabled Nixon to demonstrate U.S. resolve; but his use of violence was a way of restoring his self-esteem. Moreover, since the first raid had been unsuccessful, in the sense that it had failed to destroy COSVN, slow traffic on the Ho Chi Minh Trail, or wring concessions from Hanoi in the Paris talks, the second raid would be twice as large, another sign of Nixon's anger and frustration and his need to get even.[40]

This second raid was followed with a series of additional secret bombing attacks on a string of other Cambodian base areas. From April 1969 through early August 1969, American attacks against the North Vietnamese sanctuaries in Cambodia continued intermittently: each was approved specifically by the White House. Afterward, general authority was given; raids were conducted regularly.[41]

A striking feature of this bombing campaign was Nixon's insistence that it be kept secret. The manner in which the bombing was decided set a pattern for future White House decision making. Once Nixon and Kissinger resolved to go ahead, and the staff put together the required studies, the full National Security Council was informed in a general way, rather than consulted. The emphasis on secrecy was so great that, not only did the military men set up their own top-secret system involving a false reporting mechanism, but every effort was made to confine knowledge of the raids to the fewest possible administration officials. In the Pentagon, Secretary Laird along with the joint chiefs obviously knew about the operation. Secretary of State Rogers and Under-Secretary Elliot Richardson had been informed in general terms about the bombing decision, but neither man received the daily top-secret reports on "Menu" strikes (the code-name for the series of strikes that included Breakfast, Lunch, Dinner, and so on) or realized their full extent.[42]

The official explanation offered later for the extraordinary secrecy surrounding "Menu" bombings was that Prince Sihanouk acquiesced in them on the condition that they receive no publicity. Otherwise, American officials explained, he would be forced to make diplomatic protests, thus creating an untenable political situation for the United States. This, in fact, was partially true. While Sihanouk was later to protest to the American ambassador against American bombing in areas inhabited by Cambodians, he had no problem with the bombing of the Viet Cong sanctuaries in areas of Cambodia not inhabited by Cambodians.

Nevertheless, the evidence indicates that the "Sihanouk excuse" was merely that, an excuse; the secrecy, the wiretaps, and the burning and falsification of reports were principally intended to conceal from the American people the administration's widening of the war.[43] Even after 1970, when "Menu" had ended and Sihanouk was in exile, no longer needing protection, Nixon and other officials all continued to assure Congress, the press, and the public that the United States had scrupulously declined to attack communist positions in Cambodia before the spring of 1970. When Nixon announced the "incursion" into Cambodia on 30 April 1970, thirteen months after B-52's had begun hitting Cambodian territory, he could simply have chosen to remain silent on the issue of the bombings. Instead, he offered an outright lie: "For five years, neither the United States nor South Vietnam has moved against these enemy sanctuaries because we did not wish to violate the territory of a neutral nation."[44] Not a word was mentioned about military intelligence teams covertly crossing into Cambodia since May 1967, or about the B-52 bombings.

Both the emphasis on secrecy and the outright duplicity that followed reflected Nixon's determination not to give his critics in the media, Congress, or the anti-war movement any opportunity to attack his policies and humiliate him either by forcing him to rescind those policies or, as had happened with his predecessor, by driving him from office. In his memoirs, Nixon admitted that one reason for the secrecy "was the problem of domestic anti-war protesters. My administration was only two months old, and I wanted to provoke as little public outcry as possible at the outset."[45]

Nixon's imposition of maximum secrecy to avoid public criticism and the potential humiliation of having to alter his policies in response to his critics also made him respond violently to any indications that members of his administration were responsible for leaks. When William Beecher of the *New York Times* reported on 9 May 1969 that the United States was engaging in B-52 bombing raids on Cambodia, the White House initiated wiretaps[46] just a few hours after the report was published in an effort to find the leakers and to stop them.

The president was concerned not only about the leak of the B-52 bombing raids but also about the report published three days earlier by Beecher in which he had exposed the administration's secret deliberations concerning potential responses to the North Korean attack on the American EC-121 reconnaissance plane. Nixon may also have been worried that Beecher knew about the fact that he had become violently drunk early in the crisis. In the first week after the EC-121 had been shot down, Lawrence Eagleburger, Kissinger's personal aide, who was obviously still upset, told a friend at lunch: "Here's the President of the United States, ranting and raving – drunk in the middle of the crisis."[47] For Nixon, to have it publicly said that he had a drinking problem would have constituted another obvious source of humiliation.

By the fall of 1969 General Creighton Abrams and the JCS had accepted that "Menu" had failed in its primary military purpose: neither COSVN headquarters nor the sanctuaries themselves were destroyed. But it was having another effect. To escape the bombardment, the Vietnamese communists had begun to move deeper into Cambodia – "thus," as Abrams later acknowledged to the Senate, "bringing them into increasing conflict with the Cambodian authorities."[48]

Since the bombing had failed to solve the problem of the sanctuaries and the approximately 40,000 Viet Cong and North Vietnamese troops that were in Cambodia (a figure cited by Prince Sihanouk himself), the joint chiefs requested an invasion. Their request was deferred, and the bombing was expanded; at the same time, American diplomatic relations with Sihanouk were restored (the prince had severed them in 1963) in the hope that perhaps he could use his influence with Moscow and Peking. In January 1970 the United States paid damages for Cambodian losses incurred by the expanded bombings, and Sihanouk departed for France for his annual two-month "cure" at the baths in Grasse. From there, he was scheduled to return via Moscow and Peking where he hoped to persuade the leaders of both countries to pressure the North Vietnamese to limit the use of force in his country.

During his visit to Moscow, Sihanouk was overthrown in a military coup on 18 March by his prime minister, Lon Nol. While there is no evidence that the United States was implicated, the administration was not unhappy with this development.[49] On a 17 March memo from Kissinger, one day before the coup, which explained that Lon Nol had plans to expand the Cambodian army by ten thousand men, Nixon had written: "Let's get a plan to aid the new government on this goal." And on 19 March, the day after the coup, Nixon wrote on another Kissinger memo, "I want Helms [CIA director Richard Helms] to develop and implement a plan for maximum assistance to pro-US elements in Cambodia. Don't put this out to 303[50] or the bureaucracy. Handle [it] like our [Menu] air strike."[51]

Rogers, Laird, and Helms all advised Nixon to hold back. If the United States rushed aid to Lon Nol, it would convince Moscow, Peking, and Hanoi that the CIA had set up the coup and would give the North Vietnamese an excuse to send in main-line units to overrun Phnom Penh. Nixon reluctantly decided to hold back, at least for a while. "But he was most unhappy with himself. It was just at this time that he started watching the movie *Patton*. Patton, one could hardly doubt, would have ignored the doubters and seized the opportunity."[52]

Hanoi's decision to expand its activities in Cambodia in order to protect its supply lines was a military step that many advisers on Kissinger's NSC staff, such as Richard Sneider, had anticipated. William Watts and Laurence E. Lynn both remember warning Kissinger that an invasion of Cambodia would force the communist troops out of their sanctuaries and drive them farther west – towards Phnom Penh; in essence, the aides were arguing that the invasion would, in fact, provoke the threat that Kissinger and Nixon were using to justify it – that Hanoi had plans to invade Phnom Phenh. It was only after the invasion that the possible threat to Phnom Penh appeared. Nor did the Pentagon buy the Nixon-Kissinger theory that Phnom Phenh was directly threatened; after reviewing the available intelligence, Colonel Robert E. Pursley concluded that "there was no substantive basis" for the theory.

Evidence and arguments were less important in the White House than Nixon's belief that Hanoi was defying him[53] and in the process contributing to his sense of frustrated impotence. Indicative of the president's emotional need to act was his response, on 18 April, to a report of a Viet Cong base in a mountain area deep inside Cambodia. He made an instant command decision and snapped out his order: hit that base with a B-52 strike within two hours! But the report was unconfirmed, no operation could be mounted in that time, and the B-52 was the least appropriate weapon for such an attack. No action was taken.[54] By the last week in April, Nixon had developed a new solution: he would demonstrate his toughness by using American troops in an invasion of Cambodia.

Not only did Nixon feel angry and helpless at the behaviour of the North Vietnamese, but domestic politics at home contributed their own special brand of humiliation. The key event in this context appears to have been the Senate's rejection on 8 April of Nixon's nomination of G. Harrold Carswell, a southern judge, to the Supreme Court, following an earlier rejection of another southerner, Clement F. Haynsworth.[55]

Nixon had every reason for thinking that Haynsworth, chief judge of the Fourth Circuit Court of Appeals, would be confirmed without difficulty. His first nominee to the Supreme Court, Warren Burger, had been opposed by only three senators. To fill the next vacancy on the court, an intensive search was conducted by William Rehnquist, aide to Attorney General John Mitchell. Among the thirty potential candidates who met the exacting criteria for selection laid out by Nixon (the candidate must be a southern Republican, strict constructionist, and under sixty years of age), Haynsworth was clearly the most qualified. However, Haynsworth's suspect financial dealings and his repeated decisions against desegregation troubled some critics. In the Senate battle that ensued, Haynesworth was defeated; seventeen Republicans voted against him, including the party's leader, assistant leader, and chairman of caucus. For the first time in forty years, the Senate had failed to confirm a presidential nominee for the court.

Nixon was furious. He had put himself out on a limb by making the nomination without checking beforehand either with key Republican and Democratic leaders in the Senate or with the American Bar Association, both of whom had expected to be consulted. The Senate had sawed off the limb and left him publicly humiliated. Despite the split vote that had occurred in the Senate judiciary committee prior to its final vote, Nixon's pride would not permit him to reconsider. He remained determined to carry on

with his nominee, ignoring the pleas of leading Republican senators. In October 1969 he assured them that he would not withdraw
the nomination and referred to the rising criticism of Haynsworth
as "a vicious character assassination."[56] White House aides were reported to have been "amazed at the emotion that Haynsworth's rejection aroused in him." It was said that "in the privacy of the
White House, Nixon inveighed against the liberal press which had
built the opposition to Haynsworth, against organized labor for its
vendetta against the judge, and most of all against all those Republican senators who had betrayed their President."[57]

In the end, Nixon had to abandon Haynsworth. But he did not
put the experience behind him. Having committed himself whole-
heartedly to Haynsworth's victory, Nixon identified with his failure
and with all the hurts and humiliations that he himself had suffered at the hands of the press and other enemies over the years.
To the loss of face that Nixon had personally suffered, the response
would be aggressive and vengeful. Nixon would stand fast; if Haynsworth were unacceptable, another candidate who met exactly the
same criteria would be found.

G. Harrold Carswell's nomination was sent to the Senate on
19 January 1970, having survived the same intensive review as the
previous nomination. But by March 1970 the nominee was in serious difficulty. Under the leadership of Senator Birch Bayh, a host
of civil rights and other liberal forces had independently dug into
Carswell's record and discovered many ugly facts: he had spoken
out years earlier for white supremacy, he was involved in the incor-
poration of a white-only country club, he had harassed black plain-
tiffs and their attorneys, and his judicial decisions had often been
opposed to integration. Senators who had not initially opposed the
nomination on those grounds began to alter their positions as they
learned that Carswell frequently reversed his opinions, an indicator
of judicial incompetence, and equivocated about his country-club
connection. A massive drive to defeat Carswell began: petitions and
letters from law school deans, professors, and civil-rights groups
poured in.[58]

On 1 April Nixon received a letter from Senator William Saxbe,
hitherto uncommitted on the Carswell question, who said that he
was disturbed by recent charges of racism and mediocrity against
judge Carswell and wondered whether Nixon's silence should be
taken as indifference. Nixon denied that the judge was a racist.
"What is centrally at issue," the president continued, "is the consti-

tutional responsibility of the President to appoint members of the court – and whether this responsibility can be frustrated by those who wish to substitute their own philosophy ... for that of the one person entrusted by the Constitution with the power of appointment."[59]

Democratic and Republican senators alike responded. They pointed out that the president had only the power to nominate, and that the "consent" of the Senate was necessary to "appoint." As Senator Bayh put it, Nixon was "wrong as a matter of constitutional law, wrong as a matter of history, and wrong as a matter of public policy."[60] Bayh could have added that Nixon was wrong as a matter of politics; before the president released his letter to Saxbe, the line-up was forty-five senators against Carswell and forty-four in favour. But when the Senate voted a week later, on 8 April 1970, Carswell lost by a margin of fifty-one to forty-five.[61]

The next day, Nixon, obviously still agitated and trying to deal with his pent-up emotions, called in reporters and TV cameras and used the occasion "to issue a verbal blast unprecedented in the history of rejected Supreme Court nominations."[62] "Judge Carswell and, before him, Judge Haynsworth have been submitted to vicious assaults on their intelligence, on their honesty, and on their character. They have been falsely charged with being racists. I have reluctantly concluded that it is not possible to get confirmation for a Judge on the Supreme Court of any man who believes in the strict construction of the Constitution if he happens to come from the South." He went on, "But when you strip away all the hypocrisy, the real reason for their rejection was their legal philosophy ... and also the accident of their birth, the fact that they were born in the South." Nixon pledged that "so long as the Senate is constituted the way it is today, I will not nominate another southerner and let him be subjected to the kind of malicious character assassination accorded both Judges Haynsworth and Carswell." Nixon then concluded his speech: "I understand the bitter feeling of millions of Americans who live in the South about the act of regional discrimination that took place in the Senate yesterday ... they have my assurance that the day will come when men like Judges Carswell and Haynsworth can and will sit on the high court."[63]

In ascribing bitterness to the millions of Americans living in the south, Nixon had reacted viscerally; partly, his outburst was a calculated attempt to exploit the results of the vote for political purposes in the south, yet, more fundamentally, it was a displacement of his own bitterness about the Senate's public act of defiance of his wishes and his corresponding humiliation. As it happened, some southern senators were bitter, but mostly at the president's implication that Judge Carswell represented the best the south had to offer and that he had been turned down despite rather than because of his record. Senator Albert Gore of Tennessee, who had voted against both Haynsworth and Carswell, assailed the president's statement as "an assault on the integrity of the Senate."[64]

Nixon believed that time would ultimately vindicate his choices. But in the short run, he had lost and lost badly. His back-to-back failures had left him feeling humiliated – an almost intolerable emotion for him – and he coped as he always had before: by lashing out verbally in a way that minimized his own role in the failure and instead placed the blame on the malicious and unfair behaviour of his opponents.[65] Nixon's enraged denunciation of the fifty-one "vicious," "hypocritical," and "prejudiced" senators who had thwarted the people's wishes left members of the White House press corps feeling awkward and uncomfortable.[66]

More frustration and humiliation were to haunt Nixon in April. An especially bitter event was having to cancel plans to attend his son-in-law David's graduation at Amherst and his daughter Julie's from Smith because of the threat of anti-war demonstrations. Nixon claimed that he made the decision over the objections of Julie, whom he described as trying to hold back her tears while saying "that only a few small radical groups were involved."[67] Privately, Julie had written to Nixon aide John Ehrlichman[68] indicating her concerns: "I truly think the day will be a disaster if he comes. Smith girls are furious at the idea of massive security precautions." The pain of being unable to attend the graduation was exacerbated by taunts from the vice-president. "Don't let them intimidate you, Mr. President," Spiro Agnew remonstrated. "You may be President, but you're her father, and a father should be able to attend his daughter's graduation."[69] But the Secret Service advised Nixon that there certainly would be ugly protest demonstrations if he went either to Julie's graduation or to David's, and he reluctantly agreed to stay away from both.

The Senate contributed again to Nixon's feelings of impotence and humiliation when the foreign relations committee voted unanimously on 10 April to repeal the Gulf of Tonkin Resolution of

1964. Nixon took the position that he had inherited the war and did not need the Gulf of Tonkin Resolution to justify continuing it. Still, the committee vote, especially as it was unanimous, was another blow to his always fragile self-esteem and a further reminder that his ability to lead the country in directions he wanted to go had been sharply curtailed.[70]

The final straw was the aborted Apollo 13 moon trip on 13 April, an event that left Nixon "frustrated, angry and embarrassed."[71] Kissinger described Nixon as becoming increasingly testy and noted that Haldeman had joked that the president was in a "charming mood"; in the course of covering one subject on the telephone, Nixon had hung up on him several times.[72]

All of these developments left Nixon psychologically primed to act in a way that would demonstrate his power in the face of the abasement that he had experienced. Invading Cambodia provided just that opportunity. As if to underscore the linkage between humiliation and revenge, James David Barber comments that "Nixon moved from April and Carswell to May and Cambodia, from defeat to attack."[73]

Since the summer of 1969 Nixon had publicly committed himself to the principle of reducing American troop levels in Vietnam. Yet the president also continually restated his position that the rate of American withdrawals from Vietnam would depend on the progress of "Vietnamization" (a shift in the military burden of the war from the United States to the government of South Vietnam), the course of the Paris negotiations, and the level of enemy activity. As for the Paris talks, he reported on 20 April "with regret" that "no progress has taken place ... The enemy still demands that we unilaterally and unconditionally withdraw all American forces, that in the process we overthrow the elected Government of South Vietnam and that the United States accept a political settlement that would have the practical consequences of the forcible imposition of a Communist government upon the people of South Vietnam ... *That would mean humiliation and defeat for the United States. This we cannot and will not accept.*"[74] Nixon then went on to say that pacification was succeeding and that all American combat forces could and would be withdrawn. "The enemy has failed to win the war in Vietnam because of three basic errors in their strategy. They thought they could win a military victory. They have failed to do so. They thought they could win politically in South Vietnam. They have failed to do so. They thought they could win politically in the United States. This proved to be their most fatal miscalculation ... *We are not a weak people. We are a strong people. America has never been defeated in the proud 190-year history of this country, and we shall not be defeated in Vietnam.*"[75] Nixon's emphasis on American humiliation and the impossibility of defeat spoke to his own personal fears of being humiliated and defeated and his need to reassert publicly his own strength in the face of his enemies.

A ground assault into the Cambodian sanctuaries had always been high on the military's wish list. Sihanouk's overthrow on 18 March had removed a major obstacle, and, with Lon Nol's acquiescence, the South Vietnamese army began a series of incursions into Cambodia. On 20 March, two days after the coup, there were South Vietnamese air-force attacks and ground probes inside the country. One week later, a South Vietnamese armoured unit crossed the border; on 5 April two South Vietnamese battalions moved ten miles into Cambodia. The official policy of the U.S. government at the time was that the South Vietnamese were operating on their own without American support, but few – either in the United States or in North Vietnam – were fooled. Secretary of Defense Laird revealed to the Senate foreign relations committee six weeks later that he had "approved and recommended" the 5 April mission and others.[76]

On the morning of 21 April, Nixon was briefed on the developments in Cambodia by CIA director Richard Helms. Helms informed the president and Kissinger that the North Vietnamese army was now threatening Phnom Penh and that it stood an excellent chance of taking over the whole country; this situation, Kissinger later confided to reporters, made Lon Nol's appeal for arms very compelling.[77] It was also what Nixon wanted to hear. A move into Cambodia would accomplish the twin objectives of saving Lon Nol and destroying communist caches in the sanctuary with limited casualties for American forces.

What Helms did not say either then or at any stage during the next week was that he had just received an intelligence report on the Cambodian situation. Entitled "Stocktaking in Indochina: Longer Term Prospects," the paper concluded that even a greatly expanded American and South Vietnamese effort in Cambodia would not achieve the administration's objectives.[78] Helms never explained why he did not forward the memorandum to the White

House, but George Carver, the CIA's Vietnam specialist, testified that Helms thought it would be pointless to give the document to the president since he knew Nixon was already planning an invasion.[79]

Throughout the course of the planning for the invasion, there was a concerted effort on the part of Nixon and Kissinger to suppress "inconvenient" views. No more than a dozen senior officials were aware of the overall plan. In Washington, besides Nixon, only Kissinger, Laird, Rogers, Admiral Thomas Moorer (the acting chairman of the JCS), Helms, and Attorney General Mitchell were fully informed. Colonel Haig and a few key members of the NSC staff had access only to a certain amount of information. Even General William Westmoreland, army chief of staff, was cut out of the consultative process. J-3, the short-range-planning arm of the JCS, was brought into the picture only in the final few days; J-5, the long-range-planning staff, was kept in the dark until the end. At the State Department, Rogers was under instructions to keep the Cambodian plans entirely to himself. Under-Secretary of State Richardson, travelling in the Middle East, was caught by surprise. Marshall Green, the man in charge of Far Eastern affairs in the State Department, was deliberately eliminated from the meetings of the WASAG (Washington Special Action Group) after 20 April. In the Pacific, only General Creighton Abrams and Admiral John D. McCain plus a few of their closest aides had the full picture.[80]

In response to Helms's briefing, Nixon scheduled a meeting of the NSC the following day. "As always when he approached a crisis, Nixon was tense, keyed up, anxious and unable to sleep."[81] At 5 a.m. he got up and dictated a message to Kissinger. It began, "I think we need a bold move in Cambodia to show that we stand with Lon Nol," even though he feared that it was a futile effort. "We have really dropped the ball on this one," he said, but "we were taken in with the line that by helping him we would destroy his 'neutrality' and give the North Vietnamese an excuse to come in. Over and over again we fail to learn that the Communists never need an excuse to come in." He cited Hungary in 1956, Czechoslovakia in 1968, Laos in 1970, and Cambodia in 1970. "They [the communists] are romping in there and the only government in Cambodia in the last twenty-five years that had the guts to take a pro-Western and pro-American stand is ready to fall."[82] "In the event I decide to go on this course" [stronger support for Lon Nol],

Nixon wanted Kissinger to stress with "some of the lily-livered Ambassadors from our so-called friends in the world" that their posture on this issue would show us "who our friends are."[83] Again the graphic language Nixon used conveyed his impotence and rage at communist behaviour, as well as his sense that he was being taunted and humiliated by his enemies and, potentially, by his "so-called friends."

On 22 April Nixon presided over a lengthy NSC meeting which discussed the usual three options of doing nothing, doing something, and going all out. Secretary of State Rogers and Secretary of Defense Laird favoured a modified do-nothing approach: the United States should confine its involvement to what it was doing already, namely, giving support and advice to limited cross-border raids by the South Vietnamese army. Kissinger wanted to do something; he favoured main-force operations in Cambodia but thought they should be limited to the ARVN. The JCS wanted to go all out, using American forces to destroy communist sanctuaries.[84]

According to the military, there were two base areas in Cambodia of special concern. One was the Parrot's Beak, a sliver of land that jutted into South Vietnam and reached to within thirty-three miles of Saigon. The North Vietnamese army had been using it as a staging area for years. The second was an even larger base, called the Fishhook, about fifty miles northwest of Saigon. Intelligence analysts believed that COSVN, the communist headquarters for all operations in the south, was located there.

Rogers opposed substantial cross-border operations even by the South Vietnamese and Laird repeated his objections to any American involvement in action inside Cambodia. Normally, Nixon announced his decisions after, not during, an NSC meeting; he would deliberate and then issue instructions in writing or through intermediaries. He did this to emphasize that the NSC was an advisory not a decision-making body, and to avoid challenges to his orders. On this occasion, Nixon altered his usual practice and told his colleagues that he approved attacks on the base areas by South Vietnamese forces with U.S. support. Since the South Vietnamese could handle only one offensive, General Wheeler recommended that they go after Parrot's Beak. This led to a debate about American participation; Laird and Rogers sought to confine it to an absolute minimum, opposing even American advisers or tactical air support.[85]

At this point in the discussion, according to Kissinger, Vice-President Spiro Agnew spoke up. He complained that the whole debate was irrelevant. Either the sanctuaries were a danger or they were not. If it was worth cleaning them out, he did not understand all the pussyfooting about the American role or what was accomplished by attacking only one. He favoured an attack on both Fishhook and Parrot's Beak, including the use of American troops. His words had a significant impact on Nixon, or so Kissinger thought. "If Nixon hated anything more than being presented with a plan he had not considered, it was to be shown up in a group as being less tough than his advisers ... I have no doubt that Agnew's intervention accelerated Nixon's ultimate decision to order an attack on all the sanctuaries and use American forces."[86] The president was still smarting because of Agnew's advice that he "damn well ought to go to Smith" and see Julie graduate.[87] To be perceived as weak or shrinking from a challenge was extremely threatening to Nixon's self-image; it undermined his fragile self-esteem and threatened to expose his vulnerability.

However, at this juncture, Nixon postponed a decision. He knew that if he widened the war "it could mean personal and political catastrophe for me and my administration."[88] At the same time, Nixon was clearly frustrated at not being able to strike out and respond to all his detractors with an aggressive move. The following day, his anger mounted at the news that there had been a leak: his orders to supply Lon Nol with captured equipment had been reported in the *New York Times*. The president also learned, to his fury, that his orders to get more equipment into the CIA station in Phnom Penh had not been implemented because of bureaucratic foot-dragging. Kissinger recalled that Nixon "flew into a monumental rage," calling him that evening, April 23, at least ten times. As was his habit when extremely agitated, Nixon would bark an order and immediately hang up the phone. "He wanted our chargé, [Lloyd] Rives, relieved immediately; he ordered Marshall Green fired, on second thought his Deputy Bill Sullivan was to be transferred as well; an Air Force plane with CIA personnel aboard should be dispatched to Phnom Penh immediately; everybody with access to the cable should be given a lie-detector test; a general was to be appointed immediately to take charge of Cambodia."[89]

Tracking down his aide William Watts, who was instructed to prepare for a full day of meetings, Kissinger remarked, "Our peerless leader has flipped out."[90] In his memoirs, he observed: "In these circumstances, it was usually prudent not to argue and to wait twenty-four hours to see on which of these orders Nixon would insist after he calmed down. As it turned out, he came back to none of them."[91]

The meaning of the flurry of phone calls to Kissinger is clear: Nixon wanted to punish and humiliate his subordinates for the humiliation he had felt upon the discovery that his instructions had not been followed. Once he had vented his spleen and issued sweeping orders for changes, his self-esteem was restored; he felt powerful and grandiose, and the need to follow through was attenuated.

Further evidence of the extent to which Nixon felt humiliated by the developments of the preceding months and his visceral need to assert himself is suggested in some of the other comments he made during these calls to Kissinger, which were recorded in note form by William Watts. During one such call, Nixon, speaking of the Senate rejection of Haynsworth and Carswell, revealed his emotions in vivid fashion: "Those senators think they can push Nixon around on Haynsworth and Carswell. Well, I'll show them who's tough."[92]

During the period between 21 April, when Nixon first considered using Americans in Cambodia, and 26 April, when he made the final decision to, as he put it in his memoirs, "go for broke" and commit 32,000 American troops to the invasion, there is no evidence that Kissinger raised any objections although Laird, Rogers, and some of Kissinger's closest aides voiced heated dissent.

William Watts, Anthony Lake, and Roger Morris, all NSC staffers, were especially upset. Laurence Lynn, Jr, another senior NSC aide, told Kissinger that a Cambodian invasion would not only drive the North Vietnamese deeper into Cambodia (where Nixon had already come to believe they were) but, more important, it would make South Vietnam that much more vulnerable to a Viet Cong and North Vietnamese offensive. In an effort to persuade Lynn of the efficacy of American military intervention, Kissinger talked about the bargaining power of Nixon's seeming irrationality and said that "the Russians and North Vietnamese would run risks because of Nixon's character." By then, however, Lynn had become concerned about Nixon's real state of mind. "All of us were worried about this man's stability. We'd have glimpses of him and didn't know what to do with it."[93]

A few days before the operation, when the JCS's hastily drawn
plans for the attack were submitted to the White House, Kissinger
asked some of his staff to evaluate them. "The plan was just awful," Lynn recalls, "It was imprecise and vague. I was to write up all
the questions I could think of – about refugees, the South Vietnamese Army, security, and I even queried the proposed result of
the operation itself." Kissinger told Lynn that his list was "terrific"
and gave it to a military aide to present to the joint chiefs for a
reply. Lynn heard nothing over the next few days and eventually
asked Haig whether anything would come from his queries. Nothing did.[94]

Roger Morris, another NSC staffer, was among those who warned
Kissinger about the domestic dangers of the Cambodian operation.
Until he made his dissent known, Morris had been involved in the
flow of paper from Nixon's office to Kissinger, memoranda he later
described as "stream of consciousness excursions into courage and
aggression" that would "make extraordinary reading for historians
if they survive." Nixon published only one such paper in his memoirs, the memo he wrote during the Cambodian planning at five
o'clock in the morning of 22 April.[95] Morris commented that the
memoranda depicted "a man angry and obsessed with the idea that
the other side was trying to push him around" in Cambodia. One
read: "Now what the hell are they trying to do Henry? These intelligence reports are very disturbing. It looks as if there is an effort
here to take advantage of the weakness of the new regime, an effort
to take over large sections of the country, to upset the truce, to have
some kind of decisive, indirect effect on politics in South Vietnam."
The constant refrain was: "How are we going to look? Where will
we be after this if they do something dramatic in Cambodia? We
can't let them do this."[96] Nixon perceived developments in Cambodia as contributing to more humiliation for him; it could not be
allowed to continue.

Morris remembered Kissinger as very non-committal in his telephone talks with Nixon during that time: " 'You're right, Mr. President, but on the other hand they could simply be testing us: they
may not be going all the way.' There was a lot of 'yes, Mr. President'
in it." Kissinger was talking "not as if he were serving the President,"
Morris thought, "but as if he were treating him" as a doctor would
his patient.[97] There seemed little doubt that Kissinger was very concerned; H.R. Haldeman, White House chief of staff, recorded in his
diaries that "K [Kissinger] was very worried last night [23 April]

that P [President Nixon] is moving too rashly without thinking through the consequences."[98] But, sensitive to Nixon's narcissistic needs for affirmation and support, Kissinger was unwilling to undermine his own political position by opposing the policy.[99] His behaviour furnishes an archetypal example of the way in which narcissists such as Nixon can "get away with murder" when they are not restrained by courageous subordinates.

On the morning of 24 April, Nixon met with the chairman of the joint chiefs, General Robert Cushman, and CIA director Helms to discuss the feasibility of a combined US–ARVN operation against the Fishhook in conjunction with an ARVN offensive into the Parrot's Beak. The military favoured the plan and told the president that the destruction of COSVN and of communist supply dumps would buy valuable time for Vietnamization. They also pointed out other sanctuaries they would like to hit.[100] In the course of the morning meeting, Nixon recalled that he had been the White House coordinator for the preparation of the Bay of Pigs invasion of Cuba, which Eisenhower left for Kennedy to carry out. "Ike lost Cuba," the President remarked, "but I won't lose Cambodia."[101] Still, Nixon was not yet prepared to announce his final decision.

Kissinger urged Nixon to call an NSC meeting to give all parties an opportunity to express themselves. As he told Helms: "It is my judgment and strong recommendation that any decision must be discussed with the two Cabinet members [the secretaries of state and defense] – even if the decision has already been made and an order is in the desk drawer. You can't ram it down their throats without their having a chance to give their views."[102]

According to key participants in the decision-making process, the secretaries of state and defense were being reduced to the role of an unsuspecting audience. At the meeting set for Sunday afternoon, 26 April, Nixon's primary concern was to lessen the inevitable confrontation with Rogers and Laird to a minimum; "when pressed to the wall, his romantic streak surfaced and he would see himself as a beleaguered military commander in the tradition of Patton."[103] And like Patton, he, too, would be a man who would triumph over all obstacles and humiliations.

On the afternoon of 24 April, Nixon took a helicopter to Camp David in the company of his closest friend, Bebe Rebozo. By this stage in Nixon's presidency, it was widely rumoured among Kissinger's associates on the NSC staff that, whenever Bebe and Dick got together, the martinis flowed.[104] This time was no different. At some point that night, the president, his voice slurred, telephoned Kissinger at the White House and turned over the phone to Rebozo, who had a message from the president. Watts, horrified, listened on the line as Rebozo said to Kissinger, "The President wants you to know if this doesn't work, it's your ass." Then Kissinger heard Nixon say, "Ain't that right, Bebe?"[105]

The following day Kissinger went to Camp David to review the planning. As the president paddled in the water, Kissinger walked along the edge of the pool. Nixon, his self-esteem bolstered no doubt by Rebozo, seemed ready to take on the world. He told Kissinger that he was eager to go ahead with the Fishhook operation and began toying with the idea of going "for broke." He suggested combining an attack on the Cambodian sanctuaries with resumption of the bombing of North Vietnam as well as mining Haiphong since the opposition would be equally hysterical either way.[106]

That evening, at the White House, Nixon invited his colleagues to yet another viewing of the movie *Patton*.[107] Nixon had already seen it four or five times; he seemed to draw inspiration for drastic decisions from its portrayal of the "blood-and-guts" general who symbolized the courage that Nixon so admired.[108] At a deeper psychological level, the repeated viewing of the film seemed to reflect Nixon's need to identify with an idealized object whose strength and power he could experience as his own. Like Patton, who had been frustrated by his superior in the army, General Eisenhower, Nixon had suffered repeated frustrations and humiliations from his superior, President Eisenhower. In watching *Patton*, Nixon may have been stiffening his spine by identifying with the way in which Patton challenged an establishment that had rejected him.[109]

Late Sunday afternoon, 26 April, Nixon chaired a three-hour meeting with his principal NSC advisers – Kissinger, Rogers, Laird, Wheeler, and Helms in his working office in the Executive Office Building. Agnew was not included. Kissinger noted that, "even though he was now taking the Vice President's advice, Nixon was still smarting from Agnew's unexpected sally and was determined to be the strong man of this meeting."[110] Rather than confront Laird and Rogers directly on the issues, he pretended that he had summoned his advisers merely to listen to Helms and Wheeler's assessments of Hanoi's expansion of its base areas in Cambodia and its attempts to link them together in order to increase the insecurity of the Lon Nol government and bring about its collapse. Both Rogers and Laird fell in with the charade that it was all a planning exercise and did not take a position.[111]

Kissinger recorded that Nixon was immensely relieved at not having to deal with Laird and Rogers's objections; Nixon hated controversy. As soon as the meeting was over, Nixon instructed Kissinger to issue a directive authorizing an attack by American forces into the Fishhook area. Not content with merely initialling the directive, which was his normal practice, Nixon signed his name in full[112] as if to underline his Patton-like resolve.

Upon receipt of the presidential directive, Laird and Rogers immediately requested a meeting with the president. It was, from Nixon's perspective, a tense meeting, "because even though Rogers and Laird had by now given up hope of dissuading me from taking some action in Cambodia, they still thought they could convince me not to involve American troops."[113] Rogers was also concerned with his appearance before the Senate foreign relations committee that afternoon. He wanted to be able to testify that no Americans were involved in Cambodia; he therefore requested that the president withdraw his directive. Laird's position repeated his fear of high casualties and implied that there had been a terrible misunderstanding about Abrams's recommendation. Nixon said little and what he said was ambiguous – "a sure sign to anyone familiar with his methods that he meant to stick with his decision."[114]

Kissinger, however, prevailed upon the president to withdraw his directive for twenty-four hours to ease Rogers's problems. In the meantime, Ellsworth Bunker and General Abrams's "unvarnished views" on the two operations would be re-solicited. By early evening, the reply from Bunker and Abrams arrived. Both men strongly recommended the combined allied attack on Fishhook as the "most desirable" option, preferably in parallel with the attack on Parrot's Beak, which was the second most important target.[115] Laird also communicated once again his views in opposition to the use of American combat troops in Cambodia; in its place, he favoured the South Vietnamese operation against the Parrot's Beak.

As in most decisions with major political consequences, Nixon decided to call in John Mitchell. Kissinger, Nixon, and Mitchell spent until nearly midnight going over the memoranda and the pros and cons of the available options. The attorney general remained firmly in support of the plan and urged the president to stop wavering and start acting.[116] In the end, Nixon decided to reaffirm his original decision and to tell Laird and Rogers in the morning in front of Mitchell.[117] Mitchell's presence would serve to shore up Nixon's sense of self by allowing him to identify with a resolute figure in any ensuing confrontation with his dissenting secretaries of state and defense.

The next morning, Tuesday, 28 April, Nixon met with Mitchell and Kissinger for an hour to review the operations once again. Then Nixon requested that Kissinger leave by a side door before his meeting with Rogers and Laird. Kissinger thought that one reason for his exclusion was Nixon's desire to protect him from departmental retaliation, but that a second reason for his exclusion was more psychological: "No doubt he wanted to live up to his image of himself as the lonely embattled leader propping up faltering associates."[118]

That night, sitting alone, Nixon pulled out his yellow legal pad and made a list of the "pluses" and the "minuses" of the forthcoming operation. The advantages of the Fishhook were that it would allow the United States to withdraw more rapidly from Vietnam, divert the communists from an attack on Phnom Penh, and possibly lead Hanoi to negotiate more seriously in Paris. The disadvantages were that the communists might respond with an attack on Phnom Penh, there might be deep divisions in the United States, and the communists might break off the peace talks and attack across the demilitarized zone.[119] The "pluses" won. Early the next morning, Nixon showed his list to Kissinger. Kissinger said that he had prepared a list of his own and that it was almost identical.[120]

What Kissinger did not say is that, since he knew that Nixon's mind was already made up, his position regarding the attack would be a litmus test of his loyalty to the president. Thus, his list could have been expected to replicate Nixon's. During his discussion with Kissinger, Nixon underlined his concerns that he might be left holding the bag if problems arose. "Now that we have made the decision there must be no recriminations among us," Nixon said. "Not even if the whole thing goes wrong. In fact, *especially* if the whole thing goes wrong."[121] Although Nixon often fantasized about "the big play" and bearing the full weight of whatever consequences his decisions might produce, it is clear that he was terrified at the prospect.

Notwithstanding the fact that the "minuses" of the operation had received much stronger support than the "pluses" by the secretaries of state and defense and members of the NSC staff, Nixon was persuaded by the "plus" side even though there was little evidence that the communists were planning an attack on Phnom Penh or that American moves would lead to any modifications in Hanoi's bargaining behaviour. What Nixon factored into the equation, albeit unconsciously, was the psychological benefit that he would derive from taking action. The decision to invade would solidify Nixon's self-image as a man of courage, a Patton, while simultaneously showing his opponents that he was not someone who would accept humiliation lying down.

Operation Rock Crusher was launched against the Parrot's Beak during the night of 28 April. About fifty American advisers accompanied the initial wave, joined by twenty-two more in the first four days. On Wednesday morning, 29 April, the wire services began to report the ARVN offensive into the Parrot's Beak and unhappy Senate doves asked for assurances that Nixon did not intend to send American troops into Cambodia. The White House was silent, saying only that the president would address the nation the following night. Neither Saigon nor Washington offered the slightest hint that a parallel American attack was to start within forty-eight hours in the Fishhook. Kissinger recounts that

in the days before announcing this most fateful decision of his early Presidency, Richard Nixon was virtually alone, sitting in a darkened room in the Executive Office Building, the stereo softly playing neo-classical music – reflecting, resenting, collecting his thoughts and his anger. The Churchillian rhetoric that emerged [in the speech of 30 April] reflected less the actual importance of the decision than his undoubted sense of defiance at what he knew would be a colossal controversy over a decision he deeply believed to be right and in the making of which he received little succor from his associates.[122]

Like Patton, Nixon would show his many detractors that he was genuinely tough; the multiple humiliations that he had suffered during the previous months would be exorcised in an aggressive strike against his opponents – the North Vietnamese, the senators (who would be faced with a *fait accompli*), and the anti-war protesters.

In a subsequent conversation with New York Governor Nelson Rockefeller, Nixon explained how he had made his final decision to send in American troops:

I sat right here with two cabinet officers and my national security adviser, and I asked what we needed to do. The recommendation of the Department of Defense was the most pusillanimous little nit-picker I ever saw.[123] "Just bite off the Parrot's Beak." I said you are going to have a hell of an uproar at home if you bite off the Beak. If you are going to take the heat, go for all the marbles ... I have made some bad decisions, but a good one was this: When you bite the bullet, bite it hard – go for the big play.[124]

The verbal imagery is revealing: Nixon's feelings of impotence required him to act in a way that would demonstrate his power and satisfy his narcissistic fantasies of grandeur. But it is the grandeur of the little boy in the schoolyard who wants to win all the marbles and vanquish his opponents, or the adolescent who fantasizes becoming an athletic hero who makes the big play and earns lasting glory.

Once the decision to move ahead with a combined US–ARVN attack on the Fishhook had been made, Kissinger asked his staff to begin to consider the implications of the use of American troops. Such implications should have been considered prior to rather than after the decision was made, but then this was not a decision conceived in a rational, analytic way; rather, it was an example of a decision motivated by emotional needs.

William Watts, who was chosen to coordinate the NSC staff work on the invasion, went to Kissinger's office to tell him that he objected to the policy and could not work on it. Kissinger dressed him down, saying, "Your views represent the cowardice of the Eastern Establishment." In the White House situation-room, Watts was then confronted by Alexander Haig, who barked at him that he could not resign: "You've just had an order from your commander in chief." "Fuck you, Al," Watts said, "I just did."[125] Watts's resignation was followed in swift succession by that of Roger Morris and Anthony Lake.

Kissinger was asked at a meeting whether the invasion did not expand the war. "Look," he replied, "we're not interested in Cambodia. We're only interested in it not being used as a base." The wider justifications he cited dealt with superpower relations. "We're trying to shock the Soviets into calling a Conference," he said, "and we can't do this by appearing weak." William Safire asked whether the invasion breached the Nixon Doctrine, which called upon the states of South and Southeast Asia to take responsibility for their own defense. To this, Kissinger replied, "We wrote the goddamn doctrine, we can change it."[126] At the end of the meeting Haig stood up and shouted, "The basic substance of all this is that we have to be tough."[127] That was indeed the point. The United States would invade Cambodia to prove its toughness and to reassure the president and repair his damaged self-esteem.

Although Kissinger had angrily labelled the resignations of Lake, Watts, and Morris prior to the invasion as "the cowardice of the Eastern Establishment," he seems to have had his own misgivings. As late as the afternoon of 29 April, a day before the presidential speech, Kissinger had a final talk with Nixon. As Haig told the story afterward: "Henry tried to talk him out of it but it had gone too far." Although responsibility for the bizarre, almost manic decision making belonged chiefly to Nixon, Kissinger would remain a forceful defender of the invasion.[128]

Nixon also disregarded advice that General Abrams issue a routine announcement of the invasion from Saigon. He was apparently determined to make the most of the occasion and wrote much of his 30 April speech himself in long-hand, staying up until 5:00 a.m. that morning to complete the text. When the speech was taken over to Laird and Rogers later that day, they were horrified at what they read. "This will cause an uproar," Rogers told his staff, and Laird called Kissinger to suggest fundamental changes. Under his prodding, Kissinger did suggest some modifications but Nixon rejected almost all of them. The final speech was very much his own and ranks among the key Nixon texts. As Jonathan Schell of the *New Yorker* pointed out, it reflected his attitudes towards himself as well as his place and that of the United States in the world, and it explained much about why he acted as he did. It had almost nothing to do with the realities of Cambodia.[129]

The speech opened with a deception. The president recalled his warning ten days earlier that, if "increased enemy activity ... endangered the lives of Americans remaining in Vietnam, [he] would not hesitate to take strong and effective measures." He then went on to state that "North Vietnam has increased its military aggression in all those areas [of Indochina] and particularly in Cambodia."[130] Nixon knew that all that the communists had done was to keep moving out of the border sanctuaries, a pattern initiated long before. But the public, with no access to actual battlefield information, had no way of knowing this. Nixon's ploy was to create the impression that, after he had magnanimously ordered the new

American troop withdrawal, the North Vietnamese responded with "aggression" and thereby endangered United States forces in South Vietnam.[131]

Nixon's claim was soon demolished by, among others, Senate foreign relations committee investigators who visited Vietnam and Cambodia between 29 April and 15 May. In a special report titled "Cambodia: May 1970," James Lowenstein and Richard Moose, both highly respected Senate investigators, wrote that "neither in our briefings in Washington ... nor in the briefings and discussions we had in Vietnam on 2 and 3 May was there mention of an increased enemy threat to U.S. forces in Vietnam from the sanctuaries or of an increase in the size of enemy forces in Cambodia. Indeed, in both Washington and Saigon we were told that the size of the North Vietnamese and Vietcong forces in Cambodia had remained constant over the past six months."[132]

To bolster his public case, Nixon next plunged into an outright lie. He told his national audience that, since Cambodia had become a neutral state following the 1954 Geneva conference on Indochina, "American policy ... has been to scrupulously respect the neutrality of the Cambodian people ... For the past five years, we have provided no military assistance whatever and no economic assistance to Cambodia ... North Vietnam, on the other hand, has not respected that neutrality," establishing "military sanctuaries" that "are used for hit-and-run attacks on American and South Vietnamese forces in South Vietnam." He promised that, in the Fishhook area, American and South Vietnamese troops "will attack the headquarters for the entire Communist military operation in South Vietnam."[133]

Laird had repeatedly told Nixon that, except in the wider reaches of military fantasy, no such "key control center," as Nixon put it, existed.[134] These sanctuaries astride the Vietnamese-Cambodian border, Nixon claimed, contained "major base camps, training sites, logistics facilities, weapons and ammunition factories, airstrips, and prisoner of war compounds."[135] But Nixon grossly exaggerated the sanctuaries' importance; if, indeed, the communists had what the president claimed they had in the sanctuaries, they were never found there by anybody.

Nixon then proclaimed that "thousands" of North Vietnamese soldiers were "invading" Cambodia from the sanctuaries, "encircling the capital of Phnom Penh."[136] In fact, the westward movement of the communists in April had been the immediate result of

Sihanouk's fall – an event that had forced Hanoi to devise a new strategy. Captured communist documents revealed that there were to be "no major engagements in 1970." But the ouster of Sihanouk deprived the North Vietnamese of the north-south corridor above Sihanoukville, the Cambodian port on the Gulf of Siam, and so the new strategy was to try to retake Sihanoukville, or another harbour, and reopen the corridor to the sea.[137]

Having made the claim that Phnom Penh was being encircled by the communists, the president asserted that "Cambodia as a result of this, has sent out a call to the United States, to a number of other nations, for assistance."[138] Nixon thus sought to make it appear that the United States was responding to Lon Nol's appeals for help. But what Lon Nol had been requesting was arms and money, not an American-South Vietnamese invasion. The record shows that at no time did Washington consult with Lon Nol about a possible invasion either in the Parrot's Beak or in the Fishhook. (This was subsequently explained by administration officials in terms of the need to keep the planning secret – even from the presumed beneficiary of the imminent attacks.)

President Thieu of South Vietnam would later claim in Saigon that he and Lon Nol had reached an "agreement in principle" concerning South Vietnamese entry into Cambodia a few days before the operations were launched. But this is highly questionable because of the continued ethnic tensions between Cambodians and Vietnamese. During March and April, thousands of ethnic Vietnamese in Cambodia had been massacred by Cambodian troops; in these circumstances, it is extremely doubtful that Lon Nol would have agreed to an ARVN presence in his country. Lowenstein and Moose also noted in their Senate report that in Phnom Penh "there was some evident and understandable uneasiness at the presence of large numbers of South Vietnamese on Cambodian soil, understandable in the light of historic Cambodian fears of Vietnamese aggressiveness."[139]

Proof that the whole Cambodian operation was unrelated to any call for assistance from Phnom Penh was contained in a classified document, typed on White House stationery and titled "Points on the Cambodia Military Action," distributed to members of the president's senior staff at a meeting in the Roosevelt Room shortly before the speech was delivered. It stated: "It is a strike operation that is an integral part of our operations in Vietnam. It is not in reply to any of Lon Nol's requests for aid to Cambodia."[140]

In his address to the nation, Nixon laid out what he called "three options," again relating the Cambodian situation to the safety of American troops in Vietnam, something he regarded as an irrefutable argument. The first option, he said, would be to do "nothing," but "unless we engage in wishful thinking, the lives of Americans remaining in Vietnam after our next withdrawal of 150,000 would be gravely threatened." Pointing to the map and the sanctuary area, Nixon argued that, "if North Vietnam occupied this whole band in Cambodia or the entire country, it would mean that South Vietnam was completely outflanked and the forces of Americans in this area, as well as the South Vietnamese, would be in an untenable military position."[141]

As a strategic rationale, it was totally specious. The communists had been in the sanctuaries for years without making the situation in Vietnam any more untenable than before. Nixon was also promising the impossible: inasmuch as he was placing a sixty-day limit on the American presence in Cambodia and restricting the depth of American penetration to just over twenty miles, the incursion could not have conceivably achieved the ambitious objectives he was outlining to his television audience.

Why was the illusion of a victory so important at this juncture? The reason had nothing to do with the threat to Pnomh Penh or with the desire to strike a decisive blow against the North Vietnamese; it had everything to do, however, with Nixon's damaged self-esteem, which needed to lash out and find enemies that he could punish. The Vietnamese in Cambodia offered a relatively safe target for Nixon's wrath with the Viet Cong, the North Vietnamese, the dismal progress of the Paris negotiations, the American Senate, the news media, and the anti-war protesters.

The second option before him, Nixon went on to say, was to provide "massive military assistance to Cambodia itself." But he immediately ruled it out as impractical on the grounds that "massive amounts of military assistance could not be rapidly and effectively utilized by the small Cambodian Army against the immediate threat." Nixon then defined the third option, the one he was selecting: "Our third choice is to go to the heart of the trouble. That means cleaning out major North Vietnamese and Vietcong occupied territories – these sanctuaries which serve as bases for attacks on both Cambodia and America and South Vietnamese forces in South Vietnam." He said that, in cooperation with the armed forces of South Vietnam, attacks were being launched to clean out major enemy sanctuaries on the Cambodian-Vietnam border. "There is one area ... immediately above the Parrot's Beak, where I have concluded that a combined American and South Vietnamese operation is necessary. Tonight, American and South Vietnamese units will attack the headquarters for the entire Communist military operation in South Vietnam."[142]

Referring here to the elusive and mythical COSVN, Nixon created the impression that American troops were going to destroy the nerve centre of the entire communist force in Vietnam. And this was still another deception, for Nixon did not have the slightest idea whether COSVN really existed as a fully structured command. However, the president evidently felt that it was crucial to establish a specific target for the invasion in order to provide an easily understandable reason for the direct American involvement in the Fishhook, and he included the reference to COSVN – "the headquarters" – in his speech against the advice of his intelligence, military, and political experts, all of whom seriously doubted COSVN's very existence.

Having proclaimed the invasion's apparent objective, the president hastened to offer assurances: "This is not an invasion of Cambodia. The areas in which these attacks will be launched are completely occupied and controlled by North Vietnamese forces. Our purpose is not to occupy the areas. Once enemy forces are driven out of these sanctuaries and once their military supplies are destroyed, we will withdraw."[143]

For the balance of his speech, Nixon linked the invasion to the success of his program of withdrawing American forces from Vietnam. Yet Nixon could not resist playing the tough president addressing his nation as well as the enemy:

The answer of the enemy has been intransigence at the conference table, belligerence in Hanoi, massive military aggression in Laos and Cambodia and stepped up attacks in South Vietnam designed to increase American casualties. This attitude has become intolerable. We will not react to this threat to American lives merely by plaintive diplomatic protests. If we did, the credibility of the United States would be destroyed in every area of the world where only the power of the United States deters aggression.[144]

Nixon's feelings of frustration were as palpable as the deep-seated fear of being humiliated which he then articulated.

The action that I have announced tonight puts the leaders of North Vietnam on notice that we will be patient in working for peace; we will be conciliatory at the conference table, but we will not be humiliated. We will not be defeated. We will not allow American men by the thousands to be killed by an enemy from privileged sanctuaries ... But if the enemy response to our most conciliatory offers for peaceful negotiation continues to be to increase its attacks and humiliate and defeat us, we shall react accordingly.[145]

This was pure Nixon: a man who likened every challenge to American power as equivalent to an attack on his own fragile self, an effort to humiliate him personally. To defend himself against feelings of weakness and inadequacy, Nixon exploited the office of the presidency to nourish a grandiose and omnipotent self which, when threatened by humiliation, retaliated aggressively with all the power at its disposal.

Nixon justified the invasion as follows:

If, when the chips are down, the world's most powerful nation, the United States of America, acts like a pitiful, helpless giant, the forces of totalitarianism and anarchy will threaten free nations and free institutions throughout the world. It is not our power but our will and character that is being tested tonight ... If we fail to meet this challenge all other nations will be on notice that despite its overwhelming power the United States, when a real crisis comes, will be found wanting.[146]

For Richard Nixon, it was not only America's greatness that was being questioned, but his own grandiosity. The deeper meaning of Nixon's concern was for himself; the United States had become a narcissistic extension of himself, and he projected his own fears and weaknesses onto the body politic. Unless he took this action, he would be left feeling powerless and humiliated – the exact opposite of his idealized grandiose self. He yearned to be a Patton and resolved to act like his hero because any alternative was felt to be intolerable.

Nixon then went on to say that a Republican senator had said that the action he had taken meant that his party had lost all chance of winning the November elections and that the move against enemy sanctuaries would make him a one-term president: "No one is more aware than I am of the political consequences of the action I have taken ... [However] I know that a peace of humiliation for the United States would lead to a bigger war or surrender later ... I would rather be a one-term president and do what I believe is right than to be a two-term president at the cost of seeing America become a second-rate power and to see this nation accept the first defeat in its proud 190-year history."[147]

Nixon's message was clear: to lose Vietnam to the communists would be so humiliating that he would do whatever was necessary to avoid that possibility; he would even take actions that could risk a second term in office and contribute additional shame. In the emotional throes of his recent humiliating experiences, Nixon wanted revenge. Fear of future political embarrassment was not sufficient to stay his hand; he needed action now to bolster his plummeting self-esteem.

The implication of Nixon's remarks was that "the Cambodian crisis was not a *real* crisis. It was a test crisis."[148] At one level, this explanation was an expression of domino thinking; failure to deter anywhere, anytime, can only invite further probes by the enemy. But, at a deeper level, Cambodia was a test not only of America's will and character in facing a hostile world, but of Nixon's will and character in facing a hostile America[149] and his determination to use force against a minor and relatively unimportant military target in order to bolster his damaged sense of self worth. Acting "tough" would make him feel tough and impervious to his opponents both foreign and domestic.

The morning after the invasion, before its full impact on the United States was clear, Nixon drove with Kissinger across the Potomac for a briefing at the Pentagon. His remarks in the lobby about college anti-war protesters – "Bums, you know, blowing up campuses ... burning up the books" – were published and exacerbated the rage that was beginning to spread among students everywhere. Nixon's conduct during the briefing was even more alarming. The joint chiefs were there, as was the secretary of defense; they had assembled to inform the commander-in-chief of the progress of the operation. To their consternation, Nixon did not seem interested and cut the briefing short.[150]

For Nixon, the importance of the operation lay in his decision to order it and its expected role in replenishing and nourishing his self-esteem. Details that might intrude on his grandiose fantasies had to be suppressed. He began with an emotional harangue, using what one of those present called "locker-room language." He repeated over and over again that he was "going to clean up those sanctuaries" and he declared, "You have to electrify people with a bold decision. Bold decisions make history. Like Teddy Roosevelt charging up San Juan Hill – a small event but traumatic, and people took notice."[151] The unspoken wish was that his decision to invade Cambodia would have the same electrifying effect and cast him in a heroic mould.

General Westmoreland tried to warn Nixon that the sanctuaries could not really be cleaned up; within a month the monsoon season would make the area impassable. Nixon was unimpressed and threatened to withdraw resources from Europe if they were needed in Indochina. "Let's go blow the hell out of them," he shouted, while the joint chiefs, Laird, and Kissinger sat mute with embarrassment and concern.[152] Since he was frustrated by the elusiveness of his cherished triumph, Nixon's impulse was to retaliate aggressively.

On the heels of the invasion, a third of American colleges and universities closed or were disrupted as the rejuvenated Vietnam moratorium committee called for "immediate massive protests." The president reacted belligerently in both public and private. He assured his staff that the fact that few enemy troops had been found was not important; it was the infrastructure of the sanctuaries that he was after. "It takes ten months to build up this complex and we're tearing the living bejeesus out of it. Anything that walked is gone after that barrage and the B-52 raids." He abused members of Congress who criticized the invasion, declaring: "Don't worry about divisiveness. Having drawn the sword, don't take it out – stick it in hard … Hit 'em in the gut. No defensiveness."[153] It was Nixon the tough guy, standing firm and urging his loyal troops to redouble their efforts.

After a Reserve Officer Training Corps building was burned at Kent State University in Ohio, the national guard, ordered onto the campus the following day by Governor James Rhodes, shot fifteen students in a volley, four of them dead. The White House reaction to the killings was that they were predictable. So, too, was the response. Nearly 100,000 protesters converged on Washington. When Walter Hickel, secretary of the interior, warned Nixon (in a letter that was leaked to the press) that history showed that "youth in its protest must be heard," he was fired.

Finally, however, Nixon was forced to bend to the public mood and congressional opposition and announce concessions. He declared that United States troops would penetrate only twenty-one miles into Cambodia and would be withdrawn by 30 June. Later, he called the Cambodian invasion "the most successful operation of this long and difficult war" and in typical blame-avoidance fashion later stated that, had he bombed and mined North Vietnam as well, he could have "broken their backs."[154] By 1 July there were no more American troops left in Cambodia.

Nixon's use of Cambodia to satisfy his own narcissistic needs would have a powerful ripple effect. May 1st, 1970 marked the start of a full-fledged war that steadily ravaged Cambodia for five years. In the process, a new civil war erupted between the communist Khmer Rouge and its opponents, resulting over the next twenty years in the death of more than a million people in the "killing fields" of Cambodia. The human costs of Nixon's Cambodian policy were truly horrendous.

6 Dwight Eisenhower: The Healthy Narcissist

The Eisenhower administration's decision not to commit U.S. military forces to Indochina during the 1954 Dien Bien Phu crisis was the result of many factors; strategic, domestic, bureaucratic, cognitive, and personality variables all played a part. While some analysts focus on the pivotal impact of the president himself, especially his knowledge of military affairs and the politics of war,[1] the role of his particular personality in the making of the decisions on Dien Bien Phu has not been fully explored. In Dwight David Eisenhower, the United States had a president whose personality revealed a healthy narcissism that translated into appropriate rather than excessive or anxious self-regard.

The absence of a significant narcissistic component in Eisenhower's personality meant that his foreign-policy decisions were not unconsciously fashioned to satisfy deep-rooted narcissistic needs. He possessed a strong sense of self-esteem, the product of a pre-presidential life characterized by repeated successes. A genuinely well-liked human being whose company family and friends enjoyed, Eisenhower never experienced the sense of being unloved or excluded in the way that both Johnson and Nixon did. In contrast to both of his successors, his was a life relatively free of experiences of shame and humiliation. While such feelings were not unknown to Eisenhower, he was able to integrate them in ways that avoided the need to act them out at the policy level.

Dwight Eisenhower was born on 14 October 1890 to David and Ida Eisenhower. He was the third son, having been preceded by

Arthur in November 1886 and Edgar in January 1889. The family would continue to grow with the arrival of Roy in 1892, Paul (who died in infancy) in 1894, Earl in 1898, and Milton in 1899. As the third son in a family of six boys, Dwight always felt more comfortable with male companions.

Notwithstanding their sharply different personalities, his parents shared similar backgrounds and a common outlook on the world. Both families had emigrated from the Rhineland and were deeply religious members of a small Mennonite group known as the River Brethren. His father's family moved from Pennsylvania to Kansas when David Eisenhower (Dwight's father) was sixteen and the family prospered in the new settlement they helped establish. David grew into a quiet, serious young man who rarely smiled and, despite his father Jacob's example, expressed little interest in becoming a farmer. When David was twenty years old, Jacob reluctantly consented to finance his education at a small River Brethren school known as Lane University. At the beginning of his second year he met his bride, Ida Stover, the future president's mother.[2]

Ida Stover's ancestors had settled in Pennsylvania where they had joined the River Brethren to farm. Later, they moved south to Mount Sidney, Virginia, where Ida was born in 1862. Her parents died when she was just a child, and she went to live with relatives. Despite her early losses, she developed into an outgoing and cheerful young woman whose relationship with her brothers was very close. At the age of twenty-one she took the inheritance money left by her father and joined two of her brothers at a River Brethren colony in Kansas. In defiance of River Brethren tradition, which considered education improper for women, she subsequently bought an ebony piano and enrolled in Lane University to study music.[3] It was there that she met her future husband.

The wedding between David Jacob Eisenhower and Ida Stover took place in September 1885 and terminated university studies for both of them.[4] As a wedding present, David's father gave the new couple (as he did all his children) a 160-acre farm and $2,000 in cash. David, still not attracted to farming, mortgaged the land and, with a partner, opened a general store in Hope, Kansas. Two years later the business failed; the young couple lost everything and were left with few prospects, having depleted a sizeable inheritance. Ida believed that both the business partner and the lawyer David hired to settle the debts had cheated them, and she began to study legal books, hoping to recover some of their losses through the courts.

In the aftermath of his business failure, David left for Denison, Texas, where he found work on the railroad. Ida, who was pregnant with her second child, stayed with friends in Hope until she had given birth and then followed her husband. Soon after her arrival, she was again pregnant – a prospect that appears to have increased David's anxiety since he was already having problems supporting the family. Their third son, David Dwight, was born in the bedroom of their rented home in a working-class district. His mother soon reversed the names to avoid the confusion of having two Davids in the family.[5]

Ida was unhappy in Texas. Missing her friends and family in Kansas, she urged David to take a job offered by his brother-in-law, Chris Musser, at the Belle Springs Creamery (owned by the River Brethren) in Abilene.[6] David accepted and, before Dwight's first birthday, the family journeyed to Abilene, bringing with them their total savings of $24. The business failure had left its mark on David, and he took a long time to recover his self-confidence. He never again took a financial risk nor made any investments, save for acquiring a mortgage, and he retained a lifelong fear of debt which he tried, with imperfect results, to pass on to his sons.[7]

David's poor wages from his job at the creamery were barely adequate to provide for his growing family, and in Abilene they were considered "one of the poorest families in town."[8] Dwight and Edgar would occasionally take a wagon full of produce to the wealthier side of town to sell. Edgar later recalled resenting the way the more affluent customers treated him; "they made us feel like beggars," he said. Dwight, however, never acknowledged having such feelings.[9] After his rise to power, Eisenhower's repressed memories of his treatment at the hands of the rich and powerful would undergo a subtle reworking in his choice of a circle of wealthy friends who were at his beck-and-call for games of bridge and golf.

Despite their lack of material success or any other form of social prominence, the family remained self-sufficient and were respected around town.[10] Upon his return to Abilene after the Second World War, Dwight told the assembled crowd: "I have found out in later years we were very poor. But the glory of America is that we didn't know it then. All we knew was that our parents could say to us that opportunity was all about us. All we had to do was to reach out and take it."[11] Yet it is unlikely that Eisenhower was as oblivious to their poverty as he claimed. Lack of extra money often meant going to school in well-worn and unfashionable hand-me-downs – Dwight was the only boy in his fifth-grade picture to wear overalls. This often provoked taunting from class-mates to which Dwight would respond with his fists.[12] He soon gained a reputation as a "scrapper" who got into fights almost every day, often with boys slightly older and bigger than himself.[13] Eisenhower used his fights with older and bigger boys to restore his self-esteem and avenge his feelings of humiliation, unlike Lyndon Johnson who dealt with his early humiliations and tauntings by bragging about his imaginary achievements, or Richard Nixon who suffered in angry silence and then engaged in covertly aggressive behaviour.

As the third son, Dwight never experienced the intense attention usually afforded first children, nor did he remain the youngest for long; during his second year, Roy arrived, and his mother's attention was divided still further. Dwight grew to maturity with the ever-present knowledge that other members of the family were as important as he and that their needs would sometimes take precedence over his own.[14] Unlike both Richard Nixon and Lyndon Johnson, neither Dwight nor any of his brothers was ever singled out by their mother or their father with the responsibility of being the "someone" in the family who would avenge their humiliating circumstances by making his mark in the world.[15]

In fact, it was only very gradually that Dwight emerged from his close-knit family to assume a personality of his own, and even then it was not a striking one. Of his first seven years, no significant anecdotes survive. He was one of six sons, neither the oldest nor the youngest, and he was never encouraged to think of himself as different or special – a feature that so often occurs in the making of the narcissistic character. He was, in all respects, "normal." He cried neither more nor less than most infants. He learned to walk and talk at a normal age. There was nothing obviously precocious about him.[16] None of his biographers dispute the fact that his was an "essentially commonplace existence."[17]

If precocity was neither encouraged nor stimulated in Eisenhower's home, something else would assume great importance – a mature and confident approach to life. In the context of his consistent and predictable environment, Dwight developed an inner sense of security that prepared him to face the challenges of the outside world with confidence. In his memoirs Eisenhower recounts his earliest memory, which concerned an event that took place a few months before his fifth birthday. While visiting his aunt's farm, the young Eisenhower had several encounters with an aggressive gander that repeatedly chased him back to the house in tears. He obtained a "weapon" from his uncle, a sawed-off broom, and, after successfully confronting the gander, proudly became "the boss of the back yard." He concluded that the incident "turned out to be a rather good lesson for me because I quickly learned never to negotiate with an adversary except from a position of strength."[18] His description of this incident suggests that the young Dwight felt frightened and was unable to get his aunt or uncle to resolve the problem for him; however, since he was determined not to give up and was forced to act on his own, his sense of mastery and ego strength were enhanced. The story is also likely to have been a screen memory – a condensation of other situations in which he felt alone and frightened but was able to overcome his fears.

From his earliest years, Dwight learned from his mother that membership in the family carried certain responsibilities. All the boys had to help with the housework, gardening, and care for the animals. Dwight was apparently the hardest to rouse in the morning.[19] Ida assigned the boys chores on a rotating basis so that "each son learned all the responsibilities of running the house and none felt discriminated against." Dwight later argued that the fact that he and his brothers felt needed around the house enhanced their character development.[20] It would also have helped to develop feelings of self-esteem based on a sense of mastery.

When Dwight was in his early teens, Milton fell ill with scarlet fever; their mother stayed in the quarantined room with him for six weeks.[21] He did not appear to resent her absence and later recalled that he had taken over the cooking chores – an experience that made him feel "very important indeed. Although we didn't use the word then, cooking gave me a creative feeling."[22] In later years, Eisenhower would take enormous pride in his culinary abilities. In a situation where Dwight might have been expected to experience jealousy and anxiety over the separation from his mother, he was able – unlike Richard Nixon – to sublimate those feelings into cooking.

Dwight was deeply attached to his mother. He later recalled that his mother was "by far the greatest personal influence in our lives."[23] A friend noted that he always talked more about his mother when discussing his parents.[24] In his memoirs, Eisenhower paid her a glowing tribute: "I may exhibit a son's prejudice. But my feeling reflects the affection and respect of all who knew her. Her serenity, her open smile, her gentleness with all and her tolerance of their ways, despite an inflexible loyalty to her religious convictions and her own strict pattern of personal conduct, made even a brief visit with Ida Eisenhower memorable for a stranger. And for her sons, privileged to spend a boyhood in her company, the memories are indelible."[25]

Eisenhower's great affection for his mother was not a function of his having been singled out for special treatment. Ida consciously refused to make any sort of distinction between her boys, and she never once labelled any of them her "favourite." Once, when asked by a reporter if she was proud of her famous son (meaning Dwight), she replied, "Which one?"[26] Like Ida, David did not draw sharp distinctions between his sons and never overtly had a "favourite." Earl recalled that in conversations with his father, after all the boys had left home, David talked proudly about the accomplishments of each of his sons in equal measure.[27] As Dwight rose to prominence in the military and political worlds, his status as just another brother did not change. Often the boys would adopt their mother's line – "Which one?" – when asked about their "brother."[28] Hence, a sense of entitlement coupled with the feeling of being "special" that so often marks the narcissistic personality seems to have been conspicuously absent in Dwight Eisenhower.

The open warmth and affection that characterized Dwight's relationship with his mother was not as evident in his contacts with his father. David's work kept him away for twelve hours a day, six and sometimes seven days a week, and so he saw much less of Dwight and the other boys than did his wife. When he was at home, his quiet and serious nature (as well as fatigue from work) kept him removed and distant.[29] At the same time, he set clearly defined limits on acceptable behaviour. Drinking, smoking, and card-playing were forbidden until a son was married; afterwards, he was free to engage in any of these practices, even in his parents' home.[30] One of Dwight's principal acts of rebellion at West Point would be to smoke – against all regulations. He would also drink on occasion and he loved poker. This suggests an acting out of his inability to challenge his father openly.

If David was generally withdrawn and distant, at times his fiery temper would explode when he sensed disobedience. Ida would administer occasional spankings for minor infractions of rules or neglect of chores, but more serious matters were referred to

David, who, upon his return from work, would apply a maple switch to the offender. Dwight recalled an incident that occurred in his twelfth year, when his father discovered that Edgar had been secretly skipping school to work part-time. David arrived home from work unannounced, found the boys in the barn, and, without argument, began to whip Edgar with a piece of harness. When Dwight screamed at him to stop and attempted to restrain his arm, his father threatened him with the same treatment if he persisted. Dwight protested, "I don't think anyone ought to be whipped like that, not even a dog."

Although he admitted to having viewed Edgar's beating as "almost tragic" at the time, he was quick to defend his father as acting in their best interest: "Undoubtedly fear that his boy would seriously damage all the years of life ahead [by leaving school] provoked my father to a violent display of temper and temporary damage."[31]

When frustrated, Dwight could exhibit his father's volatile temper. Ida told her grandson, John, that Dwight was her most difficult child because of his temper and independent spirit – both of which were evident at an early age.[32] When he was ten years old, he was refused permission to go out for Halloween with his two older brothers. Dwight flew into a rage so blind that he later claimed to have no exact memory of what followed, until his father shook him back to consciousness. He had been pounding his fists into a tree and they were streaming with blood. His father spanked him and sent him to his room, where his mother found him about an hour later still sobbing and feeling hurt and abused. He recalled her soft voice as she bandaged his hands. Talking about temper and controlling it, she told him, "He that conquereth his own soul is greater than he who taketh a city."[33] She added that, in this regard, he "was the one who had most to learn." Eisenhower remembered the conversation as "one of the most valuable moments of my life."[34] In disavowing any lingering animosity towards his father and focusing on his positive relationship with his mother, he demonstrated the way in which the ego defends itself from rage and pain.

Eisenhower also recalled that his parents taught the boys never to "hate" anyone, even someone who had treated you badly or made you angry.[35] On one occasion, when Dwight was twelve, he flared up in sudden violent anger against his brother Arthur over some trifling incident. A brick was lying at his feet and, before he had regained control of himself, he seized the brick and flung it with all his might at the head of his oldest brother. Fortunately, Arthur managed to duck in time: Dwight had fully intended to hit him.[36] His temper continued to flash menacingly on occasion throughout his youth, but the emotion always seemed to be fleeting. There is no evidence of Dwight ever carrying a grudge or a vendetta; when he was upset by something or someone the anger was immediate – and then it quickly gave way to his regular balmy humour.

Dwight never attempted to deny his capacity for anger and throughout his adult life continued a very conscious battle to control his temper. When hurt or displeased by someone, he would dismiss the offender from his mind, and, if possible, sever all contact with the individual. In later years, to expunge his anger, he would write the name of a person he was upset with on a piece of paper and drop it into his bottom desk drawer. "The drawer became over the years a sort of private wastebasket for crumpled-up spite and discarded personalities. Besides, it seemed to be effective and helped me avoid harbouring useless black feelings."[37] If it was necessary to work on a regular basis with that person, he would conceal his feelings, and he studiously avoided public criticism.[38] He later told an interviewer: "I learned a long time ago, that … anybody that aspired to a position of leadership of any kind … must learn to control his temper."[39]

But controlling his temper did not mean that he could eliminate it. As president, Eisenhower informed his staff: "Once in a while you people have just got to be my safety-valve. So I'll get you in here and I will let go, but this is for you and your knowledge, and your knowledge only."[40] One White House aide, after witnessing such an explosion, commented: "My God, how could you compute the amount of adrenalin expended in those thirty seconds? I don't know why long since he hasn't had a killer of a heart attack."[41]

Apart from angry outbursts at his children's misdemeanours, David took scarcely any interest in the daily problems and accomplishments of his sons' school work or social lives, and he never pushed Dwight, or any of his other sons, to reach for extraordinary achievements.[42] Dwight recalled his father showing no emotion at the news of his West Point appointment. He thought his father was possibly a little proud, but he could not be sure because of his father's reserved nature.[43] Later Dwight and his brothers agreed that their father kept silent regarding his sons' career aspirations because he had resented his own father's attempts to pressure him into being a farmer.

In his memoirs, Dwight described his father as a "modest, studious, and intelligent person."[44] On the day of his funeral, Dwight wrote in his diary: "He was a just man, well liked, well educated, a thinker. He was undemonstrative, quiet, modest, and of exemplary habits – he never used alcohol or tobacco. He was an uncomplaining person in the face of adversity, and such plaudits as were accorded him did not inflate his ego."[45] The picture that emerges from Eisenhower's description of David is of a typical father of this era – proud, stoic, and undemonstrative, not open, warm, and affectionate.

As a youngster in Abilene, Ike's most significant challenge occurred shortly after he changed schools to enter the seventh grade. He now had to traverse the more prosperous north side of the railroad tracks and found himself in the middle of long-established hostilities. Dwight was picked out, through mob consensus, to represent the south side in the traditional north-south brawl that marked every new class. Soon he and his mob-picked rival, Wesley Merifield, were pushed together. As Dwight recalled, "neither of us had the courage to say 'I won't fight.'"

Dwight, the slightly smaller of the two, took a bad beating early on, but he refused to give up and soon was making up ground.[46] After more than an hour of stubborn combat, both boys were battered and exhausted. As Eisenhower recalled, "Wes said, 'I can't lick you.' I said the same thing. And that was that." The fight, one of the longest on record for these two groups of boys, ended in a draw.[47] His older brother Arthur later observed, "That was Father in Dwight. Beaten to a pulp. But never licked." That night, Dwight remained silent while Ida soothed his swollen face with warm towels. Edgar howled for revenge and demanded to be told who had done it. Dwight's only comment was: "It was a fair fight."[48] Such a fight established his credentials among his older siblings and his class-mates as a gutsy kid who could not be easily intimidated.

Eisenhower's developing sense of self-worth was also enhanced by his parents' overall agreement in their management of the children. In sharp contrast to both the Nixon and Johnson families, Ike described how his parents "maintained a genuine partnership in raising their six sons. Father was the breadwinner, Supreme Court, and Lord High Executioner. Mother was tutor and manager of our household. Their partnership was ideal … I never heard a cross word pass between them. Never did I hear them disagree on a value judgment in family, social, or economic affairs."[49] The other boys also claimed never to have heard their father and mother so much as raise their voices at each other or disagree. Such uniformity of parental views probably owed a great deal to their similar backgrounds and outlooks on the world as well as to the deference Ida showed David. Ida Eisenhower respected her husband and his values and the marriage was a happy one; she had no need to treat Dwight or any of her other sons as special – she did not see them as destined to recompense her for her unhappy life with her husband. This was in marked contrast to the way in which both Rebekah Johnson and Hannah Nixon treated Lyndon and Richard respectively.

Apart from his prowess with his fists, Dwight's life at school as a youngster was unremarkable. He seems to have achieved average marks with an average effort. One school-mate recalled: "In his school work, Dwight was not outstanding. He made about average marks in grade school, and slightly better than average in high school with the exception of history and mathematics." In these two classes he excelled.[50] His high school football coach described him as "just another average chap."[51]

What did distinguish Eisenhower from some of his class-mates, however, was his passion for knowledge. It was not so much ideas that stimulated him as a hunger for concrete information. Vagueness seems to have exasperated him.[52] Not surprisingly, Dwight's favourite subjects were plane geometry and history, both replete with either precision or facts. He performed so well in history class that his teacher gave him extra assignments to keep him from getting bored.[53] One of his young teachers was often ill-prepared in his subject, and Dwight seemed to take a cruel delight in correcting him in class when he committed errors or lacked information.[54]

Sports were the ruling passion of Dwight's life at this time,[55] and he demonstrated the depth of his attachment when he sustained a slight injury to his leg which developed into a serious infection. It was diagnosed as "blood poisoning." As the disease progressed, and Dwight succumbed to frequent losses of consciousness, the doctors recommended amputation. Dwight, whose lucidity was sporadic, was horrified at the prospect. He enlisted Edgar to prevent the amputation should he not remain conscious, telling him: "I'd rather be dead than crippled, and not be able to play ball." His parents, distrustful of surgery anyway, respected his decision, and, after a few tense weeks, the disease stopped its advance. The illness kept him away from school so long, however, that he had to repeat the year.[56]

Dwight's south-side origins kept him from joining the fraternity, the Bums of Lawsy Lou, which was made up mostly of more wealthy north-side students. But his accomplishments as an athlete and his sunny disposition helped make up for what he lacked in social standing and Ike received invitations to some of the fraternity's parties and picnics.[57] He finished high school (not a common occurrence for males in that era) by working part-time and during the summer to support his education.[58] One of his high school teachers recalled that he was "good-natured and popular with his classmates, a good student but no prodigy."[59]

After graduating from high school in May 1909, Eisenhower spent more than a year working at a creamery to help support Edgar on his way to university.[60] Although Ike seemed a little aimless during this period, he claimed that he was "determined to go to college but ... [had] only a sketchy notion of how this might be done."[61]

It was during his second year out of high school that Everett "Swede" Hazlett convinced Eisenhower to try with him for an appointment to Annapolis Naval Academy.[62] The two had not known each other well before this time, having attended different high schools, but Swede later wrote that "I liked him most for his sterling qualities – he was calm, frank, laconic and sensible, and not in the least affected by being the school hero ... He had qualities of leadership of the best sort, combined with the most likeable human traits – candour, honesty, horse-sense and a keen sense of humor."[63]

Eisenhower wrote the competitive examination for both Annapolis (scoring first among those who competed) and West Point (scoring second). Because of an age restriction, he was barred from attending Annapolis, but he did win the appointment to West Point after the leading candidate failed the physical.[64] Hazlett was disappointed that they could not attend Annapolis together, and he urged Eisenhower to lie about his age since no proof was required. Dwight decided, however, that he would not "look a gift horse in the mouth." He accepted the West Point appointment and began his studies there in June 1911.[65]

Amid the harsh realities of cadet life, Eisenhower's first battle was with his temper; he recalled that he strengthened himself with the reminder: "Where else could you get a college education without cost?"[66] When he became a "yearling" – a member of the next to lowest class – he participated only sporadically in hazing the new freshmen or, as they were known, "plebes." One day, when a plebe accidentally ran into him, he was particularly hard on the young cadet and ended up insulting him. Afterwards he regretted the incident. He told his room-mate that night that never again would he "crawl" (correct harshly) another plebe, and he never did.[67]

Surrounded by many plebes of upper- and upper-middle class origins, Eisenhower reverted to his familiar "boy from the wrong side of the tracks" role, but this time it was with a much more experienced and talented group of contemporaries.[68] He was impatient with snobbish or pretentious cadets, and he made no excuses about his humble origins. This attitude, and his winning personality, soon turned him into an unofficial leader in the cadets' activities during their limited free time.[69]

Eisenhower also gained their respect for his athletic prowess. He later acknowledged: "It would be difficult to overemphasize the importance that I attached to participation in sports."[70] In his first year, he narrowly missed making the varsity squad in football and baseball. He worked hard at both over the season and earnestly applied the coach's suggestions. In his second year, Eisenhower played consistently on the varsity football team and seemed to have two very bright seasons ahead of him. However, near the end of the year, he sustained a minor injury to his knee, and after a short stay in hospital he was released with instructions to take it easy.

A few days later, during a riding drill, an instructor berated him for holding back in a dismount exercise. Eisenhower, ashamed and angered by the criticism, ignored the whispered advice of friends who urged him to explain his physical condition. "I've got to do it," he told his room-mate, "he as good as called me a liar."[71] He pushed ahead with the exercise, and soon the knee buckled under him – badly damaged.[72]

After the injury, which ended his football career, Dwight was "despondent and several times had to be prevented from resigning [from the military] by the persuasive efforts of classmates. Life seemed to have little meaning; a need to excel was almost gone."[73] He lost motivation for his studies, dropping from fifty-seventh in a class of 212 in his first year to eighty-first in a class of 177 the year he hurt his knee.[74]

During this period, Eisenhower wrote to his Abilene friend Rudy Norman: "The fellows that used to call me 'Sunny Jim' call me 'Gloomy Face' now ... I sure hate to be so helpless and worthless."[75] The injury was as much a narcissistic wound as a physical one. Dwight's self-esteem, which was closely bound up with his athleticism, had been seriously undermined. His response to the perceived humiliation was not to lash out against the instructor but to think of withdrawing – a sign of his depleted self-esteem and attendant depression.

Eisenhower began to smoke, in violation of regulations. This behaviour added demerits to what had already become his regular practice of flaunting academy regulations; he rarely kept his room or his dress as neat as required and was frequently late.[76] This was his way of thumbing his nose at authority – and all the surrogate fathers who thought they knew best. At the same time, he clearly identified with many of their values. When he was the duty officer, a number of his infractions were self-reported; for all his laxness in discipline, he took the honour code very seriously.[77]

Eisenhower soon found an outlet that restored his self-esteem. Coaching football tapped his energy and competitiveness and developed his organizational skills, concentration, willingness to work hard, and, most important, ability to lead a team.[78] Those lessons would stay with him throughout his life. "I believe that football, perhaps more than any other sport, tends to instill in men the feeling that victory comes through hard – almost slavish – work, team play, self-confidence, and an enthusiasm that amounts to dedication."[79]

Eisenhower later claimed to have identified strongly with the West Point tradition from the very beginning. In his memoirs, he wrote that at the end of his first day at West Point, when he took the oath that would make him a cadet, the country and its flag took on a new meaning: "From here on it would be the nation I would be serving, not myself."[80] He was proud of his new role and at the end of his second year he wore his uniform around town.[81]

At West Point, Eisenhower was in an even more isolated and conservative atmosphere than he had been in Abilene, and the military's prejudices and assumptions were reflected in his outlook: he valued the group over the individual, respected organization, had disdain for commercial pursuits and contempt for politics and politicians, and, most important, was strongly committed to duty and the ideal of disinterested public service.[82] These themes would reappear repeatedly throughout Eisenhower's career, prompting one observer to label him "a sucker for duty."[83] Much of this fit well with what he had learned from his parents and his sports training. After he graduated from West Point in June 1915, Eisenhower's commitment to these ideals, and to the military as a profession, would continue to grow.

Eisenhower met his wife-to-be, Mamie Geneva Doud, at San Antonio in October 1915, during his first assignment after graduation. Mamie was the second of four daughters from a comfortable and close-knit family. Brought up by a strict but caring father, and a mother who was devoted to her, she became "a tactful, orderly child, shy about being the beauty of the family." Though she was popular and often planned dates weeks in advance, she had never before been involved in a serious romance.[84]

The day after they met, Ike called the Doud home every fifteen minutes until Mamie got home. When she finally did, he was only able to arrange a date for four weeks ahead since Mamie already had dates for all the other nights. For the next three weeks, Ike called two or three times a day urging Mamie to rearrange her schedule. She refused his advances but did drop the hint that she was usually home by five and that he should drop by some time. He did – often.[85] Mamie recalled: "I had a few other beaux, and I wasn't about to give them up immediately. But Ike was never easily discouraged. He simply out-persisted the competition."[86] In that sense, his behaviour was no different than that of his successors, Lyndon Johnson and Richard Nixon, both of whom pursued their wives-to-be ardently and refused to take no for an answer.

On the income of a debt-ridden second lieutenant, the courtship between Dwight and Mamie remained simple.[87] Eisenhower proposed on Valentine's Day, 1916, almost three months after they had met.[88] When he approached Mamie's father to ask for his daughter's hand, Mr Doud expressed his approval of the engagement but asked that they wait for some time since he had not expected his daughter to marry so young. Out of respect for his wishes, the wedding was planned for November, when Mamie would be twenty.[89]

Soon after these plans were made, Eisenhower received a positive response to a request he had submitted, months earlier, for transfer to the aviation section – a move that promised excitement and a

50 per cent increase in pay. When he recounted his good fortune to his fiancée's family, Mr Doud told him that if he was so irresponsible as to enter the "flying business" – something the Douds considered a dangerous experiment – just as he was about to be married, he and his wife would have to revoke their consent. Eisenhower recalled: "That night I left in a glum frame of mind. For the next couple of days, I pondered the matter in misery."

Finally, he told the Douds that he was willing to give up aviation. He later said that this experience "brought me face to face with myself and caused me to make a decision that I have never recanted nor regretted. The decision was to perform every duty given me in the Army to the best of my ability and to do the best I could to make a creditable record, no matter what the nature of the duty."[90] Instead of harbouring resentment against his future father-in-law for the sacrifice he had been forced to make, Eisenhower suppressed his anger and psychologically transformed his decision from a painful obligation into an act of personal responsibility. In the process, his father-in-law's fiat had become an army order.

Mamie and Dwight's wedding took place on 1 July 1916, in the Douds' spacious Denver home. It was earlier than originally planned because of the increasing likelihood that the United States would enter the war and Dwight would be sent overseas. After a brief honeymoon, Mamie moved into her husband's three-room military quarters at Fort Sam, San Antonio.

About a month later, Dwight came home one day and began silently packing. Mamie, realizing what this meant, protested: "You're not going to leave me this soon after our wedding day, are you?" He hugged her, saying: "Mamie, there is something you must understand. My country comes first and always will; you come second."[91] Concerned for his new wife's safety when she was alone, he bought her a .45 pistol and showed her how to use it.[92]

The Great War brought further separations – Eisenhower was first posted to Camp Wilson, some twenty miles from San Antonio – and personal life continued to take a back seat to professional responsibilities. But worse was to come. In late 1917 Eisenhower was forced to leave his wife for reassignment to Fort Ogelthorpe, Georgia, to instruct officer candidates. The move took place just four days before Mamie gave birth to their first son, Doud Dwight, (known as "Icky") on 24 September. After the birth, the couple remained separated for quite some time. Ike returned and met his son only after Mamie collapsed in a near-fatal coma just before

Christmas.[93] With a later assignment to a new camp at Fort Leavenworth, Kansas, which was closer to his family, Eisenhower was able to spend a few evenings at home.[94] From there he moved to Camp Meade, Maryland, and was afterwards given command of Camp Colt near Gettysburg, Pennsylvania, where Mamie and their son joined him.

The first three years of marriage, then, were characterized mostly by separations and Dwight and Mamie did not establish any normal pattern of home life until the summer of 1920, when Eisenhower was transferred back to Camp Meade. That base had been converted into the army tank-training school, and Dwight and Mamie's time there gave them the opportunity for what Eisenhower called "a fuller family life than we'd ever known."[95] Their son, Icky – three years old at the time – was his parents' pride and joy and was popular with the tank corps and football team.[96]

Just before the end of that year, Icky died of scarlet fever, an event that Eisenhower later called "a tragedy from which we never recovered." Ike was filled with guilt for his previous absences: "I blamed myself because I had often taken his presence for granted, even though I was proud of him and of all the evidence that he was developing as a fine, normal boy ... This was the greatest disappointment and disaster in my life, the one I have never been able to forget completely."[97] Although the birth of their second son, John, a year and a half later "did much to fill the gap,"[98] Mamie recalled that "when Icky died ... for a long time it was as if a shining light had gone out in Ike's life. Throughout all the years that followed, the memory of those bleak days was a deep inner pain that never seemed to diminish much."[99]

For the next half century, Ike sent flowers to Mamie every year on Icky's birthday. They arranged to have the boy's remains laid beside them in their own burial plot.[100] Although Mamie repressed her grief, and was not even able to cry for their lost son, Ike "gave vent openly to his devastation ... to such a degree that Mamie feared for his health."[101] Given Mamie's inhibited mourning style, her husband's demonstrative expression of his grief could have seemed excessive. But an ability to grieve openly and to mourn fully are important indicators of a stable, well-integrated ego.

As a family man, Eisenhower was, in some ways, much like his own father. Mamie observed that "Ike was not a demonstrative man with any of his family – not even with me. Often when he came home from work, his greeting would be merely an affectionate pinch or a pat on the back. It was enough. He didn't have to tell me a dozen times a day how he felt about me."[102]

When the United States entered the First World War, Eisenhower still had less than two years of commissioned service. Nevertheless, he was put in charge of various training camps – Fort Oglethorpe, Fort Leavenworth, Camp Meade, and Camp Colt – to prepare new recruits. He performed his job with such diligence and skill that he acquired a reputation as a young officer "with special qualities as an instructor." What he really desired, however, was an assignment overseas. He applied for such duty directly on several occasions, only to be repeatedly refused. After one such request, he received a reprimand in the form of a letter from the adjutant-general which informed him that the War Department did not approve of his applications for special duty and that his role was to obey orders. "This made me furious and when the Colonel [who read him the letter] proceeded to add several reprimands of his own, I reverted to the old, red-necked cadet." He informed the colonel that, with all due respect, it was not his place to be adding to the War Department's reprimand since he had not been involved in the "offence." Surprisingly, the colonel agreed.[103]

Despite such a show of arrogance to his superiors, Eisenhower seems to have been concerned with his reputation as an officer. At one point early in the training, Eisenhower failed to follow a minor detail of procedure, and he ended up with a bill of $22.04 for missing equipment. He later recalled: "More humiliating than costly, in a way, I felt that in that nebulous region called the War Department, I had been found wanting."[104] Eisenhower's sensitivity to feelings of humiliation led him to redouble his efforts to correct his mistakes rather than exact revenge from his tormentors.

With the end of each training assignment, he would receive another, while the men he trained headed overseas. He described the early months of 1918 as a "dead end" period. "I could see myself, years later, silent at class reunions while others reminisced of battle. For a man who likes to talk as much as I, that would have been intolerable punishment. It looked to me as if anyone who was denied the opportunity to fight might as well get out of the Army at the end of the war."[105] Yet this lack of enthusiasm was kept under wraps. A junior officer, serving under Eisenhower in 1918, described him as "one of the most efficient and best Army officers in the country … He knows his job, is enthusiastic, can tell us what he wants us to do and is pretty human, though wickedly harsh and abrupt."[106]

The former rule-breaker became a strict disciplinarian, no doubt the result of an identification with his superiors. When he received orders to train a tank battalion to take overseas, he was elated. He laboured over their training and the details of departure. His efficiency impressed his superiors with his organizational abilities and won him the task of training the next group of recruits. Denied an overseas assignment once again, Eisenhower reported: "My mood was black." Yet he carried out his new assignment with the tank corps with his usual rigorousness, claiming that here he "really began to learn about responsibility."[107] It was an important position to give to a captain only twenty-seven years of age, but he was not happy to be there.[108]

Finally, Eisenhower received orders to go overseas, with a departure date scheduled for November 1918. Then, he was offered a promotion if he stayed in the United States, to which he replied that he was willing to take a reduction in rank if his present rank stood in the way of him being sent overseas. Just as he was to depart, the imminent German defeat put an end to all troop transfers. When he was informed by the ship's captain that they would not be sailing, Eisenhower's temper erupted.[109] His anger was mingled with disappointment and resentment since, as a professional soldier, he did not expect to see another such war in his lifetime and so would have no war stories for his son.[110] He briefly considered leaving the army to try his luck in civilian life.[111] Yet, in the eyes of others, Eisenhower's war years had been a success, and he later received the Distinguished Service Cross for his training work.[112]

After the war, Eisenhower returned to his permanent rank of a major – where he would remain for sixteen years. It is said that "he made almost no decisions between his twenty-eighth and fifty-first birthdays, except to stay in the minuscule Army and do his best."[113] During the inter-war period, Eisenhower served under some of the most domineering generals in the army – George Patton, Fox Conner, John J. Pershing, Douglas MacArthur, and George C. Marshall.[114] Experience with such forceful superiors did much to temper his youthful spirit of independence with skills of tact and compromise.[115]

Eisenhower continued working with tanks and became a true enthusiast of the new weapon. In 1920 he summarized his conclusions

– which were two decades ahead of current military doctrine – in the *Infantry Journal*. For his rare show of creative thinking, he was called before the chief of infantry and "told that my ideas were not only wrong but dangerous and that henceforth I would keep them to myself. Particularly, I was not to publish anything incompatible with solid infantry doctrine. If I did, I would be hauled before a court-martial."[116]

After the rejection of his tank ideas and Icky's death (which occurred around the same time), Eisenhower's spirits were somewhat restored by a tour of duty in Panama, from early 1922 to September 1924, which he described as "one of the most interesting and constructive [periods] of my life. The main reason was the presence of one man, General Fox Conner."[117] Conner inspired Eisenhower to read serious military literature and to seek new challenges in his profession, and Eisenhower took up the extra curricular study with vigour – much to the astonishment of many of his contemporaries, who were languishing in the lull of a peace-time army.[118] Eisenhower called his three years with Conner "a sort of graduate school in military affairs and the humanities ... In a lifetime of association with great and good men, he is the one more or less invisible figure to whom I owe an incalculable debt."[119]

In August 1925, shortly after leaving the Canal Zone, Fox Conner pulled some strings to get Eisenhower into the command and general staff school at Fort Leavenworth. Eisenhower was ecstatic.[120] However, he worried because he was going to Leavenworth without the usual preparatory-school training that most other participants had received. Leavenworth had a reputation for its pressure – many students suffered nervous breakdowns and suicides occurred on occasion – and Eisenhower wanted to be prepared. Conner assured him that his three years in Panama had been more than enough preparation, but Eisenhower still studied sample problems in his free time. At the school he established a study routine with one other student – shunning the traditional study-group approach – and found the pressure "exhilarating." He graduated first in his class of 275 officers. (His study partner finished second.[121])

In the summer of 1926 the Eisenhower family held a reunion that brought the six boys together for the first time since Arthur had left home; Dwight found all his brothers to be doing better financially and with brighter prospects than him. But he displayed no envy; he had travelled more than all of them put together and had had more schooling. As well, his career had presented him with challenging problems and brought him into contact with interesting people.[122]

After Leavenworth, he was briefly assigned to General Pershing's staff to write a guidebook to the battle sites of the First World War. The result won him the admiration of Pershing, who reported that he had shown "unusual intelligence and constant devotion to duty."[123] Having completed the guidebook, Dwight was chosen to attend the Army War College in Washington, a "gentlemen's graduate school" for officers. There, he studied problems in national policy and objectives, including political, budgetary, interservice, and foreign affairs issues. He also initiated and revived many of the friendships that were to be useful in his later career and that helped him advance through the informal peer-rating process.[124] Upon graduating from the college on 30 June 1928, again at the head of his class,[125] Eisenhower was asked to return to the Battlefield Monuments Commission to revise his booklet. As this meant touring the battlefields of France, he accepted with alacrity and took Mamie with him.[126]

When his stint with the Monuments Commission was completed, Eisenhower decided to stay in Washington to assume the post of assistant secretary of war, an opportunity that gave him insight into the workings of Washington. He remained in Washington for his next position, serving as an aide to General Douglas MacArthur with "duties [that] were beginning to verge on the political, even to the edge of partisan politics."[127] In the early 1930s MacArthur wrote a fitness report on Eisenhower: "This is the best officer in the Army. When the next war comes, he should go right to the top."[128]

Despite the good impression he was making, Eisenhower seemed to be less enthralled with his career when he and three of his brothers spent some time together during the winter of 1934. He had not had a promotion in a decade and was not due for one for a long time. He seriously contemplated leaving the army; after the work on the guidebook and writing speeches for MacArthur, he had been offered a well-paying job as military editor for a newspaper. Eisenhower also confided his disappointment to Swede Hazlett in 1935.[129] Ultimately, he decided to stay with the army, probably because that was the line of work for which he felt best suited.

Politics continued to play a major role in Eisenhower's assignments; his next tour of duty was with MacArthur to prepare the Philippines militarily for independence. Eisenhower had preferred to return to service with the troops, which he admitted could have been "simply a preference for the known over the unknown,"[130] but he complied when MacArthur made the request an order. In the Philippines, Eisenhower began to acquire a reputation for diplomacy, aided by the fact that he did not manifest any trace of the racism displayed by some Americans. He conferred with President Manuel Quezon of the Philippines regularly and became one of his confidants.[131]

When Britain declared war on Germany, Eisenhower knew that the United States could not stay out of the conflict for long. He immediately requested a transfer back to the United States – despite the protests of MacArthur. President Quezon offered to let him write his own contract if he remained. Eisenhower replied: "Mr. President, your offer is flattering. But no amount of money can make me change my mind. My entire life has been given to this one thing, my country and my profession. I want to be there if what I fear is going to come about actually happens."[132] Before he left the Philippines, Eisenhower was offered a $60,000-a-year job seeking havens for Jewish refugees from Nazi Germany. He was tempted, but "by this time, I had become so committed to my profession that I declined."[133]

Eisenhower was then stationed at Fort Lewis, Washington, on active duty with troops. "No better assignment than mine could have been asked by a professional soldier at a time when much of the world was already at war and the eventual involvement of the United States daily became more probable."[134] He was in robust health; according to some, he looked ten years younger than he was and "exuded self-confidence."[135] He had been officially informed that he was ranked at or near the top among field officers, and he knew many commanders had sought him for their staffs.[136] He was popular with the men serving under him, and he worked hard for them.[137] His experience, although strenuous and exhausting, "fortified my conviction that I belonged with troops; with them I was always happy."[138]

Eisenhower worried, however, that he would be denied the command position he so desperately wanted because of his rank and his reputation as a superb staff officer.[139] He received a telegram from his study partner at Leavenworth which read, "I need you in War Plans Division. Do you seriously object to being detailed on the War Dept General Staff and assigned here?" The prospect of being stuck at a desk job, once again, for the duration of the war caused Eisenhower to have an attack of shingles, a skin disease often associated with extreme nervousness or anxiety. (It was the only attack in his lifetime.)[140] Caught between the demands of friendship and his own career plans, Eisenhower dealt with his conflict by somatizing – developing physical symptoms for his emotional anxieties.

Eisenhower laboured over his reply to his old friend: "Your telegram … sent me into a tailspin." He told him that he was flattered by his use of the word "need" in reference to himself, but that he preferred to stay with the troops. As a result of his experience of the previous few months, he had "completely reassured myself that I am capable of handling command jobs" and just needed a chance to prove it to his superiors.[141] Eisenhower recalled that he "did not want to be considered as a slacker or a cry baby, but I honestly felt that after all my years of almost constant staff assignments, I really deserved troop duty."[142] Once again, we have evidence of Eisenhower's healthy narcissism – an accurate appreciation of his talents and abilities and a determination where possible not to see them ignored. The request was withdrawn, but Eisenhower seemed destined to remain a staff officer.

With the rapid expansion of the armed forces, Eisenhower became chief-of-staff of the Third Army in October 1940. In this position he began to gain public recognition, receiving much credit for the brilliant planning which was instrumental in the victory of the Third Army in its "invasion" of Louisiana during the largest peacetime military manoeuvres in American history.[143] The newsmen who covered his theatre were attracted to Eisenhower by his modesty, openness, and honesty. Rather than attempt to hide deficiencies or problems, he frankly admitted them and expressed the hope that the reporters would alert the rest of the country to what was needed.[144] He also established good relations between himself and his troops by allowing anyone to approach him with a comment or complaint. He wrote to a friend: "Handling an Army staff that has had very little chance to whip itself together has its tough points – in spite of which I am having a good time. But I would like a command of my own."[145]

After the Japanese attack on Pearl Harbor on 7 December 1941, General Marshall called Eisenhower to the War Department in Washington. Eisenhower recalled: "This message was a hard blow … Being ordered to a city where I had already served a total of eight years would mean, I thought, a virtual repetition of my experience in World War I." He left for Washington with a heavy heart.[146] Once there, he applied himself to monitoring the Allied position in the Far East[147] and completed his tasks with his usual thoroughness.[148] But he quickly became frustrated with the pretentiousness of staff workers in the War Department. On 4 January 1942 he wrote in his diary: "Tempers are short. There are lots of amateur strategists on the job, and prima donnas everywhere. I'd give anything to be back in the field."[149]

During a meeting that took place soon after Eisenhower started at the War Department, General Marshall explained that he would reverse the practice of the First World War and favour field commanders for promotions over the staff officers. Turning to Eisenhower, he added: "Take your case. I know that you were recommended by one general for division command and by another for corps command. That's all very well. I'm glad they have that opinion of you, but you are going to stay right here and fill your position, and that's that." Eisenhower got up to leave but, before he had reached the door, he regained control of his emotions. He turned and flashed a sheepish grin before leaving.[150] He expressed his rage in his diary, but the next day he tore out the page and wrote a new entry. "Anger cannot win, it cannot even think clearly ... So, for many years I've made it a religion never to indulge myself, but yesterday I failed."[151] Several days later, Eisenhower was promoted to major-general on the recommendation of Marshall.

Marshall eventually became so impressed with Eisenhower's ability that he tentatively decided to give him the European command; but first he sent Eisenhower and some others to be examined by the British command. When Marshall asked Churchill what he thought of them, the prime minister's positive response confirmed Marshall in his decision on Eisenhower.[152] Although Marshall had said nothing, Eisenhower suspected, before he left, that he was a candidate for command. He wanted it, and he had confided his aspirations to his wife and his orderly.[153] As well, his correspondence during this period displays his confidence that he could successfully undertake the responsibilities of command.[154]

Once chosen for command (11 June 1942), Eisenhower jumped ahead of 365 other officers who had seniority over him. In his entire military career, he had never held an independent command, having always served under a strong-willed and decisive superior. This would be his test.[155] "The transfer from staff to command duty would have been welcomed by any soldier; but the weight of responsibility involved was so great as to obliterate any thought of personal elation and so critical as to compel complete absorption in the job at hand."[156]

Eisenhower does not seem to have gloried in the increased exposure and influence his new position brought him; he had little need to magnify his own importance as a way of maintaining his self-esteem. In fact, Ike was filled with considerable uncertainty over whether he was to be retained in command and whether the missions he was planning would go ahead. But, instead of allowing those concerns to impair his performance, Eisenhower intensified his focus on the task at hand.

Eisenhower had not been in London long when he was chosen to command the Allied expedition in North Africa, code-named "Torch."[157] Throughout the planning stages of the operation, he was repeatedly informed by his army associates that he had taken on an impossible task. Not discouraged by such talk, he continued to carry out his assigned duties and was pleased to observe "a daily and noticeable growth of co-operation, comradeship, faith, and optimism in Torch headquarters."[158] As he had done in his football days, Eisenhower worked hard to create a team effort. "British and Americans were unconsciously, in their absorption in common problems, shedding their shells of mutual distrust and suspicion."[159] When animosity between British and American units emerged under the strain of battle over a British corps commander's public criticism of the Americans' fighting ability, Eisenhower put it in perspective. He later wrote: "Nothing creates trouble between allies so often or so easily as unnecessary talk – particularly when it belittles one of them. A family squabble is always exaggerated beyond its true importance."[160]

During his rapid rise to prominence, Eisenhower never lost his sense of "naive wonder" at the positions of leadership that were entrusted to him. When he established his headquarters in Gibraltar to plan and oversee the invasion of North Africa, his initial reaction was one of amusement at being an American with operational command of this symbol of the British empire. He wrote: "I simply must have a grandchild or I'll never have the fun of telling this when I'm fishing, grey-bearded, on the banks of a quiet bayou in the deep South."[161] Missing from his musings is any sense of entitlement or grandiosity. Eisenhower's visions were not of grandeur but of a peaceful old age with his family.

The leadership role that Eisenhower assumed brought him increasingly into a political role. After the initial landings in North Africa in early November 1942, the Allied armies began to meet some local French resistance, and it was determined that the one man who held the power to order a French cease-fire was Admiral Jean-Louis Darlan, one of the Vichy French who had collaborated with the Nazis. The question was whether or not to negotiate with him. Eisenhower called it "the first major political decision I had ever felt called on to make."[162] Believing that the benefits of dealing with the enemy outweighed the costs in additional casualties and the loss of precious time, Eisenhower decided to recognize Darlan as the head of the existing civil government in North Africa, on condition that he agreed to follow orders. In a letter to Marshall explaining his actions, Eisenhower admitted to having an "appreciation of all the political problems created by the necessity we have met of dealing with Darlan," but he felt that the potential gains were worth the risk.[163] Marshall, Roosevelt, and Churchill eventually agreed.

None the less, Eisenhower took considerable heat from the media over his handling of the Darlan affair. Trying to react stoically, he wrote to his son: "From what I hear of what has been appearing in the newspapers, you are learning that it is easy enough for a man to be a newspaper hero one day and a bum the next. The answer is that just as one must not let his head get swelled too much by a bit of acclaim, he must not be too upset and irritated when the pack turns on him."[164] Eisenhower intuitively understood that the goal of the healthy individual is to be able, more or less, to regulate his self-esteem without taking flight into mania or depression.

But his feeling of irritation remained. He told a British aide: "I can't understand why these long-haired, starry-eyed guys keep gunning for me. I'm no reactionary. Christ on the mountain! I'm as idealistic as hell."[165] Years later, Eisenhower recalled: "Most of the time, I was too busy to worry about personal problems. But when the furor was at its height, I did reflect uneasily that sensational charges of incompetence as a political man, a role for which I had little training and little liking, could end my career. If I were through, I would feel sorry for myself, probably, and angry at the critics. Nor would I have excused them."[166] Here Eisenhower demonstrated a capacity to be in touch with his affective world. He recognized that, had things gone awry, he would have experienced self-pity, anger, and a lack of forgiveness. At the same time, he was careful to mask his emotions publicly.

Eisenhower's biggest military challenge in North Africa was the battle for Tunisia. His gamble on an all-out early effort to capture it had failed, and the Allies were left in an over-extended position. The tenuously held Allied positions combined with faulty intelligence reports led to disastrous losses at the battle for Kasserine Pass. Eisenhower refused to consider retreat to a more secure position because, he claimed, the "moral effect of retreat upon the population of North Africa" would be a loss of confidence in the Allies.[167] Carefully ignored in Eisenhower's stance was the impact that a retreat would have had upon Allied confidence in his leadership capabilities. As a commander leading troops for the first time, Eisenhower could not have been insensitive to the damage a retreat would have wreaked on his reputation and self-esteem.

Ike did take Tunisia eventually, in May 1943, and followed that battle with landings in Sicily in July and on the Italian mainland in September – flawed but ultimately successful campaigns. The increased combat experience reinforced Eisenhower's self-confidence and optimism.[168] After the victory in Tunisia, his letters to his wife lost their tone of "mild uncertainty," to be replaced by more frequent expressions of confidence.[169]

Throughout the war, Eisenhower maintained a phenomenal pace; he worked extremely long hours, made repeated trips to the front, spoke personally with almost everyone who wanted to see him, and slept less than five hours per night. In December 1942 Eisenhower found that his "shorter and shorter hours of sleep [were becoming] broken by an unaccustomed nervousness. I definitely felt a deterioration in vigor that I could not overcome." That he was anxious is revealed by some of his efforts to alleviate the emotional pressures he experienced. Throughout the war, he smoked continually – four packs a day. Nor was he able to derive much pleasure from his accomplishments. After the hard-won victory at Tunisia, he wrote to General Marshall: "Sometimes I think it would be most comforting to have a disposition that would permit relaxation – even possibly a feeling of self-satisfaction – as definite steps of a difficult job are completed. Unfortunately, I always anticipate and discount, in my own mind, accomplishment of the several steps and am, therefore, mentally racing ahead into the next one ... I am so impatient and irritated because of the slowness with which the next phase can unfold that I make myself quite unhappy."[170] The picture that emerges is of a man almost compulsively driven and unsure as to whether he can continue to master the challenges facing him.

Near the end of the Mediterranean campaign, Eisenhower was informed that his next posting would most likely be a return to a Washington desk job, albeit as chief-of-staff of the army, so that Marshall could command "Overlord" (the planned landing in France). His diary entries on this topic betray no sense of injustice or ill-treatment. On the contrary, he considered it "flattering" to even be considered for the same job as the extremely capable Marshall.[171] However, the amount of diary space and time he dedicated to reporting these rumours indicates that Eisenhower was deeply concerned about his personal future. President Roosevelt's son, James, recalled Ike's "nagging worry" about being "kicked upstairs into a desk job in the Pentagon." Eisenhower even offered to become one of the field commanders under Marshall rather than return to Washington.[172]

Roosevelt met with Churchill and Stalin at Teheran in November 1943, and, over the clear preferences of both men, he chose Eisenhower to be supreme commander of "Overlord." The president later told his son that, while he "thought Marshall the wisest of the generals," he selected Eisenhower as supreme commander because "Eisenhower is the best politician among the military men. He is a natural leader who can convince men to follow him."[173]

Before returning to London, Eisenhower spent two weeks in the United States for meetings and personal business. At a family reunion, held during the visit, Dwight's brothers noticed in him "a new, quiet self-confidence that gave him an air of serenity."[174] Eisenhower called the visit "a rejuvenating experience – until then I had not fully realized how far war tends to carry its participants away from the interests, objectives, and concerns of normal life."[175]

The most significant military decision that Eisenhower made during the war was the "O.K., let's go" that launched the D-Day armada. Foul weather had been playing havoc with the invasion schedule, and Eisenhower delayed his decision until the last possible moment, awaiting a weather report that the storm would lift just long enough for beach-heads to be established. The entire operation went forward on his decision.[176] Shortly afterwards, Eisenhower wrote a letter, to be made public only if the landing was a failure, accepting full responsibility for the operation.[177] His willingness to take responsibility for his errors, rather than searching for scapegoats, marks him as a person with good ego strengths. The more narcissistically vulnerable an individual, the less he or she can tolerate any admission of error, since it challenges the sense of omnipotence and grandiosity which is used as a defense against feelings of inadequacy and worthlessness.

Although Eisenhower was willing to accept responsibility for his mistakes, he resented the absence of plaudits for his performance. He complained in his diary about the British columnists' portrayal of his role in the Mediterranean: "They don't use the words 'initiative' and 'boldness' in talking of me, but often do in speaking of Alex [Alexander] and Monty [Montgomery] ... We had a happy family, and to all the commanders in chief must go the great share of the operational credit. But it wearies me to be thought of as timid, when I've had to do things that were so risky as to be almost crazy. Oh hum."[178] Despite his irritation at not having his strengths fully appreciated, Eisenhower did not become punitive or attempt to get back at the hurtful columnists – his self-esteem was sufficiently stable that he could acknowledge his disappointment somewhat philosophically, as the "oh hum" suggests.

Eisenhower managed to sustain good personal relationships with most of the important and strong-willed men working under him.[179] Able to tolerate divergent opinions, he was careful in dealing with his subordinates to seek out words and phrases that would not cause insult to anyone – a trait that caused many of his subordinates (British and American) to believe that Eisenhower always agreed with the last man he talked to. "Eisenhower's great weakness in this situation was ... his eagerness to be well liked coupled with his desire to keep everyone happy." However, he never gave way on any matters of substantive importance.[180] He also battled to keep his legendary temper in check: "The complications of Allied command were intriguing. It's just as well; otherwise they might have been infuriating."[181] As a result of such efforts, Eisenhower enjoyed good relations with his troops that were unmatched by the other commanders in the war.[182]

During the Battle of the Bulge in December 1944, British Field Marshal Montgomery announced that he would not launch a counter-attack until two days after the set date. Eisenhower was furious and ready to send Montgomery home. In an attempt to control his temper, Eisenhower would shred cloth handkerchiefs with his hands hidden beneath the desk during meetings; the day he received the news from Montgomery, three handkerchiefs met their maker.

After the battle, Montgomery gave a press conference which left the impression that the British troops had come to the rescue of the Americans. Eisenhower later wrote: "This incident caused me more distress and worry than did any similar one of the war." It also raised the ire of Omar Bradley, the American general who fought across the Bulge from Montgomery.[183] Once again, through quiet diplomacy, Eisenhower fought to keep the peace by refraining from an untrammelled expression of his anger.

But there were limits on the extent to which Eisenhower was prepared to control his feelings. He blamed the Germans for the extensive death and destruction of the war and his hatred of the Nazis grew more intense as a result of the sights he saw inside Germany itself. On 12 April 1945 Eisenhower toured the concentration camps of Ohrdruf Nord and Buchenwald; many of those present were overwhelmed and could not complete the tour. Eisenhower later wrote: "I have never felt able to describe my emotional reactions when I first came face to face with indisputable evidence of Nazi brutality and ruthless disregard of every shred of decency ... I am certain, however, that I have never at any other time experienced an equal sense of shock."[184] Eisenhower's letters to Mamie at that time contained such statements as "The German is a beast" and "God, I hate the Germans."[185] There was no mention of his own German ancestry, which may have been too painful to acknowledge.

By the end of the war, Eisenhower's rage at Nazi barbarism was at its peak. He refused to meet with a Nazi general to accept the surrender, instead sending a subordinate to sign the papers. He wanted Germany to be humiliated and made to pay first for starting the war and then prolonging it after defeat was assured; to this end he supported the "Morgenthau Plan," which proposed eliminating Germany's industrial capacity.[186] Here was a man capable of intensely felt emotions – rage and bitterness against the Germans and a wish to punish them for their terrible crimes. But because Eisenhower was not a rage-filled narcissistic personality, his intense dislike of the Germans was to lessen over time. During a brief stint as military governor of Germany after the armistice was signed, Eisenhower manifested a very different attitude towards the Germans. One observer, Robert Bowie, recalled that in dealing with his former wartime adversaries Eisenhower "created an immediate sense of friendliness with the Germans and avoided any memory or recollection of prior relationships which could have made it awkward."[187]

The great victory Eisenhower had helped bring about did not seem to inflate his self-importance. Many individuals on his staff composed flowery messages to inform the combined chiefs-of-staff of the Nazi surrender. Eisenhower rejected all of these and sent an unpretentious, factual note: "The mission of this Allied force was fulfilled at 0241, local time, 7 May 1945."[188] His "Victory Order of the Day," issued 8 May, emphasized future unity, not past accomplishments: "Let us have no part in the profitless quarrels in which other men will inevitably engage as to what country, what service, won the European war."[189] He later wrote: "Like so many other men and women who had been at war physically or emotionally, exhaustion rather than exultation was my first reaction to victory in Europe ... I had been liberated, too. In a deep sag of reaction, I luxuriated in the freedom from decisions about the life and death of human beings."[190]

Eisenhower was still unaware of the acclaim and adulation that he was about to receive. As the victorious supreme commander, he was adored by the American public, though few knew very much about him.[191] For some, his modest reaction to the acclaim awarded him after the war was evidence of great humility.[192] Others have suggested that the explanations for his behaviour were far more complex. "Eisenhower was never particularly modest, much less humble, about an accomplishment which he believed deserving of praise. The reason he failed to anticipate the future fanfares was that, in sharp contrast to some of his field commanders, General Eisenhower was lacking in arrogance and theatricality ... he was self-confident, but he was not cursed with an overweening sense of self-importance."[193]

Before returning to the United States, Eisenhower went to London at the invitation of Churchill to be honoured by the British people.[194] It was his first major public speech and received international attention. In the talk, Eisenhower stated that "humility must always be the portion of any man who receives acclaim earned in blood of his followers and sacrifices of his friends."[195]

At the conclusion of the war, Eisenhower reluctantly accepted the position of chief-of-staff of the army in Washington. He recalled that "no personal enthusiasm marked my promotion"[196]; he agreed to take the job only after the president affirmed the existence of a special need for him and promised his tour would be short. To his wife, he often expressed his desire to retire and to apply himself to teaching young people about the changes wrought by the atom bomb.[197]

In November 1945 he wrote to his friend Swede Hazlett: "For myself, there is nothing I want so much as opportunity to retire ... The job I am taking now represents nothing but straight duty. Naturally I will do it as well as I know how."[198] A year later, Eisenhower expressed his dismay: "It has been a most difficult period for me, with far more frustrations than progress." He seemed to long for the wartime command structure where, in spite of difficulties, "the job is always clearly outlined."[199]

Eisenhower's frustration was a result of the tasks he had to perform in his new role. While he strongly favoured universal military training and continued Allied unity, he was assigned to oversee the demobilization of the American armed forces and was helpless to prevent the huge budget cuts imposed on them, cuts that made it impossible to maintain a significant military presence overseas. "Eisenhower was out of step with his countrymen. And he knew it."[200]

His work in Washington brought him into contact with the country's top political figures, enabling him to see the political process function at close range. During these years he began to associate with his "gang" – a group of wealthy and influential men – with whom he played golf and bridge. Eisenhower was greatly impressed by financial success, although he was not interested in amassing wealth himself.[201] That such men sought his company and arranged their schedules to suit him may have satisfied an unconscious need to prove that he had triumphed over his humble origins and was the de facto leader of the fraternity, the "Bums of Lawsy Lou," that had rejected him.

During his tour as chief-of-staff, Eisenhower was repeatedly offered jobs in the private sector; all of these offers promised him many times more than his military salary for the holding of nominal posts. Eisenhower turned them down. After rejecting several invitations to publish his memoirs, he eventually agreed because he was persuaded by the argument that "you owe it to yourself, to the country, and to history, to tell the personal story of your European campaign on a factual basis." Eisenhower struck a deal in which he wrote the book and sold all the rights for one lump sum. He then noted in his diary: "Long ago I determined that, if ever I should publish a war memoir for which I should be paid, I would remember with substantial presents some of the people who served me so faithfully and unselfishly during the war." He then wrote out a list of such people and the sums to be given them.[202]

But Eisenhower was not impervious to the value of money. He recognized that his memoirs would provide "the one chance in my lifetime to build security for my family. The soldier leaves the Army as poor as he enters it."[203] With the aid of a special tax arrangement, the work brought him about half a million dollars after taxes.[204]

Working sixteen-hour days, he completed the book in seven weeks. "I refused superlatives or purple adjectives and would not indulge in the kind of personal criticism or disparagement of others that had badly marred many military accounts."[205] In fact, he told one associate that any time he mentioned any individual it would be "with an expression of respect and even admiration."[206] The resulting book was descriptive rather than analytical. Eisenhower defended all the major decisions of the War Department and himself, but he did admit mistakes – such as the thin defense that allowed the Battle of the Bulge break-out. However, he carefully concealed his inner thoughts and emotions, and, true to his word, did not engage in any criticism of other personalities – an approach that offended no one.

During the Potsdam Conference in July 1945, President Truman made a proposition that Eisenhower said struck him in his "emotional vitals." Truman told him: "General, there is nothing that you may want that I won't try to help you get. That definitely and specifically includes the presidency in 1948." Eisenhower treated it as a joke, and lightly replied: "Mr. President, I don't know who will be your opponent for the presidency, but it will not be I."[207] He was more emphatic when questioned about his intentions during his 1945 visit to Abilene: "In the strongest language you can command, you can state that I have no political ambitions at all."[208]

On the surface, Eisenhower had adopted the military's open disdain for politics and politicians. Yet he displayed an increasing political consciousness. Ike began to think and write (in private) about the issues of the day, and he came to believe that he possessed the analytical capabilities to deal with them. All the while, he ingratiated himself with the country's top business and political figures.[209] Despite Eisenhower's many assertions to the contrary, Harry Butcher, who worked closely with Eisenhower throughout the war, believed that "he wants it [the presidency] so bad he can taste it!"[210] In September 1947 Eisenhower wrote to "Beetle" Smith: "I do not believe that you or I or anyone else has the right to state, categorically, that he will not perform any duty that his country might demand of him."[211] If Eisenhower could frame the decision to seek the presidency in terms of duty, this would make his ambition more acceptable to him.

Eisenhower's internal struggle was clearly visible in a letter he wrote refusing to allow his name to be entered in the New Hampshire primary. Eisenhower stated that he had not flatly refused to run, because this would violate "that concept of duty which calls upon every good citizen to place no limitations upon his readiness to serve in any designated capacity." However, he stated that the military must remain subservient to the civilian government, and this could only be maintained if "life-long professional soldiers, in the absence of some obvious and overriding reason, abstain from seeking high public office." He concluded, "My decision to remove myself completely from the political scene is definite and positive."[212]

At the same time that Eisenhower refused to seek the presidency of the United States, he was wrestling with a decision regarding the acceptance of another presidency – that of Columbia University. In July 1947 he wrote to Beetle Smith: "It was almost the first decision I ever had to make in my life that was directly concerned with myself."[213] In another letter, he told Swede Hazlett that "going to Columbia is merely to change the location of my headquarters; perhaps it would be more accurate to say that I am changing the method by which I will continue to strive for the same goals."[214] He accepted the job because he felt that "he needed a new forum from which to influence public opinion," and that his time at Columbia was simply a "rite of passage," an essential step in his education for the presidency.[215]

While at Columbia, Eisenhower's many prepared and extemporaneous speeches kept him in the public limelight; during his first year there, he "averaged an important talk every other day" that allowed him to present his views on all manner of international and domestic concerns.[216] The faculty became irritated by his frequent public speeches which "were becoming increasingly to sound like those of a Republican campaigning for the presidency." In one speech to the faculty, he expounded on the communist threat, saying that "this is not just a casual argument against slightly different philosophies. This is a war of light against darkness, freedom against slavery, Godliness against atheism."[217]

Eisenhower's speech-making activities stimulated his supporters to urge him to run for office. In July 1949 Eisenhower recorded in his diary his impressions of a visit from New York governor Thomas Dewey:

The governor says that I am a public possession, that such standing as I have in the affections or respect of our citizenry is likewise public property. All of this, though, must be carefully guarded to use in the service of all the people.

(Although I'm merely repeating someone else's exposition, the mere writing of such things almost makes me dive under the table) ...

It all seems unreal and forced to me, but I'm not egotistical enough to give any kind of an irrevocable, arbitrary answer at this moment.[218]

At the same time as he was recording his ambivalence at becoming an icon, Eisenhower was deeply interested in the nature of the public's "affections or respect" for him. During 1948 he had received 20,000 letters, mostly urging him to run for president, which he turned over to a Columbia sociologist for analysis. Eisenhower went through the report with him line by line to discover what it was about himself that people liked and why they urged him to seek the presidency. Eighty-five per cent of correspondents expressed support for him because of his personal qualities – sincerity, human warmth, and competence – rather than his achievements. Many cited the fact that, despite his military competence, he was non-militaristic.[219]

The frequency with which Eisenhower listed his reasons for staying out of politics in his diary suggests that he may have been trying to convince himself. In November 1949 he wrote: "I am not, now or in the future, going willingly into politics. If ever I do so it will be as the result of a series of circumstances that crush all my arguments ... that there appears to me to be such compelling reasons to enter the political field that refusal to do so would always thereafter mean to me that I'd failed to do my duty." Yet he seemed to recognize the weakness of his own argument: "I must say that, as of this moment, my imagination cannot conjure up any picture of emergency, disaster, or danger that would point irrevocably to me as the sole saviour of the United States. Put that way, the thing sounds silly."[220]

Eisenhower's psychological struggle is unmistakeable. But to have acknowledged to himself that he might want to wield the power of the presidency was unacceptable: he would then be no better than the petty politicians he professed to disdain. It was much easier to deny his ambitious, competitive nature and see the job of president as a compelling but unpleasant duty that he could not, in good conscience, ignore.

Although he often claimed that he did not want the presidency, Eisenhower never once said, publicly or privately, that he felt unqualified to be president – an omission that was indicative of his enormous self-confidence and sense of mastery.[221] Whatever narcissism Eisenhower exhibited was by no means unhealthy or pathological; it reflected the superb talents he had demonstrated as supreme commander in the Second World War.

In December 1950 President Truman asked Eisenhower to become commander of the NATO forces then being assembled in Europe. As Eisenhower recalled it, Truman "put the message as a request. But he was the President of the United States and I told him that my own convenience had nothing to do with it; I had been a soldier all my life and by law was still an active soldier. I would report at any time he said."[222] He received a leave of absence from his duties at Columbia and prepared himself for the move. Reflecting on his change of plans, he wrote: "I do not think it is particularly important where I am working as long as I feel I am doing the best I can in what I definitely believe to be a world crisis."[223]

At the end of January 1951 Eisenhower returned briefly to Washington to report his findings on the situation in Europe. While there, he arranged a meeting with Senator Robert Taft, the leading Republican candidate for the presidency, to solicit his support for U.S. military participation in NATO. He also claimed that he intended finally to make an unambiguous, irreversible statement indicating that he would not enter political life. Prior to the meeting, he had prepared a statement so strongly worded that "if made public, any political future for me thereafter would be impossible." However, at the meeting, Senator Taft refused to give an unqualified endorsement for the concept of collective security. "This aroused my fears that isolationism was stronger in congress than I had previously suspected." Eisenhower then destroyed his prepared statement since "in the absence of the assurance I had been seeking, it would be silly for me to throw away whatever political influence I might possess to help keep us on the right track."[224]

In his political differences with Senator Taft, Eisenhower had found justification for remaining a potential presidential candidate; political office would be sought not to satisfy his egoism or his narcissism but to keep the country "on the right track." In this fashion,

Eisenhower was able to deny, even to himself, the extent of his ambition and his belief that he was superbly qualified to be president.

When Eisenhower returned to Europe in February 1951 to assume his full responsibilities as commander of Supreme Headquarters Allied Powers Europe, he continued to express a lack of interest in politics while simultaneously widening his range of political contacts. He wrote in his diary: "One good thing about this dismaying and unattractive assignment is that I should be finally and fully removed from the personal political ambitions of others, which are reflected, often, in their presentations to me."[225] Eisenhower's duties served both to acquaint him personally with some of the civilian heads of government and ministers whom he did not already know, and "to prevent his drive for the Republican presidential nomination from cresting too early." [226]

He was also assiduous in protecting his most important political asset – his image. In May 1951 he wrote: "While I'm determined to stay aloof from all the current snarling and fighting in the United States, I'm most of all determined never to get into the 'personality' kind of argument."[227] He expressed his concern about his reputation to a friend: "I think I pretty well hit my peak in history when I accepted the German surrender."[228] In December he confided to an aide that he believed his participation in a race for political nomination "would do much to destroy such reputation I have had for a disinterested and loyal public servant."[229]

To enter politics without damage to his reputation and his own self-image as a man above the political fray and the grubby activities of politicians, Eisenhower envisioned a broad "call to duty" from the American people – as had happened with one of his boyhood heroes, George Washington. But there is an element of grandiosity in that idea – Eisenhower as the people's saviour. In October 1951 he recorded these thoughts in his diary: "The only way I could leave this duty is to believe that a section of the United States want me to undertake a higher one. This could be a real draft, something that all agree cannot happen. In this I take real comfort because it will at least eliminate the necessity of my making any personal decision as to my own suitability."[230]

Privately, Eisenhower considered accepting a draft but refused to fight for the nomination. On 23 January 1952 he made public a reply to one of his supporters explaining that he had not issued a flat refusal to accept the nomination if it were offered because "such an expression would smack of effrontery." He seemed completely oblivious to the fact that refusing to contest the nomination could also be interpreted as a form of hubris. His second reason for not issuing a strong rejection was "a persistent doubt that I could phrase a flat refusal without appearing to violate that concept of duty to country which calls upon every good citizen to place no limitations upon his readiness to serve in any designated capacity." Finally, he cited the necessity of a division between civilian government and the military. He concluded that "my decision to remove myself completely from the political scene is definite and positive."[231]

Despite such statements, Eisenhower already had one foot in the race: early in January 1952 his name had been entered in the primaries. He then made a public statement confirming his "Republican voting record." He said that he would leave his present duty if called to a higher one, including a nomination by the Republican Party, but he would not abandon his European responsibilities to join in the campaign for the nomination.[232]

Eisenhower wanted the nomination by acclamation, a route that would remove the indignity of his having to scramble for delegates.[233] In his diary, he seemed angered by even having to make this partial concession: "Time and again I've told anyone who'd listen that I will not seek a nomination. I don't give a d—— how impossible a 'draft' may be. I'm willing to go part way in trying to recognize a 'duty,' but I do not have to seek one, and I will not."[234]

For Eisenhower, the appeal of duty met "the demands of conscience ... in part by maintaining the feeling of sacrifice – the person confirms that he is doing his duty by the fact that he does not enjoy it. Thus reluctance is a defense."[235] By refusing to acknowledge his own drive for power, prestige, and influence, Eisenhower could keep his idealized self-image intact and satisfy the demands of his superego (conscience) that he not behave in a grandiose or exhibitionistic fashion.

In February, Eisenhower watched a film of the "Eisenhower Rally" at Madison Square Garden that the famous aviator Jacqueline Cochran had brought him: "Viewing it finally developed into a real emotional experience for Mamie and me. I've not been so upset in years. Clearly to be seen is the mass longing of America for some kind of reasonable solution for her nagging, persistent, and almost terrifying problems. It's a real experience to realize that one could become a symbol for many thousands of the hope they have."[236]

After seeing the film, Cochran offered the following toast: "To the President." As she recalled, "I was the first person to ever say this to him and he burst into tears ... Tears were just running out of his eyes, he was so overwhelmed." Then Eisenhower announced that he was going to declare himself for the nomination.[237] Eisenhower's tears at Cochran's toast reveal that, for him, the prospect of becoming president aroused profound emotions: he would become the embodiment of mass longings and aspirations – a thought that was both gratifying and, because of the potential for failure, terrifying.

His reaction to his first-ballot nomination victory was not a sense of personal triumph or elation. His brother Arthur recalled that "Dwight was the calmest fellow in the room at the time of the nomination."[238] Other guests who were with him after the nomination reported that he seemed very "everyday" and relaxed.[239] This was not wholly surprising given his ambivalence about expressing pleasure in seeking the power of the presidency.

His first act after winning the nomination – breaking party tradition and against the wishes of his advisers – was to meet with his rival Senator Taft and so reunite the "team" for the common Republican cause.[240] For Eisenhower, Taft was not a personal enemy who had to be vindictively punished, but a colleague with whom he had differences of opinion that could now be set aside.

Nor was the presidency the *raison d'être* for Eisenhower's life as it would be for both Johnson and Nixon. His professional identity had been formed by the military. His brother Earl felt that one of the hardest tasks for Ike was to resign his commission as general and thereby end forty years of military service. Earl commented that "there were near-tears at that moment in the eyes of all members of the family."[241] Mamie recalled that she had "never seen Ike look worse, or be more deeply moved" than the day he returned from a surprise ceremony at the Pentagon to honour his resignation. She said that, as he recounted the events to her, he had an "immeasurable sadness" written on his face.[242]

During the campaign for the presidency, Eisenhower held to his long-established practice of avoiding personal disagreements with political figures.[243] He campaigned only on the broad issues, letting Nixon deliver the personal attacks against individuals. In 1954 Eisenhower wrote to a friend:

I developed a practice which, so far as I know, I have never violated. That practice is to avoid public mention of any name unless it can be done with favorable intent and connotation, reserve all criticism for the private conference; speak only good in public ... A leader's job is to get others to go along with him in the promotion of something. To do this he needs their goodwill. To destroy goodwill, it is only necessary to criticize publicly. This creates in the criticized one a subconscious desire to "get even." Such effects can last for a very long period.[244]

What Eisenhower had intuitively grasped was the relationship between the experience of being shamed and humiliated and the concomitant desire for revenge to alleviate the painful feelings of low self-worth. He was determined to avoid becoming the target of such revenge. But he was not above allowing Nixon to take the low road in attacking political opponents and incurring the inevitable political flak. As president, Eisenhower encouraged his subordinates to announce controversial initiatives, an approach that allowed him to distance himself publicly from the unpopular actions of his administration and to maintain his standing with the people.

When Truman launched personal attacks on Eisenhower, the latter's legendary temper emerged – but only in private. Although Eisenhower claimed to do what his West Point wrestling coach had told him – get up off the canvas with a smile – he grew very upset about Truman's campaign rhetoric. He often wondered aloud "if I can stand sitting next to him" in the inaugural procession. Bitterly, he recalled Truman's words to him: "This politics is a dirty game, but nothing will affect us and our relationship."[245] Eisenhower never forgave the former president for what he felt were low blows and for treating him as an ordinary political opponent.[246] What hurt Eisenhower most was the sense of betrayal – Truman had urged him to run in 1948 and was now attacking him. Lurking just below the surface was Eisenhower's sense of entitlement that, as a military hero and reluctant candidate, he deserved better treatment than a mere politician might receive.

Those issues may have been operative, in part, in Eisenhower's relations with Nixon. When Nixon had been chosen to be the vice-presidential candidate, Eisenhower scarcely knew him. They had held no philosophical or political discussions of any substance; they had never played cards together, or shared a meal or a drink. At thirty-nine years of age, Nixon was young enough to be Eisenhower's son. Eisenhower's reputation rested on a lifetime of accomplishments as manager, organizer, commander: Nixon's reputation, aside from his slashing campaign style, rested on a single investigation, that of Alger Hiss. Basically, Eisenhower owed Nixon nothing and only hoped that he would be an asset rather than a liability.

As noted in chapter 4, after Nixon came under attack for his alleged slush fund, Eisenhower's sense of fair play would not permit him to dump his running-mate without allowing him a public hearing on national TV. But he was certainly not prepared to embrace Nixon too closely lest he damage his candidacy. When Nixon, furious over Eisenhower's apparent vacillation, told him "to shit or get off the pot," the outburst left a scar. Eisenhower never forgot Nixon's temerity on this occasion. No one, not Churchill, not de Gaulle, not FDR, not Marshall had ever presumed to talk to Eisenhower in such a fashion.

To add insult to injury, in the "Checkers" speech Nixon had called on Adlai Stevenson, the Democratic Party's presidential candidate, and John Sparkman, the Democratic vice-presidential candidate, to make full revelations of their financial history, because, as Nixon said, "a man who's going to be President and a man who's to be Vice-President must have the confidence of all the people." Eisenhower was livid: he recognized that Nixon had turned the spotlight on him, since, if three out of the four candidates made their finances public property, Eisenhower would have to do so too. From the time of this incident onward, the relationship between the two men was characterized by tension, hostility, and mistrust. Eisenhower resented Nixon's lack of deference and his willingness to embarrass his boss to serve his own ends, while Nixon could never forgive nor forget Eisenhower for not backing him unconditionally.[247]

While waiting for the returns on election night, Eisenhower was confident; regarding his anticipated victory with a sense of equanimity, he even had a nap before the decisive results came in. Ike's older brother Arthur recalled: "I didn't see him particularly changed when the outcome of the election was announced."[248] But the size of Eisenhower's landslide victory was not matched by an equal enthusiasm for other Republican candidates. The victory had been a personal one for the new president; the nation had expressed its admiration for the man – rather than for the party he now headed.[249]

Eisenhower entered the Oval Office with confidence that his life experiences had prepared him well for the challenges of the presidency. On 21 January 1953 he recorded his impressions of his new job in his diary: "My first day at the president's desk. Plenty of worries and difficult problems. But such has been my portion for a long time – the result is that this just seems (today) like a continuation of all I've been doing since July 1941 – even before that."[250]

If Eisenhower found no change in his daily duties, others found no change in the man. In separate interviews, his brothers all agreed that the great powers and responsibilities that had been entrusted to him as military commander and president had not changed his basic personality or created any trace of arrogance in him.[251] Milton later wrote that, despite his national and international fame, Ike "never lost the modesty that characterized him as a youth."[252] He also never lost the emotional reserve that had characterized him as an adult. As one of Eisenhower's close associates observed, "his daily demeanor stayed singularly barren of full and open expressions of inner thought and direction."[253]

As he had done as a commanding general, Eisenhower sought out successful and ambitious men for his new team.[254] None of the people Eisenhower asked refused to join his cabinet – a unique statistic in the modern presidency.[255] He applied many quasi-military techniques of organization to the White House – appointing a "chief-of-staff" (Sherman Adams) and delegating much authority to cabinet members. Lacking any need to inflate his own ego by surrounding himself with individuals who could be denigrated, Eisenhower sought to "build up" the men who worked with him.[256]

A few days after his election, Eisenhower held a meeting with his cabinet members which set the tone for the many that were to follow. After reading the latest draft of his inaugural address, he cut short the applause that followed: "I read it far more for your blue pencils than I did for your applause ... One reason I wanted to read it now is so that you can think it over and be ready to tear it to pieces."[257]

He once told reporters: "I am not one of the desk-pounding types that likes to stick out his jaw and look like he is bossing the show."[258] In fact, Eisenhower had a visceral dislike of "yes-men." During a cabinet meeting early in his first term, when the discussion turned to examining ways to cut spending, Lodge suggested reducing grants to the states for highway programs. Eisenhower replied that "my personal opinion is that we should spend more for highways." Lodge offered a withdrawal and fell silent – not the response the president had sought. "It's open to discussion," he informed Lodge, adding, "I've given way on a number of personal opinions to this gang."[259]

He once commented to his brother Milton: "I don't see that anything is hurt by the presence in the highest councils of different kinds of thinking. It is in the combination of these various attitudes that we hammer out acceptable policies; enthusiasts for anything go too far."[260] His self-esteem was sufficiently robust that he was not threatened by the expression of dissenting views from his colleagues. And he often displayed a willingness to reopen matters that had already been settled, and to change the decision or its details if the evidence warranted it. Nor did he avoid unpleasant issues either; the aide who prepared the agendas for seven years of cabinet meetings never once received a complaint from Eisenhower or directions not to put something on the table for discussion.[261]

Eisenhower downplayed his own role in discussions and decisions. He often preceded his political analysis with the disclaimer, "I am no politician as you well know, but ..."[262] Frequently he would delay his entry into a discussion so as not to limit, prematurely, the expression of opinion by making his own position known. When he did speak up, his words carried extra weight because of his position and the fact that they were supported by "a range of acquaintanceship with things and with people [that] seemed no less than dazzling."[263]

Walter Bedell Smith, who had many occasions to observe Eisenhower's interaction with subordinates during the war and in the White House, observed that "one of his most successful methods in dealing with individuals is to assume that he himself is lacking in detailed knowledge and liable to make an error and is seeking advice ... He actually values the recommendations and suggestions he receives, although his own better information and sounder judgment might cause them to be disregarded."[264]

Eisenhower demanded much from his team but in return gave them the support they needed; each of his subordinates was permitted one serious mistake.[265] He was also willing to take the fall when it seemed to be best for the team. In February 1953 a slight mix-up over the timing of the announcement of the resignation of the American ambassador to Great Britain made it look as though the United States had not consulted its ally about his replacement. This was politically embarrassing for the British government, and Eisenhower chose to "advise Anthony [Eden] ... to lay the blame for this whole unfortunate occurrence squarely on me. He will have the logical explanation that my lack of formal experience in the political world was the reason for the blunder. Actually, I was the one who cautioned against anything like this happening, but manifestly I can take the blame without hurting anything or anybody; whereas if the secretary of state would have to shoulder it, his position would be badly damaged."[266] The president's decision and his analysis of its costs and benefits reveals his considerable ego strength. Noticeably absent is any need to be perceived as perfect; his narcissism did not require him to be omnipotent.

Eisenhower worked hard to achieve consensus and compromise among his advisers. His brother Milton observed that this leadership style "extended throughout his war years and subsequent years. It was very natural for him when he became president to keep on working cooperatively for a consensus. That was an exceedingly sincere and constant effort."[267] Less sympathetic observers have claimed that this "sincere and constant effort" stemmed from a need to be liked, a need that led him to agree with every adviser or associate he spoke with and even to support contradictory opinions. They argue that his determination to make everyone happy frequently prevented Eisenhower from making clean-cut decisions; in wanting popularity above all else, he often appeared less concerned with any "specific achievement" of his administration than with "his adulation by the American people."[268]

Eisenhower did not seem to be unduly upset by criticism of his policies or programs. He was a regular reader of newspapers and news magazines – although he denied ever looking at them – but never sent an angry letter to an editor. (On occasion he would send a note of praise to the publisher.) Only his closest friends would hear about it when he was upset by a press report. As long as the criticism was aimed at the policy, and not at himself or another individual, he generally did not get too upset.[269] But occasionally, he did take policy criticisms personally. When Ken Crawford of *Newsweek* wrote an article critical of the administration, Eisenhower commented, "I don't understand how he could write a piece like that because I've always regarded him as a friend of mine." An aide replied: "Well, he admires you and he is a friend of yours. His trouble is that he hates Republicans." Eisenhower grinned and remarked: "He may have something there."[270]

The first major crisis that Eisenhower had to confront during his presidency was the Korean War. Eisenhower had supported Truman's initial decision to intervene, calling it "wise and necessary,"[271] but by 1952 the war had bogged down into a stalemate and, as the casualty lists continued, it was becoming increasingly unpopular.

The communists had indicated a willingness to reconvene the armistice talks with the United Nations team at Panmunjom and seemed ready to settle for a division of Korea at the thirty-eighth parallel. When Secretary of State John Foster Dulles wanted to reject the offer, Eisenhower lost his patience, telling an aide: "If Mr. Dulles and all his sophisticated advisers really mean that they can not talk peace seriously, then I am in the wrong pew. For if it's war we should be talking about, I know the people to give me advice on that – and they're not in the State Department. Now either we cut out all this fooling around and make a serious bid for peace – or we forget the whole thing."[272]

Dulles believed that it was possible to secure a much more satisfactory settlement and that, if a "political settlement" to ensure the unification of Korea did not follow a cease-fire, the United States should break the armistice. Eisenhower was adamant: "The American people, will never stand for such a move."[273] The vast majority of his advisers, Republican colleagues, and most Democrats urged that he allow the stalemate to continue.[274]

Eisenhower refused to commit himself either to the hard line General MacArthur and Dulles had proposed or to a prolongation of the stalemate. As a way of reviving the stalled truce talks, Eisenhower decided to "let the Communist authorities understand that, in the absence of satisfactory progress, we intended to move decisively without inhibition in our use of weapons, and would no longer be responsible for confining hostilities to the Korean Peninsula ... we dropped the word, discreetly, of our intention. We felt quite sure it would reach Soviet and Chinese Communist ears."[275] He also made the threat credible by having atomic weapons shipped into the area.[276]

American threats seem to have had the desired effect. Soon after, negotiations were restarted and, after some haggling over specifics, a deal was worked out for an exchange of sick and wounded prisoners that was acceptable to both sides. With this major question out of the way, negotiators began to address the issue of a final cease-fire line.[277] Eisenhower's decision to pursue a cease-fire required him to reject almost all the advice he received.[278] He felt secure enough in his own analysis of the situation not to rely upon the options proposed by his advisers or to concur with their opinions.

Syngman Rhee, the South Korean leader, complained to Eisenhower that an armistice arrangement which would allow the Chinese communists to remain in the country would be "a death sentence for Korea without protest."[279] On the eve of the signing of the truce, he allowed 25,000 prisoners of war who were about to be exchanged with the communists to escape. Eisenhower's position was further complicated when several members of the Republican old guard came out publicly in Rhee's defense.[280]

An infuriated Eisenhower called Rhee's move "so foolish as to be fantastic."[281] In his diary on 24 July 1953, he wrote: "Of course the fact remains that the probable enemy is the communists, but Rhee has been such an unsatisfactory ally that it is difficult indeed to avoid excoriating him in the strongest of terms."[282] Privately, Eisenhower expressed to Rhee his great disappointment and even threatened the withdrawal of UN troops if such behaviour continued.

He was, however, unprepared to act on this threat, and he refused the advice of several of his associates that the United States evacuate its forces in the event of further difficulties with Rhee. Publicly, Eisenhower downplayed any rift between the Allies that would encourage the communists. He also instructed the assistant secretary of state for Far Eastern affairs, Walter Robertson, to discuss the situation with Rhee and persuade him to cooperate – which Rhee eventually did.[283] By avoiding the opportunity to humiliate his recalcitrant ally, Eisenhower was able to effect a rapprochement rather than a rupture. Once again, Eisenhower's healthy ego allowed him to determine his priorities without the intrusion of aggressive impulses and the desire for revenge.

With the conclusion of the Korean armistice, Dwight Eisenhower had achieved an almost uninterrupted string of victories. From the frightened child who had conquered his aunt's backyard, he had gone on to succeed in the schoolyard and on the sports field. He had risen through the ranks of the military to become supreme commander of the largest victorious fighting force the world had ever seen, and, shortly afterwards, he had switched fields and entered politics from the top – becoming president after an overwhelming election triumph. In his first year in office, he ended the Korean War.

With each of these accomplishments, Eisenhower's self-esteem and confidence grew. He began 1954 still riding the crest of success, and, when confronted with the crisis in Indochina, he was able to face it unencumbered emotionally by the kinds of narcissistic needs that were to bedevil his successors.

7 Eisenhower and Dien Bien Phu

Throughout his life, Dwight D. Eisenhower was a self-confident, secure individual with a well-functioning ego. A warm and supportive relationship with parents and siblings enabled him to develop solid friendships and meet the challenge of his studies at school and later at West Point. Those disappointments and setbacks that he encountered were addressed and either mourned or sublimated, not left to fester in ways that contributed to narcissistic rage and low self-esteem. Although Eisenhower possessed a fiery temper, he learned later in life to vent his anger in a secure setting and not carry it around with him in the form of a grudge. As a military commander, he demonstrated his willingness to confront opponents when the need arose; at the same time, he was devoid of any need to "prove" himself by demeaning his associates. Blessed with intelligence, a talent for command and administration, and a capacity for friendship, Eisenhower had only very few life experiences that could be described as humiliating.

During the Indochina crisis of 1954,[1] Eisenhower drew upon his considerable ego strengths to engage in a decision-making process that featured a careful assessment of the costs and benefits of each of the various options. Unlike Johnson, his Indochina decisions were not influenced by psychological needs to bolster his self-esteem by acquiescing in the advice tendered by his advisers. And unlike Nixon, he did not feel the need to act as a response to prior experiences of shame and humiliation.

Although Eisenhower's anti-communist credentials were impeccable, in foreign policy he was a strong pragmatist. Preferring to settle conflicts with diplomacy, he did not, however, oppose the use of force when he thought it was merited. He firmly believed that "the United States possessed a moral obligation to employ its power in order to contain international communism."[2] That said, for Eisenhower, communism was better contained not by military means but by creating the right conditions to make it "wither away." During the 1954 Indochina conflict, Eisenhower considered the case for force on its merits and probable costs as defined by these principles.

Among the difficult foreign-policy issues that confronted Eisenhower in his first year and a half in the White House, the French-Indochina War loomed large. As part of the struggle against Japan during the Second World War, American intelligence had worked with Ho Chi Minh's "Vietnam Doc-Lap Kong Minh Hoi" (Revolutionary League for the Independence of Vietnam, known as the Viet Minh) to expel Japanese forces from Vietnam. Shortly after the end of the war, on 2 September 1945, Vietnam declared its independence. Three weeks later the French returned, and five and half months later, on 6 March 1946, concluded a preliminary accord with the Vietnamese that seemed to open the door to a political compromise. Negotiations stalled, however, and, after months of unproductive dialogue, bloodshed ensued. Following a vicious French naval bombardment of Haiphong in November 1946, the Viet Minh forces launched a retaliatory strike in December and the French-Indochina War began in earnest.

As the atmosphere of the Cold War intensified, fears of communist expansion became the overriding preoccupation of American foreign-policy makers. Concern about the balance of East-West power in Europe led them to funnel substantial sums of aid money to France – indirectly assisting French military action in Indochina. By 1950, with the defeat of the Kuomintang fresh in memory and the Korean War just under way, the assumptions of the domino theory convinced Washington that if Indochina fell the rest of Southeast Asia would also be imperilled. Even among those who acknowledged that the war in Indochina and the insurgencies in Burma, Malaya, and Indonesia might be indigenous, most were persuaded that, in an increasingly polarized world, the mere existence of those revolutions and their leftist orientation meant that Southeast Asia was "the target of a coordinated offensive directed by the Kremlin."[3]

In 1950 the United States began to fund directly the French war effort in Indochina, and, from 1950 until 1953, its commitment grew from $130 million to $800 million (40 per cent of the total cost of the war in 1951 and 80 per cent by 1954). Policy makers, increasingly committed to the domino theory, agreed that Southeast Asia must not be permitted to fall into the hands of the communists like a ripe plum, and that a continued French presence was essential to the defense of the region.[4] France and the United States were now joined in the war effort, yet each had different goals; Washington sought to halt the march of communism in the area, while France hoped to prevent the disintegration of the French empire.[5]

Eisenhower recognized early on that "saving" Indochina would be a formidable task. On 17 March 1951 he wrote in his diary: "If they [the French] quit and Indochina falls to Commies, it is easily possible that the entire Southeast Asia and Indonesia will go, soon to be followed by India ... I'd favour heavy reinforcement to get the thing over at once; but I'm convinced that no military victory is possible in that kind of theatre. Even if Indochina were completely cleared of Communists, right across the border is China with inexhaustible manpower."[6]

Despite Eisenhower's recognition that American military intervention was unlikely to alter the outcome of the fighting in Indochina, he was tempted to become involved because of his Cold War beliefs. He dismissed Ho Chi Minh as "of course, a hard-core communist" and called the war "a clear case of freedom defending itself from communist aggression."[7]

In the president's mind, France held the key to stopping the advance of communist forces in Southeast Asia. The problem for the United States was to support and benefit from the anti-communist aspect of the French struggle without sliding into support for French colonialism.[8] The most obvious way of developing the allegiance of the Vietnamese people was to grant independence to the Associated States (Tonkin, Annam, and Cochin China) and construct an indigenous army with a native army corps. As NATO commander in 1951, Eisenhower had urged this position upon the French to no avail.[9]

Under mounting pressure to do something or withdraw, the French government of Premier Joseph Laniel appointed General Henri Navarre in early 1953 to command French forces in Indochina. Shortly thereafter, the new French commander presented the so-called Navarre Plan for American approval. Tailored to meet many of the specifications set down earlier by the American Joint Chiefs of Staff, it called for a vast augmentation of the Vietnamese national army, the establishment of a new training program, and the commitment of an additional nine battalions of French regulars to Indochina. Navarre proposed to withdraw his scattered forces from their isolated garrisons, combine them with the new forces, and initiate a major offensive to drive the Viet Minh from the Red River Delta. He hoped to inflict major casualties by forcing the Viet Minh to engage in large-scale set-piece battles that would limit the effectiveness of their guerrilla-style warfare.

The JCS called the proposals "a marked improvement in French military thinking."[10] After extracting a formal French promise to pursue the Navarre Plan with determination, the administration, on 9 September 1953, agreed to provide France with an additional $385 million to implement it.[11] Support for France had come to mean support for Premier Laniel since "no succeeding government would take a stronger position than his on the defense of Indochina, or in support of the European Defense Community."[12]

During Eisenhower's first year and a half in power, ratification of the European Defense Community (EDC) Treaty, which France had been delaying since 1951, was a major American foreign-policy goal. Throughout this time "Paris held the treaty hostage, promising to ensure either its passage or defeat depending on U.S. cooperativeness in Indochina."[13] Laniel's survival was deemed crucial to the treaty's future, just as it was to Indochina's. In a report dated 5 August 1953, the U.S. State Department had articulated its concerns that, if the Laniel government fell, "it [would] almost certainly be succeeded by a government committed to seek a settlement on terms dangerous to the security of the U.S. and the Free World ... Under present conditions any negotiated settlement would mean the eventual loss to Communism not only of Indochina but of the whole of Southeast Asia." The report concluded that the "loss of Indochina would be critical to the security of the U.S ... . If the French actually decided to withdraw, the U.S. would have to consider most seriously whether to take over in this area."[14]

In December 1953, the Viet Minh invaded central and southern Laos and prepared for a major strike into northern Laos. In response, the French altered their plans and air-dropped 12,000 of their finest troops into an isolated outpost called Dien Bien Phu. Eisenhower later recalled that he was "horror-stricken" by the move, since he was "well acquainted with the almost invariable fate of troops invested in an isolated fortress," and he instructed both the State and Defense departments to communicate his concerns to their French counterparts.[15] Soon after the French had installed themselves at Dien Bien Phu, more than 50,000 Viet Minh soldiers, under the leadership of commander Ngo Nguyen Giap, attacked with enormous force, raising serious doubts about the wisdom of French military strategy.[16] More important, in light of the worsening French position, the U.S. Defense Department began to give concerted attention to the question of how far "the U.S. was prepared to go in terms of force commitments to ensure that Indochina stayed out of Communist hands."[17]

The Eisenhower administration addressed the impending crisis in Indochina on 8 January 1954 at its regular National Security Council meeting. CIA director Allen Dulles began what was to become his regular practice of briefing all those present on the military situation in Indochina, especially concerning Dien Bien Phu. At that juncture, three Viet Minh divisions had surrounded the French forces, having begun an unexpectedly intense siege. Dulles argued that the Viet Minh sought political gains from this battle, believing that a military victory would undermine the French will to fight.

On the question of involving U.S. ground forces in the conflict, Eisenhower's position was clear. In his view, "the key to winning this war was to get the Vietnamese to fight. There was just no sense in even talking about United States forces replacing the French in Indochina. If we did so, the Vietnamese could be expected to transfer their hatred of the French to us." He added, "I cannot tell you ... how bitterly opposed I am to such a course of action. This war in Indochina would absorb our troops by divisions!"[18]

In an effort to increase the range and quality of advice he was receiving, the president, on 16 January, instructed Under-Secretary of State Walter Bedell Smith, CIA Director Allen Dulles, Deputy-Secretary of Defense Roger Kyes, special assistant to the president C.C. Jackson, and the chairman of the JCS, Admiral Arthur Radford, to create what came to be known as the Special Committee (or Smith group). Their mandate was to analyse the situation in Southeast Asia and formulate an "area plan" to deal with all of the region, not just Indochina or Vietnam. Eisenhower informed the group that it was to be "self contained ... and that neither NSC nor OMB [Office of Management and Budget] need be cut in on the deliberations." At a later meeting of the Smith committee General Graves B. Erskine, a respected intelligence specialist, was chosen to head a "working group" (later called the Erskine group) comprised of members of the Smith group.

At its 29 January meeting, the Smith committee redrafted a list of future policy options; under pressure from Radford, it included the option of engaging U.S. combat forces, and it also turned its attention to the "urgent French requests" for aircraft and 400 U.S. technicians. None of the participants objected to sending the aircraft, but Roger Kyes and Allen Dulles opposed the request for technicians on the grounds that sending personnel would lead to the need to send combat troops and that acquiescing so readily to French demands would limit American bargaining power with France. To ease the worries of the dissenters, the committee recommended that the United States send the planes and 200 technicians to "be used at bases where they would be secure from capture and would not be exposed to combat." Eisenhower concurred with the group's recommendation and the first active American military personnel were sent to the French-Indochina War.[19]

When a CBS broadcast (4 February) revealed the existence of the Smith committee and the plan to send technicians, Eisenhower reacted with fury at this latest leak of classified information.[20] Congress was also upset that no one on the armed services or foreign relations committees of either the House or the Senate had been previously informed of the existence of the Smith committee or the plan to send material and technicians. It felt (with some justification) that it was being side-stepped in the planning and decision-making process, and it demanded that such behaviour not be repeated.[21]

In response, Eisenhower ordered Under-Secretary Bedell Smith to consult with Congress before proceeding with any further recommendations or actions. He then met personally with Senate Republican leaders on 8 February to soothe their sensibilities and restore confidence in the administration. Eisenhower drew upon his personal authority in military matters, telling the senators: "Don't think I like to send them there, but after all ... we can't get anywhere in Asia by just sitting here in Washington and doing nothing. My God, we must not lose Asia – we've got to look the thing right in the face."[22] He called the move a "small project to serve a very large purpose – that is to prevent all of Southeast Asia from falling to the Communists."

In order to avoid another cut in the Indochina appropriations, Eisenhower vowed to remove American military mechanics by

15 June, at which time they would be replaced by civilians. The promise was enough to convince Republican leaders on Capitol Hill to support the president's decision.[23]

Eisenhower had manoeuvred around Congress and was now trying to avoid alienating it. In an effort to smooth ruffled feathers, he met with congressmen personally, appearing to make concessions and promising more consultations in the future.[24] Eisenhower's method of handling Congress illustrated his desire to avoid head-on confrontations if possible; his wartime experiences had shown him the folly of quarrels with strong and stubborn personalities.

NSC meetings in the ensuing two weeks focused on the need to find an indigenous Vietnamese leader to counter Ho Chi Minh's popularity and the overwhelming perception on the part of the Vietnamese people that what was taking place was a French colonial war. Highlighting the need for a popular indigenous leader, Eisenhower recounted a conversation he had with the Vietnamese ambassador, who reported that only "perhaps two or three percent" of the people of Vietnam believed the French promises of genuine independence. In the ambassador's view, the United States had to find some way to win over the Vietnamese population and instill some spirit into the French.[25]

Meanwhile, Secretary of State Dulles, who had been meeting in Berlin with the foreign ministers of Great Britain, France, and the Soviet Union since 25 January, was under increasing pressure to agree to hold a multinational conference in Geneva, with the participation of the People's Republic of China, to discuss prospects for uniting Korea and for peace in Indochina. Dulles informed Georges Bidault, the French foreign minister, that the United States was strenuously opposed to any negotiation on Indochina, since he felt that it would inspire the Viet Minh to increase their efforts while deflating French commitment. He threatened that the United States might not attend the proposed conference if the topic of Indochina were to be discussed. Bidault replied that the political climate in France demanded negotiations, and he waved the carrot of French ratification of the EDC Treaty under Dulles's nose. Dulles, who vehemently opposed an international conference, grudgingly consented to preserve Allied unity.

In the weeks that followed the decision to hold an international conference on Indochina, Eisenhower continued to examine various policy options advocating what would later come to be known

as "united action." Under-Secretary Bedell Smith submitted a
report to Eisenhower from the Erskine group on 11 March that
called the need for an area plan "essential"; in a supplemental
report six days later, the group proposed joint American, British,
and French efforts in Indochina. The State Department's policy-
planning staff advanced a similar concept in a memorandum dated
23 March.[26] Eisenhower encouraged the development of all these
reports but refused to commit himself to any specific course of
action. When asked about possible American involvement in
Indochina, the president side-stepped the question and the responsibility for the decision. "There is going to be no involvement of
America in war unless it is a result of the constitutional process that
is placed upon Congress to declare it."[27]

On 13 March a large-scale Viet Minh assault began at Dien Bien
Phu, and two hill outposts, Gabrielle and Beatrice, were quickly
seized. Military experts had underestimated the Viet Minh's ability
to get artillery up to the high ground around the fortress, and, on
15 March, the fortress's airfield was rendered inoperative, making
parachute drops the only means of resupply. Within five days, the
equivalent of two French battalions were killed or wounded, while a
third battalion deserted, reducing the fortress to a nearly indefensible state.[28] Five days later, Allen Dulles reported to the NSC that
recent intelligence estimates gave Dien Bien Phu only a 50–50
chance of holding out.[29]

The chairman of the French chiefs of staff, General Paul Ely, flew
to Washington on 20 March, at the invitation of Admiral Radford,
to brief the U.S. defense establishment on the situation in Indochina.[30] Two days later, Eisenhower met with Ely and Radford and
agreed to a French request for military hardware. He was non-committal, however, concerning the possibility of U.S. intervention. Ely
(no doubt encouraged by Radford) left with the impression that
Eisenhower had ordered Radford to provide anything the French
government asked for, without limit, in order to save Dien Bien
Phu.[31] In his memoirs, Eisenhower downplayed Ely's visit by making only a single passing reference to it.[32]

The following day, 23 March, Ely, meeting with Radford and
Dulles, submitted a request in writing for information as to what
type of American response could be anticipated if the Chinese
were to intervene in Indochina. Secretary of State Dulles believed
that this request stemmed more from a desire to obtain a bargaining chip for Geneva than from any honest fear that a strike was

imminent, and so he diplomatically avoided committing the administration to any fixed course of action. After the meeting, Radford revived Ely's hope for a bombing raid by implying that the position of the president might be different from that of Dulles.[33]

In a memorandum to Eisenhower, Radford voiced his concerns that the measures taken by the French to improve their military situation would prove both inadequate and too late to prevent a progressive deterioration of the situation. He feared that the end result would be the loss of all Southeast Asia to communist domination. He urged the administration to act promptly and with force to a possible frantic and belated request by the French for U.S. intervention.[34]

Dulles reiterated his refusal to commit the United States to a fixed course of action, in response to a possible Chinese intervention, on the grounds that "we could not afford thus to engage the prestige of the United States and suffer a defeat which would have world-wide repercussions."[35]

After his meeting in the Oval Office with Eisenhower on 24 March, Dulles reported that the president was in agreement that the United States should not get involved in any fighting in Indochina unless there were the political preconditions necessary for a successful outcome. Clearly, Eisenhower was not insensitive to the humiliation the United States and his administration would suffer if the country entered the conflict and did not obtain a victory; however, he did not wholly exclude the possibility of a single strike "if it were almost certain this would produce decisive results." Dulles then proposed an alternative strategy of harassing the Chinese along the seacoast and from Formosa. As this plan conformed nicely with the administration's "New Look" policy – the nuclear weapons strategy based on the doctrine of massive retaliation, which emphasized the role of threats and brinkmanship – Eisenhower seemed interested. Still, he told Dulles that he must not say anything in his pronouncements on the subject that could be construed as "an explicit promise that we might not be able to live up to."[36] Eisenhower was not about to discard any of his options prematurely or allow his secretary of state to circumscribe his freedom of manoeuvre.

On his last scheduled day in Washington, 25 March, General Ely encountered a hostile reception from the JCS. Army Chief of Staff Matthew B. Ridgway, who was particularly unresponsive, opposed injecting U.S. forces or funds into the conflict under any circumstances because of France's lacklustre commitment to the war.

Having left it to his subordinates to assume a tough posture and ask hard questions, Eisenhower reserved the role of benefactor for himself by finally approving virtually every item of American military hardware on Ely's shopping list.[37]

Radford convinced Ely to extend his stay by twenty-four hours for a meeting that, as it turned out, would sow the seeds of frantic French requests for U.S. intervention just prior to the fall of Dien Bien Phu. Ely claimed that, during their discussion, Radford informally proposed that American B-29s and carrier-based aircraft make massive night-time air strikes, possibly using tactical atomic weapons, against the perimeter of Dien Bien Phu to relieve the siege. Ely claimed that Radford told him that, if the French requested such assistance, he would do all he could to convince Eisenhower to support the plan.[38]

Radford subsequently denied having made any such offer.[39] While it is possible that language difficulties or selective memory may account for the different versions of this meeting, the most probable explanation is that Radford did convey the impression that Eisenhower would support a request for intervention. Nor was the fault entirely Radford's. The United States did wish to prevent a Viet Minh victory; the military was in the process of developing an operational plan, and Eisenhower had frequently appeared to support Radford's position. On this basis, the admiral may have felt that he would likely be able to obtain approval for Operation Vulture (Vautour).[40] Eisenhower's proclivity to think out loud and explore multiple options during the early stages of discussion was about to backfire.

When Ely returned to France and reported to Paris on the "ouverture extraordinaire" of Radford, he realized that no decision had been made. Paradoxically, Radford's assurances made Ely feel that he would have more difficulty getting his own government to make the request than Radford would have in obtaining Eisenhower's support for it.[41] French confidence that the president was ready to intervene was probably reinforced by Eisenhower's 24 March press conference in which he declared Southeast Asia to be "of the most transcendent importance," adding, "this fighting going on in Indochina, no matter how it started, has very manifestly become again one of the battlegrounds of people that want to live their own lives against this encroachment of Communist aggression."[42]

At an NSC meeting on 25 March, the participants turned their attention to a JCS memo which stated that "continuation of the fighting with the objective of seeking a military victory appears as the only alternative to acceptance of a compromise settlement." It recommended that the NSC consider the extent to which the United States would be willing to commit its resources in support of the Associated States in the effort to prevent the loss of Indochina to the communists irrespective of France's role. Then, the memo listed four possible scenarios for American involvement: in concert with the French; in the absence of the French; in concert with other allies; or, if necessary, unilaterally.[43]

Eisenhower was not about to be pressed hastily into action; he observed that, if the French could move only by air, "it seemed sufficient indication that the population of Vietnam did not wish to be free of Communist domination."[44] He also stated that the extent of congressional support would have to be canvassed "in the event that it seemed desirable to intervene in Indochina." He then argued that the United States or other free world nations could not go all-out in support of the Associated States without UN approval and assistance. Since this was highly unlikely, owing to the foreseeable opposition of the Asian-Arab bloc, Eisenhower's position suggested his less than wholehearted enthusiasm for American military involvement.

Another possibility Eisenhower considered was that the government of Vietnam could extend an invitation to the free nations of Southeast Asia, the United States, Britain, and France to come to its aid through a mutual-defense treaty – an option that would probably get the necessary votes to pass the Senate. (This idea would eventually grow into the Southeast Asia Treaty Organization.) The meeting ended with the president's statement that "the collapse of Indochina would produce a chain reaction which would result in the fall of all of Southeast Asia to the Communists."[45] His ambivalence was transparent: intervention was problematic, but so, too, were the risks inherent in the collapse of Indochina.

At a cabinet meeting on 26 March, Dulles opined that the battle for Dien Bien Phu was of only minor military importance; the Viet Minh would gain no significant advantage even if they took the fortress. While acknowledging the considerable psychological effect a defeat at Dien Bien Phu would have on the French, the secretary of state felt that Navarre and Laniel's strong determination to avoid a humiliating defeat could stimulate their willingness to accede to U.S. demands for Indochinese independence and an American role in planning strategy and training troops. In his view, the United States should offer to help France win the war, thus ruling out partition, withdrawal, or a continuation of the stalemate. The crux of Dulles's argument was a call for a conditional U.S. offer of assistance to Laniel based upon his acceptance of American stipulations; he was opposed, however, to immediate, unqualified action to save Dien Bien Phu.[46]

Unlike Dulles, Eisenhower had little to say. Throughout the cabinet's lengthy discussion of Dien Bien Phu, the president made only a few remarks, preferring to listen to what his advisers had to offer him. This behaviour was not atypical at cabinet meetings, but it stood in sharp contrast to Eisenhower's greater volubility during meetings of the National Security Council. However, in the few remarks that the president did offer, he revealed considerable pessimism about the chances for victory in Indochina.[47]

Although the war in Indochina was beginning to demand an increasing amount of the president's attention, it was still not his primary focus. Much of Eisenhower's time in the last days of March was dedicated to his writing the "fear speech" to counteract the "communists in government" hysteria fomented by Senator Joseph McCarthy. It was left to Dulles to concentrate more directly on the crisis, but he maintained daily contact with Eisenhower. The president continued to encourage various ideas and options on Indochina without committing himself to any of them. During this period, he told Dulles that he had not ruled out the option of a unilateral strike, while continuing to spur his advisers to consider various forms of multilateral intervention.[48]

Eisenhower's appreciation of the importance of maintaining and even encouraging a broad range of responses to a given problem would serve him well during the Indochina crisis. Nixon maintained that his boss "was not shackled to a one-track mind." Instead, "he always applied two, three or four lines of reasoning to a single problem and he usually preferred the indirect approach where it would serve him better than the direct attack on the problem."[49]

On the morning of 29 March, Eisenhower, Dulles, and Nixon met with Republican legislative leaders. The official record of this meeting does not indicate that Indochina was discussed, but Nixon, in his memoirs, claimed that the president noted the possibility of diversionary tactics, such as an attack by Chiang Kai-shek's forces on Hainan or a naval blockade along China's coast, should the situation at Dien Bien Phu become desperate. Nixon quotes Eisenhower as having said: "'I am bringing this up at this time because at any time within the space of forty-eight hours, it might be necessary to move into the battle of Dien Bien Phu in order to keep it from going against us, and in that case I will be calling in the Democrats as well as our Republican leaders to inform them of the actions we're taking.'"[50]

That evening, Dulles delivered a speech entitled "The Threat of a Red Asia" to the Overseas Press Club in New York. In it, he outlined the economic and strategic importance of the area within the context of the domino theory, arguing, "If the Communist forces were to win uncontested control over Indochina or any substantial part thereof, they would surely resume the same pattern of aggression against the other free peoples in that area." Then he added ominously, "The imposition on Southeast Asia of the political system of Communist Russia and its Chinese Communist ally, by whatever means, would be a grave threat to the whole free community. The United States feels that the possibility should not be passively accepted but should be met by united action. This might involve serious risks."[51]

As Eisenhower had edited and approved drafts of Dulles's speech, he may have agreed with its broad outlines. However, the emphasis in the speech on the perils of communist rule over any part of Southeast Asia gained "by whatever means" implied that any negotiated settlement would lead the United States to break with its French ally – a break Eisenhower did not seem ready to accept.[52] At his regular press conference on 31 March, Eisenhower stated, "It is in the united action of all nations and peoples and countries affected in that region that we can successfully oppose the encroachment of communism." The administration's goal, he suggested, was to make its friends strong enough to take care of local situations by themselves, with American financial, moral, political, and, where the vital interests of the United States demanded it, military assistance.[53]

The president's press conference underscored the need to engage the people of Indochina in the struggle against communism; more important, it spelled out his reluctance to commit American ground forces unilaterally, except in those situations in which undefined "vital interests" were involved. Although Eisenhower had permitted Dulles to take a hard line, he carefully softened it in the press conference.

"United action" was seen as a more attractive option because it dealt with some of the perceived flaws of unilateral intervention. If the United States acted as part of a unified group, which, it was hoped, would include nations from the region, that would undercut embarrassing charges of American imperialism as well as eliminate the potentially humiliating outcome of intervening unilaterally and failing to achieve victory. It would also allow the administration to support France and curb the advance of communism in the area.

In his memoirs, Eisenhower recalled that early in 1954 he held three conditions to be essential for intervention: a legal right under international law, accompanied by a request from the French government which "would have to reflect, without question, the desire of the local governments"; support from Congress; and "a favorable climate of Free World opinion."[54]

In retrospect, it seems clear that the president envisaged "united action" as a way of preparing Americans for the possibility of intervention in the event of a French defeat, Chinese intervention, or the collapse of Geneva, while seeking to ensure that if such intervention were to occur it would enjoy public and congressional support and the United States would not have to fight alone.[55] "United action" kept Eisenhower's options open without tying him down to any specific commitments since the concept remained so ill-defined.

In response to a second Viet Minh assault on Dien Bien Phu on 30 March, Admiral Radford called a special executive meeting of the JCS. While the French had stood their ground, the decisive battle had begun and its outcome seemed to be a question of weeks.[56] Present at the JCS meeting were the three service chiefs and the marine corps commandant; Radford polled them as to whether the United States should make a unilateral offer to provide air and naval support. The result was a unanimous "no" vote. General Matthew Ridgway, the strongest dissenting voice, believed that if the United States undertook air attacks, ground forces would soon have to follow.[57] The "no" vote deprived the JCS chairman of his most crucial support and shifted the balance of power within the administration so that the advocates of non-intervention outnumbered supporters of intervention by more than two to one.[58]

Yet the president was reluctant to disavow unilateral intervention publicly. As the situation on the ground at Dien Bien Phu worsened, it was obvious that a decision would have to be made. At the regularly scheduled JCS meeting on 1 April, Radford again pushed his case for unilateral intervention, but Eisenhower, well aware of the outcome of the JCS vote of the day before, clipped Radford's wings – telling him that the question of how or whether to save Dien Bien Phu was one for "statesmen" to decide and not the military.[59] Had he sought to encourage the idea of unilateral intervention, Eisenhower could easily have used this opportunity to signal his support for Radford's position. At the same time, the president recognized that he must be careful to say nothing to damage the morale of France or the Associated States. If defeatism was to become too widespread in France and Indochina, Navarre could surrender all or most of Vietnam to the communists even before the Geneva conference took place.

After the meeting concluded, Eisenhower met with some members of the NSC in his office. Unfortunately, no minutes from this meeting have survived, but, immediately after its conclusion, Dulles and Radford (presumably on orders from Eisenhower) started contacting top congressional leaders to sound out their views on the circumstances deemed necessary for them to support intervention.[60] Dulles and Radford planned to inform them on the activities that could be undertaken with sea and air power to deter the Chinese communists so that "they won't think of further adventures in Southeast Asia." They both agreed that it was necessary to stress that what had to be done could be done without the use of American ground troops.[61]

That same day at lunch, Eisenhower mused aloud that the situation might develop so that it would be necessary to send in squadrons of planes unilaterally, adding immediately that "we'd have to deny it forever." Uttering these thoughts in the presence of two important newspaper editors was more than sufficient to torpedo any such covert strategy.[62] In fact, this was to be the last time Eisenhower mentioned unilateral intervention as a real possibility.

On 2 April the president met with Dulles, Radford, Cutler, and Wilson to discuss the upcoming meeting with selected members of Congress. Dulles presented a draft congressional resolution which would authorize the president, upon his own determination, to use U.S. naval and air forces to aid those resisting aggression in Southeast Asia and to prevent the expansion of that aggression. Eisenhower approved of the contents of the draft, but he told Dulles not to present it to the congressional leaders since the "tactical procedure should be to develop first the thinking of Congressional leaders without actually submitting in the first instance a resolution drafted by ourselves." Dulles then claimed that his resolution was designed only to clarify what the administration thought was desirable. The president agreed that this was important but still did not explicitly articulate a commitment to the unilateral use of naval and air forces.[63] This may have been an indication that Eisenhower had ruled out unilateral intervention, "successfully tuck[ing] his own position behind the banner of separation of powers,"[64] or it may have been an attempt "to avoid the potential appearance of a setback" should Congress not accept it.[65] If the latter, then the president would have avoided a potentially embarrassing outcome by disassociating himself from a plea for intervention that might have been rejected.

Radford continued to advocate an immediate military use of force in the area, having again sought such a motion from the JCS that very day, while Dulles and Wilson opposed the move.[66] They both emphasized that the primary value of gaining congressional approval for unilateral military action would be to deter the Chinese and to strengthen the American bargaining position with the French and British. (Eisenhower did not challenge this view.) Faced with the opposition of most of the JCS, Radford retreated, stating that it was probably too late to rescue Dien Bien Phu and that any congressional authorization would not be acted upon immediately. However, he added that the French position could deteriorate after the fall of the fortress and advance congressional approval might be useful to speed intervention in this case.[67] It is also possible that Radford adopted a softer line because he had sensed that the president was not in favour of a unilateral strike.[68]

The meeting of Dulles and Radford (along with Under-Secretary of State Walter Bedell Smith, Deputy Secretary of Defense Roger Kyes, Navy Secretary Robert Anderson, and State Department congressional liaison Thurston Morton) with a bipartisan group of eight congressional leaders took place on 3 April in Dulles's office. Eisenhower distanced himself from the controversy by going to Camp David for the weekend. The congressmen showed their reluctance to approve what appeared to be a request for unilateral intervention. They stated that they wanted "no more Koreas" and that, once the U.S. flag and prestige were involved, it would not be possible to limit the military to an air and sea role. Radford acknowledged that it was too late for air strikes to save Dien Bien Phu and that the other JCS members were against such a mission. During the discussion that followed, the congressional leaders insisted on three conditions: there should be no congressional action until

Dulles had obtained commitments of a political and material nature from the Allies; the French government must promise to keep its forces in the fight; and France must also move more quickly in the granting of independence to the Associated States.[69]

Dulles reported the results of the meeting to the president that afternoon. Eisenhower agreed with Dulles that Congress had raised valid objections to unilateral American intervention, and he stated that he felt "the stakes [in Indochina] concern others more than us."[70] Years later in his memoirs, Eisenhower wrote: "There was nothing in these preconditions or in this congressional viewpoint with which I could disagree; my judgment entirely coincided with theirs."[71]

This meeting seems to have been critical in torpedoing the option of unilateral American intervention. It appears as though the president had decided to oppose unilateral intervention and used congressional opposition to justify his position.[72] If Eisenhower had been a staunch supporter of unilateral American intervention, he could have attended the meeting with congressional leaders and, drawing upon his influence on Capitol Hill, explained his reasons for wanting unilateral intervention, or at the very least made phone calls to key congressional leaders.[73] Alternatively, he could have proceeded with intervention on the basis of executive action and explained his decision afterward (as he had done when sending technicians in January, or as he would later do in Guatemala).[74]

By arranging the 3 April meeting, Eisenhower isolated Radford, Nixon, and other supporters of unilateral intervention by demonstrating congressional reluctance to adopt the unilateral option.[75] Instead, he built domestic support for his preferred approach of multilateral intervention, while making it appear as though it was the work of Congress. At the same time, he won over congressional leaders by making them feel that they were in control of the situation and that their opinions were being respected.[76] Had he explicitly ruled out unilateral intervention, however, it might have triggered additional communist pressure. It would also have undercut the morale of the French and the non-communist forces in the Associated States, whom Eisenhower relied upon to keep up the military pressure until a long-term political solution could be set in place.[77]

To say "no" publicly to unilateral intervention would also have risked political humiliation for the president. The opposition and those advocating an "Asia-First" perspective in his own party would have seen such a move as abandoning the area to the communists; it would have left him open to charges of being "soft on communism" and of having "lost Indochina." Instead, he arranged a meeting that he knew would construct roadblocks. In this way he could shift the blame for the "loss" of Indochina to Congress. By his "hidden-hand" technique,[78] Eisenhower avoided tying himself directly to a policy of abstinence that could be viewed as unacceptable.

In a 1979 interview, Thurston Morton, one of the participants in the meeting, was asked whether he thought the response of the congressmen had influenced the decision not to intervene. "No, I don't think so ... The fact that the President had reservations is what stopped it."[79]

When he returned from Camp David on the evening of 4 April, Eisenhower convened a meeting at the White House where, for the first time, he heard the complete list of conditions set out by Congress. Sherman Adams, the only participant to give an account of this meeting, recalled:

Eisenhower ... agreed with Dulles and Radford on a plan to send American forces to Indochina under certain strict conditions. It was to be, first and most important, a joint action with the British, including Australia and New Zealand troops, and, if possible, participating units from such Far Eastern countries as the Philippines and Thailand so that the forces would have to continue to fight in Indochina and bear a full share of responsibility until the war is over. Eisenhower was also concerned that American intervention in Indochina might be interpreted as protection of French colonialism. He added a condition that would guarantee future independence to the Indo-Chinese states of Vietnam, Laos and Cambodia.[80]

By making his conditions for intervention even more demanding than Congress's had been, Eisenhower further lessened the likelihood of ever having to intervene.

At the same time, the French military was becoming increasingly desperate. In the midst of the second Viet Minh offensive, General Navarre decided that a massive American air strike was Dien Bien Phu's only chance for survival. Late in the evening of 4 April, the French government sent a diplomatic note through the American embassy in Paris stating that the "immediate armed intervention of US carrier aircraft at Dien Bien Phu is now necessary to save the situation." To strengthen its request, it stated that "Radford had given him [Ely] his personal assurance that if [the] situation at Dien Bien Phu required US naval air support he would do his best to obtain such help from [the] US government."

Dulles informed Eisenhower of the French request the next morning. The president exploded in fury. Dulles recorded Eisenhower as saying that he "supposes Radford thought he was talking to someone in confidence – but says he should never have told a foreign country he would do his best because they then start putting pressure on us." The fate of Dien Bien Phu, which the president had allowed Congress to leave to the French and the British, threatened to become Eisenhower's responsibility because of Radford's rash talk. This revived the president's anger over the French handling of the war, and he referred to their request for air strikes as just one in a line of French "whims."

Eisenhower categorically refused the French request to intervene with American air power, agreeing with Dulles's analysis that the United States "cannot risk [its] prestige in defeat." He added: "Such a move is impossible. In the absence of some kind of arrangement getting support of Congress, it would be completely unconstitutional and indefensible." The president's opposition to American intervention in the war was unmistakeable: "We cannot engage in active war," he commented angrily, suggesting, instead, that Dulles explore alternative ways to aid the French.[81]

To be sure, concerns of "prestige" were not totally absent from Eisenhower's deliberations. He did seek to avoid losing military and political conflicts lest failure result in a "loss of face." But he responded to those concerns by attempting to alter the situation – urging his secretary of state to find other means to help the French. Unlike Nixon, Eisenhower was not tempted to pursue a military option to inflate his self-esteem by inflicting damage on the enemy. Nor is there any evidence of a desire to seek revenge against the Viet Minh when events in Indochina unfolded in a manner contrary to his wishes.[82]

Radford's apparent promise to Ely to obtain American intervention was embarrassing and politically damaging; if the French believed that the president had the power to override the objections of Congress, his strategy of refusing to intervene without congressional approval would be perceived as bogus – resulting in a collapse in French morale before Geneva. Eisenhower's fury with Radford may have been a displacement of his own guilt for having failed to disabuse Radford of the belief that he had the president's support for an American bombing of Viet Minh positions at Dien Bien Phu.[83]

Dulles contacted Radford, and they agreed that it was necessary to inform Congress more fully about the American stake in Indochina. That afternoon, Dulles reported to the House foreign affairs committee on a top-secret intelligence report that documented communist China's aid to the Viet Minh. He described the situation as "fraught with danger, not only to the immediate area but to the security of the United States and its allies in the Pacific area," and he urged the committee to support the administration's "united action" policy and continued aid to Indochina.[84]

On 6 April Eisenhower called an emergency NSC meeting to announce his decision not to intervene unilaterally. First, however, the council's planning board presented its report on the preconditions of American intervention – a task it had been assigned by the NSC on 25 March. It recommended the use of U.S. ground forces, if necessary, in one of four ways: joint U.S.-French action; U.S.-French action in conjunction with the Associated States; unilateral U.S. action; U.S. action in conjunction with other Allies should the French withdraw. These were the same four scenarios that the JCS had submitted to the council on 25 March. But this report made it clear that any intervention would be costly, concluding, "Once U.S. forces have been committed, disengagement will not be possible short of victory."[85]

The NSC then heard a report from the Smith committee (prepared by the Erskine group) which called the defeat of the Viet Minh "essential if the spread of Communist influence in Southeast Asia is to be halted" and urged the administration to accept nothing short of a military victory. If French assistance could not be obtained, the report continued, the United States should oppose any negotiated settlement in Geneva and arrange with the governments of the Associated States for the United States to continue the war in Indochina. Every effort should be made to obtain the participation of other interested nations, but the report concluded that the United States should proceed on its own if such support failed to materialize.[86]

Eisenhower was unruffled by these hawkish reports and remained steadfast in his opposition to unilateral intervention. In his decision to reject Operation Vulture, the costs and benefits were carefully appraised. The president was convinced that the conditions he desired for intervention, effectiveness and secrecy, could not be met.[87] In his memoirs, he defended his decision not to intervene:

Willingness to fight for freedom, no matter where the battle may be, has always been a characteristic of our people, but the conditions then prevailing in Indochina were such as to make unilateral American intervention nothing less than sheer folly ... Had the circumstances lent themselves to a logical use of military force, the task of explaining to the American public the necessity for sacrifice would have been an acceptable one. But the losses would have been heavy, and ... there never arose a situation justifying intervention.[88]

Although cognizant of the risk that the Republican right-wing (supporters of unilateral intervention) and some Democrats would use his refusal to act to embarrass him, Eisenhower was able to set aside such considerations and base his decision upon more objective cost-benefit calculations. In the absence of any deep-seated concerns with issues of self-esteem, his decision making was not impaired by personal psychological needs that distorted his judgment. Thus, he was better able to reach decisions that closely approximated a rational analytic model than his successors Johnson and Nixon would be.

In its debate that same day, 6 April, the Senate, displaying strenuous opposition to unilateral U.S. intervention, indicated a willingness to authorize intervention as part of a coalition of committed allies as long as "united action" did not turn into a cover for another Korean-style war. Success, the members stressed, was dependent upon genuine guarantees of independence for the Associated States. Most important, the Senate was adamant in demanding that Congress be kept informed and included in the decision-making process.[89] By insisting that the Congress, not the president, held the power to declare war, the senators conveniently removed responsibility for not intervening from Eisenhower's shoulders, shifting it instead to other nations.

When questioned by a reporter the following day about the importance of Indochina to the West, Eisenhower replied that "the possible consequences of the loss [of Indochina] are just incalculable to the free world." He then added that "this problem could not be handled by one country alone" but required "a concert of readiness to react in whatever way it was necessary." He told his listeners, "We are 160 million of the most productive and the most intelligent people on earth; therefore why are we going around being too scared?" But he refused to comment on a reporter's question as to whether the United States would "go it alone."[90]

Eisenhower's verbal aggressiveness at this press conference served the dual purpose of sounding threatening to the communists and increasing public awareness of the seriousness of the situation. This could be safely done since congressional demands now shielded him from having to follow through unilaterally – an option that obviously did not appeal to him since he had given his private "no" in the NSC meeting the day before. However, he refused to rule it out explicitly when asked, giving the impression that it was still under consideration. Privately, he was still pushing the coalition idea, trying to make conditions more favourable for intervention.[91]

The most serious obstacle to multilateral intervention was obtaining British participation, a precondition that Eisenhower had insisted upon at the 4 April meeting. On 2 April Dulles had met with British Ambassador Roger M. Makins, who told him that his government supported a negotiated settlement and favoured partition of Vietnam.[92] In a cable dated 4 April, the president addressed the subject of the Geneva conference and concluded, "There is no negotiated solution of the Indochina problem which in its essence would not be either a face-saving device to cover a French surrender or a face-saving device to cover a Communist retirement." The first alternative was unacceptable. The way to achieve the second alternative was, Eisenhower stated, through an "ad hoc grouping or coalition composed of nations which have a vital concern in the checking of Communist expansion in the area ... The important thing is that the coalition must be strong and it must be willing to join the fight if necessary."

The Allies were completely opposed to the formation of a coalition; on 6 April the French government formally rejected internationalizing the war effort, and the British followed suit the next day. Both governments felt that pursuing a coalition at this point would serve only to hinder the possibility of an acceptable armistice at Geneva.[93]

Dulles was visibly disappointed with the Allied response and remarked that, if the United States lacked the support of its Allies, it would have to decide on its own what policies would best serve American interests and security.[94] Dulles flew to London on 10 April to persuade Eden to agree to join a planning group to develop the idea of a coalition. At the conclusion of these meetings, a communiqué was issued which indicated the willingness of the countries principally concerned to examine the possibility of establishing a collective-defense mechanism to assure the peace, security, and freedom of Southeast Asia and the western Pacific.[95]

Dulles cabled Eisenhower that the communiqué indicated "a large measure of acceptance of our view of the danger and the necessity for united action." However, on the same day that Dulles left London, Eden reported to parliament that there had been no change in British policy, and that the communiqué did not represent any form of commitment to the American plan, only a willingness to explore possibilities. The British would not take any action before the Geneva conference, which they still believed could produce a reasonable settlement. This drained the life out of what Dulles had believed was a preliminary British commitment.[96]

Dulles then flew to Paris for talks with Georges Bidault and other French leaders. Upon his arrival, he gave the impression that the British had promised more than the contents of the communiqué suggested, and that, as a result, a coalition was taking shape. In an attempt to erase the taint of colonialism that still hung over the war, Dulles obtained the very meager statement that "the independence of the three Associated States within the French Union, which new agreements are soon to complete, is at stake in these battles." Eisenhower accepted this watered-down promise of independence and hoped that a colonial war had been transformed into a war against communism. In his memoirs, he highlighted the promise of "independence" and the "concessions on the part of the French" and concluded that "the Vietnamese had been satisfied."[97]

Dulles's trip appeared to have accomplished little in the way of concrete results; the United States was still isolated in its search for partners to form a coalition. Yet, when the secretary of state arrived back in the United States, he claimed that a ten-nation alliance was "taking definite form." He then set about organizing a meeting on 20 April for prospective members to discuss the formation of the new security organization.[98]

Vice-President Nixon, speaking off the record at a meeting of the American Society of Newspaper Editors on 16 April, stated that "to avoid further Communist expansion in Asia and Indochina we must take the risk now by putting our boys in, I think the Executive has to take the politically unpopular decision to do it."[99] At the time, this statement was widely viewed as a "trial balloon" for the administration to test public reaction to possible intervention.[100] However, it seems that Nixon had acted on his own initiative. Earlier, he had told the French ambassador that he shared Radford's view of the benefits of a massive air strike to save Dien Bien Phu.[101]

Nixon's comments appeared to have caught the president by surprise; it is now generally agreed that Eisenhower neither orchestrated the statement to test public reaction nor was informed about it in advance. However, Eisenhower did not openly challenge or refute Nixon's statement; rather, he sought to minimize the damage by telling the State Department to "clarify" U.S. policy "without cutting the ground from under Nixon."[102] He did not reprimand Nixon personally, preferring to put a positive interpretation on an incident that could have been politically embarrassing for him. Sherman Adams reported that Eisenhower called Nixon and "told him not to be upset. Trying to cheer him up, the president reassured him that the uproar over his comment had been all to the good because it awakened the country to the seriousness of the situation in Indochina."[103]

Years later, Eisenhower played down the incident in his memoirs, saying that "this [sending troops] was always a possibility; the question was under constant study."[104] He may have kept silent to avoid displaying divisions in the administration, but it is more likely that he saw some value (as did Dulles) in Nixon's statement: having the communists believe that the United States might yet intervene could force them to moderate their demands at Geneva. The president seems to have been willing, temporarily, to lose some domestic and Allied support in order to intimidate the communists. Yet his motivations continue to be something of a mystery, since he remained silent throughout the episode and subsequently.

Dulles returned to Europe on 21 April to participate in regularly scheduled NATO meetings, but his main activity was to lobby the Allied governments to support "united action." With the Geneva conference set to convene in six days, Dulles thought it was crucial that the western Allies present a united front. As soon as he arrived, the French began to apply pressure. On 22 April Bidault requested massive U.S. air intervention. He put a new emotional slant on the request by emphasizing that the strikes were to save the lives of the French soldiers at Dien Bien Phu. Bidault implied that he might favour internationalizing the war if U.S. action would save Dien Bien Phu. Dulles tried to turn the conversation to organizing a long-term defense coalition, but Bidault retorted, "If Dien Bien

Phu fell the French would want to pull out entirely from Southeast Asia, and assume no continuing commitments."

The following day at lunch with Dulles, Laniel explicitly tied the fate of Dien Bien Phu to France's future involvement in Southeast Asia and the EDC. He admitted the illogic of the position but added that Dien Bien Phu "had become a tremendously emotional thing and Frenchmen were no longer capable of reasoning about it." He refused to moderate his position since he believed that his government would not survive the collapse of the fortress.[105] Later that afternoon, the French request was repeated with more force by Bidault, who interrupted the afternoon's meetings to show Dulles a note from General Navarre which stated that the only alternative to the immediate implementation of Operation Vulture was a cease-fire. Dulles, recognizing that Bidault was "close to the breaking point," replied he could not personally respond to such a request but would pass it to Eisenhower.[106]

In a second message, two hours later, Dulles expanded on his perception of the situation: "There is, of course, no military or logical reason why loss of Dien Bien Phu should lead to collapse of French will, in relation both to Indochina and EDC. It seems to me that Dien Bien Phu has become a symbol out of all proportion to its military importance."[107] That evening, Eisenhower phoned Bedell Smith and "agreed that Foster's position should stand unchanged. There would be no intervention without allies."[108]

Dulles then wrote Bidault, stating that air strikes were beyond the constitutional powers of the president because they would constitute active belligerency and therefore would require congressional approval, which in turn was conditional on the formation of a coalition. Intervention, he concluded, was still possible but only through collective action.[109]

In his efforts to create a coalition, Dulles (joined by Radford, who had just arrived in Geneva) met with Eden on 24 April and told him that the knowledge that a "common defense system was in prospect" would strengthen the West's bargaining position at Geneva and deter the communists. Furthermore, Dulles added, Eisenhower was ready to ask Congress for authorization to intervene if the British government would agree to participate. Eden was firmly opposed. He doubted the usefulness of air strikes at such a late date and feared that such an attack could bring China directly into the conflict, which in turn could bring in the Soviets under the Sino-Soviet Treaty of 1950.[110]

In a letter dated 24 April, Bidault again petitioned Dulles for air strikes to save the French position at Dien Bien Phu. In response to the French request, Eisenhower had Bedell Smith inform French Ambassador Henri Bonnet that, if the British agreed to participate, the administration would request congressional authorization for a 28 April air strike on Dien Bien Phu.[111] Eisenhower's decision shifted responsibility for the air strike to the British, who, as the president had expected, rejected the proposal.[112]

Arriving in Geneva, Eden met with Dulles and told him that the British would not participate in any intervention plans but would be willing to undertake a secret study of military options to defend the other nations of Southeast Asia (excluding Indochina).[113] The British refusal, coupled with Eisenhower's insistence on their participation, ended any real possibility of intervention at Dien Bien Phu. Dulles informed the president that, in his opinion, air strikes might not save the fortress and would put a great strain on relations with Britain and the Commonwealth countries. In addition, there was insufficient time to arrange political understandings with France and the political risk could not be justified. Most important, he added, "once our prestige is committed in battle, our negotiation position in these matters would be almost negligible."[114]

Some scholars believe that Eisenhower was genuinely interested in intervention and see this as the point where, frustrated by the Allies' reluctance to cooperate, he resigned himself to a negotiated settlement at Geneva.[115] Other analysts have speculated that the president was never really interested in intervening, even as part of a coalition effort, and that he made the offer of intervention knowing that the British would refuse to go along with it. In this way, responsibility for the failure to intervene was transferred from him to the British. These scholars observe that Eisenhower gave Dulles little assistance in his campaign to formulate a coalition, and that he wrote to Churchill and Laniel only once throughout the entire ordeal.[116] The message to Laniel did not even mention a coalition but merely encouraged him to announce that France would keep fighting after the fall of Dien Bien Phu.[117] If Eisenhower's goal had been the creation of a coalition capable of intervening, he did very little to make it a reality.

Still others have argued that the president was not opposed in principle to intervention at Dien Bien Phu but only to intervention under the prevailing circumstances, and that he would have intervened had his preconditions been met.[118] In a personal letter of

26 April to General Alfred Gruenther, the head Allied commander in Europe, Eisenhower stated that for a Western power to contemplate going to Asia militarily, without the participation of local Asian peoples, would be "to lay ourselves open to the charge of imperialism and colonialism or – at the very least – of objectionable paternalism."[119] In essence, Eisenhower was arguing that intervention under such circumstances would be politically damaging – too high a price to pay for minimal gain.

The alternative that Eisenhower presented was a plan which, based on the premise that "the loss of Dien Bien Phu does not necessarily mean the loss of the Indochina war," called for concerned nations to begin "conferring at once on means of successfully stopping the Communist advances in Southeast Asia." In addition, it required the participation of the French army and assurances of "freedom of political action to Indochina promptly upon attainment of victory." Eisenhower concluded that "the general security and peaceful purposes and aims of such a concert of nations should be announced publicly – as in NATO. Then we possibly wouldn't have to fight."[120] The president apparently hoped that, as NATO had done in Western Europe, a new NATO-like alliance in Southeast Asia would stem communist aggression and obviate the need for any loss of American lives.

Privately, Eisenhower placed most of the responsibility for inaction on the French. In a letter to Swede Hazlett on 27 April, Eisenhower accused the French of using "weasel words in promising independence" to the Associated States. "Through this one reason as much as anything else [they] have suffered reverses that have been really inexcusable." He continued to complain that the French wanted the Americans to act "as junior partners and provide materials, etc., while they themselves retain authority in that region." Eisenhower would not be party to "any such notion."[121] While neither the president nor his secretary of state wanted France humiliated at Dien Bien Phu, they felt that such a defeat, even with its attendant risks, would be less of an evil than to risk American prestige in support of a doomed fortress of colonialism.[122]

At a meeting with Republican congressional leaders the same day, Eisenhower conceded that Dien Bien Phu would probably fall within the week. He also told his listeners that, "if we were to put one combat soldier into Indo-China, then our entire prestige would be at stake, not only in that area but throughout the world." He then made it clear that he had no intention of sending in American ground forces unilaterally, but he warned that there was still a possibility that some U.S. units might become involved. He concluded that that "the free world must understand that our most effective role did not lie in furnishing ground troops ... The French have asked us to send planes to Dien Bien Phu ... but we are not going to be involved alone in a power move against the Russians."[123] Eisenhower's proposed solution was "to lead the free world into a voluntary association which would make further Communist encroachment impossible."[124] He stated that the United States "must keep up [the] pressure for collective security and show determination of the free world to oppose chipping away of any part of the free world."

Recognizing that the president's reluctance to act seemed at variance with his anti-communist beliefs, Republican congressional leaders agreed that the administration must take appropriate steps to avoid being tarred with the onus of "losing" Indochina as the Democrats had been blamed for the "loss" of China.[125] Though Eisenhower himself was cognizant of the problems he faced, he was able to resist the pressure of the "bombers" and the fear of being shamed and humiliated as a result of his inaction. At the same time, he understood the need for a fig-leaf to cover his unwillingness to become involved in the fighting at Dien Bien Phu. In order to avoid having to say "no" and being censured for the loss of Vietnam, Eisenhower hid behind congressional insistence upon British participation.

The president again met the press on 29 April and was asked to explain an earlier comment he had made about Geneva being the search for a "modus vivendi."[126] He replied that, between the unacceptable (the complete loss of Indochina to the communists) and the unattainable (a satisfactory peace settlement and stable relationship with the communists), there was probably a middle path. Later, he denied that this meant he favoured partition: "I didn't mean ... to endorse, even by indirection, any specific means of getting along. I have no particular method that I am thinking about at the moment." Eisenhower claimed that he had done all he could as chief executive without exceeding his constitutional authority. But his remarks outraged the French, who viewed them as a "betrayal." Bidault complained that the American position left him with "just a two of clubs and a three of diamonds" with which to negotiate.[127]

Later that same day, Bedell Smith reported to the president on the state of affairs at Geneva. Eden's position was that the British were prepared to guarantee any peace agreement that the French made but they would not join any regional-defense agreement until after Geneva. Australia and New Zealand had retreated from their initial positions of support for a regional-defense arrangement. The good news was that the French had signed a preliminary agreement for independence with the Associated States. In his memoirs, Eisenhower stated that, under the conditions then existing, Geneva would probably result in "a pragmatic and workable rather than a desirable arrangement."[128]

At the 29 April NSC meeting,[129] Eisenhower fought what was virtually a one-man battle against his security advisers to enforce his decision against war and intervention. In Geneva, even Dulles challenged the president's reasoning via a message he sent to Bedell Smith. According to the official minutes of the meeting, Eisenhower retorted that, "in spite of the views of the Secretary of State," to intervene unilaterally seemed "quite beyond his comprehension." Radford pushed for intervention, as did Smith, Nixon, Stassen, and (via messages to Radford and Smith) the American ambassador to France, Douglas Dillon. For nearly two hours, the president rebuffed their arguments one by one, supported only by one comment each from Kyes and General Robert Cutler, special assistant secretary for national security affairs. Director of Foreign Aid Operations Harold Stassen launched the most heated exchange with the president, arguing strenuously that the United States should intervene in Indochina, without the British if necessary, if the French withdrew; Congress and the American public would support such intervention "if the Commander-in-Chief made it clear to them that ... [it] was necessary to save Southeast Asia from Communism." In a not so subtle challenge to the president's manhood, Stassen urged him not to let "the appalling weakness of both the British and the French ... render the United States inactive and impotent." Eisenhower countered Stassen's analysis by stating he did not feel the mood in Congress was anywhere close to supporting such a move. Moreover, he added, if the United States went in alone "we would in the eyes of many Asiatic peoples merely replace French colonialism with American colonialism" and be engaging in "an attempt to police the entire world ... We should be everywhere accused of imperialistic ambitions." Even if it were desirable, Eisenhower continued, the military force for such an intervention would not be immediately available. He then raised the grave risk of a war with China and the USSR which would have to be fought without allies. "The concept of leadership implied associates. Without allies and associates, the leader is just an adventurer like Genghis Khan." In this last comment, Eisenhower's lack of grandiosity and omnipotence can be observed in his rejection of a policy of "going it alone." Nor did he believe that the United States should focus on its own aims without considering the goals and desires of other nations, since those same nations could be crucial to achieving American objectives. Eisenhower closed the exchange with Stassen by pushing him into a corner. He asked if the "right decision was not rather to launch a world war. If our allies were going to fall away in any case, it might be better for the United States to leap over the smaller obstacles and hit the biggest one with all the power we had."

Other participants also pleaded the case for intervention. Smith inquired about air strikes with other Asian nations. Eisenhower replied that this was not possible since Australia was unwilling to participate. Nixon then proposed sending "an Air Force contingent representing a unified alliance [which] would have the double effect of letting the Communists know that we were going to resist further expansion in the area, and of bolstering the morale of the French and Vietnamese troops." Such a move Nixon claimed, could be taken in the context of a Pacific coalition without the British.[130] The president stated that he would recommend this course to Congress if he could be sure the French would keep their troops in the fighting. (This was a safe proposal, considering that the French had given every indication they would find a way to pull out at Geneva.)

After the ensuing debate in which his counsellors had pressed him as hard as they could to intervene – either by air strikes to save the French position in Indochina or by land forces to prevent a "giveaway" at Geneva – the only step Eisenhower would agree to take was to allow acting secretary of state Smith to discuss the possibility of going ahead with other interested countries, even though Britain had backed out of the coalition. To Smith and the other pro-interventionists, the compromise offered the chance that warlike responses from ambassadors Percy Spender and Leslie Munro of Australia and New Zealand respectively, and the returning Dulles, might persuade the president to change his position at the next meeting of the National Security Council.[131]

Eisenhower accepted the proposal in the knowledge that it bound him to do nothing but wait for events to unfold.[132] Dulles would also be able to say to the French, by way of encouragement, that the United States had not made its final decision regarding intervention. But, in fact, the 29 April meeting was the final occasion at which substantive policy options regarding Indochina were considered in the NSC forum. After this, the NSC's role was reduced to being a vehicle for briefings, possibly because the president wished to avoid a repetition of the intense and protracted challenges he had endured at its hands.

None the less, this meeting was strikingly illustrative of the fact that, although Eisenhower sought diverse counsel, he was careful never to relinquish control of the decision-making process or to allow his advisers to dictate policy. Because of his lengthy experience in positions of authority, he was not overwhelmed by the magnitude of the responsibilities facing him. Confident in his own decision-making abilities, and in his powers of analysis, Eisenhower was able to stand firm in the face of heated opposition and, in sharp contrast to Lyndon Johnson, ignore the advice of his more hawkish advisers.

Dulles returned from Europe on 4 May and met with Eisenhower, MacArthur, and Cutler the next morning to report on the course of his talks with the British and French. Dulles "spoke of how galling it was to the U.S. to be the centre of the Red attack at Geneva, without any of our Western friends speaking up in general debate in our defense." He said that he told Eden "how disappointed we are in [the] British repudiating the position they had taken in the communiqués,"[133] which the Americans had interpreted as a commitment to a coalition approach. Eisenhower suggested that "Dulles give a chronology of the U.S. actions to Congress in his bipartisan briefing, to show that throughout we had adhered to the principle of collective security" and to the position that "no unilateral intervention by the U.S., overtly, would be tolerable, because it would place a colonial stigma on the U.S., and because it would exhaust the U.S. eventually." Eisenhower "did not want Dulles to undercut or repudiate the U.K. publicly, but merely show the factual record."[134]

After outlining to Eisenhower the divisions within the French leadership, Dulles concluded that "there is no French policy at the present time." He continued, "The French fear ... if the U.S. is brought into the struggle, France will not have a free hand to 'sell out and get out.'" Therefore, he believed that "conditions did not justify the U.S. entry into Indochina as a belligerent at this time." Eisenhower firmly agreed. The president commented that European allies were willing to let the United States pull their chestnuts out of the fire but will also "let us be called imperialists and colonialists." Once again, they agreed to continue efforts at a regional grouping. But, at Eisenhower's suggestion, it was resolved to find out secretly where the British and American positions were in agreement and then to proceed with talks with a broader group.[135] The decision against intervention was continuing to crystallize with a remarkable lack of fireworks or dramatics.

Afterwards, Dulles informed congressional leaders that the administration had decided against intervention since the three preconditions had not been met. He added that the situation was such that, even if the United States did enter the conflict, it did not appear possible to obtain a successful outcome. He believed that the United States should attempt to establish a coalition-defense arrangement for Southeast Asia as soon as possible, and that it should not "write off" the British and French as allies. The congressmen expressed general agreement with the administration's actions and plans thus far.[136]

At a press conference later the same day, Eisenhower deflected attention from the actions of the administration. He stated that the Indochina portion of the Geneva conference was being organized and that a large measure of the initiative now rested with France and the Associated States. He affirmed that efforts at realizing a Southeast Asia security arrangement were under way, adding that this process could bear directly upon the course of events in Geneva.[137] In all these pronouncements, the Allies were held up as ultimately responsible for the position of the administration.

At the next day's NSC meeting, the topic of U.S. intervention was largely by-passed; instead, Eisenhower turned his attention to the issue of bargaining tactics at Geneva. The possibility of a demarcation line was discussed and the need to maintain the territorial integrity of Laos and Cambodia re-emphasized. The president stated that he had "no objection to the French making use of the idea of U.S. intervention as a means of influencing the Communists," but he added that the American delegation itself should not engage in such talk because, if "U.S. officials began talking of U.S. unilateral intervention, such talk would be completely inconsistent with our whole foreign policy."[138]

The Indochina phase of the Geneva conference opened on 8 May – the day after Dien Bien Phu was overrun following fifty-five days of siege. Allied unity was in a shambles. In Paris and Washington most of the resentment was aimed at London for sabotaging "united action." The Eisenhower administration, recognizing that France had few bargaining chips, saw little hope of preventing it from calling a cease-fire, pulling its troops out of the war, and negotiating away at least part of Indochina. The French government submitted a proposal to demilitarize Cambodia and Laos and to move opposing troops to separate zones in Vietnam – the first step towards partition. In his memoirs, Eisenhower claimed that he was worried by these proposals since they lacked adequate enforcement measures and partition would lead to "enslavement of millions in the northern partitioned area."[139] The NSC resolved that "the United States will not associate itself with any French proposal directed toward cease-fire in advance of a satisfactory armistice agreement."[140]

Efforts to implement "united action" continued, but with little genuine conviction that they would succeed. Dulles once again approached French Ambassador Bonnet to explore "internationalization" of the war – a conversation that had taken place many times before, but this time it produced different results. On 10 May Ambassador Dillon cabled the secretary of state to inform him that Laniel was inquiring about the kind of military action the United States was willing to take in Indochina and that he was also seeking U.S. advice on how to protect the French Expeditionary Corps. Dulles told Radford that Laniel's attitude was significant since it was the first sign that the French were willing to discuss any specifics of the military situation.[141]

Dulles and Radford consulted with Eisenhower at the White House, and together they formalized the preconditions for U.S. intervention to present to the French. The administration indicated that it was prepared to intervene provided that the following conditions were met: U.S. military participation was formally requested by France and the Associated States; Thailand, Philippines, Australia, New Zealand, and the United Kingdom also received similar invitations, and the U.S. was satisfied that the first two would accept at once with the rest to follow shortly thereafter; the United Nations became involved, perhaps by request from Laos, Cambodia, or Thailand, through a peace-observation commission; France guaranteed to the Associated States complete independence, including an unqualified option to withdraw from the French Union at any time; France undertook not to withdraw its forces from Indochina during the period of "united action" so that U.S. forces – principally air and sea – and others would be supplementary and not in substitution; agreement was reached on the training of native troops and on a command structure for "united action." In addition, Eisenhower declared that these conditions would have to be endorsed by the National Assembly (so any successor French government would have to adhere to them). If this were done, the president added, he would appear before Congress and request a resolution that would "enable him to use the armed forces of the U.S. to support the free governments that we recognize in that area."[142]

To insist that Laniel, who headed a weak and faltering coalition with only a two-vote majority, obtain the approval of a war-weary National Assembly for a surrender of French control over Indochina was to demand the impossible. These preconditions were "so formidable that they could be judged only as having been carefully calculated to impede, if not indeed to preclude, American military involvement."[143] More than anything else, they suggested a government that seemed less than eager to commit its military forces.[144]

Premier Laniel, after reviewing the American terms for intervention, once again rejected the stipulation giving the Associated States the right to withdraw from the French Union.[145] France's continued refusal to grant independence to the area hardened Eisenhower's unwillingness to fulfil any requests that would strengthen the French position there. In his memoirs, Eisenhower again focused on American anti-colonialism: "The standing of the United States as the most powerful of the anticolonial powers is an asset of incalculable value to the Free World ... Never, throughout the long and sometimes frustrating search for an effective means of defeating the Communist struggle for power in Indochina, did we lose sight of the importance of America's moral position."[146] Eisenhower, ever the pragmatist, understood that it was one thing to fight communism, quite another to fight it with outdated colonialism.

After its final preconditions for intervention were rejected, the administration awaited further developments from Geneva and the battlefield – which had moved to the Red River Delta.[147] Dulles announced publicly, on 8 June, that the administration did not propose to seek authorization from Congress for intervention in Indochina. Eisenhower made a similar statement at a press conference two days later. In a meeting with French Ambassador Bonnet on 9 June, Dulles explained that the United States could not allow the French government to hold a permanent option regarding U.S. intervention for purposes of internal manoeuvring or negotiating at Geneva.[148] Three days later, Laniel's government fell on a vote on the Indochina question and was replaced by a government headed by Pierre Mendes-France, who publicly set himself a one-month deadline to reach a settlement.

Fearing that the new French government would give away too much to the communists in its desire for peace, the administration recalled Under-Secretary Smith from Geneva on 20 June, leaving foreign service officer U. Alexis Johnson to head the delegation.[149] With partition becoming more probable, Eisenhower was increasingly put on the defensive for his decision not to intervene. He was forced to deflect accusations, articulated by Senator William Knowland, that negotiations were a search for a "Far East Munich" by stating that the two situations were not comparable; Munich had been an ill-conceived attempt to avoid war by appeasing an aggressor, while partition would be an acceptance of the military fact of French defeat at war.[150]

Although scattered cries of "Munich" continued on Capitol Hill,[151] Eisenhower did not feel compelled to respond with a show of force in Indochina, as Nixon and Johnson were to do subsequently. Instead, he carefully arranged for a third party to appear to take the responsibility for non-intervention – Congress in the case of "Operation Vulture" and Britain in the case of "united action." In this way, Eisenhower distanced himself publicly from his more controversial decisions and avoided the political and psychological costs for the "loss" of North Vietnam.

When Premier Mendes-France requested that Dulles return to Geneva or send Smith as a gesture to show American support, thus enabling the French to avoid even harsher terms from the communists, Eisenhower expressed concern that "if we do go and if we sound off against the settlement, as we should, then are we not dividing the free world and being put in the position of splitting publicly with France and probably with the U.K?" Nevertheless, Eisenhower felt that the United States should have a high-level American representative at Geneva: "Otherwise, the stories from Geneva will be entirely colored by Red propaganda and also by propaganda of our allies, particularly the French, who will then blame us for everything that goes wrong."[152]

During the night of 21–22 July, arrangements for a cease-fire agreement, a "Final Declaration" establishing temporary partition at the 17th parallel, and the scheduling of nation-wide elections following unification in 1956 were concluded in Geneva. There

were only limited protests in Congress.[153] Eisenhower announced
that "the United States has not itself been a party to or bound by
the decisions taken by the conference ... [but] will not use force to
disturb the settlement."[154] In his memoirs, the president admitted
that "by and large, the settlement obtained by the French Union
at Geneva in 1954 was the best it could get under the circumstances."[155] In August, however, Eisenhower paid the predictable
cost when the French National Assembly defeated the proposed
EDC treaty by a vote of 319 to 264.[156]

These events were followed by the creation of the Southeast
Asian Treaty Organization (SEATO) on 8 September, which, in an
attached protocol, extended a vague commitment to the security of
South Vietnam, Laos, and Cambodia – all of which had been forbidden from joining any military alliance by the Geneva agreement. SEATO was the "institutional embodiment of the principles
of 'united action' that Eisenhower and Dulles championed, but
could not put into effect, during the Dien Bien Phu crisis."[157]

The president affirmed that SEATO's creation meant that "the
dilemma of finding a moral, legal, and practical basis for helping
our friends of the region need not face us again."[158] He had also
provided himself with a counter-argument and defense against those
who may have wanted to label him "soft on communism" for allowing the "loss" of the northern half of Vietnam.

Paradoxically, Eisenhower's continuing support and aid to the
non-communist portion of Vietnam after partition would result in
"the continuation of an American presence that tied American
interests to Indochina almost as surely as would have the use of
troops."[159] As president, Eisenhower never acquired any intimate
understanding of Vietnamese society and thus raised no objections
when Ngo Dinh Diem, a Catholic, proposed to head the government of the southern half of Vietnam, which was predominantly
Buddhist. American aid to Diem's government between 1955 and
1961 surpassed a billion dollars, of which 78 per cent was for the
military. The United States became South Vietnam's principal
backer when it took over training of the Vietnamese military, and it
supported Diem's decision not to hold elections in 1956. Such actions closely linked American prestige to a government that was
never able to enlist the support of its people.[160]

Commentators writing during and immediately following Eisenhower's presidency generally perceived him as a figurehead who

did not fully embrace the responsibilities of his office but rather delegated authority among his subordinates and advisers. Many of the early accounts of the Indochina crisis scarcely mentioned Eisenhower's role, while those that did suggested that his contribution was heavily dependent on the advice of his advisers and was often inconsistent.[161]

Contemporary observers of the relationship between Eisenhower and Secretary of State John Foster Dulles interpreted Dulles's higher visibility and outspokenness as evidence that he was the principal architect of the administration's foreign policy. Certainly, Eisenhower did little to discourage that interpretation, emphasizing the high level of agreement between Dulles's views and his own. For example, at a press conference on 12 May 1954, Eisenhower stated: "I think I have assured this group several times that I know of no important announcement made by either one of us in this regard that isn't the result of long and serious conferences. If there are any differences ever detectable in our utterances, it must be because of language and not because of any intent."[162] Quasi-insider Sherman Adams put forward a similar analysis of the Eisenhower-Dulles relationship in his memoirs. Adams claimed that the president established the broad themes of foreign policy and that "within that framework Eisenhower delegated to Dulles the responsibility of developing the specific policy including the decision where the administration would stand and what course of action would be followed in each international crisis."[163]

Yet a much different picture of Eisenhower's role emerges from recently declassified government documents. These documents make it abundantly clear that Eisenhower was deeply involved with foreign-policy issues, though he often concealed his involvement by taking action indirectly.[164] Furthermore, the same documents reveal not only that Eisenhower retained final authority but that he kept a tight rein on his voluble secretary of state.[165] Throughout the 1954 Indochina crisis, Dulles and Eisenhower maintained a regular dialogue that involved almost daily meetings or briefings. But access and the frequency of meetings did not translate into an all-powerful role for the secretary of state. They may have "jointly perfected policies, but Eisenhower made the final decisions and Dulles executed them."[166]

Eisenhower's concealment of his activist role reflected his ambivalence about the nature of the presidency. While he wanted to exercise power in order to shape the political issues of his administration, he also wished to be perceived as a calm, reassuring voice to the nation. This prompted him to publicize the non-controversial, ceremonial aspects of his office while concealing the more political part. His more vocal subordinates (Dulles and Radford) were left publicly to take the unpopular stands for which he would then take the credit for moderating.[167] They acted as lightning-rods that drew the political heat away from Eisenhower who, by his "hidden-hand" technique, protected himself from becoming the target of potential acrimony and divisiveness.[168]

Shielded from public opprobrium by this façade, Eisenhower made full use of his advisers by actively encouraging various groups and individuals to formulate opinions independent of one another, even when those opinions directly contradicted his own. He used the ideas, options, and objections raised by those around him to explore the merits of different policy choices and to probe for weaknesses in his own position. Unlike Nixon, who avoided information and advice that challenged his own preferred position, or Johnson, who went along with his advisers' recommendations in order to retain their support, Eisenhower invited opposing perspectives and opinions even when preparing to ignore them.

The evidence suggests that the president played a critical role in all of the major decisions during the Indochina crisis of 1954; he opposed the involvement of ground troops and rejected the French request for air strikes; he initiated discussion on a multilateral approach that eventually resulted in the "united action" plan and the formation of SEATO; and he decided on the status of the negotiating team at Geneva and set its mandates and guidelines.

Eisenhower was a secure and self-confident individual with a well-functioning ego. As a result, his decision-making was not impaired by fears of shame and humiliation over the "loss" of North Vietnam. Unlike Johnson, he could tolerate the lack of support from many of his key advisers and remain true to his own convictions. That Eisenhower was very impressed by Dulles's comprehensive knowledge of world affairs is incontrovertible; but he was not prepared to play second fiddle, even to his secretary of state. He once told journalist Emmet Hughes that "there's only one man I know who has seen more of the world and talked with more people and knows more than he does – and that's me."[169] Given this flattering self-portrait, it is not surprising that the president would feel supremely comfortable in challenging the more hawkish positions of Dulles and Radford on Vietnam and in ultimately deciding not to assist the French. Eisenhower's confidence in his ability to deal with foreign-policy issues was in sharp contrast with Johnson's anxieties in this area. It allowed Eisenhower to reject the advice of his senior advisers – unlike Johnson, who finally acquiesced even though he intuitively grasped that his decisions to escalate the war in Vietnam would create more problems than they would solve.

Nor did Eisenhower, in contrast to Nixon, feel the need to act out previous experiences of shame and humiliation. Defeats on the battlefield or at the negotiating table were perceived as setbacks to his policy, not personal attacks. His temper flared on occasion, but the emotion always passed quickly, and there is no evidence of Eisenhower acting out of anger to punish his opponents during the Indochina crisis.

In Eisenhower's personality and character, then, the unconscious influence of narcissistic vulnerabilities that coloured the Vietnam foreign policy of Johnson and Nixon was largely absent. He was able to judge, in a more objective fashion than his successors, the most effective ways of realizing his goals with the fewest costs. His determination to avoid expanding the U.S. military commitment to France required him to make compromises he did not like; but he was able to avoid committing American forces to a war that, as both Johnson and Nixon would painfully discover, could not be won.

Conclusion

Lyndon Johnson's decisions to escalate the level of American military involvement in the Vietnam War in 1965, and Richard Nixon's decisions to bomb and invade Cambodia in 1969–70, stand in sharp relief to Dwight Eisenhower's earlier decision in 1954 not to commit American forces to the French defense of Dien Bien Phu. In 1954 and 1965 presidents Eisenhower and Johnson each expressed concerns about the costs of becoming embroiled in an Asian land war, and each was subjected to considerable pressure by their respective civilian and military advisers to act. Eisenhower resisted the pressure; Johnson did not. In the case of President Nixon, the pressure to bomb and invade Cambodia was largely self-induced; it was a Nixon-initiated policy that was opposed by a majority of his advisers.

In situations where presidents are faced with massive political pressure to take certain actions, decision makers may find their room for manoeuvre seriously constrained; this was not the case in 1954, 1965, and 1969–70. The domestic political environment in which Eisenhower, Johnson, and Nixon functioned in those years was sufficiently malleable to give them genuine freedom of choice.[1] In 1954 opinion was divided between those who feared greater involvement in Indochina and those who believed that containing the spread of communism required the United States to help its beleaguered French ally. In 1965 Vietnam was not high on the public's agenda. While it is true that public-opinion polls revealed that many Americans supported the war effort, Johnson did have a real choice. In 1969–70, Nixon's decisions to bomb and invade Cambodia were taken largely in secret and without any solicitation of public support. In all three instances, there was no ground swell of popular opinion demanding the action that each president finally chose. The domestic political environment was not a significant determinant of policy; its fluidity made it possible for personality variables to play a significant part.

Nor can the presidents' advisory systems be assigned a major explanatory role in these presidential decisions. Eisenhower's advisory system was carefully structured, with policy options subjected to detailed and meticulous examination; yet the president ultimately chose to ignore the advice his advisers tendered.[2] In contrast, debates among Johnson's advisers were desultory and loosely organized. Although Johnson's advisory system left something to be desired in terms of careful cost-benefit analyses of competing options, Johnson was exposed to rigorous critiques of the various choices open to him. Nevertheless, he chose to listen to those who advocated bombing North Vietnam and committing American ground troops to South Vietnam, a reflection more of his excessive deference, for psychological reasons, to the opinions of his Kennedy advisers – McNamara, Bundy, and Rusk – than to the nature of his advisory system. That Nixon's advisory system was inadequate and poorly functioning is also true. But it was not the product of inadvertence or flawed design. Rather, it reflected the deliberate attempt of the president and his national security adviser to make foreign policy themselves with as little input as possible from the State Department.[3] In each of these three cases, the structure of the president's advisory system reflected the wishes of the incumbent; its limitations, ultimately, were a product of the personality of the office holder as reflected in his decision-making style.

A detailed analysis of the personality traits and character of presidents Eisenhower, Johnson, and Nixon reveals significant contrasts. Eisenhower emerges as a healthy, well-functioning individual with a secure and adaptive ego structure. He was highly intelligent and self-confident, with a warm and engaging personality. Possessing a quiet confidence in his intrinsic self-worth, Eisenhower was not driven by a need to curry favour or to be popular with his associates. He was almost effortlessly well liked by his peers, his superiors, and his subordinates. At the same time, Eisenhower was no saint. His associates were well aware of his capacity for angry outbursts. Stupidity, arrogance, and incompetence infuriated him. But he did not remain angry for long, and once unleashed his anger abated. When he experienced hurt or anger as a result of criticisms directed against himself or his policies, he was able to tolerate those upsetting emotions; he did not behave punitively towards those who had offended him, nor did he take pleasure in humiliating them or others in order to restore his own self-esteem.

When faced with the Viet Minh assault on Dien Bien Phu and France's request for American military assistance, Eisenhower did not interpret North Vietnamese behaviour as an attack on him personally or as a challenge to his machismo, as would Nixon. Nor did he overvalue the opinions of his hawkish advisers because of his feelings of inadequacy and fear of humiliation, as would Johnson. He explored various options through a careful cost-benefit analysis and was prepared to oppose American intervention on that basis.[4]

In contrast to Eisenhower and Nixon, Johnson lacked self-confidence in the realm of foreign affairs. His political strengths and interests lay in the field of domestic policy, where his narcissistic personality traits of grandiosity and omnipotence were "reparative" rather than "destructive"[5] and so produced the remarkable legislative achievements of the Great Society. Given his deficient knowledge and expertise in the international sphere, Johnson relied heavily on his foreign-policy advisers. And, despite the existence of competing options and concerns about funding for his Great Society programs, he chose to align himself with those who advocated bombing North Vietnam and committing American combat forces. It was not an easy choice; powerful strategic and domestic arguments were mounted both for and against escalation. Adding to the military and strategic arguments in favour of widening the war was Johnson's fear of being humiliated by his colleagues should he fail to support their position, and his desire to appear decisive and courageous in the eyes of the American people.

As a narcissistic personality, Johnson oscillated between feelings of grandiosity and inferiority. To maintain his omnipotent, grandiose self, Johnson needed the mirroring approval of those around him, particularly those whom he admired; in 1964, these were his Kennedy advisers. Having suffered numerous humiliations at their hands as vice-president, he needed to be perceived by the "Harvards" as deserving of the slain president's mantle. At a conscious level, Johnson was concerned to avoid their backbiting and possible defection from the administration – a prospect that carried humiliating potential for electoral losses. At an unconscious level, his self-esteem was dependent on maintaining his advisers' respect; loss of their regard was experienced as a narcissistic wound. For both conscious and unconscious reasons, Johnson's narcissistic preoccupation with issues of shame and humiliation led him to silence his own doubts about the efficacy of escalation and to choose a policy of expanding the war.

Johnson's decision to intensify American involvement in the war was also facilitated by a second component of his narcissism: his search for an idealized parental "imago" or good internal object to restore his sense of completeness. In idealizing Robert McNamara and, to a lesser extent, McGeorge Bundy and Dean Rusk, Johnson enhanced his self-esteem through the unconscious fantasy of being connected with a perfect object. To have rejected their counsel would have involved a process of de-idealization with its concomitant feelings of disappointment and emptiness.

Unlike Johnson, Nixon possessed both an intimate knowledge of international affairs and complete confidence in his ability to conduct foreign policy. That was his preferred area of expertise, and his years as vice-president had provided him with significant exposure to many of the world's leaders and to foreign-policy issues in general. Nixon, like Johnson, alternated between feelings of omnipotence and insignificance; however, whereas Johnson's narcissism in the foreign-policy arena was expressed in the search for mirroring and idealizing transferences with his advisers, Nixon's narcissism presented more of the "glass bubble" phenomenon. He often behaved as though he were impervious to others, with a self-sufficient grandiosity; the opinions of colleagues were frequently ignored or devalued. Yet underneath Nixon's veneer was a psychological self that was intensely vulnerable to being shamed and humiliated and that reacted with rage to such experiences.

Nixon perceived any challenge to his policies, such as the North Vietnamese spring offensive in South Vietnam that began in February 1969, the opposition of the anti-war protesters, the Senate's refusal to confirm two of his Supreme Court nominees and its curtailment of presidential war powers through its repeal of the Gulf of Tonkin resolution, as an expression of his opponents' ambitions to humiliate him personally. Given Nixon's narcissistic rage at his perceived treatment by his "enemies," and the political challenges from the Senate and the peace activists that would have accompanied a direct assault on North Vietnam,[6] Cambodia became the convenient displacement-object for Nixon's anger, rage, and frustration.

But why did Johnson and Nixon become narcissistic characters while Eisenhower did not? Although innate constitutional endowment cannot be ruled out, it is more fruitful to look at the impact of early childhood environment on the development of personality and character. In the making of the narcissistic character, the young child is frequently singled out as "special" and the message that is communicated, early on, is that love is contingent on performance – the child's ongoing demonstration that he or she is, in fact, singular and extraordinary. Thus the message that the narcissistically vulnerable child learns is that he or she is not inherently lovable and that parental love must be constantly earned and can be easily withdrawn. The mothers of both Lyndon Johnson and Richard Nixon communicated to them that they were, in fact, "special" and that their expectations for them were of a different order than the ones they held for their other children.

Lyndon Johnson was the first-born in a family that came to number five children; he was followed by two sisters, then a brother, and finally another sister. The prototype of the intellectually precocious and gifted child, he was adored by his mother particularly because his intellect and charm seemed in such marked contrast to her husband's crude, raucous, and drunken ways. Rebekah expected Lyndon to become a professor; his father, Sam, wanted him be a politician and a legislator. The sense that he was special, inculcated in him by his mother, came under assault, however, as he was forced to contend with the time she devoted to his siblings. He also had to deal with his mother's anger, as well as with her withdrawal of love when he proved to be an indifferent student unable to satisfy her narcissistic yearnings for a person in her life who would make something of himself and thus be different from her husband. All this was to erode his self-esteem and lead him to compensate for feelings of inferiority through the creation of a grandiose and omnipotent self that would be immune to feelings of shame or humiliation.

But it was difficult for Johnson to retain that sense of uniqueness when faced with the evidence that his father thought him a lazy good-for-nothing, his classmates found him obnoxious, and his family was regarded with scorn and contempt. Repeatedly humiliated in his efforts to inflate his self-esteem, he decided on a political career since it seemed to promise the possibility of recreating his sense of superiority through electoral triumphs over a series of rivals. Successive victories at the ballot-box would be the ultimate testimony that he was extraordinary and that he was loved. Oedipal issues were also involved. Electoral success would provide the crowning oedipal victory, with father, the hapless politician, dethroned by the son who would then be number one in mother's eyes.

Although Richard Nixon was the second-born child in a family of five sons, many of the dynamics that were operative in his home were the same ones that had been evident in Johnson's. Nixon's mother, Hannah, like Rebekah Johnson, was better educated and more socially prominent than the man she chose to marry. Their marriage, like that of the Johnsons, was a struggle marked by constant financial worries and the failure of Nixon's father to provide an adequate living or intellectual companionship for his more intelligent and ambitious wife.

Unlike the Eisenhower family in which no child appeared to be significantly more intelligent or gifted than the others, Richard Nixon was definitely different from his siblings. His older brother Harold, by all accounts an easy-going and warm child, lacked Richard's intellectual precocity, as did his younger and quite average brothers. Hannah recognized Richard's distinctive gifts and taught him to read before he entered kindergarten. She pushed him to achieve, even to the point of arranging for his three siblings[7] to share a room while Richard was given a room of his own. The message was clear: Richard was "special," and his particular niche in the family was to satisfy his mother's narcissistic need that he make something of his life so that hers could be imbued with meaning beyond scraping a living from their tiny grocery store.

To ensure his mother's continued interest in and concern for him, Richard, unlike Lyndon, applied himself ceaselessly to his studies. With Arthur's death in 1925 (at age seven), and Harold's death in 1933 (at age twenty-four), Nixon's drive intensified. It was fuelled partly by survivor guilt; his successes would help compensate his mother for her other losses and alleviate his guilt for unconscious homicidal wishes towards his brother Harold, the object of so much of his mother's attention. The deaths of Harold and Arthur, along with his father's demonstrable inadequacy as a husband and provider, furnished Richard with enhanced opportunities to satisfy his narcissistic needs and his oedipal fantasies of being special to his mother.

But there was a price to be paid. To be perceived by mother as hard-working, undemanding, and dependable, and to avoid being beaten by an abusive father, Nixon had to control both his feelings and his needs. He grew up with an intense concern about maintaining control of himself, confessing, "I have a fetish about disciplining myself."[8] At its best, control, rooted in the anal stage of development, leads to autonomy, but at its worst, it leads to overcontrol, to rigidity, and to a constricting fear of "letting go." Nixon's notorious body rigidity, with its mechanical gestures, suggested a desperate need to control himself lest his emotions surface and shame him. Privately, however, as both the Watergate tapes and the Haldeman diaries reveal, he was enormously angry and full of rage, with a habit of fulminating against Jews, blacks, Democrats, and many others. But even in public, his use of anal metaphors such as "kicking butt" was indicative of the links between his anality and aggression.

Lyndon Johnson and Richard Nixon came from homes in which the father was impatient, angry, and, most important, devalued. The mother was more intelligent and more cultured and suffered from the emotional, intellectual, and financial limitations of her husband. Both Rebekah Johnson and Hannah Nixon focused their attention on one son, Lyndon and Richard respectively, in order to provide themselves with a sense of achievement. That son was loved insofar as he satisfied his mother's ambition. Maternal love was contingent on performance and even then grudgingly given.

Both Johnson and Nixon had difficulty making friends. Lyndon's gregarious nature, however, prompted him to surround himself with associates, many of whom he either idealized or devalued as a way of shoring up his self-esteem. In contrast, Nixon was more of a loner; his compulsion to be autonomous and in control did not permit him to relate easily to people or to inspire affection or love. In this friendless space, his envy and rage were projected onto others, who were seen as harmful and dangerous and against whom protection was necessary lest they attack his vulnerable self. As an adult, he became increasingly reserved and suspicious and had difficulty trusting others. Not surprisingly, Nixon preferred to make decisions largely on his own, as Cambodia demonstrated. His narcissistic and obsessional character had become infused with paranoia.

Dwight Eisenhower was also born into a poor family but did not suffer the humiliation of severe privation or community contempt. As the third son in a family that would comprise six boys,[9] all of whom were intelligent and talented and developed successful careers, neither Dwight's arrival nor his particular talents singled him out for unusual attention by his parents or his siblings. He was, according to his biographers, a likeable, scrappy kid who developed a close, mutually supportive relationship with his brothers. Indicative of the lack of distinctive treatment that he enjoyed, even as an adult, was the discussion that surrounded a planned family reunion after he had become the supreme allied commander in Europe. No one in his family, least of all Eisenhower, assumed that his schedule should take precedence over that of his brothers; no one thought of him as "special."[10]

As was the case with Johnson and Nixon, Eisenhower was particularly close to his mother and saw his father as somewhat stern and removed. But David Eisenhower, his father, unlike Sam Johnson and Frank Nixon, was never an object of scorn or derision. He and his wife, Ida, had a stable and secure relationship, and notwithstanding David's early financial reverses, he remained respected and admired by his family. Ida loved her children but never looked to any of them, including Dwight, to achieve or accomplish in order to compensate for whatever she may have perceived as her husband's inadequacies.

In that environment, Eisenhower grew up with a sense of being loved for himself; he also grew up with an awareness that, as a middle child in a family of boys, competition and sibling rivalry were core ingredients of family dynamics. His mother saw her sons' childhood fights as a normal part of growing up and she almost never intervened to take sides or play favourites. Eisenhower's childhood experiences gave him a sense of comfort and camaraderie with other men, an attitude that expressed itself in his choice of a military career and in a well-honed competitive spirit that was based on a mature appreciation of his strengths and weaknesses.

As someone whose narcissism was appropriate and healthy, Eisenhower did not oscillate between feelings of inadequacy and grandiosity; his self-esteem was largely stable. Since his self-expectations were reasonable, rather than grandiose, he was less prone to experience feelings of shame and humiliation when he failed to live up to them. Thus he was able to tolerate failure and disappointment much better than Johnson and Nixon were; he never had to lash out at his enemies to restore his self-esteem.

To be singled out by a parent as extraordinary by virtue of one special attribute, and to feel that love is heavily contingent on what one "achieves" rather than on what one "is," constitutes a major ingredient in the creation of the narcissistic personality. Typically, such people function extremely well in their careers, although they often suffer tremendous oscillations in their self-esteem, ranging from grandiose illusions of omnipotence to debilitating feelings of shame and humiliation when reality pierces their grandiosity. Lyndon Johnson and Richard Nixon are classic examples of this phenomenon. Although previously humiliated by Kennedy's advisers, Johnson would not give up in his quest for their love and admiration; to avoid their contempt and scorn, he stifled his own reservations, ignored the critics, and allowed his decisions on Vietnam in 1965 to be coloured by his narcissistic needs.

In 1970 Richard Nixon, humiliated by the North Vietnamese, the Senate, and the peace activists, had given up his efforts to be either accepted or respected by his "enemies." His narcissism had been so wounded that he could only lash out and punish his detractors by deciding, virtually on his own initiative, to bomb and invade Cambodia. Such behaviour would demonstrate his strength and resolve and silence his inner fears about being passive and dependent[11]; equally important, it would restore his self-esteem by allowing him to "get even" with his enemies for their failure to provide him with the mirroring he so desperately craved. Thus his actions were unconsciously designed to buttress his grandiose and omnipotent self and deny his fragile, dependent self; he would behave as he saw fit, without having to wait for anyone else's approval or permission.

If the escalation of the Vietnam War in 1965 and the bombing and invasion of Cambodia in 1969–70 reflect, in part, the impact of Johnson and Nixon's narcissistic concerns with issues of shame and humiliation, how can we explain Johnson's subsequent decisions to halt the bombing of North Vietnam and refuse to seek another term as president, and Nixon's later decision to accept an end to the war on terms that did not ensure a "just and lasting peace"? What role, if any, did their narcissistic personalities play in these decisions?

Lyndon Johnson's decisions, announced on 31 March 1968, were the product of a number of interrelated factors that included military-strategic, financial, and domestic-political concerns.[12] But personality factors involving issues of shame and humiliation were also significantly implicated. Having finally recognized that continuing his aggressive policies would only exacerbate his feelings of shame and humiliation, Johnson decided to behave in a less aggressive manner to avoid the potential for still further humiliation. This time he would de-escalate rather than escalate his involvement; but his actions continued to be governed by his psychological need to avoid shame and humiliation. The behaviour would be different, but the underlying motivations would be the same.

From a military-strategic perspective, the Tet offensive of 31 January 1968, which saw the North Vietnamese launch a series of massive, coordinated attacks throughout the cities and towns of South Vietnam, put a lie to the administration's year-end claims of progress and further eroded public support for the war. It also forced a full-scale reconsideration of the military strategy undertaken by the administration, particularly in light of the requests made by General Westmoreland for an additional 205,000 troops.

Domestic factors, such as the lack of congressional support, the financial implications of escalating the conflict, the possibility of new riots and turmoil in the cities, the New Hampshire primaries, and the role of his advisers were also important in influencing Johnson's decision. Johnson had asked his senior colleagues from the Senate, Richard Russell, John Stennis, Scoop Jackson, and Stuart Symington, if they thought Congress would support a call-up of the reserves, and he was told that it would not. Mike Mansfield, who had succeeded Lyndon Johnson as Senate majority leader, also warned that the administration had reached the end of the line on increases in American troop levels.[13]

Spelling out the brutal fiscal and economic implications of the build-up of the reserves, Treasury Secretary Henry Fowler underscored the need for an economic surtax to finance the war. British devaluation of the pound in late 1967 had triggered a general deterioration in the gold market and a crisis of confidence in the dollar. By the middle of March, the gold market was in a state of panic and speculation was rife that the United States, too, might be forced to devalue. Without the surtax, the American economy would be in jeopardy, but there were few indicators that Congress or the American public would support it.[14]

Although principal responsibility for dealing with racial violence in the cities rested with the nation's mayors and governors, Johnson feared being asked to send in federal troops (as had occurred in 1967) and then having to face the criticism that he was over- or under-reacting with one eye on election day.[15] At the same time, the New Hampshire primaries brought home to Johnson just how vulnerable his Vietnam war policy had made him. On 13 March 1968 Senator Eugene McCarthy shocked the nation by winning 42.4 per cent of the primary vote to Johnson's 49.5. When the final results were tabulated, the president of the United States had won the primary by only 230 votes, and McCarthy had captured twenty of the twenty-six delegates. McCarthy's victory revealed sufficient discontent with Johnson to encourage Robert Kennedy to announce his candidacy for the presidency on 16 March 1968. The erosion of public support threatened to overwhelm Johnson, leading Harry McPherson, presidential adviser and chief speech-writer, to write to Johnson that continuing the status quo would "lead either to Kennedy's nomination or Nixon's election or both."[16]

But the evidence suggests that, notwithstanding all of these pressures, Johnson was strongly resistant to the idea of halting the bombing as a way of stimulating Hanoi to negotiate. He rationalized that it could endanger the lives of his troops, and in mid-March he told his aides, "I'm telling you now I'm not going to stop the bombing. Now I don't want to hear any more about it."[17]

The president had not wanted war in Vietnam; but, having committed himself to it, the investment of his personal prestige made it extremely difficult for him to back down.[18] His wish to stay the course was a matter of pride. For he saw no alternative that did not require him to admit failure or defeat[19] – both humiliating choices to a man such as Johnson. In fact, Johnson seemed headed towards another escalation. Harry McPherson's second draft of the president's Vietnam speech, scheduled for 31 March, was even tougher than the first. It contained such statements as "the American people … do not engage in craven retreats from responsibility, whatever the year."[20]

Instrumental in persuading Johnson to rethink his Vietnam war strategy was his new secretary of defense, Clark Clifford, an old and valued Johnson friend whose hawkish views had recommended him to Johnson as a replacement for McNamara. Within the short space of a month, however, as he absorbed the meaning of the Tet offensive, Clifford became increasingly convinced that a marked change in direction was necessary. Since, in his view, the military had no acceptable rationale for the troop increase, no idea whether more troops might be needed or when, if ever, the South Vietnamese would be ready to carry the main burden of the war, their request should not be met.[21]

Supporting Clifford's strategic assessment were the views of the senior adviser group, the so-called "Wise Men." This group, which had supported a hard-line position in November 1967, received new briefings on 25 March from State and Defense department officials. The following day, McGeorge Bundy, who had been designated spokesman, told the president that the majority[22] believed that the United States must take steps to disengage and that there should be no substantial troop reinforcement or any expansion of the conflict. The effect on the president was considerable. Although Johnson had known for two weeks that Dean Acheson had started to change his views, his position, ex officio, as the leader of the foreign policy establishment had "an unquestionable impact on the President," as did Cyrus Vance's signficant reversal of his opinions.[23]

At a meeting with generals Wheeler and Abrams that same day, Johnson sought to stifle potential military criticism of the peace moves by playing to their sympathy, pointing out the "abominable" fiscal situation, the panic and demoralization in the country, near-universal opposition in the press, and his own overwhelming disapproval in the polls. He concluded that if he refused to alter course "I will go down the drain."[24]

But three days before his 31 March speech, the president, although clearly shaken by the advice of the "Wise Men," still had not indicated any change in his hard-line position. Clifford persuaded Secretary of State Rusk and W.W. Rostow, Johnson's national security assistant, that presidential speech-writer Harry McPherson should prepare another, softer draft of the address indicating American willingness to stop the bombing of North Vietnam, except for the area north of the demilitarized zone. Johnson then could choose between the two drafts.[25]

Johnson selected the softer draft; on 31 March the public learned that only 13,500 new ground troops would be sent to Vietnam (not the original number of 205,000 requested by Westmoreland and Wheeler) as part of a policy to rely more heavily on South Vietnamese efforts, and that Ambassador Averell Harriman had been appointed as Johnson's special adviser to the peace talks.[26] But there was little evidence that Johnson had rethought the goals of the war. Militarily, the means were being scaled back without modifying the ends. There was no acknowledgment that the war had been a mistake or that the speech heralded a U.S. withdrawal from Vietnam. Rather, it seemed to have been designed to quiet the forces of domestic dissension,[27] thus curbing additional personal attacks on the president's self-image.

The most dramatic aspect of Johnson's speech, however, was his concluding remarks in which both his advisers and the public learned that he would not run again for president. It was clearly a difficult and painful decision for Johnson, fraught with the potential for humiliation, since the American people might well assume that he was being driven from office by the Tet offensive and Bobby Kennedy's entry into the presidential race.

What finally tipped the balance was Johnson's recognition that his position had become untenable. He worried that, if he left office and went back to Texas, he could be accused of acting like a coward; but if he stayed, he risked the possibility of Robert Kennedy reclaiming "the throne in the memory of his brother"[28] or Nixon's trouncing him at the ballot-box.

Both choices seemed equally agonizing to a man with Johnson's narcissistic sensibilities. Faced with mounting evidence of public opposition to any extension of the war, as well as the change of heart by Clifford and the "Wise Men," Johnson had a sufficiently strong ego to accept the new realities. However, it was his narcissism that enabled him to rationalize that he could alter course and withdraw from politics without being seen as a coward. What mattered was not what his generation would think or say about his decisions, but what history would say about his presidency. If he were able to demonstrate that he had fostered domestic peace, provided for the national security, and improved the general welfare as a result of his decision to stop the bombing and withdraw from the presidential race, his burning ambition to be seen as a great president could still be rewarded. Posterity, he reasoned, would see his withdrawal as an act of courage; this action would stop civil disorders and protests against "Johnson's war," it would free him to pursue peace negotiations with Hanoi without such a strategy being seen as an election ploy, and it would end Republican stalling on a tax increase and thus protect the stability of the dollar and the U.S. economy.[29] All of these results would help secure Johnson the favorable judgment of history while foreclosing, in the short term, the humiliating possibility that his own party would fail to give him the nomination. Johnson's bombing halt and withdrawal from the presidential race were designed to avoid the shameful prospect of further humiliation – the same concern that had motivated his earlier decisions to escalate the war in 1965.

Notwithstanding his commitment to "peace with honor" in Vietnam, by January 1973 Nixon was forced to accept an agreement that failed to ensure either peace or the continued viability of the South Vietnamese government. What role did Nixon's narcissistic vulnerability to feelings of shame and humiliation play in facilitating this outcome? In the aftermath of the failed 1970 Cambodian invasion, the Nixon administration continued the secret negotiations that had begun in February 1970; but for nearly three years the American and North Vietnamese bargaining positions remained far apart.[30] To inhibit public opposition to the war, the administration announced the withdrawal of 150,000 American troops in September 1970 as well as plans for the continued phased withdrawal of all American forces from South Vietnam as it stepped up its policy of Vietnamization. Yet anti-war protests continued and members of the Senate called for a specific withdrawal date. Rather than risk being humiliated and scorned by further attacks on his policies, Nixon decided to adopt a policy of accommodation. By August 1972 the last U.S. combat unit was withdrawn, and by the end of 1972 only 24,200 American personnel remained in South Vietnam.

Following his landslide electoral victory on 7 November 1972, Nixon resolved to end the war with "honor" before his inauguration. In October 1972, after nearly three years of on-again, off-again discussions with the North Vietnamese, Kissinger negotiated an agreement with Le Duc Tho (a key member of the North Vietnamese government), only to see it categorically rejected by President Thieu, who insisted on sixty-nine changes, the overwhelming number of which were, in Kissinger's words, "preposterous."[31] But two were substantive: at least some of the North Vietnamese army should leave the country, and movement across the demilitarized zone should be prohibited. The latter amounted to a demand that North Vietnam recognize South Vietnam as a sovereign nation with the 17th parallel as its legal boundary, thus undercutting Hanoi's contention that Vietnam was one country. To gain the support of President Thieu, Nixon tried to reopen negotiations with Hanoi but was met by a hardening of North Vietnamese demands.

Clearly humiliated by both Thieu and the North Vietnamese refusal to do his bidding, Nixon responded viscerally. He initiated intense B-52 bombing raids against North Vietnam in an effort to win further concessions from the North Vietnamese and persuade Thieu that, in the aftermath of an agreement, the United States could be relied upon to come to the assistance of its ally.[32] Between 18 and 29 December, over 3,420 bombing and support sorties were flown. So widespread was the damage in the residential areas of Hanoi (2,196 civilians were killed and 1,577 wounded) that domestic and international critics charged that the "Christmas Bombing" was "an unnecessary, irrational act of fury representing the belligerence that Nixon felt towards all his real and perceived enemies, foreign and domestic."[33] In the *New York Times*, James Reston called it "war by tantrum," while Anthony Lewis charged that Nixon was acting "like a maddened tyrant."[34]

Confronted by an enormous domestic and international outcry, and determined to avoid being shamed by further attacks on his character and behaviour, Nixon suspended the bombing on 29 December and announced that the Paris negotiations would be resumed. Thieu was told that, if he refused to accept the terms of the October agreement, the United States on its own would seek a settlement with the enemy and the two sides would go their separate ways.[35] Thieu finally bowed to American pressure and promises of further military action against North Vietnam should the agreement be violated. On 27 January, eight years after the massive U.S. combat build-up had begun, the United States signed the Paris Agreement on Ending the War and Restoring Peace in Vietnam.

In the aftermath of the agreement, Nixon later wrote that he had expected to feel relief and satisfaction but instead found himself experiencing "sadness, apprehension and impatience."[36] It was not surprising. He had been forced to accept an outcome to the war that he knew was humiliating without being able to respond aggressively. A continuation of the fighting would only invite further humiliation from the North Vietnamese and his fellow Americans.

Although Nixon often vehemently asserted that he had achieved "peace with honor," it was a difficult claim to sustain. Seven years earlier, when pressed by reporters to explain what kind of a settlement he would accept in Vietnam, he had held up the Korean armistice of 1953 as his model.[37] What he had been forced to accept was far short of that goal.

The Korean agreement had left 60,000 American troops in South Korea; the Vietnam agreement left no American troops in South Vietnam. The Korean settlement had left no communist troops in South Korea; the Vietnam settlement left 160,000 communist troops in South Vietnam. The Korean agreement had established the 38th parallel as a dividing line so heavily fortified on both sides that twenty years later almost no living thing had crossed it; the Vietnam agreement designated the 17th parallel as a border, but the North Vietnamese army controlled both sides of it and moved back and forth without any interference. The Korean arrangements had left President Rhee with enough control of his country that he could ban the Communist Party; the Vietnam arrangements forced President Thieu to accept communist membership on the National Council of Reconciliation.[38]

Thieu, understandably, regarded the settlement as little short of a surrender and feared that the cease-fire would last only until the POWs were returned to the Americans. Nixon also recognized that the verdict of history might, justifiably, be harsh, and that he could be subject to the humiliating charge of having betrayed an ally. To that end, speech-writer Patrick J. Buchanan was instructed to draft a speech in which Nixon would be portrayed as a great president, the leading "peacemaker" in a long war. He would be depicted as courageous, tough, and wise. Congressional critics who had advocated the simple withdrawal of U.S. troops from Vietnam would be portrayed as promoting a plan for cutting and running, the equivalent of abject, dishonorable defeat and surrender. And Nixon's peace with a cease-fire would be described not as a "bug out" but as an arrangement that assured the right of the South Vietnamese to determine their own future without the communists imposing a government on them.[39] In this way, the president hoped to avoid the humiliation of being tarred with losing Vietnam. Having failed to achieve "peace with honor," Nixon would satisfy his narcissism and reinflate his self-esteem by inventing one.

The broader policy implications of this study suggest that leaders with a narcissistic personality structure manifesting itself in a strong sensitivity to issues of shame and humiliation may be influenced in the making of foreign-policy decisions by unconscious efforts to avoid shame-inducing experiences and alleviate painful feelings of low self-worth. However, this does not mean that they are always incapable of "reality testing," lack ego strengths, or are insensitive to the impact of external and domestic variables in their calculations. Rather, concerns over issues of shame and humiliation may act as prism through which assessments of the environment will be made, or, in cases where advice is ambiguous or divided, tilt the balance in a particular direction. In contrast, leaders whose personality structures exhibit less of a narcissistic component will be more likely to reach decisions based on the interplay of a wide range of environmental and cognitive variables without the distorting filter of their emotional needs.

Given the relationship among feelings of shame and humiliation, narcissistic rage, and aggressive behaviour, in those circumstances in which narcissistic political leaders feel humiliated by the behaviour of external actors, they may choose aggressive foreign-policy responses as a way of restoring their self-esteem. The greater the latitude that narcissistic leaders have in the making of decisions – that is, the more autocratic or dictatorial the system in which they operate – the greater the possibility of that outcome.

Narcissistic personalities may favour aggressive foreign policies to avoid shame and humiliation for failing to act (Johnson in 1965) or after they have been shamed and humiliated (Nixon 1969–70). However, once they have experienced intense shame and humiliation, they may be strongly motivated to avoid a repetition of such experiences. Thus, Johnson halted the bombing and withdrew from the presidential race, while Nixon chose to end the war. Narcissistic preoccupations were still in evidence, but not the use of aggression to restore self-esteem. In both instances, however, Johnson and Nixon remained fearful that their behaviour might still be subject to scorn and derision. And so each man justified his actions in ways that protected his narcissistic sense of self.

In an assessment of the role of narcissism and the impact of shame and humiliation on behaviour, what is critical is not only the type of policy that is advocated but the reasons underlying its choice. Healthy narcissists may decide either to eschew violence or to behave belligerently for reasons that are unrelated to issues of shame and humiliation, as Eisenhower's Dien Bien Phu decisions and his military role in the Second World War demonstrated. Humiliated and angry narcissists, such as Johnson and Nixon, may oscillate between aggressive and non-aggressive behaviour, as both these presidents' Vietnam policies revealed; but the underlying dynamic fuelling such actions remains constant – a narcissistic preoccupation with issues of shame and humiliation.

Since the personality of political leaders can have such a profound impact upon the policies of their states, we need to pay much greater attention to that factor. Cognitive abilities may be important, but, if highly charged emotional states colour leaders' perceptions of their environment, the outcome will be policies that reflect that bias to the detriment of more reasoned choices.

Notes

INTRODUCTION

1 See, for example, Kolko, *Anatomy of War*, which focuses on a combination of the international system of nation-states and conditions in the American political environment.

2 For studies that explore the dynamics of the Cold War, ideology, and the doctrine of containment, see: Kalb and Abel, *The Roots of Involvement*; Hoopes, *The Limits of Intervention*; Zagoria, *Vietnam Triangle*; Gelb with Betts, *The Irony of Vietnam*; Glad and Taber, "Images, Learning and the Decision to Use Force," 56–82.

3 For those addressing domestic politics, see Kolko, *The Roots of American Foreign Policy*; Klare, *War Without End*; Ellsberg, "The Quagmire Myth," 217–74.

4 See Barnet, "The Game of Nations"; Thomson, Jr, "How Could Vietnam Happen?"; Halberstam, *The Best and the Brightest*; Schlesinger, Jr, *The Bitter Heritage*; Barrett, *Uncertain Warriors*.

5 For an examination of the impact of "group think," see Janis, "Escalation of the Vietnam War," 97–130.

6 See, for example, Khong, "Korea and the Vietnam Decisions of 1965," and *Analogies at War*.

7 The following are some of the books that include a discussion of the impact of the personalities of Johnson, Nixon, and/or Eisenhower on their Vietnam policies: Barber, *The Presidential Character*; Berman, *Planning and Tragedy*; Burke *et al.*, *How Presidents Test Reality*; Greenstein,

The Hidden-Hand Presidency; Herring, *America's Longest War,* and *LBJ and Vietnam*; Hersh, *The Price of Power*; Kearns, *Lyndon Johnson and the American Dream*; Kissinger, *White House Years.*

8 Notable exceptions are those studies that focus on the roles of the national security adviser and the secretary of defense. See, for example, Hersh, *The Price of Power*, Isaacson, *Kissinger*; Kissinger, *White House Years*; McNamara, *In Retrospect.*

9 Baudry, "Character, Character Type," 656.

10 I made a deliberate decision to exclude John F. Kennedy's foreign-policy decisions on Vietnam, largely because I was looking at critical decisions to escalate the conflict that involved or would have involved a major shift in American policy. Kennedy never made a final decision – positive or negative – to supply combat troops to South Vietnam. What he did was to order the relevant government departments to be prepared for the introduction of combat troops, should they prove to be necessary, while steadily expanding the size of the military-assistance mission (2,000 at the end of 1961, 15,500 at the end of 1963) by sending in combat-support units, air-combat and helicopter teams, more military advisers and instructors, and 600 of the green-beret Special Forces to train and lead the South Vietnamese in anti-guerrilla tactics.

   Had Kennedy lived longer, he might well have escalated the American commitment to Vietnam, since, like Johnson, he was highly narcissistic. For an examination of the role that shame and humiliation played in an earlier Kennedy decision, see B. Steinberg, "Shame and Humiliation in the Cuban Missile Crisis," 653–90.

CHAPTER ONE

1 See Lewis, *Shame and Guilt*; Lynd, *On Shame*; Nathanson, ed., *The Many Faces of Shame*; Piers and Singer, *Shame and Guilt*; Wurmser, *The Mask of Shame.*

2 Levin, "Some Metapsychological Considerations," 355–62.

3 Wurmser, *The Mask of Shame,* 53.

4 Sandler, Holder, and Meers, "The Ego Ideal," 139–58.

5 Lynd, *On Shame.*

6 Piers and Singer, *Shame and Guilt,* 23–9; Jacobson, *The Self and the Object World*; Lewis, *Shame and Guilt,* 37.

7 Wurmser, "Shame, The Veiled Companion," 76. Kohut challenges the view that ego/ego ideal tensions are necessary for shame, arguing that many shame-prone people do not possess strong ideals; most

are exhibitionistic and driven by ambition. From his perspective, shame is a reaction to the loss of grandiosity and omnipotence of early childhood and later to the loss of "narcissistic supplies" (those which make self-love possible) afforded by idealized objects which take the role of real loved objects. See "The Psychoanalytic Treatment of Narcissistic Personality Disorders," and *The Analysis of the Self.*

8 Kris, "Helping Patients," 605–20.

9 Spero, "Shame," 262–3. In structural terms, humiliation can be understood as involving a conflict between ego and super-ego or external world, whereas shame involves a conflict between ego and ego ideal [Stamm, "The Meaning of Humiliation," 425–6].

10 Morrison, "Working with Shame," 479–505.

11 Wurmser, *The Mask of Shame*, 51.

12 S. Freud, *Further Remarks; Three Essays; Inhibitions, Symptoms and Anxiety;* Abraham, "Restrictions and Transformation," 169–234; Fenichel, *The Psychoanalytic Theory of Neurosis,* 139; Jacobson, *The Self and the Object World,* 43–4.

13 S. Freud, *Further Remarks.*

14 S. Freud *Three essays.*

15 Ibid., 157; Abraham, "Restrictions and Transformation," 169–234.

16 Jacobson, *The Self and the Object World,* 43–4; Fenichel, *The Psychoanalytic Theory of Neurosis,* 233.

17 Erikson, *Childhood and Society,* 254.

18 Rank, "Emotion and Denial," 9–25.

19 Kaufman, *Shame,* 1985.

20 Levin, "The Psychology of Shame," 355–62; Wurmser, *The Mask of Shame.*

21 Alexander, "Remarks," 41–9.

22 S. Freud, *Beyond the Pleasure Principle,* 20–1.

23 Grunberger, *Narcissism,* 268–9.

24 Alford, "Mastery and Retreat," 571–89.

25 Wurmser, *The Mask of Shame,* 49.

26 Bursten, "Some Narcissistic Personality Types," 294.

27 For a perspective that stresses the positive dimensions of the narcissistic quest, see Alford, *Narcissism.*

28 The American Psychiatric Association lists the following diagnostic criteria for identifying the narcissistic personality disorder: a) grandiose sense of self-importance or uniqueness, exaggeration of achievements or talents; b) preoccupation with fantasies of unlimited success, brilliance, beauty, or ideal love; c) exhibitionism – the person requires constant attention and admiration; d) cool indifference or marked

feelings of rage, inferiority, shame, humiliation, or emptiness in response to criticism, indifference of others, or defeat. In addition, at
least two of the following are characteristic of the narcissistic personality: 1) feelings of entitlement – expectation of special favours without
assuming reciprocal responsibilties; 2) interpersonal exploitativeness –
taking advantage of others to indulge one's own desires and disregard
for the personal integrity and rights of others; 3) relationships that
characteristically alternate between the extremes of over-idealization
and devaluation; 4) lack of empathy – inability to recognize how others
feel. See *Diagnostic and Statistical Manual,* 315–17.

29 Kernberg and Kohut both address primitive narcissism, with Kernberg, *Borderline Conditions,* referring to it as "malignant narcissism,"
and Kohut, *The Analysis of the Self,* describing it as "archaic narcissism."

30 See Kernberg, *Borderline Conditions.*

31 Post, "Current Concepts of the Narcissistic Personality," 104.

32 Volkan, "Narcissistic Personality Disorder," 332–50.

33 Repression involves the attempt to repel, or to confine to the unconscious, thoughts, images, or memories which would incur the risk of
provoking unpleasure of ego or super-ego demands. Regression involves the transition to modes of expression that are at an earlier developmental level as regards to complexity, structure, and differentiation.
Reaction-formation involves the replacement of a distressing idea by a
counter-symptom or idea. Projection is a process whereby qualities,
feelings, and wishes which the subject refuses to recognize or rejects in
himself/herself are expelled from the self and located in another person or thing. Introjection is the process whereby, in fantasy, the subject
transposes objects and their inherent qualities from the "outside" to
the "inside" of himself/herself. Idealization is the process in which the
object's qualities and value are elevated to the point of perfection.
Identification with the aggressor is the process whereby the subject
faced with an external threat (typically represented by criticism or aggressive behaviour) identifies himself/herself with the aggressor. See A.
Freud, *The Ego and the Mechanisms of Defense*; Laplanche and Pontalis,
The Language of Psychoanalysis.

34 Kernberg, *Borderline Conditions,* 238.

35 Post, "Current Concepts of the Narcissistic Personality," 99–100.

36 See Volkan and Itzkowitz, *The Immortal Ataturk.*

37 Storr, *Human Aggression,* 85–7.

38 For an excellent summary of the diverse accounts of narcissism offered
by S. Freud, M. Klein, Fairbairn, Guntrip, Kohut, Kernberg, Rothstein,
Grunberger, and Chasseguet-Smirgel, see Alford, *Narcissism,* 21–71.

39 S. Freud, *On Narcissism*, 88.

40 Ibid., 91.

41 Alford, *Narcissism*, 26.

42 Although Freud did not distinguish between the "ego ideal" and the "ideal ego," some post-Freudian psychoanalysts, such as Herrmann Nunberg, Daniel Lagache, and Jacques Lacan, have argued for differentiating between the two. In their view, what distinguishes the "ideal ego" from the "ego ideal" is the absence of a super-ego component in the former, coupled with greater narcissistic elements. They regard the "ideal ego" as a narcissistic ideal of omnipotence involving a primary identification with an omnipotent object, namely the mother. See Laplanche and Pontalis, *The Language of Psychoanalysis*, 201–2.

43 Rothstein, *The Narcissistic Pursuit*.

44 Alford, *Narcissism*.

45 Kernberg, *Borderline Conditions*, 231.

46 Ibid., 235.

47 Ibid., 235.

48 Klein, "Envy and Gratitude," 216–17.

49 Mitchell, *Relational Concepts*, 182–3.

50 Ibid., 183.

51 Kernberg, *Borderline Conditions*, 235.

52 See Kernberg, *Borderline Conditions*; *Severe Personality Disorders*; *Aggression in Personality Disorders*; Volkan, *Primitive Internalized Object Relations*; "Narcissistic Personality Disorders."

53 Kernberg, *Borderline Conditions*, 233–4, 265.

54 Kohut, *The Analysis of the Self*, 25.

55 Kernberg, *Borderline Conditions*, 233.

56 Blos, "Modifications in the Classical Psychoanalytic Model of Adolescence," 486.

57 For an analysis of the process of idealization beginning in infancy, see Klein, "Notes on Some Schizoid Mechanisms," 7. "Persecutory anxiety" is anxiety that relates to the feeling of being persecuted or attacked by bad objects. These bad objects (that is, individuals) may be the product either of a child's fantasies – revolving around "internal objects" or the external environment – "external objects" alone, or both.

58 Blos, *Father and Son*, 147.

59 Psychoanalysts who have explored the role of the non-destructive aspects of aggression as an adaptive instinct, or as activity directed toward motility, mastery, separation-individuation, and self-preservation, include: Hendrick, "Instinct and the Ego," 33–58; "Work and the Pleasure Principle," 311–29; Heimann and Valenstein, "The Psychoanalytic

Concept of Aggression," 31–5; Joseph, "Aggression Re-defined,"
197–213; Winnicott, "Aggression in Relation to Emotional Development," 204–18; Storr, *Human Aggression*; Rangell, "Aggression, Oedipus," 3–11. More recent observational infant research strongly
supports these findings. See Lichtenberg, *Psychoanalysis and Infant
Research*; and Parens, *The Development of Aggression*.

60 Stone, "Reflections on the Psychoanalytic Concept of Aggression,"
195–243.

61 Klein, "On the Theory of Anxiety and Guilt," 25–42.

62 A. Freud, *The Ego and the Mechanisms of Defense*, 167.

63 Kernberg, *Borderline Conditions*, 234.

64 Kernberg, *Severe Personality Disorders*, 186.

65 Mitchell, "Aggression and the Endangered Self," 361.

66 Kernberg, *Severe Personality Disorders*, 195.

67 Sandler, "Panel Discussion on 'Aggression,' " 13–19.

68 S. Freud, *New Introductory Lectures*, 103.

69 A. Freud, *The Ego and the Mechanisms of Defense*, 115.

70 Sullivan, *The Interpersonal Theory*.

71 Fairbairn, *An Object Relations Theory*.

72 Guntrip, *Schizoid Phenomena*, 149–50.

73 Mitchell, *Hope and Dread*, 166.

74 Mitscherlich, "Psychoanalysis and the Aggression of Large Groups,"
161–7.

75 Mitchell, "Aggression and the Endangered Self," 366.

76 Hartmann, Kris, and Loewenstein, "Notes on the Theory of Aggression," 9–36.

77 A. Reich, "Pathogenic Forms of Self-Esteem Regulation," 215–31.

78 R. Waelder, "Critical Discussion," 97–109.

79 Because the infantile self is weak and has no durable structure, it requires the participation of others to provide a sense of cohesion, con-
stancy, and resilience. Kohut terms these others, who from the infant's
perspective are not yet differentiated from the self, "selfobjects," since
they are objectively separate people who serve functions that will be
later performed by the individual's own psychic structure. To the extent that parents are unable to provide the infant with cohesion, con-
stancy, and empathy, the result will be a degree of self object failure in
the infant.

80 Kohut, "Thoughts on Narcissism," 360–400.

81 Kohut, "Thoughts on Narcissism." In *Borderline Conditions*, Kernberg
emphasizes the manner in which the object of the wounded narcissist's

intense unremitting anger experiences the chronic-rage reactions of the wounded narcissist.

82 Kohut, *The Restoration of the Self.*

83 Parens, *The Development of Aggression in Early Childhood*, 106–8.

84 Kohut, "Thoughts on Narcissism," 386.

85 Rochlin, *Man's Aggression.*

86 Post, "Current Concepts of the Narcissistic Personality," 114.

87 Rochlin, *Man's Aggression*, 185–201.

88 Ibid., 258.

89 See Pruitt's analysis of this phenomenon among the general population in "Aggressive Behavior," 287–93.

CHAPTER TWO

1 Kearns, *Lyndon Johnson*, 20.

2 R. Johnson, *A Family Album*, 25, 29; Steinberg, *Sam Johnson's Boy*, 10–11; Caro, *The Path to Power*, 51; Dallek, *Lone Star Rising*, 27.

3 Kearns, *Lyndon Johnson*, 22.

4 R. Johnson, *A Family Album* 17–18; Dallek, *Lone Star Rising*, 31, n.2.

5 R. Johnson, *A Family Album*, 18; Steinberg, *Sam Johnson's Boy*, 13; Caro, *The Path to Power*, 66; Dallek, *Lone Star Rising*, 31–2.

6 Dallek, *Lone Star Rising*, 32.

7 R. Johnson, *A Family Album*, 18–19.

8 Kearns, *Lyndon Johnson*, 25; Dallek, *Lone Star Rising*, 32–3.

9 Dallek, *Lone Star Rising*, 33.

10 Ibid., 33–4.

11 Steinberg, *Sam Johnson's Boy*, 23; Caro, *The Path to Power*, 69.

12 Kearns, *Lyndon Johnson*, 26; Dallek, *Lone Star Rising*, 34.

13 Kearns, *Lyndon Johnson*, 24.

14 Ibid.

15 Ibid., 24–5.

16 Quoted in Jones, *The Life and Works of Sigmund Freud*, 6.

17 Kearns, *Lyndon Johnson*, 27.

18 Ibid., 25.

19 Dallek, *Lone Star Rising*, 37–8; Kearns, *Lyndon Johnson*, 40.

20 Kearns, *Lyndon Johnson*, 40.

21 Halberstam, *The Best and the Brightest*, 443–4.

22 Caro, *The Path to Power*, 102.

23 Dugger, *Politician*, 73; Dallek, *Lone Star Rising*, 39.

24 Kearns, *Lyndon Johnson*, 38.

25 Steinberg, *Sam Johnson's Boy*, 699; Caro, *The Path to Power*, 100.

26 Kearns, *Lyndon Johnson*, 38; Dallek, *Lone Star Rising*, 39.

27 Steinberg, *Sam Johnson's Boy*, 21; Caro, *The Path to Power*, 73.

28 Kearns, *Lyndon Johnson*, 36–7; Caro, *The Path to Power*, 74; Dallek, *Lone Star Rising*, 50.

29 Caro, *The Path to Power*, 61–3; Dugger, *Politician*, 73; Dallek, *Lone Star Rising*, 47–8.

30 Caro, *The Path to Power*, 98–112.

31 Ibid., 94.

32 Ibid., 95–6.

33 Ibid., 97.

34 Kearns, *Lyndon Johnson*, 24; Caro, *The Path to Power*, 111.

35 Caro, *The Path to Power*, 111.

36 Ibid., 112.

37 Ibid., 113.

38 Ibid.

39 Ibid., 120.

40 Steinberg, *Sam Johnson's Boy*, 27.

41 Conkin, *Big Daddy*, 32; Dallek, *Lone Star Rising*, 57.

42 Ibid., 32–3.

43 Kearns, *Lyndon Johnson*, 43.

44 Caro, *The Path to Power*, 125–7.

45 Ibid., 128.

46 Kearns, *Lyndon Johnson*, 44.

47 Caro, *The Path to Power*, 133–4.

48 Steinberg, *Sam Johnson's Boy*, 34; Caro, *The Path to Power*, 134–6; Dallek, *Lone Star Rising*, 61.

49 Dallek, *Lone Star Rising*, 63.

50 Caro, *The Path to Power*, 141–2; Dallek, *Lone Star Rising*, 63–4.

51 Clifford with Holbrooke, *Counsel to the President*, 385.

52 Kearns, *Lyndon Johnson*, 41.

53 Caro, *The Path to Power*, 153.

54 Steinberg, *Sam Johnson's Boy*, 43; Caro, *The Path to Power*, 153–4; Dallek, *Lone Star Rising*, 70.

55 Caro, *The Path to Power*, 155.

56 Ibid., 156.

57 Ibid.

58 Ibid.

59 Ibid., 159.

60 S. Johnson, *My Brother Lyndon*, 29; Kearns, *Lyndon Johnson*, 57; Caro, *The Path to Power* 161–3; Dallek, *Lone Star Rising*, 81.

61 Caro, *The Path to Power,* 163.

62 Dallek, *Lone Star Rising,* 81.

63 Caro, *The Path to Power,* 163.

64 Ibid., 172–3; Dallek, *Lone Star Rising,* 81.

65 Caro, *The Path to Power,* 162.

66 Kearns, *Lyndon Johnson,* 57.

67 S. Johnson, *My Brother Lyndon,* 29.

68 Kearns, *Lyndon Johnson,* 57–8.

69 Steinberg, *Sam Johnson's Boy,* 57–8; Caro, *The Path to Power,* 206–10; Dallek, *Lone Star Rising,* 90–1.

70 Caro, *The Path to Power,* 211; Dallek, *Lone Star Rising,* 90.

71 Caro, *The Path to Power,* 229.

72 Ibid., 335.

73 Ibid., 235–59; Dallek, *Lone Star Rising,* 96–102.

74 Kearns, *Lyndon Johnson,* 41.

75 Caro, *The Path to Power,* 363.

76 Ibid., 431–6; Dallek, *Lone Star Rising,* 150–6.

77 Johnson's aides recall that at night, while signing the hundreds of letters that they had prepared for his signature, his right hand would bleed through the cracks in his skin. Wrapping a small towel around his hand to avoid staining the letters with blood, he insisted on signing every one. Sherman Birdwell, Oral History II; Gene Latimer, Oral History, 17 August 1971.

78 Caro, *The Path to Power,* 552.

79 Ibid., 571.

80 Dallek, *Lone Star Rising,* 188.

81 Ibid., 189.

82 Dugger, *Politician,* 254.

83 Dallek, *Lone Star Rising,* 190–1.

84 Miller, *Lyndon,* 103; Dugger, *Politician,* 233; Caro, *The Path to Power,* 733, Dallek, *Lone Star Rising,* 221.

85 Caro, *Means of Ascent,* 5–8.

86 Caro, *The Path to Power,* 734–40; Dugger, *Politician,* 234–5; Miller 104–5; *Roosevelt Presidential Press Conferences,* 1 July 1941, 6–7; Dallek, *Lone Star Rising,* 223.

87 Dugger, *Politician,* 235; Dallek, *Lone Star Rising,* 224.

88 Rowe, Jr, Oral History, 9 and 16 September 1969.

89 Miller, *Lyndon,* 106; Dallek, *Lone Star Rising,* 224.

90 Dugger, *Politician,* 236; Kearns, *Lyndon Johnson,* 93–4; Dallek, *Lone Star Rising,* 225.

91 Caro, *Means of Ascent,* 39–45; Dallek, *Lone Star Rising,* 236–9.

92 Halberstam, *The Best and the Brightest*, 449.

93 Caro, *Means of Ascent*, 80.

94 Ibid., 88.

95 See Caro, *Means of Ascent*, 80–118; Dallek, *Lone Star Rising*, 247–52; Wheeler and Lambert, "The Man Who Is the President," 62; Barron, "Special Report."

96 Halberstam, *The Best and the Brightest*, 434; Caro, *Means of Ascent*, 111.

97 Caro, *The Path to Power*, 759.

98 Ibid., 761–2.

99 Dallek, *Lone Star Rising*, 279.

100 Caro, *Means of Ascent*, 126.

101 Ibid., 134–5.

102 Ibid.

103 Ibid., 134.

104 Steinberg, *Sam Johnson's Boy*, 240.

105 Dallek, *Lone Star Rising*, 297.

106 Kearns, *Lyndon Johnson*, 100.

107 Caro, *Means of Ascent*, 206–23; Dallek, *Lone Star Rising*, 303–13.

108 Caro, *Means of Ascent*, 300; Dallek, *Lone Star Rising*, 862.

109 Caro, *Means of Ascent*, 300.

110 Dallek, *Lone Star Rising*, 319.

111 Ibid., 327.

112 Ibid., 328.

113 For more information on the procedures and the attendent controversy, see Caro, *Means of Ascent*, 318–59, 367–395; Dallek, *Lone Star Rising*, 328–44.

114 Steinberg, *Sam Johnson's Boy*, 272; Caro, *Means of Ascent*, 398–9; Dallek, *Lone Star Rising*, 346.

115 Dugger, *Politician*, 341; Caro, *Means of Ascent*, 401–2.

116 Caro, *Means of Ascent*, 402.

117 Ibid., 400–2.

118 Steinberg, *Sam Johnson's Boy*, 320–1; Dallek, *Lone Star Rising*, 392–3.

119 Kearns, *Lyndon Johnson*, 102–16; Caro, *Means of Ascent*, 411–12; Dallek, *Lone Star Rising*, 468–83.

120 Kearns, *Lyndon Johnson*, 121.

121 Ibid., 120–1.

122 Ibid., 122.

123 Dallek, *Lone Star Rising*, 544–5.

124 For details regarding Johnson's perceptions of Kennedy's inadequacies, see Goodwin, *The Fitzgeralds and the Kennedys*, 780; Dallek, *Lone Star Rising*, 555.

125 Dallek, *Lone Star Rising*, 555–6; Goodwin, *The Fitzgeralds and the Kennedys*, 790; Evans and Novak, *Lyndon B. Johnson*, 232.

126 Dallek, *Lone Star Rising*, 559.

127 Ibid., 560.

128 Ibid., 575.

129 Schlesinger, Jr, *A Thousand Days*, 48.

130 Evans and Novak, *Lyndon B. Johnson*, 280; Kearns, *Lyndon Johnson*, 161.

131 Kearns, *Lyndon Johnson*, 161.

132 Guthman and Shulman, eds., *Robert Kennedy*, 316–17; Dallek, *Lone Star Rising*, 578.

133 Dallek, *Lone Star Rising*, 579.

134 Guthman and Shulman, eds., *Robert Kennedy*, 21–2; Dallek, *Lone Star Rising*, 580.

135 Dallek, *Lone Star Rising*, 580.

136 Ibid.

137 Ibid.

138 Ibid., 581.

139 Guthman and Shulman, eds., *Robert Kennedy*, 22; see also White, *The Making of the President 1964*, 413–14.

140 Miller, *Lyndon*, 319–20.

141 Dallek, *Lone Star Rising*, 583–6.

142 LBJ to Connally, 18 October 1960, "Senate Papers."

143 Rowe to Humphrey, 22 November 1960, Rowe, Jr., *Rowe Papers*.

144 Evans and Novak, *Lyndon B. Johnson*, 305–8; Kearns, *Lyndon Johnson*, 164.

145 Kearns, *Lyndon Johnson*, 164–5.

146 Ibid., 165.

147 Schlesinger, Jr, *A Thousand Days*, 649.

148 Evans and Novak, *Lyndon B. Johnson*, 313; Kearns, *Lyndon Johnson*, 165.

149 Evans and Novak, *Lyndon B. Johnson*, 308–9; Kearns, *Lyndon Johnson*, 165, n.10.

150 Evans and Novak, *Lyndon B. Johnson*, 314.

151 Ibid., 314.

152 Kearns, *Lyndon Johnson*, 165–6.

153 Ibid., 166.

154 Ibid., 166–7.

155 Ibid., 164.

156 S. Johnson, *My Brother Lyndon*, 108.

157 Muslin and Jobe, *Lyndon Johnson*, 193–4.

158 Evans and Novak, *Lyndon B. Johnson*, 332.

159 Ibid.

160 Kearns, *Lyndon Johnson*, 170.

161 Ibid., 174–6.

162 Ibid., 175.

163 Ibid., 177–8.

164 Wills, *The Kennedy Imprisonment*, 189.

165 Ibid., 189.

166 Evans and Novak, *Lyndon B. Johnson*, 354.

167 Clifford with Holbrooke, *Counsel to the President*, 396.

168 Evans and Novak, *Lyndon B. Johnson*, 446.

169 Halberstam, *The Best and the Brightest*, 407.

170 Ibid., 533–6.

171 Ibid., 333.

172 Solberg, *Hubert Humphrey*, 265–6.

173 Eisele, *Almost to the Presidency*, 234.

174 For a description of the various ways that Johnson personalized foreign policy, see Kearns, *Lyndon Johnson*, 193–6.

175 Wicker, *LBJ and JFK*, 204.

CHAPTER THREE

1 Khong, *Analogies At War*, 137.

2 See, for example, Neustadt and May, *Thinking in Time*; Vertzberger, *The World in Their Minds*; Khong, *Analogies At War*.

3 Herring observes that Johnson attempted throughout his career to position himself comfortably in the middle, and on Vietnam he did the same. *LBJ and Vietnam*, 47–8.

4 Irving Janis, *Groupthink*, 98.

5 Solberg, *Hubert Humphrey*, 270–82; Barrett, "The Mythology Surrounding Lyndon Johnson," 637–63. For a more extensive treatment of the details of the relationship of each of these men with Johnson and the nature of their advice, see Barrett, *Uncertain Warriors*, 13–61.

6 See Barrett, "The Mythology Surrounding Lyndon Johnson," 660–3.

7 See, for example, Herring, *America's Longest War*, 113.

8 Humphrey, *The Education of a Public Man*, 289.

9 Halberstam, *The Best and the Brightest*, 373.

10 Shapley, *Promise and Power*, 277. Dean Acheson recounts that Johnson, to compensate for his humiliating dependency on his advisers, publicly humiliated McNamara to his face at a meeting, "squeezing him like an orange" [ibid., 278].

11 Humphrey, *The Education of a Public Man*, 288.

12 Harris, "A Policy-Maker's View," 39.

13 Ball, Oral History, 1–26, 34.

14 Russell, letter to L. Wolfson, 4 January 1966.

15 Barrett, "The Mythology Surrounding Lyndon Johnson," 662.

16 Mansfield, letter to the president, 27 July 1965.

17 L. Johnson, letter to Mansfield, 28 July 1965, International Series–Vietnam, Subject file 23–31 July 1965, Russell Memorial Library, University of Georgia, Athens, Georgia.

18 Even after McNamara's changed views on the Vietnam War led to his departure from the cabinet in 1967, Johnson rewarded him with the presidency of the World Bank. For details, see McNamara, *In Retrospect*, 311–13.

19 Barrett, "The Mythology Surrounding Lyndon Johnson," 663.

20 George Reedy, *Lyndon B. Johnson*, 147.

21 Ibid.

22 Ibid.

23 Kahin, *Intervention*, 132, n.28.

24 Ibid., 166.

25 Berman, *Planning a Tragedy*, 28.

26 Westmoreland, "Vietnam in Perspective," 21–4.

27 Controversy over what President Kennedy would have done vis à vis Vietnam had he lived continues unabated. Some argue that he was growing increasingly concerned about the divisions within the South Vietnamese political elites and the demand for greater American involvement, and that he would have decided on a American withdrawal in the context of a Laotian-like solution as soon as his re-election was secured. See O'Donnell and Powers, *Johnny We Hardly Knew Ye*, 16–18; McNamara, *In Retrospect*, also makes this argument without any substantiating evidence. Others are less persuaded; they point to the possibility that he would also have been strongly influenced by his advisers and reluctant to incur the opprobrium and humiliation that could have attended the "loss" of Vietnam. See Schlesinger, Jr, review of *JFK and Vietnam*, 3, 31.

28 Kalb and Abel, *The Roots of American Involvement*, 153.

29 Porter, ed., *Vietnam*, #166.

30 *Pentagon Papers*, Gravel, ed., 78, n.2.

31 Kahin, *Intervention*, 214, n.29.

32 Critics would later cite Tonkin Gulf as a trumped-up crisis designed by the administration as a pretext for escalation. See Gelb with Betts, *The Irony of Vietnam*, 100–5; Goulden, *Truth Is the First Casualty*, 91–160.

33 Kahin, *Intervention*, 221.

34 By 1984 "unimpeachable" proof had emerged that there had never been a second attack. For the details of Vice-Admiral James B. Stockdale's account of what happened that evening, see *Washington Post,* 16 October 1984; Kahin, *Intervention,* 222–3.

35 Ball, *The Past Has Another Pattern,* 379.

36 L. Johnson, *The Vantage Point,* 120.

37 Ibid.

38 Kahin, *Intervention,* 240. For Johnson's reaction to the alleged Gulf of Tonkin attack on 18 September, see McGeorge Bundy, Memorandum for the Record, "The Gulf of Tonkin Incident, September 18," 20 September 1964, as cited in Kahin, *Intervention,* 240, n.7.

39 Kahin, *Intervention,* 240.

40 Thomson, Jr, "How Could Vietnam Happen"? 52–3.

41 Kahin, *Intervention,* 241.

42 Ball, *The Past Has Another Pattern,* 380–3; Kahin, *Intervention,* 241–2.

43 Kahin, *Intervention,* 242.

44 Halberstam, *The Best and the Brightest,* 499.

45 Kahin, *Intervention,* 243.

46 Ball, *The Past Has Another Pattern,* 383.

47 Kahin, *Intervention,* 243.

48 Quotes are from Revised Draft 11/21/64, as amended 11/26/64, W.P. Bundy/J. McNaughton, "Courses of Action in South-East Asia," in *Pentagon Papers,* Gravel, ed., 3: 656–66.

49 *Pentagon Papers,* Gravel, ed., 3: 114–15; Berman, *Planning a Tragedy,* 34; Kahin, *Intervention,* 273–4.

50 Kahin, *Intervention,* 274–5.

51 Halberstam, *The Best and the Brightest,* 505.

52 Ibid., 499.

53 *The Pentagon Papers,* Gravel, ed., 3: 262.

54 Cable from President Johnson to Taylor, 30 December 1964, NSC History, as cited in Burke and Greenstein, *How Presidents Test Reality,* 124.

55 Halberstam, *The Best and the Brightest,* 512.

56 Ibid., 500.

57 Ibid. Later, when Alsop was virtually the only columnist in Washington still supporting the war, Johnson would read his columns and attack him for having closed off the administration's options in Vietnam. He suspected that it was the Bundys, old Alsop friends, who were the source of the leaks.

58 President's Meeting with Congressional Leaders, 22 January 1965, File of McGeorge Bundy, Misc. Meetings.

59 Kahin, *Intervention*, 271.

60 The Bundy Memorandum as cited in Kahin, *Intervention*, 272–3; McNamara, *In Retrospect*, 167–8.

61 Kahin, *Intervention*, 273–4.

62 Ibid., 275, n.29.

63 Cooper, *The Lost Crusade*, 256.

64 Cooper, Oral History, interview of January 1969, 14.

65 Kahin, *Intervention*, 276–7.

66 Ibid., 277.

67 This includes George Ball, who stated that, "faced with a unanimous view, I saw no option but to go along" [Ball, *The Past Has Another Pattern*, 390].

68 L. Johnson, *Vantage Point*, 125.

69 Halberstam, *The Best and the Brightest*, 522.

70 *Pentagon Papers*, Gravel, ed., 3: 286.

71 L. Johnson, *Vantage Point*, 128.

72 Kahin, *Intervention*, 281.

73 *Pentagon Papers*, Gravel, ed., 3: 309–11.

74 Kahin, *Intervention*, 281–3.

75 *Pentagon Papers*, Gravel, ed., 3: 309–11.

76 Kahin, *Intervention*, 283.

77 In his memoirs, Hubert Humphrey documented the way in which his opposition to escalating the war in Vietnam, even as expressed in confidential memos to Lyndon Johnson, was rewarded with his being frozen out of those meetings in which policy was discussed and decisions taken [Humphrey, *The Education of a Public Man*, 318–30]. See also Halberstam, *The Best and the Brightest*, 533–6; Eisele, *Almost to the Presidency*, 230–40.

78 Ball, ms., cited in Berman, *Planning a Tragedy*, 45.

79 Kahin, *Intervention*, 286.

80 Ibid., 286–7.

81 L. Johnson, *Vantage Point*, 130–1.

82 *New York Times*, 16 February 1965.

83 Ball, *The Past Has Another Pattern*, 392.

84 Ibid. In his account of the Vietnam tragedy, McNamara consigned Ball's memorandum to a footnote, without any discussion of his strenuous opposition to it. He explained Johnson's decision to begin the sustained bombing of Vietnam as a product of his "fears about failure in Vietnam ... overriding whatever hesitation he still harbored about South Vietnam's instability." See *In Retrospect*, 69–75.

85 Halberstam, *The Best and the Brightest*, 530.

86 Kearns, *Lyndon Johnson and the American Dream*, 252–3.

87 Ibid., 253.

88 Halberstam, *The Best and the Brightest*, 532.

89 Ibid. For a detailed analysis of the complex relationship between Ball and Johnson, which endured until the president's death in 1971, see David L. DiLeo, *George Ball, Vietnam, and the Rethinking of Containment.*

90 Halberstam, *The Best and the Brightest*, 531.

91 Humphrey, *The Education of a Public Man*, 318–29; Eisele, *Almost to the Presidency*, 230–4.

92 Kahin, *Intervention*, 292–305.

93 Burke *et al.*, *How Presidents Test Reality*, 160.

94 Handwritten notes by McGeorge Bundy, 10 March 1965, Papers of McGeorge Bundy.

95 Gibbons, *The U.S. Government and the Vietnam War*, ch. 3.

96 Kahin, *Intervention*, 312.

97 Ibid.

98 Ibid.

99 L. Johnson, "Peace Without Conquest," address to Johns Hopkins University, Baltimore, Maryland, 7 April 1965, *Public Papers of the Presidents 1965*, 394–5.

100 Those present at the meeting included Ambassador Maxwell Taylor, General William Westmoreland, Robert McNamara, Admiral Ulysses G. Sharp, commander-in-chief, Pacific (CINCPAC), General Earle Wheeler (chairman of the JCS), William Bundy and John McNaughton.

101 Kahin, *Intervention*, 319.

102 See McNamara, *In Retrospect*, 182–3.

103 Ball, *The Past Has Another Pattern*, 393.

104 Quoted in Kahin, *Intervention*, 327.

105 Ball, *The Past Has Another Pattern*, 393–4.

106 Ibid., 394.

107 Kahin, *Intervention*, 320. Johnson's decision to approve the use of American ground forces may have been enhanced by his handling of the crisis in the Dominican Republic. There, 22,000 U.S. troops had restored the existing government to power and, in Johnson's view, prevented the establishment of a communist regime and a second Cuba. A decision to escalate the war in Vietnam would, he hoped, have similar felicitous results [Halberstam, *The Best and the Brightest*, 573–4].

108 Kahin, *Intervention*, 336.

109 Berman, *Planning a Tragedy*, 68; Burke and Greenstein, *How Presidents Test Reality*, 198.

110 Burke *et al.*, *How Presidents Test Reality*, 198; Kahin, *Intervention*, 347–8.

111 Kahin, *Intervention*, 349.

112 Ball, *The Past Has Another Pattern*, 396.

113 Ibid.

114 Ibid., 395–6.

115 Berman, *Planning a Tragedy*, 75.

116 Ibid., 75.

117 Ibid., 86–7; Ball, *The Past Has Another Pattern*, 397.

118 Memorandum to the President, 1 July 1965, NSC History, Deployment of Forces.

119 Memorandum from the Secretary of Defense, 30 June 1965, NSC Meeting File, Deployment of Forces; McNamara, *In Retrospect*, 192–4.

120 Burke *et al.*, *How Presidents Test Reality*, 207; Kahin, *Intervention*, 353–4.

121 Burke *et al.*, *How Presidents Test Reality*, 206.

122 *Pentagon Papers, New York Times* ed., 449–54.

123 Burke and Greenstein, *How Presidents Test Reality*, 206.

124 *Pentagon Papers, New York Times* ed., 450; Ball, *The Past Has Another Pattern*, 398. Emphasis is from Ball's memorandum to the president.

125 McGeorge Bundy, "Holding on in South Vietnam," NSC History – Troop Deployment, 30 June 1965.

126 When Robert Kennedy reversed himself and became an opponent of the war, Johnson was outraged at what he felt was a betrayal and an attempt to make him look foolish. His sense of Kennedy as the "enemy" helped stiffen his unwillingness to consider any change in his Vietnam policies [Kearns, *Lyndon Johnson*, 259].

127 Burke *et al.*, *How Presidents Test Reality*, 209.

128 Dwight D. Eisenhower, Memorandum of Telephone Conversation, 2 July 1965, Post-Presidential Papers.

129 My thanks to Alexander George, who drew my attention to this explanation for the advice that Eisenhower offered Johnson. See also Gacek, *The Logic of Force*, who analyses the tension between the "never againers" and the "limited war" school and traces their impact on U.S. crisis decisions since the Korean War.

130 Kahin, *Intervention*, 360–1. See chapter 7 for a further discussion of this issue.

131 William Bundy, unpubl. ms., cited in Burke *et al.*, *How Presidents Test Reality*, 212–13; Kahin, *Intervention*, 361.

132 L. Johnson, *Vantage Point*, 144.

133 Those present at the meeting were Secretary of State Dean Rusk, Secretary of Defense Robert McNamara, national security assistant McGeorge Bundy, Under-Secretary of State George Ball, CIA Director

William Raborn, assistant secretary of state for Far Eastern affairs William Bundy, deputy secretary of defense Cyrus Vance, assistant secretary of defense for international security affairs John McNaughton, JCS Chairman Earle Wheeler, newly appointed ambassador Henry Cabot Lodge, United States Information Agency Director Carl Rowan and his deputy Leonard Marks, six other departmental and White House aides, and a non-governmental adviser whom Johnson held in special esteem, Clark Clifford.

Three records of this meeting exist: an unsigned account from the NSC files rendered in abbreviated, semi-verbatim style (NSC, "Cabinet Room, Wednesday, July 21, 1965"); the slightly less comprehensive but apparently verbatim record of the president's aide Jack Valenti, *A Very Human President*, 319–56; and the extensive and more inclusive summary by Chester Cooper, the most recently declassified of the three ("Meetings on Vietnam, July 21, 1965"). For a careful weaving together of the three accounts, see Kahin, *Intervention*, 368–78.

134 Valenti, *A Very Human President*, 318–63; Berman, *Planning a Tragedy*, 105–6.

135 Ball, ms., cited in Berman, *Planning a Tragedy*, 106.

136 Valenti, *A Very Human President*, 331–56.

137 Ibid., 328–9.

138 Berman, *Planning a Tragedy*, 108.

139 Valenti, *A Very Human President*, 333–4.

140 Ibid., 334–5; Ball, *The Past Has Another Pattern*, 401.

141 Ibid.

142 Kahin, *Intervention*, 375–6.

143 Valenti, *A Very Human President*, 335–6.

144 Those present included McGeorge Bundy, Clark Clifford, Robert McNamara, Cyrus Vance, presidential aide Jack Valenti, and senior military spokesmen: General Earle G. Wheeler, General Harold K. Johnson, army chief of staff, General John P. McConnell, air force chief of staff, Admiral David L. McDonald, chief of naval operations, General Wallace M. Greene, Jr, commandant of the Marine corps, Harold Brown, secretary of the air force, Paul Nitze, secretary of the navy, Stanley Resor, secretary of the army, and Eugene M. Zuckert, assistant secretary of the air force. The fullest account of this meeting is from the Cabinet Room, 22 July 1965, Meeting Notes File, Lyndon B. Johnson Library, Austin, Texas.

145 Valenti, *A Very Human President*, 341.

146 Ibid., 340–2.

147 Ibid., 348–9.

148 Ibid., 349.

149 Clifford with Holbrooke, *Counsel to the President,* 411–22.

150 Ball, *The Past Has Another Pattern,* 402–3; Kahin, *Intervention,* 386–7.

151 Kahin, *Intervention,* 387–8.

152 Ibid., 388–90.

153 Berman, *Planning a Tragedy,* 124.

154 McNamara has been extremely critical of Johnson's refusal to tell the American people that the new troop deployments would entail roughly $10 billion in additional expenditures through fiscal year 1966 and would also require additional taxes to pay for the war and thus avert inflation. In his view, "Johnson felt trapped between two bitter choices: subterfuge versus the twin dangers of escalatory pressure and the loss of his social programs" [*In Retrospect,* 205–6].

155 Mansfield, "Meeting on Vietnam."

156 L. Johnson, *Vantage Point,* 149.

157 Berman, *Planning a Tragedy,* 99–100.

158 William Bundy, Oral History.

159 Kahin, *Intervention,* 366–7.

160 Ball, *The Past Has Another Pattern,* 389.

161 Thomson, "How Could Vietnam Happen?" 52; see also Wicker, *LBJ and JFK,* 199.

162 Teger, *et al., Too Much Invested to Quit,* 2.

163 Brown, "The Effects of Need to Maintain Face," 107.

164 Kearns, *Lyndon Johnson,* 270–1.

165 Ibid., 295–6.

166 Berman, *Planning a Tragedy,* 146.

167 L. Johnson, Oral History, 12 August 1969.

168 Ball, ms., cited in Berman, *Intervention,* 149–50.

CHAPTER FOUR

1 Ambrose, *Nixon,* vol. 1: 13–14; Aitken, *Nixon: A Life,* 7–10.

2 Timberlake, *Oral History,* 22; Brodie, *Fawn Brodie Collection,* 38.

3 Abrahamsen, *Nixon vs. Nixon,* 24.

4 Morris, *Richard Milhous Nixon,* 42.

5 Parsons, *Oral History,* 3.

6 Morris, *Richard Milhous Nixon,* 41.

7 Abrahamsen, *Nixon vs. Nixon,* 24–5.

8 Itzkowitz and Dod, *Richard Milhous Nixon,* 169.

9 Alsop, *Nixon and Rockefeller,* 195.

10 Harlow, "The Man and the Political Leader," 9–10; Wicker, *One of Us*, 31.

11 Sidey, "The Man and Foreign Policy," 301.

12 Kornitzer, *The Real Nixon*, 57.

13 Volkan, Itzkovitz, and Dod, *Richard Milhous Nixon*, 153.

14 Barber, *The Presidential Character*, 401.

15 Abrahamsen, *Nixon vs. Nixon*, 60.

16 Brodie, *Richard Nixon*, 77.

17 Ambrose, *Richard Nixon*, vol 1: 32.

18 Barber, *The Presidential Character*, 397.

19 Brodie, *Richard Nixon*, 56.

20 Morris, *Richard Milhous Nixon*, 66; Mazo, *Richard Nixon*, 20–1.

21 Spalding, *The Nixon Nobody Knows*, 44.

22 Morris, *Richard Milhous Nixon*, 66–7.

23 Aitken, *Nixon*, 16.

24 H. Nixon, "Richard Nixon," 212.

25 Ibid.

26 Wildermuth, *Oral History*, 2.

27 Ibid., 27–8.

28 Randall, *Oral History*, 21.

29 De Toledano, *One Man Alone*, 21.

30 Morris, *Richard Milhous Nixon*, 100–1.

31 Kornitzer, *The Real Nixon*, 121.

32 Mazlish, *In Search of Nixon*, 122.

33 H. Nixon, "Richard Nixon."

34 Brodie, *Richard Nixon*, 116.

35 Kornitzer, *The Real Nixon*, 326.

36 Kornitzer, "My Son," 9f.

37 Beeson, *Oral History*, 23.

38 West to Fawn Brodie, cited in Brodie, *Richard Nixon*, 40, n.20.

39 Kornitzer, *The Real Nixon*, 79; Spalding, *The Nixon Nobody Knows*, 3; Nixon, *RN: Memoirs*, 6.

40 Kornitzer, *The Real Nixon*, 78.

41 Brodie, *Richard Nixon* 40.

42 Barber, *The Presidential Character*, 405.

43 Kornitzer, *The Real Nixon*, 79.

44 West interview, in Brodie, *The Fawn Brodie Collection*.

45 Mazlish, *In Search of Nixon*, 29.

46 Brodie, *Richard Nixon*, 44.

47 Kornitzer, *The Real Nixon*, 57.

48 White, *The Making of the President, 1968*, 63; Safire, *Before the Fall*, 80; Price, *With Nixon*, 45.

49 Brodie, *Richard Nixon* 45.

50 Nixon to David Frost, 23 March 1977, cited in Brodie, *Richard Nixon* 45.

51 Brodie, *Richard Nixon*, 502.

52 *Los Angeles Times*, 10 May 1959; H. Nixon, "Richard Nixon," 216.

53 Brodie, *Richard Nixon*, 60.

54 Ambrose, *Richard Nixon*, vol. 1: 64.

55 Costello, *The Facts about Nixon*, 24.

56 Kornitzer, *The Real Nixon*, 110.

57 Ambrose, *Richard Nixon*, vol. 1: 65.

58 Weymouth, "The Word from Mamma Buff," 200–4.

59 Ola Welch Jobe interview, in Brodie, *The Fawn Brodie Collection*.

60 Mazlish, *In Search of Nixon*, 63.

61 David, *The Lonely Lady*, 57.

62 Ola Welch Jobe interview, in Brodie, *The Fawn Brodie Collection*.

63 Mazlish, *In Search of Nixon*, 64.

64 Morgan, "Whittier '34," *Los Angeles Times*, 10 May 1970.

65 Shearer, "Richard Nixon and Ola-Florence Welch," *Parade*, 28 June 1970.

66 Ola Welch Jobe interview, in Brodie, *The Fawn Brodie Collection*.

67 Morris, *Richard Milhous Nixon*, 168.

68 Ibid., 169.

69 Ibid., 219.

70 Ibid.

71 Ibid., 220.

72 J. Eisenhower, *Pat Nixon*, 59.

73 Ibid., 66.

74 Tom Dixon interview, in Brodie, *The Fawn Brodie Collection*.

75 Smith, "Ordeal!" 129.

76 Sherwood interview, in Brodie, *The Fawn Brodie Collection*.

77 Tom Dixon interview, in ibid.

78 McCullah St. Johns interview, in Morris, *Richard Milhous Nixon*, 594.

79 Brodie, *Richard Nixon*, 237, n.22.

80 Ibid., 237, n.22.

81 Ibid., 237.

82 Ibid., 237, n.22.

83 Tom Dixon interview, in Brodie, *The Fawn Brodie Collection*.

84 R. Nixon, *RN: Memoirs*, 240.

85 *Public Papers of the Presidents 1974*, 632.

86 Brodie, *Richard Nixon*, 143.

87 Ibid., 237, n.22.

88 Mazlish, *In Search of Nixon*, 37; Brodie, *Richard Nixon*, 132.

89 *Public Papers of the Presidents 1969*, 419.

90 Spalding, *The Nixon Nobody Knows*, 135.

91 For the details of this case, see Abrahamsen, *Nixon vs. Nixon*, 122–8; Brodie, *Richard Nixon*, 134–9; Ambrose, *Nixon*, vol. 1: 88; Morris, *Richard Milhous Nixon*, 189–92.

92 Morris, *Richard Milhous Nixon*, 191–2.

93 R. Nixon, *RN: Memoirs*, 22.

94 Morris, *Richard Milhous Nixon*, 194.

95 Ambrose, *Nixon*, vol. 1: 89; Morris, *Richard Milhous Nixon*, 196.

96 Tom Bewley interview, in Brodie, *The Fawn Brodie Collection*.

97 Evlyn Dorn, quoted in Morris, *Richard Milhous Nixon*, 196.

98 Tom Bewley interview, in Brodie, *The Fawn Brodie Collection*.

99 Morris, *Richard Milhous Nixon*, 197.

100 Ibid.

101 Mildred Jackson Johns interview, in Brodie, *The Fawn Brodie Collection*.

102 *Whittier Daily News*, inaugural edition, 18 January 1969.

103 Morris, *Richard Milhous Nixon*, 203.

104 Ambrose, *Nixon*, vol. 1: 117–40; Morris, *Richard Milhous Nixon*, 257–337.

105 Ambrose, *Nixon*, vol. 1: 209–23; Morris, *Richard Milhous Nixon*, 538–621.

106 *San Diego Journal*, 6 May 1950; Morris, *Richard Milhous Nixon*, 561.

107 R. Nixon, *RN: Memoirs*, 77.

108 W. Arnold, *Back When It All Began*, 12–13.

109 Nixon's well-known distaste for women who wore slacks or pants was also a reflection of his castration anxiety. It raised questions as to who actually possessed the phallus, the woman or the man.

110 Thomas Mellon interview, Earl Warren Oral History Project, cited in Morris, *Richard Milhous Nixon*, 710.

111 J. Eisenhower *Pat Nixon*, 116; Morris, *Richard Milhous Nixon*, 733.

112 Nixon, *RN: Memoirs*, 87.

113 R. Nixon, *In the Arena*, 319.

114 Morris, *Richard Milhous Nixon*, 743.

115 R. Nixon, *Six Crises*, 76.

116 Ibid., 87.

117 Ibid., 92–3.

118 Ibid., 93.

119 Lyon, *Eisenhower,* 456; Morris, *Richard Milhous Nixon,* 791.

120 R. Nixon, *Six Crises,* 93.

121 Kornitzer, *The Real Nixon,* 192–3.

122 R. Nixon, *Six Crises* 100–1; *RN: Memoirs,* 97–9.

123 Morris, *Richard Milhous Nixon,* 803.

124 R. Nixon, *Six Crises,* 99.

125 Ibid., 100.

126 Wills, *Nixon Agonistes,* 103.

127 R. Nixon, *Six Crises,* 100.

128 R. Nixon, *RN: Memoirs,* 98. A bowdlerized version of this conversation is given in R. Nixon, *Six Crises,* 100, where it is referred to as "fish or cut bait." At that time, Nixon may have worried about the potentially negative impact on his future political career plans of his use of vulgar language against an American hero. By 1978, those considerations no longer seemed relevant.

129 R. Nixon, *RN: Memoirs,* 98.

130 R. Nixon, *Six Crises,* 101.

131 R. Nixon, *RN: Memoirs,* 102–3.

132 R. Nixon, *Six Crises,* 110; *RN: Memoirs,* 102–3.

133 Mazo, *Richard Nixon,* 127–8.

134 On the "Checkers" speech and reaction to it, see De Toledano, *One Man Alone,* 149–52; Ambrose, *Nixon,* vol. 1: 284–91; Parmet, *Richard Nixon and His America,* 245–51; Wicker, *One of Us,* 97–100. As for Eisenhower, he was not only embarrassed; he was also angered by Nixon's demands that Stevenson and Sparkman publish their financial holdings. He knew that he would be required to follow suit and that the public would learn that his candidature had long been handsomely bankrolled by wealthy friends and that he had been permitted by the Internal Revenue Service to publish *Crusade in Europe* with a special tax advantage [Aitken, *Nixon: A Life,* 217; Brodie, *Richard Nixon,* 285, n.50]. See also chapter 6.

135 R. Nixon, *RN: Memoirs,* 105.

136 R. Nixon, *Six Crises,* 120; *RN: Memoirs,* 106.

137 Morris, *Richard Milhous Nixon,* 840.

138 Mazo, *Richard Nixon,* 133.

139 R. Nixon, *Six Crises,* 122.

140 R. Nixon, *RN: Memoirs,* 106.

141 Ibid., 109.

142 Mazo, *Richard Nixon,* 125–6; Brodie, *Richard Nixon,* 288.

143 *New York Times,* 15 December 1953.

144 Brodie, *Richard Nixon,* 318.

145 R. Nixon, *RN: Memoirs*, 134.

146 Brodie, *Richard Nixon*, 319.

147 Ibid.

148 R. Nixon, *Six Crises*, 152.

149 Ibid.

150 Ibid., 158.

151 Ibid., 160.

152 Ibid., 160.

153 Ibid., 161–2.

154 Ibid., 164.

155 R. Nixon, *RN: Memoirs*, 167.

156 For the narcissistic character, responses to humiliating experiences often oscillate between withdrawal, in which damaged narcissism is repaired in hurtful silence, and aggression, in which damaged narcissism is repaired by utilizing aggression to repair self-esteem.

157 Wills, *Nixon Agonistes*, 122–3.

158 Ibid., 123.

159 Ibid., 124; Wicker, *One of Us*, 218.

160 Wills, *Nixon Agonistes*, 124.

161 Ibid., 125.

162 R. Nixon, *Six Crises*, 321.

163 Ambrose, *Nixon*, vol. 1: 558, n.5.

164 Slater, *The Ike I Knew*, 230–1; Ambrose, *Nixon*, vol. 1: 558.

165 Ambrose, *Eisenhower*, vol. 2: 604.

166 Finch, "The Cabinet and the Nixon Presidency," 261.

167 In a letter to the author, 15 July 1991.

168 Ambrose, *Nixon*, vol. 1: 559.

169 Ambrose, *Nixon*, vol. 1: 559; Wicker, *One of Us*, 224–5.

170 Nixon, *Six Crises*, 339.

171 Goldwater, *With No Apologies*, 216; Brodie, *Richard Nixon*, 259–360.

172 Halberstam, *The Powers That Be*, 336; Brodie, *Richard Nixon*, 360.

173 R. Nixon, *RN: Memoirs*, 222.

174 See Wicker, *One of Us*, 243.

175 In Illinois, Nixon lost by 10,000 votes; in Missouri, his margin of defeat was 35,000.

176 Nixon, *RN: Memoirs*, 224–6.

177 Dr Arnold Hutchnecker, who had treated Nixon for psychosomatic complaints, has his own theory. He feels that his professional silence concerning what was in fact Nixon's excellent health cost Nixon the election. Had he been prepared to reveal that Nixon's health was excellent, when he was called by a reporter from Associated Press ten

days before the election, that would have forced a disclosure from Kennedy's physician that he was suffering from Addison's disease. Given Eisenhower's heart attack, and public concern about the health of a presidential incumbent, Nixon might have picked up enough additional votes to win the election [interview with the author, 1 September 1991].

178 Wicker, *One of Us*, 261.

179 White, *The Making of the President, 1968*, 69–70.

180 Wicker, *One of Us*, 261–2.

181 Nixon, *RN: Memoirs* 231–2.

182 Ambrose, *Nixon*, vol. 1: 651.

183 Nixon, *RN: Memoirs*, 245.

184 Witcover, *The Resurrection of Richard Nixon*, 23.

185 J. Eisenhower, *Pat Nixon*, 215–16.

186 R. Nixon, *RN: Memoirs*, 240.

187 J. Eisenhower, *Pat Nixon*, 216.

188 Ibid.

CHAPTER FIVE

1 Barber, *The Presidential Character*, 362.

2 Mazo and Hess, *Nixon*, 172.

3 R. Nixon, *Six Crises*, 217, 219, 229, 235.

4 R. Nixon, *Six Crises*, 244, 245, 254. 257, 271.

5 Ibid., 271.

6 Barber, *The Presidential Character*, 363–4.

7 Ibid., 364.

8 Hersh, *The Price of Power*, 53; Shawcross, *Sideshow*, 90.

9 Szulc, *The Illusion of Peace*, 62.

10 Decision makers not prone to feelings of shame and humiliation could have been equally opposed to withdrawal at this juncture, but it is one of the hallmarks of the shame-prone decision maker that he does not engage in serious cost-benefit analysis because emotional needs determine his choices.

11 For a detailed analysis of the preparation of NSSM-1 and the White House response, see Szulc, *The Illusion of Peace*, 24–7.

12 Ibid., 27.

13 Isaacson, *Kissinger*, 172; Hersh, *The Price of Power*, 54.

14 Abrams replaced General William Westmoreland as United States commander in Vietnam in the second half of 1968.

15 Shawcross, *Sideshow*, 91–2.

16 Hersh, *The Price of Power,* 55.

17 Karnow, *Vietnam,* 591.

18 R. Nixon, *RN: Memoirs,* 380. According to Hersh, *The Price of Power,* 58, the evidence is clear that North Vietnamese and Viet Cong attacks were in response to a previously authorized increase in American operations. Pentagon statistics show that the number of battalion-sized operations initiated by American units rose from 727 in November 1968, the month the Johnson administration's bombing halt began, to 1,077 in January 1969 – an increase of nearly 48 per cent. Some of these operations were among the most brutal of the war in terms of civilian casualties in the south.

19 Hersh, *The Price of Power,* 58; Isaacson, *Kissinger,* 173.

20 Kissinger, *White House Years,* 242.

21 Ibid., 243; Isaacson, *Kissinger,* 174.

22 Ibid.

23 Kissinger, *White House Years,* 243.

24 Ibid.

25 Ibid., 244.

26 Ibid.; Isaacson, *Kissinger,* 174.

27 Kissinger, *White House Years,* 244.

28 Ibid., 245.

29 Ibid.

30 Ibid.; Isaacson, *Kissinger,* 174.

31 General Earle Wheeler was chairman of the Joint Chiefs of Staff.

32 Kissinger, *White House Years,* 246.

33 Ibid., 247, 313–21.

34 R. Nixon, *RN: Memoirs,* 383. Contrary to Nixon's belief that the North Koreans had shot down the EC-121 in a deliberate act of defiance, a series of highly classified intelligence intercepts monitored by the National Security Council concluded soon after the attack that the incident was apparently a command-and-control error involving a single North Korean airplane. There was no evidence that the North Korean government knew of the attack in advance, as it had, for example, before the *Pueblo* was seized in January 1968 [Hersh, *The Price of Power,* 69–70].

35 Hersh, *The Price of Power,* 66–77; R. Nixon, *RN: Memoirs,* 383.

36 Kissinger, *White House Years,* 247. Excessive concerns about feeling "weak" or inadequate are characteristic of narcissistic individuals who are prone to feelings of shame/humiliation.

37 News Summaries 3/23/69, cited in Ambrose, *Nixon,* vol. 2: 271, n.71.

38 Karnow, *Vietnam,* 591.

39 Ibid.

40 Ambrose, *Nixon*, vol. 2: 272, n.75.

41 Kissinger, *White House Years*, 248–9.

42 Szulc, *The Illusion of Peace*, 54–8.

43 Shawcross, *Sideshow*, 94.

44 *Public Papers of the Presidents 1970*, 407.

45 R. Nixon, *RN: Memoirs*, 382.

46 Those wiretapped included members of the National Security Council, the cabinet, various journalists and broadcasters – virtually anyone deemed a potential enemy.

47 Hersh, *The Price of Power*, 88. Isaacson notes that Nixon's drinking became unsettling to Kissinger, who would "poke fun at 'my drunken' friend the way people joke about things that truly scare them." The drinking also disturbed Kissinger's staff, who often listened in on the late-night conversations between Nixon and Kissinger [Kissinger, *White House Years*, 262–3].

48 Cited in Shawcross, *Sideshow*, 113.

49 Ambrose, *Nixon*, vol. 2: 336; Hersh, *The Price of Power*, 176; Shawcross, *Sideshow*, 113–17.

50 The 303 Committee, by then renamed the 40 Committee, was the inter-agency committee supervising covert intelligence activities.

51 Kissinger, *White House Years*, 465.

52 Ambrose, *Nixon*, vol. 2: 337.

53 Hersh, *The Price of Power*, 187.

54 Kissinger, *White House Years*, 473.

55 Mazlish, *In Search of Richard Nixon*, 128–30; Szulc, *The Illusion of Peace*, 252–3.

56 Evans, Jr, and Novak, *Nixon in the White House*, 162.

57 Ibid., 163.

58 Barber, *The Presidential Character*, 427.

59 *New York Times*, 2 April 1970.

60 Ibid., 3 April 1970.

61 Ambrose, *Nixon*, vol. 2: 337.

62 Ibid., 337–8.

63 *Public Papers of the Presidents 1970*, 373–7.

64 *New York Times*, 11 April 1970.

65 Mazlish, *In Search of Richard Nixon*, 130–1.

66 Shawcross, *Sideshow*, 134.

67 R. Nixon, *RN: Memoirs*, 447–8.

68 Ehrlichman, *Witness to Power*, 62.

69 R. Nixon, *RN: Memoirs*, 448.

70 Ambrose, *Nixon*, vol. 2: 338–9.

71 Ibid., 339.

72 Kissinger, *White House Years*, 483.

73 Barber, *The Presidential Character*, 429.

74 *Public Papers of the Presidents 1970*, 373–4. Emphasis added.

75 Ibid., 377. Emphasis added.

76 Hersh, *The Price of Power*, 178.

77 Shawcross, *Sideshow*, 137.

78 Ibid.

79 Ibid.

80 Szulc, *The Illusion of Peace*, 253.

81 Ambrose, *Nixon*, vol. 2: 340.

82 R. Nixon, *RN: Memoirs*, 448–9.

83 Kissinger, *White House Years*, 489.

84 Ibid., 490; Isaacson, *Kissinger*, 261.

85 Kissinger, *White House Years*, 491.

86 Ibid., 492–3.

87 Shawcross, *Sideshow*, 410; Kissinger, *White House Years*, 488–92; Isaac-son, *Kissinger*, 261.

88 R. Nixon, *RN: Memoirs*, 450.

89 Kissinger, *White House Years*, 495.

90 Isaacson, *Kissinger*, 362.

91 Kissinger, *White House Years*, 495.

92 Hersh, *The Price of Power*, 187–8.

93 Ibid., 188.

94 Ibid., 189.

95 R. Nixon, *RN: Memoirs*, 448–9.

96 Hersh, *The Price of Power*, 189.

97 Ibid., 189–90.

98 Haldeman, *The Haldeman Diaries*, 154.

99 For details on Kissinger's political calculations, see Szulc, *The Illusion of Peace*, 283.

100 Kissinger, *White House Years*, 493.

101 Szulc, *The Illusion of Peace*, 257.

102 Kissinger, *White House Years*, 497.

103 Ibid.

104 Ambrose, *Nixon*, vol. 2: 342.

105 Hersh, *The Price of Power*, 190; Morris, *Uncertain Greatness*, 147; Brodie, *Richard Nixon*, 477; Ambrose, *Nixon*, vol. 2: 342; Karnow, *Vietnam*, 609; Isaacson, *Kissinger*, 262.

106 Kissinger, *White House Years*, 498.

107 Ibid.

108 Szulc, *The Illusion of Peace*, 258.

109 Wills, *The Kennedy Imprisonment*, 193–4.

110 Kissinger, *White House Years*, 499.

111 Ibid.

112 Ibid.

113 R. Nixon, *RN: Memoirs*, 450.

114 Kissinger, *White House Years*, 500.

115 Ibid., 501; R. Nixon, *RN: Memoirs*, 450.

116 Ambrose, *Nixon*, vol. 2: 343.

117 Kissinger, *White House Years*, 502.

118 Ibid.; Isaacson, *Kissinger*, 267.

119 Szulc, *The Illusion of Peace*, 258.

120 Kissinger, *White House Years*, 503.

121 R. Nixon, *RN: Memoirs*, 451.

122 Kissinger, *White House Years*, 503.

123 Karnow, *Vietnam*, 608; Shawcross, *Sideshow*, 144.

124 Shawcross, *Sideshow*, 144.

125 Ibid.

126 Ibid.; Karnow, *Vietnam*, 609. On the Nixon Doctrine, see *Congressional Record*, 28 July 1969, S–8637–40, reproduced in Senate Foreign Relations Committee Report, "Background Information Relating to Southeast Asia and Vietnam," December 1974, 356–67.

127 Shawcross, *Sideshow*, 145.

128 Morris, *Uncertain Greatness*, 174–5.

129 Shawcross, *Sideshow*, 146.

130 *Public Papers of the Presidents 1970*, 405–6.

131 Szulc, *The Illusion of Peace*, 261.

132 Shawcross, *Sideshow*, 261.

133 *Public Papers of the Presidents 1970*, 407.

134 Shawcross, *Sideshow*, 146–7.

135 *Public Papers of the Presidents, 1970*, 406.

136 Ibid.

137 Szulc, *The Illusion of Peace*, 263.

138 *Public Papers of the Presidents 1970*, 406.

139 Szulc, *The Illusion of Peace*, 264.

140 Ibid., 265.

141 *Public Papers of the Presidents 1970*, 407.

142 Ibid.

143 Ibid., 407–8.

144 Ibid., 408.

145 Ibid., 408–9.

146 Ibid., 408.

147 Ibid., 409–10.

148 Schell, *The Time of Illusion*, 91.

149 Mazlish, *In Search of Richard Nixon*, 131–2; Schell, *The Time of Illusion*, 93.

150 Shawcross, *Sideshow*, 152.

151 Ibid.

152 Ibid.

153 Ibid., 152–3.

154 Isaacson, *Kissinger*, 271–2.

CHAPTER SIX

1 See, for example, Billings-Yun, *Decision Against War*; Anderson, ed., *Shadow on the White House*, 43–62.

2 D. Eisenhower, *At Ease*, 66–7; F. Miller, *Eisenhower*, 35–7; Ambrose, *Eisenhower*, vol. 1: 14–15; Lee, *Dwight D. Eisenhower*, 4.

3 F. Miller, *Eisenhower* 30–3; Ambrose, *Eisenhower*, vol. 1: 15–16; Davis, *Soldier of Democracy*, 32–3; Lee, *Dwight D. Eisenhower*, 4–5; Neal, *The Eisenhowers*, 8.

4 Later, Ida's son Earl (Dwight's younger brother) would call it a "tragedy" that their mother had married and started a family before finishing school [Kornitzer, *The Great American Heritage*, 10]. David, like his wife, would regret having not continued with university; he later took engineering courses by correspondence [F. Miller, *Eisenhower*, 45]. This experience left the couple with a strong desire to see their sons pursue a university education [Kornitzer, *The Great American Heritage*, 23].

5 F. Miller, *Eisenhower*, 37–8, 49–51; Davis, *Soldier of Democracy*, 42, 65; Lyon, *Eisenhower*, 35; Ambrose, *Eisenhower*, vol. 1: 17–18.

6 Davis, *Soldier of Democracy*, 43–4; Lee, *Dwight D. Eisenhower*, 6–7.

7 Lee, *Dwight D. Eisenhower*, 5–6.

8 Neal, *The Eisenhowers*, 12.

9 Davis, *Soldier of Democracy*, 73–4; Kornitzer, *The Great American Heritage*, 35; Neal, *The Eisenhowers*, 15.

10 Ambrose, *Eisenhower*, vol. 1: 18–19.

11 Neal, *The Eisenhowers*, 12.

12 Ibid., 14–15; Davis, *Soldier of Democracy*, 73.

13 Ambrose, *Eisenhower*, vol. 1: 29.

14 Davis, *Soldier of Democracy*, 66. Throughout his life, family ties remained important to Eisenhower. He consistently remembered birthdays and other family events with cards and messages [Kornitzer, *The Great American Heritage*, 96]. And, except when he was out of the country, he managed to visit Abilene at least once a year. Family reunions were significant events which were held as often as possible [Ambrose, *Eisenhower*, vol. 1: 69].

15 Lee, *Dwight D. Eisenhower*, 21.

16 Davis, *Soldier of Democracy*, 65–6.

17 Lyon, *Eisenhower*, 33; Kornitzer, *The Great American Heritage*, 93; Davis, *Soldier of Democracy*, 65; Lee, *Dwight D. Eisenhower*, 12.

18 D. Eisenhower, *At Ease*, 37–8.

19 Davis, *Soldier of Democracy*, 53.

20 D. Eisenhower, *At Ease*, 39–40.

21 Davis, *Soldier of Democracy*, 56–8.

22 D. Eisenhower, *At Ease*, 95.

23 Ibid., 44.

24 Orin Snyder Oral History Interview, 6 October 1964.

25 D. Eisenhower, *At Ease*, 292.

26 Kornitzer, *The Great American Heritage*, 249–51.

27 Ibid., 258.

28 Ibid., 304.

29 All the sons commented on their father's quiet and serious manner. Arthur recalled: "I never saw him in tears or overcome by any emotion" [Kornitzer, *The Great American Heritage*, 19].

30 Ibid., 265; Ambrose, *Eisenhower*, vol. 1: 20.

31 D. Eisenhower, *At Ease*, 43–4.

32 J.S. Eisenhower, *Strictly Personal*, 15.

33 Earl also recalled hearing this same lecture from their mother [Kornitzer, *The Great American Heritage*, 48–9].

34 D. Eisenhower, *At Ease*, 57–8.

35 Kornitzer, *The Great American Heritage*, 25–6.

36 Davis, *Soldier of Democracy*, 68.

37 D. Eisenhower, *At Ease*, 58.

38 Ambrose, *Eisenhower*, vol. 2: 13.

39 Greenstein, *The Hidden-Hand Presidency*, 44.

40 "Five Presidents on the Presidency," CBS News 1973, as quoted in Greenstein, *The Hidden-Hand Presidency*, 43.

41 Hughes, *The Ordeal of Power*, 149.

42 Barber, *The Presidential Character*, 167.

43 Kornitzer, *The Great American Heritage*, 87–8.

44 D. Eisenhower, *At Ease*, 289.

45 Ferrell, ed., *The Eisenhower Diaries*, 51.

46 Neal, *The Eisenhowers*, 15.

47 D. Eisenhower, *At Ease*, 99.

48 Kornitzer, *The Great American Heritage*, 45–6.

49 D. Eisenhower, *At Ease*, 38.

50 F. Miller, *Eisenhower*, 78.

51 Ibid., 73–83; Davis, *Soldier of Democracy*, 84–5.

52 Davis, *Soldier of Democracy*, 67.

53 Ambrose, *Eisenhower*, vol. 1: 32.

54 Davis, *Soldier of Democracy*, 84; Lee, *Dwight D. Eisenhower*, 19.

55 For his high-school accomplishments on the sports field and in athletic organizations, see D. Eisenhower, *At Ease*, 103.

56 A school-mate who remembered the incident insisted that both the duration and danger of the illness have been greatly exaggerated [Lee, *Dwight D. Eisenhower*, 15; D. Eisenhower, *At Ease*, 101–2; Kornitzer, *The Great American Heritage*, 43–4].

57 Davis, *Soldier of Democracy*, 85.

58 Lee, *Dwight D. Eisenhower*, 17.

59 F. Miller, *Eisenhower*, 75.

60 Neal, *The Eisenhowers*, 18.

61 D. Eisenhower, *At Ease*, 106.

62 Dwight and Swede remained friends until the latter's death in 1958. Eisenhower recalled that Swede was one of the people to whom he "opened up."

63 McCann, *Man From Abilene*, 58–9.

64 D. Eisenhower, *At Ease*, 108–10.

65 Davis, *Soldier of Democracy*, 113; McCann, *Man from Abilene*, 60.

66 D. Eisenhower, *At Ease*, 14.

67 Ibid., 28; Ambrose, *Eisenhower*, vol. 1: 45.

68 Lyon, *Eisenhower*, 43.

69 F. Miller, *Eisenhower*, 133.

70 D. Eisenhower, *At Ease*, 16.

71 Neal, *The Eisenhowers*, 26.

72 Lee, *Dwight D. Eisenhower*, 31.

73 D. Eisenhower, *At Ease*, 24–6.

74 Ambrose, *Eisenhower*, vol. 1: 50.

75 Neal, *The Eisenhowers*, 27.

76 Ambrose, *Eisenhower*, vol. 1: 47–8.

77 Lee, *Dwight D. Eisenhower*, 33. At graduation he stood 125th in discipline out of 162 men – while academically he was 61st [D. Eisenhower, *At Ease*, 22].

78 Ambrose, *Eisenhower*, vol. 1: 51.

79 D. Eisenhower, *At Ease*, 16.

80 Ibid., 14.

81 Neal, *The Eisenhowers*, 28.

82 Griffith, "Dwight D. Eisenhower and the Corporate Commonwealth," 88; Ambrose, *Eisenhower*, vol. 1: 52–4.

83 Barber, *The Presidential Character*, 159.

84 Brandon, *Mamie Doud Eisenhower*, 47–8, 66.

85 Ambrose, *Eisenhower*, vol. 1: 58.

86 Ramsay, *Ike*, 7.

87 D. Eisenhower, *At Ease*, 116.

88 Brandon, *Mamie Doud Eisenhower*, 59.

89 D. Eisenhower, *At Ease*, 119.

90 Ibid., 119–20.

91 Ramsey, *Ike*, 5–6.

92 D. Eisenhower, *At Ease*, 126.

93 Brandon, *Mamie Doud Eisenhower*, 80–7.

94 D. Eisenhower, *At Ease*, 150.

95 Ibid., 178.

96 Ambrose, *Eisenhower*, vol. 1: 74.

97 D. Eisenhower, *At Ease*, 179.

98 Ibid., 191.

99 Ramsey, *Ike*, 10–11.

100 Ambrose, *Eisenhower*, vol. 1: 75.

101 Brandon, *Mamie Doud Eisenhower*, 122.

102 Ramsey, *Ike*, 16.

103 D. Eisenhower, *At Ease*, 134.

104 Ibid., 132.

105 Ibid., 136–7.

106 Greenstein, *The Hidden-Hand Presidency*, 32.

107 D. Eisenhower, *At Ease*, 138–9.

108 Lee, *Dwight D. Eisenhower*, 44–5.

109 F. Miller, *Eisenhower*, 169.

110 Ambrose, *Eisenhower*, vol. 1: 65.

111 D. Eisenhower, *At Ease*, 151, 155.

112 Lee, *Dwight D. Eisenhower*, 45.

113 Ambrose, *Eisenhower*, vol. 1: 67.

114 Ibid., 73.

115 McCann, *Man from Abilene*, 106.

116 D. Eisenhower, *At Ease*, 172.

117 Ibid., 182.

118 McCann, *Man from Abilene*, 80; Ambrose, *Eisenhower*, vol. 1: 76.

119 D. Eisenhower, *At Ease*, 185.

120 Ibid., 195–7.

121 Ibid., 198–200; Lyon, *Eisenhower*, 61; Lee, *Dwight D. Eisenhower*, 54.

122 Ambrose, *Eisenhower*, vol. 1: 69–70.

123 Lee, *Dwight D. Eisenhower*, 56.

124 Lyon, *Eisenhower*, 62.

125 D. Eisenhower, *At Ease*, 201; Lee, *Dwight D. Eisenhower*, 56.

126 Lee, *Dwight D. Eisenhower*, 57.

127 D. Eisenhower, *At Ease*, 209.

128 MacArthur's efficiency reports in the Eisenhower Library, quoted in Ambrose, *Eisenhower*, vol. 1: 93.

129 Neal, *The Eisenhowers*, 93–4; Davis, *Soldier of Democracy*, 240.

130 D. Eisenhower, *At Ease*, 216.

131 Lee, *Dwight D. Eisenhower*, 61–3.

132 President Quezon reappeared later, while Eisenhower was working at the War Plans division, to offer him a honorarium and citation for his services. Eisenhower refused the honorarium but accepted the citation on the grounds that it "would be of great and more lasting value to me and my family than any amount of money his government could possibly present to me" [Ferrell, ed., *The Eisenhower Diaries*, 63].

133 D. Eisenhower, *At Ease*, 225, 227.

134 D. Eisenhower, *Crusade in Europe*, 6.

135 Ambrose, *Eisenhower*, vol. 1: 121–2.

136 Lyon, *Eisenhower*, 81.

137 Ambrose, *Eisenhower*, vol. 1: 122–3.

138 D. Eisenhower, *At Ease*, 230.

139 Ambrose, *Eisenhower*, vol. 1: 125–6.

140 McCann, *Man from Abilene*, 30.

141 Ibid., 25–9.

142 D. Eisenhower, *At Ease*, 230–2.

143 Davis, *Soldier of Democracy*, 265–74.

144 Ambrose, *Eisenhower*, vol. 1: 129–30.

145 D. Eisenhower, *At Ease*, 236–7.

146 D. Eisenhower, *Crusade in Europe*, 14.

147 Ibid., 18–22.

148 Ambrose, *The Supreme Commander*, 22.

149 Ferrell, ed., *The Eisenhower Diaries*, 40.

150 D. Eisenhower, *At Ease*, 249–50; Ambrose, *Supreme Commander*, 21.

151 Ferrell, ed., *The Eisenhower Diaries*, 52.

152 Neal, *The Eisenhowers*, 127.

153 Lyon, *Eisenhower*, 122.

154 McCann, *Man from Abilene*, 42.

155 Lee, *Dwight D. Eisenhower*, 72–3; Ambrose, *Supreme Commander*, 51.

156 D. Eisenhower, *Crusade in Europe*, 51.

157 Ibid., 71.

158 Ibid., 89.

159 Ibid.

160 Ibid., 151.

161 Ferrell, ed., *The Eisenhower Diaries*, 81.

162 D. Eisenhower, *Crusade in Europe*, 107.

163 Greenstein, *The Hidden-Hand Presidency*, 25–6.

164 Ambrose, *Supreme Commander*, 130.

165 MacMillan, *The Blast of War*, 174.

166 D. Eisenhower, *At Ease*, 250.

167 D. Eisenhower, *Crusade in Europe*, 125.

168 Lyon, *Eisenhower*, 266; Lee, *Dwight D. Eisenhower*, 86.

169 J.S. Eisenhower, ed., *Letters to Mamie*, 10.

170 McCann, *Man from Abilene*, 113.

171 Ferrell, ed., *The Eisenhower Diaries*, 103–5.

172 Neal, *The Eisenhowers*, 171–2.

173 Cook, *The Declassified Eisenhower*, 63–4. See also Lyon, *Portrait of a Hero*, 255.

174 Lee, *Dwight D. Eisenhower*, 95.

175 D. Eisenhower, *Crusade in Europe*, 219.

176 Ibid., 250.

177 Neal, *The Eisenhowers*, 188.

178 Ferrell, ed., *The Eisenhower Diaries*, 111.

179 Ambrose, *Supreme Commander*, 664–5. Two notable exceptions were his relations with General George Patton and Field Marshal Bernard Montgomery. During the Sicilian campaign, Patton verbally and physically abused two enlisted men who were in hospital for shell-shocked nerves, an action for which he could have faced court-martial. After Patton publicly commented at a press conference that de-Nazification was being overdone and the Nazis were just another political party, Eisenhower's tolerance evaporated – Patton was now expendable. He told Patton: "The war's over and I don't want to hurt you – but I can't let you be making such ridiculous statements.

I'm going to give you a new job" [Ambrose, *Supreme Commander*, 342]. More serious problems occurred with Eisenhower's primary British subordinate, Field Marshall Montgomery. Montgomery frequently insinuated that Eisenhower's strategy was flawed and accused him of playing politics in his refusal to support Montgomery's battle plans [Montgomery, *The Memoirs of Field Marshal the Viscount Montgomery of Alamein*, 243].

180 Ambrose, *Eisenhower*, vol. 1: 342–4.

181 D. Eisenhower, *Crusade in Europe*, 314.

182 Lyon, *Eisenhower*, 268.

183 Lee, *Dwight D. Eisenhower*, 108–9; D. Eisenhower, *Crusade in Europe*, 356; Bradley, *A Soldier's Story*, 486–8.

184 D. Eisenhower, *Crusade in Europe*, 408–9.

185 J.S. Eisenhower, ed., *Letters to Mamie*, 209–10.

186 Morgenthau claimed that his plan grew out of a conversation with Eisenhower. However, Eisenhower also remembered telling Morgenthau that the Germans must be left the capacity to make a living so they would not become a charity case. See Ambrose, *Eisenhower*, vol. 1: 422.

187 Greenstein, *The Hidden-Hand Presidency*, 31.

188 Lee, *Dwight D. Eisenhower*, 114.

189 McCann, *Man from Abilene*, 118.

190 D. Eisenhower, *At Ease*, 283.

191 Lyon, *Eisenhower*, 345–6.

192 Lee, *Dwight D. Eisenhower*, 115.

193 Lyon, *Eisenhower*, 7–8. Illustrative of the sense of balance that Eisenhower tried to maintain is a poem that he would often quote (author unknown) which reads in part: "Sometime, when you're feeling important/Sometime, when your ego's in bloom/Sometime, when you take it for granted/You're the best qualified in the room/... Take a bucket, fill it with water/Put your hand in – clear up to the wrist/Now pull it out; the hole that remains/Is a measure of how you'll be missed ..." [J.S. Eisenhower, *Strictly Personal*, 389]. It is difficult to imagine either Lyndon Johnson or Richard Nixon quoting a similar poem to himself, given the degree of narcissism each man exhibited.

194 Eisenhower also received the Order of Merit from King George VI of England, the first American to be so honoured. Similar incidents and acclaim followed him on his return tours to France and the United States. On a later trip, Eisenhower (along with Montgomery) was awarded the Russian Order of Victory, a Soviet decoration that had

never before been awarded to a foreigner [D. Eisenhower, *Crusade in Europe*, 437; Lyon, *The Eisenhowers*, 23].

195 D. Eisenhower, *At Ease*, 285.

196 Ibid., 301.

197 Brandon, *Mamie Doud Eisenhower*, 239.

198 McCann, *Man from Abilene*, 129.

199 Ferrell, ed., *The Eisenhower Diaries*, 137.

200 Cook, *The Declassified Eisenhower*, 59.

201 Lee, *Dwight D. Eisenhower*, 128–9.

202 Ferrell, ed., *The Eisenhower Diaries*, 147.

203 Neal, *The Eisenhowers*, 241.

204 Lee, *Dwight D. Eisenhower*, 133.

205 D. Eisenhower, *At Ease*, 312.

206 Greenstein, *The Hidden-Hand Presidency*, 74.

207 D. Eisenhower, *Crusade in Europe*, 444.

208 Neal, *The Eisenhowers*, 232.

209 Ferrell, ed., *The Eisenhower Diaries*, xii.

210 Lyon, *Eisenhower*, 348.

211 McCann, *Man from Abilene*, 141.

212 D. Eisenhower, *At Ease*, 319; Lee, *Dwight D. Eisenhower*, 131.

213 McCann, *Man from Abilene*, 161.

214 Ibid., 165.

215 Cook, *The Declassified Eisenhower*, 59–62.

216 McCann, *Man from Abilene*, 175–8.

217 Lee, *Dwight D. Eisenhower*, 135.

218 Ferrell, ed., *The Eisenhower Diaries*, 161–2.

219 Greenstein, *The Hidden-Hand Presidency*, 96–8; Parmet, *Eisenhower and the American Crusades*, 18.

220 Ferrell, ed., *The Eisenhower Diaries*, 164–5.

221 Ambrose, *Eisenhower*, vol. 1: 460–1.

222 D. Eisenhower, *At Ease*, 344.

223 Ferrell, ed., *The Eisenhower Diaries*, 180.

224 D. Eisenhower, *At Ease*, 353.

225 Ferrell, ed., *The Eisenhower Diaries*, 189.

226 Lee, *Dwight D. Eisenhower*, 138.

227 Ferrell, ed., *The Eisenhower Diaries*, 193.

228 Neal, *The Eisenhowers*, 265.

229 Parmet, *Eisenhower and the American Crusades*, 47.

230 Ferrell, ed., *The Eisenhower Diaries*, 199.

231 McCann, *Man from Abilene*, 149–51.

232 Ibid., 235–6.
233 Ambrose, *Eisenhower*, vol. 1: 518.
234 Ferrell, ed., *The Eisenhower Diaries*, 209.
235 Barber, *The Presidential Character*, 172.
236 Ferrell, ed., *The Eisenhower Diaries*, 214.
237 Ambrose, *Eisenhower*, vol. 1: 523.
238 Kornitzer, *The Great American Heritage*, 68.
239 Brandon, *Mamie Doud Eisenhower*, 289–90.
240 Ambrose, *Eisenhower*, vol. 1: 541; Neal, *The Eisenhowers*, 285–6; During
    the early years of his presidency, Eisenhower worked hard to gain the
    support of Taft and his followers [Neal, *The Eisenhowers*, 322–3].
241 Kornitzer, *The Great American Heritage*, 197–8.
242 Brandon, *Mamie Doud Eisenhower*, 294.
243 Greenstein, *The Hidden-Hand Presidency*, 29.
244 Ibid., 74.
245 Hughes, *The Ordeal of Power*, 54.
246 Lee, *Dwight D. Eisenhower*, 167.
247 For this analysis, see Ambrose, *Eisenhower*, vol. 1: 554–61.
248 Kornitzer, *The Great American Heritage*, 68; Emmet Hughes, who worked
    closely with Eisenhower during both his election campaigns, recalled
    the "emotional insurance" Eisenhower engaged in, such as his com-
    ment in September 1956: "Hell, if the people were to decide not to
    re-elect me, I sure couldn't feel desperately unhappy about it." But on
    election night (1956), Eisenhower had changed his tune: "You rem-
    ember that story of Nelson dying, he looked around and asked, 'Are
    there any of them still left?' I guess that's me. When I get in a battle, I
    just want to win the whole thing … six or seven states we can't help. But
    I don't want to lose any more. Don't want any of them 'left' – like
    Nelson. That's the way I feel" [Hughes, *The Ordeal of Power*, 192, 228].
249 Hughes, *The Ordeal of Power*, 47; Parmet, *Eisenhower and the American
    Crusades*, 145–6.
250 Ferrell, ed., *The Presidential Diaries*, 225.
251 Kornitzer, *The Great American Heritage*, 198–9.
252 M. Eisenhower, *The President Is Calling*, 186.
253 Hughes, *The Ordeal of Power*, 153–4.
254 Ambrose, *Eisenhower*, vol 2: 19–20.
255 Greenstein, *The Hidden-Hand Presidency*, 32, including footnote.
256 M. Eisenhower, *The President is Calling*, 273.
257 Greenstein, *The Hidden-Hand Presidency*, 109.
258 Lee, *Dwight D. Eisenhower*, 173.

259 Ambrose, *Eisenhower,* vol. 2: 79–80.

260 Greenstein, *The Hidden-Hand Presidency,* 120.

261 Ibid., 115–17.

262 Ibid., 111.

263 Hughes, *The Ordeal of Power,* 135.

264 Greenstein, *The Hidden-Hand Presidency,* 34.

265 Lee, *Dwight D. Eisenhower,* 179.

266 Ferrell, ed., *The Eisenhower Diaries,* 232.

267 M. Eisenhower, "Portrait of a Brother," 14.

268 See Cook, *The Declassified Eisenhower,* 153; Divine, *Eisenhower and the Cold War,* 9.

269 Ambrose, *Eisenhower,* vol. 2: 26–7.

270 Ibid., 55.

271 Lee, *Dwight D. Eisenhower,* 142.

272 Ambrose, *Eisenhower,* vol. 2: 92–3.

273 Ibid., 97.

274 Ibid., 107.

275 D. Eisenhower, *Mandate for Change,* 181.

276 Neal, *The Eisenhowers,* 306.

277 D. Eisenhower, *Mandate for Change,* 181–3.

278 Ambrose, *Eisenhower,* vol. 2: 107.

279 D. Eisenhower, *Mandate for Change,* 183.

280 Parmet, *Eisenhower and the American Crusades,* 314.

281 Hughes, *The Ordeal of Power,* 119.

282 Ferrell, ed., *The Eisenhower Diaries,* 248.

283 D. Eisenhower, *Mandate for Change* 183–7; Parmet, *Eisenhower and the American Crusades,* 313–15.

CHAPTER SEVEN

1 All dates mentioned in the chapter will be 1954 unless otherwise indicated. It should also be noted that, for the sake of consistency, alternate spellings of Dien Bien Phu (Dienbienphu) and Indochina (Indo-China) have all been standardized.

2 Melanson, "The Foundations of Eisenhower's Foreign Policy," 43.

3 Herring, *America's Longest War,* 10.

4 NSC 124/2, 24 June 1952, *Pentagon Papers,* Gravel, ed., vol. 1, 385–6. This strategic interest was emphasized to Eisenhower in the briefing he received from the outgoing secretary of state, Dean Acheson. See Billings-Yun, *Decision Against War,* 1–2.

5 Gibbons, *The U.S. Government and the Vietnam War,* 25–6; Hammer, *The Struggle for Indochina,* 313; Gelb with Betts, *The Irony of Vietnam,* 53; C. Alexander, *Holding The Line,* 77–8.

6 Ferrell, ed., *The Eisenhower Diaries,* 190.

7 D. Eisenhower, *Mandate for Change,* 333, 336.

8 Eisenhower's extensive international experience had bred in him a determined belief in the need to cultivate and support allies, especially those in Western Europe. He had many friends among the leaders of Western European nations and identified strongly with them because of their shared experiences in the Second World War.

9 Divine, *Eisenhower and the Cold War,* 42.

10 *Pentagon Papers,* Gravel, ed., vol. 1: 410–11.

11 Memorandum of the 161st meeting of the NSC, 9 September 1953, Foreign Relations of the United States (FRUS), 1952–54, vol. 13: 810–12; *Pentagon Papers,* Gravel, ed., vol. 1: 405–6.

12 D. Eisenhower, *Mandate for Change,* 343.

13 Billings-Yun, *Decision Against War,* 7.

14 *Pentagon Papers,* Gravel, ed., vol. 1: 407; (FRUS), 1952–54, vol. 13: 714–18; Radford claimed to support this conclusion [Radford, *From Pearl Harbor to Vietnam,* 364].

15 Billings-Yun, *Decision Against War,* 24, n.47; D. Eisenhower, *Mandate for Change,* 339–40.

16 Fall, *Hell in a Very Small Place,* 1–52; C. Alexander, *Holding the Line,* 78; Divine, *Eisenhower and the Cold War,* 40; Radford, *From Pearl Harbor to Vietnam,* 377.

17 *Pentagon Papers,* Gravel, ed., vol. 1: 89.

18 Memorandum of the 179th meeting of the NSC, 8 January 1954, FRUS, 1952–54, vol. 13: 947–54.

19 Memorandum of the Meeting of the President's Special Committee on Indochina, Washington, 29 January 1954, FRUS, 1952–54, vol. 13: 1002–6; *Pentagon Papers,* Gravel, ed., vol. 1: 443–7. There had been American Military Assistance Advisory Group (MAAG) officers in Saigon for some time, but they were extremely limited in their movements and access to information and therefore were not considered "active."

20 In response to angry inquiries about the source of the leak, Smith replied: "All one could say was that this secret had been kept quite a bit longer than most others" [Memorandum of discussion at the 183rd meeting of the NSC, 4 February 1954, FRUS, 1952–54, vol. 13: 1016; Immerman, "Between the Unattainable and the Unacceptable," 126].

21 Gibbons, *The U.S. Government and the Vietnam War,* 158–9; Gurtov, *The First Vietnam Crisis,* 69–70; Immerman, "Between the Unattainable and the Unacceptable," 126; Billings-Yun, *Decision Against War,* 26.

22 Hagerty Diary, 8 February 1954, James C. Hagerty Papers.

23 Minnich, Memorandum on Legislative Conference, 8 February 1954, FRUS, 1952–54, vol. 13: 1023–5. Eisenhower almost never consulted with his secretary of defense, Charles E. Wilson, on the substantive aspects of defense policy but employed him more as a manager and administrator to run the defense establishment [Fred I. Greenstein, *The Hidden-Hand Presidency,* 85].

24 Billings-Yun, *Decision Against War,* 26–7.

25 Memorandum of Discussion at the 183rd and 184th Meetings of the NSC, 4 February 1954 and 11 February 1954, FRUS, 1952–54, vol. 13: 1013–17, 1035–9.

26 Report by the President's Special Committee on Indochina, 2 March 1954, FRUS, 1952–54, vol. 13: 1109–10; Memorandum from the Special Committee, NSC, *Pentagon Papers,* Gravel, ed., vol. 1: 453; Memorandum by Charles Stelae of the Policy Planning Staff, 23 March 1954, FRUS, 1952–54, vol. 13: 1146–8.

27 *Public Papers of the Presidents 1954,* 306.

28 Herring, *America's Longest War,* 29; Buttinger, *Vietnam,* 358; Gurtov, *The First Vietnam Crisis,* 78; Gibbons, *The U.S. Government and the Vietnam War,* 170; Immerman, "Between the Unattainable and the Unacceptable," 128; Bator, *Vietnam,* 30.

29 See Memorandum of Discussion of the 189th Meeting of the NSC, 18 March 1954, FRUS, 1952–54, vol. 13: 1146–8; D. Eisenhower, *Mandate for Change,* 344; Herring, *America's Longest War,* 29.

30 Ely, *L'Indochine Dans La Tourmente,* 59–81; Radford, *From Pearl Harbor to Vietnam,* 391–7. Secondary sources for the Ely visit include Gibbons, *The U.S. Government and Vietnam,* 171–3; Lacouture and Devillers, *End of a War,* 72–5; Immerman, "Between the Unattainable and the Unacceptable," 129–32; Gurtov, *The First Vietnam Crisis,* 78–9; Bator, *Vietnam,* 31–2; Billings-Yun, *Decision Against War,* 29–52.

31 Ely, *L'Indochine Dans La Tourmente,* 73; Billings-Yun, *The Decision Against War,* 33–7; Bator, *Vietnam,* 32.

32 D. Eisenhower, *Mandate for Change,* 345.

33 Memorandum by General Paul Ely to Admiral Radford, Pentagon Papers, Gravel, ed., vol. 1: 458–9; Radford, *From Pearl Harbor to Vietnam,* 393–6; Billings-Yun, *Decision Against War,* 37–40.

34 Memorandum by the Chairman of the Joint Chiefs of Staff (Radford) to the President, 24 March 1954, *Pentagon Papers*, Gravel, ed., vol. 1: 459–60; Radford, *From Pearl Harbor to Vietnam*, 397.

35 Memorandum by the Secretary of State to the President, 23 March 1954, FRUS, 1952–54, vol. 13: 1132.

36 Memorandum of Conversation with the President, 24 March 1954, FRUS, 1952–54, vol. 13: 1150.

37 Billings-Yun, *Decision Against War*, 45–8; Burke *et al.*, *How Presidents Test Reality*, 43.

38 Ely, *L'Indochine Dans La Tourmente*, 76–7, 82–3. For the origins of Operation Vulture see *Pentagon Papers*, Gravel, ed., vol. 1: 97–8; Fall, *Hell in a Very Small Place*, 301; Lacouture and Devillers, *End of a War*, 74–5.

39 Radford, *From Pearl Harbor to Vietnam*, 392–5; Radford, Memorandum for the President's Special Committee on Indochina, *Pentagon Papers*, Gravel, ed., vol. 1: , 455–8; Herring and Immerman, "Eisenhower, Dulles, and Dien Bien Phu," 347–8.

40 Immerman, "Between the Unattainable and the Unacceptable," 131.

41 Ely, *L'Indochine Dans La Tourmente*, 83–4; Radford, *From Pearl Harbor to Vietnam*, 400–1; Lacouture and Devillers, *End of a War*, 75–6; Bator, *Vietnam*, 36 (including footnote.).

42 *Public Papers of the Presidents 1954*, 341.

43 Memorandum for the Secretary of Defense, 12 March 1954, *Pentagon Papers*, Gravel, ed., vol. 1: 448–51; FRUS, 1952–54, vol. 16: 471–2.

44 J. Arnold, *The First Domino*, 158.

45 Memorandum of Discussion of the 190th Meeting of the NSC, 25 March 1954, FRUS, 1952–54, vol. 13: 1163–8.

46 Billings-Yun, *Decision Against War*, 58–9, n.8.

47 Ibid., 59.

48 Ibid., 60.

49 R. Nixon, *Six Crises*, 161.

50 R. Nixon, *RN: Memoirs*, 151; FRUS, 1952–54, vol. 13: 1181; Gibbons, *The U.S. Government and Vietnam*, 180.

51 For the full text of Dulles's speech, see *Department of State Bulletin*, 12 April 1954, 539–42.

52 Divine, *Eisenhower and the Cold War*, 43.

53 *Public Papers of the Presidents 1954*, 366.

54 D. Eisenhower, *Mandate for Change*, 340. Unpublished opinion polls commissioned by the State Department inquiring whether people would support multilateral intervention returned a 69 per cent ap-proval rating [Department of State, "Special Report on American

Opinion," 22 July 1954, box 42, file: Southeast Asia 1953–61, National Archives].

55 Immerman, "Between the Unattainable and the Unacceptable," 133; Herring and Immerman, "Eisenhower, Dulles and Dienbienphu," 350.

56 Fall, *Hell in a Very Small Place*, 191–213; D. Eisenhower, *Mandate for Change*, 345; Gibbons, *The U.S. Government and Vietnam*, 182.

57 Ridgway, *Soldier*, 275–7.

58 Immerman, "Between the Unattainable and the Unacceptable," 133; Burke *et al.*, *How Presidents Test Reality*, 48; Billings-Yun, *Decision Against War*, 70–3.

59 Memorandum of Discussion of the 191st Meeting of the NSC, 1 April 1954, FRUS, 1952–54, vol. 13: 1200–2.

60 According to the most popular account of that meeting, Eisenhower's decision to place the Dien Bien Phu question before the congressional leadership offers incontrovertible evidence that the JCS, apart from Radford, had won the president's support for the difficult decision of saying "no" [see especially Roberts, "The Day We Didn't Go to War"]. A more sophisticated interpretation suggests that "Eisenhower had merely found another way to delay and evade responsibility for the un-congenial decision of saying no ... He already had decided to let history take its course unaided at Dien Bien Phu. Rather than announcing that controversial decision, though, he would leave it to time – and Congress to settle" [Billings-Yun, *Decision Against War*, 82–3].

61 Telephone conversation with Admiral Radford, 1 April 1954, 3:01 p.m., John Foster Dulles's Papers, quoted in Burke *et al.*, *How Presidents Test Reality*, 49; Billings-Yun, *Decision Against War*, 82.

62 Hagerty Diary, 1 April 1954, James C. Hagerty Papers; FRUS, 1952–54, vol. 13: 1204 (including footnote.).

63 Draft Prepared in the Department of State, 2 April 1954, FRUS, 1952–54, vol. 13: 1211–12; Memorandum of a Conversation with the President, 2 April 1954, FRUS, 1952–54, 1210–11.

64 Billings-Yun, *Decision Against War*, 84.

65 Immerman, "Between the Unattainable and the Unacceptable," 134–5.

66 For an account of why other members of the JCS voted against the proposal, see FRUS, 1952–54, vol. 13: 1220–3; Gibbons, *The U.S. Government and Vietnam*, 186–7; Immerman, "Between the Unattainable and the Unacceptable," 133–4.

67 Memorandum of a Conversation with the President, 2 April 1954, FRUS, 1952–54: 1210–11.

68 Burke et al., *How Presidents Test Reality*, 54; Billings-Yun, *Decision Against War*, 85.

69 Memorandum for the File of the Secretary of State, 3 April 1954, FRUS, 1952–54, vol. 13: 1224–5.

70 Telephone conversation between the President and the Secretary of State, 3 April 1954, FRUS, 1952–54, vol. 13: 1230.

71 D. Eisenhower, *Mandate for Change*, 347.

72 See Anderson, *Trapped by Success*, 38.

73 Roberts interviewed the congressional leaders who attended the meeting and concluded that, if Eisenhower had asked forcefully for the power to intervene, Congress would have granted it [Roberts, "The Day We Didn't Go to War," 35].

74 Billings-Yun, *Decision Against War*, 93–5.

75 Hoopes, *The Devil and John Foster Dulles*, 211–12.

76 Gelb, with Betts, *The Irony of Vietnam*, 57.

77 Billings-Yun, *Decision Against War*, 76–8.

78 See Greenstein, *The Hidden-Hand Presidency*.

79 Congressional Research Service Interview with Thruston Morton, 29 January 1979, quoted in Gibbons, *The U.S. Government and Vietnam*, 195.

80 Adams, *First Hand Report*, 121–2.

81 Memorandum of Presidential Telephone Conversation, 5 April 1954, FRUS, 1952–54, vol. 13: 1241–2.

82 Khong concluded that "Eisenhower saw no need to demonstrate the credibility of American power or the credibility of America's commitment. The former hardly needed demonstration. The United States had just recently used its military might to stop communist aggression in South Korea and did so at severe costs to itself even though the Korean peninsula had earlier been written off as not central to the defense perimeter of the United States. Equally important, Eisenhower wanted to know if U.S. power could succeed in stopping the Vietminh before committing American prestige to Vietnam – the containment policy and the domino effect notwithstanding" ["Credibility and the Trauma of Vietnam," 232–3].

83 Billings-Yun, *Decision Against War*, 107, n.12, 171.

84 "Dulles Warns Red China Nears Open Aggression in Indo-China," *New York Times*, 6 April 1954.

85 *Pentagon Papers*, Gravel, ed., vol. 1: 462–71.

86 Ibid.

87 Saunders, "Military Force," 107.

88 D. Eisenhower, *Mandate for Change*, 373.

89 Gibbons, *The U.S. Government and Vietnam*, 203–7; FRUS, 1952–54, vol. 13: 1266; Gelb with Betts, *The Irony of Vietnam*, 58–9.

90 Press conference of 7 April 1954, *Public Papers of the Presidents 1954*, 383–7.

91 Billings-Yun, *Decision Against War*, 119–20; Immerman, "Between the Unattainable and the Unacceptable," 138; Bator, *Vietnam*, 55.

92 Bator, *Vietnam*, 48–9.

93 Lacouture and Devillers, *End of a War*, 84–5; Gurtov, *The First Vietnam Crisis*, 99–100; Buttinger, *Vietnam*, 367; Bator, *Vietnam*, 56; D. Eisenhower, *Mandate for Change*, 347.

94 Hoopes, *The Devil and John Foster Dulles*, 213.

95 Secretary of State to the Department of State, 13 April 1954, FRUS, 1952–54, vol. 13: 1321 (including n.3).

96 "Secretary of State to the President," 13 April 1954, FRUS, 1952–54, vol. 13, 1322–3; D. Eisenhower, *Mandate for Change*, 348–9.

97 D. Eisenhower, *Mandate for Change*, 348.

98 Pusey, *Eisenhower the President*, 155; Gurtov, *The First Vietnam Crisis*, 104–5; Gardner, 227–8.

99 D. Eisenhower, *Mandate for Change*, 353.

100 Gurtov, *The First Vietnam Crisis*, 106–7; Pusey, *Eisenhower the President*, 153.

101 Lacouture and Devillers, *End of a War*, 92.

102 Hagerty Diary, 16–19 April, 1954, James C. Hagerty Papers.

103 Adams, *First Hand Report*, 122.

104 D. Eisenhower, *Mandate for Change*, 353.

105 MacArthur, Memorandum of Conversation with Laniel *et al.*, 23 April 1954, FRUS, 1952–54, vol. 13: 1371–3.

106 Secretary of State to the Department of State, 23 April 1954, FRUS, 1952–54, vol. 13: 1374.

107 Ibid.; Gurtov, *The First Vietnam Crisis*, 105–6.

108 D. Eisenhower, *Mandate for Change*, 351.

109 Dulles to Bidault, April 24, 1954, FRUS, 1952–54, vol. 13: 1398–9.

110 Eden, *Full Circle*, 111–15; Memorandum of Conversation by Assistant Secretary of State for European Affairs Merchant, 26 April 1954, FRUS, 1952–54, vol. 13: 1386–91.

111 Burke *et al.*, *How Presidents Test Reality*, 80–1; Eden, *Full Circle*, 117–119; Lacouture and Devillers, *End of a War*, 95.

112 For the discussions that took place in the British cabinet, see Gilbert, *Winston S. Churchill*, vol. 7: 973.

113 Memorandum of Conversation by the Special Adviser to the U.S. Delegation, Merchant, 27 April 1954, FRUS, 1952–54, vol. 16: 578.

114 The Secretary of State to the Acting Secretary of State, FRUS, 1952–54, vol. 13, 25 April 1954, 1404–5; Herring and Immerman, "Eisenhower, Dulles, and Dien Bien Phu," 359–60.

115 Gurtov, *The First Vietnam Crisis*, 112–13; J. Arnold, *The First Domino*, 167–8.

116 Billings-Yun, *Decision Against War*, 143–5; Burke *et al.*, *How Presidents Test Reality*, 81.

117 FRUS, 1952–54, vol. 13: 1383.

118 C. Alexander, *Holding the Line*, 79; Immerman, "Between the Unattainable and the Unacceptable," 144.

119 Eisenhower to Gruenther, 26 April 1954, FRUS, 1952–54, vol. 13: 1419–21; D. Eisenhower, *Mandate for Change*, 352–3.

120 Ibid.

121 Eisenhower to Hazlett, 27 April 1954, FRUS, vol. 13: 1427–8.

122 Gardner Lloyd, *Approaching Vietnam*, 247.

123 Adams, *First Hand Report*, 104.

124 Memorandum by the Assistant Staff Secretary (Minnich) to the President (undated) FRUS, 1952–54, vol. 13: 1413.

125 Hagerty Diary, 26 April 1954; James C. Hagerty Papers; FRUS, 1952–54, vol. 13, 1410–12; Memorandum by Assistant Staff Secretary (Minnich) to the President (undated), FRUS, 1952–54, vol. 13: 1413.

126 *Public Papers of the Presidents 1954*, 428.

127 Ibid., 427–8, 436; D. Eisenhower, *Mandate for Change*, 353.

128 Australia at the time was in the midst of a closely contested election and its leaders were reluctant to take any firm public stands before the election had been concluded at the end of May. New Zealand was hesitant to go ahead without Britain [Eisenhower, *Mandate for Change*, 353–4].

129 Memorandum of discussion at the 194th Meeting of the National Security Council, 29 April 1954, FRUS, vol. 13: 1431–45.

130 R. Nixon, *RN: Memoirs*, 154.

131 Billings-Yun, *Decision Against War*, 153.

132 Ibid., 153, n.9, 178.

133 For details of Dulles's meeting with Eden, see Memorandum of Conversation with Mr. Eden, FRUS, 1952–54, vol. 16: 622–5.

134 Memorandum of Conference at the White House, 5 May 1954, FRUS, 1952–54, vol. 13: 1466–70.

135 Ibid.

136 Record of the Secretary of State's Briefing for Members of Congress, FRUS, 1952–54, vol. 13: 1471–7.

137 *Public Papers of the Presidents 1954*, 450–9; FRUS, 1952–54, vol. 13: 1470.

138 Memorandum of the Discussion at the 195th Meeting of the NSC, 6 May 1954, FRUS, 1952–54, vol. 13: 1488.

139 D. Eisenhower, *Mandate for Change*, 357.

140 FRUS, 1952–54, vol. 13: 1509. This position had originated from a JCS proposal that read: "The United States will not associate itself with any French proposal directed toward cease-fire in advance of a satisfactory political settlement." Eisenhower initially agreed with the wording but wanted to add the phrase "because of the proof given in Korea that the communists will not be bound militarily by the terms of an armistice" [Radford, *From Pearl Harbor to Vietnam*, 413–14].

141 The Ambassador in France [Dillon] to the Secretary of State, 10 May 1954, FRUS, 1952–54, vol. 13: 1526–7; Dulles telephone conversation with Radford, 10 May 1954, FRUS, 1952–54, vol. 13: 1562.

142 FRUS, 1952–54, vol. 13: 1534–5.

143 Hoopes, *The Devil and John Foster Dulles*, 229.

144 Eisenhower later wrote in his memoirs that these were "the preconditions under which I *might* ask Congress for authority to use armed forces of the United States" (italics in original). He added that, at that point, he was still concerned about the possibility of communist China intervening in response to American intervention and the strain on the United States's relationship with Britain [D. Eisenhower, *Mandate for Change*, 159]. This suggests that, even if the preconditions had been met, Eisenhower would still have retained serious reservations about intervening militarily.

145 The Ambassador in France [Dillon] to the Secretary of State, 14 May 1954, FRUS, 1952–54, vol. 13: 1567.

146 D. Eisenhower, *Mandate for Change*, 373–4.

147 Eisenhower was consistent with his earlier decisions when faced with the threat of Chinese intervention. The JCS, led by Radford, urged the use of atomic weapons directly against China should it intervene [*Pentagon Papers*, Gravel, ed., vol. 1, 511–12; FRUS, 1952–54, vol. 13: 1590–2]. On 1 June, Robert Cutler, special assistant to the president for national security affairs, reported that the president "said the United States would not intervene in China on any basis except united action. He would not be responsible for going into China alone unless a joint Congressional resolution ordered him to do so ... Unilateral action by the United States in cases of this kind would destroy us" [Memorandum of Conversation between the President and Robert Cutler, FRUS, 1952–54, vol. 13: 1648; Pentagon Papers, Gravel, ed.,

vol. 1: 129 (including footnote)]. This position was formulated into official policy the next day, at a meeting in the Oval Office, [FRUS, 1952–54, vol. 13: 1658] and approved by the NSC on 3 June [D. Eisenhower, *Mandate for Change*, 361–2]. Once again, Eisenhower displayed his proclivity for examining the risks involved in an aggressive course of action, rather than being driven to respond viscerally by emotionally motivated needs.

148 FRUS, 1952–54, vol. 13: 1670; *Public Papers of the Presidents 1954*, 545–54; cable from Dulles to U.S. delegation at Geneva, 9 June, FRUS, 1952–54, vol. 16: 1100.

149 On 10 June, Eisenhower had told Smith that, "if France should insist on continuing negotiations in spite of their obvious futility, our best move would be to reduce our delegation in stature rather than completely withdraw it" [D. Eisenhower, *Mandate for Change*, 365].

150 Memorandum by the Special Assistant to the President for National Security Affairs Robert Cutler, 23 June 1954, FRUS, 1952–54, vol. 13: 1730–3; D. Eisenhower, *Mandate for Change*, 366; Eisenhower's comments appeared in Bryce Harlow, Memorandum for the Record, 23 June 1954.

151 *Washington Post*, 5 July 1954.

152 Hagerty Diary, 8, 9 July 1954, James C. Hagerty Papers; FRUS, 1952–54, vol. 13: 1797–8.

153 Gibbons, *The U.S. Government and the Vietnam War*, 257; Billings-Yun, *Decision Against War*, 157–8.

154 The president's news conference of 21 July 1954, *Public Papers of the Presidents 1954*, 168.

155 D. Eisenhower, *Mandate for Change*, 374–5.

156 Adams, *First Hand Report*, 106.

157 Khong, *Analogies At War*, 113.

158 Gibbons, *The U.S. Government and the Vietnam War*, 271–81; D. Eisenhower, *Mandate for Change*, 374.

159 Saunders, "Military Force," 114.

160 Gibbons, *The U.S. Government and the Vietnam War*, 259–64; Billings-Yun, *Decision Against War*, 158–9; Immerman, "Between the Unattainable and the Unacceptable," 145.

161 See, for example, Rostow, *The United States in the World Arena*, 392–5; Buttinger, *Vietnam*, 365.

162 When he made this particular statement, Eisenhower was discussing the possible inclusion of the Associated States in the proposed Southeast Asia defense coalition [*Public Papers of the Presidents 1954*, 107]. In his memoirs, Nixon claimed that Eisenhower had said privately

that he and Dulles agreed "all the way" on the question sending troops to Vietnam [*RN: Memoirs,* 155].

163 Adams, *First Hand Report,* 80–1.

164 See for example, Greenstein, *The Hidden-Hand Presidency,* 57; Billings-Yun, *Decision Against War,* 18–20; Immerman, "Between the Unattainable and the Unacceptable," 120–1; Brinkley, "Do We Like Ike?" 110–19.

165 See Immerman, "Eisenhower and Dulles," 21–38.

166 Greenstein, *The Hidden-Hand Presidency,* 87.

167 Burke *et al., How Presidents Test Reality,* 11.

168 This is a core argument that Greenstein makes in *The Hidden-Hand Presidency.*

169 Winthrop Aldrich interview, Columbia Oral History Project.

CONCLUSION

1 For a discussion of the effects of the political environment on the Eisenhower and Johnson presidencies, see Burke *et al., How Presidents Test Reality,* 268–73.

2 For a more detailed analysis of the comparisons between the Eisenhower and Johnson advisory systems, see ibid., 256–8.

3 The decisions to initiate the bombing and invasion of Cambodia were Nixon's; Kissinger supported both, but less from a sense of real enthusiasm than as a way to consolidate his political and personal relationship with the president. See Szulc, *The Illusion of Power,* 283; R. Nixon, *RN: Memoirs,* 380–5, 445–54; Kissinger, *White House Years,* 239–54, 483–529.

4 In 1965 Eisenhower would recommend escalating the war, but his advice reflected the logic of the "never again" school of strategic thinking (see Gacek, *The Logic of Force*). It had nothing to do with narcissistic concerns involving either the avoidance of shame and humiliation or the need to restore self-esteem through aggressive behaviour.

5 Volkan and Itzkowitz note that narcissistic leaders may be "destructive" or "reparative" and may alternate roles depending on the circumstances. The reparative leader wants adoration from his "valued" followers and may attempt to uplift them in order to be build an impressively high level of support. For an analysis of the "reparative" aspects of narcissism as exemplified in the leadership role of Kemal Ataturk, see Volkan and Itzkowitz, *The Immortal Ataturk,* especially 355–9.

6 As Berkowitz notes: "A frustrating event increases the probability that the thwarted organism will act aggressively soon afterward" ["The Frustration-Aggression Hypothesis Revisited," 2].

7 The fourth son, Edward, was born in 1926 when Richard was thirteen.

8 Mazo, *Richard Nixon*, 5.

9 A seventh son, Paul, the fifth to be born, died in infancy.

10 Kornitzer, *The Great American Heritage*, 255.

11 Mazlish, *In Search of Nixon*, 118.

12 In his memoirs, Johnson implied that his health was also an issue. He wrote that he found the work of the presidency "demanding and unrelenting" and felt that his constitution could not survive another four years of "long hours and unremitting tensions" [*The Vantage Point*, 425–6].

13 Clifford with Holbrooke, *Counsel to the President*, 497–8.

14 See L. Johnson, *The Vantage Point*, 426; Clifford with Holbrooke, *Counsel to the President*, 495; Kearns, *Lyndon Johnson and the American Dream*, 347.

15 L. Johnson, *The Vantage Point*, 426.

16 See Berman, *Lyndon Johnson's War*, 187.

17 Ibid., 188.

18 For an understanding of the process of "effort justification," see Milburn and Christie, "Effort Justification," 236–51.

19 Herring, *America's Longest War*, 181.

20 Clifford with Holbrooke, *Counsel to the President*, 506.

21 See Hoopes, *The Limits of Intervention*, 202–24; Berman, *Lyndon Johnson's War*, 176–203; Clifford with Holbrooke, *Counsel to the President*, 501–26.

22 The majority consisted of Dean Acheson, George Ball, Arthur Dean, Cy Vance, Douglas Dillon, and McGeorge Bundy; opposing the recommendations were generals Omar Bradley and Maxwell Taylor, Robert Murphy, and Justice Abe Fortas. For an account of that meeting, see Clifford with Holbrooke, *Counsel to the President*, 511–19.

23 Clifford with Holbrooke, *Counsel to the President*, 518.

24 Herring, *LBJ and Vietnam*, 163.

25 Clifford with Holbrooke, *Counsel to the President*, 519–21.

26 For the text of the president's address on the Vietnam War, see *New York Times*, 1 April 1968.

27 Herring, "The Reluctant Warrior," 102–3.

28 LBJ interview with Doris Kearns, in *Lyndon Johnson and the American Dream*, 343.

29 I am indebted to Doris Kearns, *Lyndon Johnson and the American Dream*, 342–5, for this insightful analysis.

30 For analyses exploring the peace negotiations, see Ambrose, *Nixon*, vols. 1 and 2; Duiker, *The Communist Road to Power in Vietnam*; Goodman, *The Lost Peace*; Hersh, *The Price of Power*; Isaacson, *Kissinger*; Kissinger, *White House Years*; R. Nixon, *RN: Memoirs*; Porter, *A Peace Denied*; Tang with Chanoff and Toai, *A Viet Cong Memoir*; Turley, *The Second Indochina War*; Szulc, *The Illusion of Peace*.

31 Kissinger, *White House Years*, 1,417.

32 Although Kissinger had taken the lead in urging renewed bombing, he favoured using the smaller and more precise fighter-bombers such as the F-111 or the F-4 for targets in civilian areas. Nixon, urged on by Alexander Haig, the president's chief of staff, opted for an all-out attack [Isaacson, *Kissinger*, 461–74].

33 Kimball, "Peace with Honor," 174–5.

34 Cited in Ambrose, *Nixon*, vol. 3: 41.

35 Kissinger, *White House Years*, 1,459–60; R. Nixon, *RN: Memoirs*, 737.

36 R. Nixon, *RN: Memoirs*, 757.

37 Ambrose, *Nixon*, vol. 3: 53–4.

38 For the comparison between the Korean and Vietnam agreements, see Ambrose, *Nixon*, vol. 3: 54.

39 See Safire, *Before the Fall*, 14, 26; Kimball, "Peace with Honor," 176–7.

Bibliography

Abraham, Karl. "Restrictions and Transformation of Scoptophilia in Psycho-neurotics with Remarks on Analogous Phenomena in Folk-psychology," in *Selected Papers on Psychoanalysis*. New York: Basic Books 1953: 169–234.

Abrahamsen, David. *Nixon vs. Nixon – A Psychological Inquest*. New York: Farrar, Straus, and Giroux 1976.

Adams, Sherman. *First Hand Report: The Story of the Eisenhower Administration*. New York: Harper 1961.

Aitken, Jonathan. *Nixon: A Life*. London: Weidenfeld and Nicolson 1993.

Aldrich, Winthrop. Columbia Oral History Project. New York: Columbia University.

Alexander, Charles C. *Holding the Line: The Eisenhower Era, 1952–1961*. Bloomington: Indiana University Press 1975.

Alexander, Franz. "Remarks about the Relation of Inferiority Feelings to Guilt Feelings." *International Journal of Psychoanalysis* 19 (1938): 41–9.

Alford, C. Fred. "Mastery and Retreat: Psychological Sources of the Appeal of Ronald Reagan." *Political Psychology* 9 (1988), no. 4: 571–89.

– *Narcissism: Socrates, the Frankfurt School, and Psychoanalytic Theory*. New Haven: Yale University Press 1988.

Alsop, Stewart. *Nixon and Rockefeller: A Double Portrait*. Garden City, New York: Doubleday 1960.

Ambrose, Stephen E. *The Supreme Commander: The War Years of General Dwight D. Eisenhower*. Garden City, New York: Doubleday 1970.

– *Eisenhower: Soldier, General of the Army, President-Elect, 1890–1952*. New York: Simon and Schuster 1983.

– *Eisenhower: The President.* New York: Simon and Schuster 1984.

– *Nixon: The Education of a Politician 1913–1962.* New York: Simon and Schuster 1987.

– *Nixon: The Triumph of a Politician 1962–1972.* New York: Simon and Schuster 1989.

– *Nixon: Ruin and Recovery 1973–1990.* New York: Simon and Schuster 1991.

American Psychiatric Association. *Diagnostic and Statistical Manual of Mental Disorders.* 3rd. ed., revised. Washington, D.C.: American Psychiatric Association 1980.

Anderson, David L. *Trapped by Success: The Eisenhower Administration and Vietnam, 1953–1961.* New York: Columbia University Press 1991.

– ed. *Shadow on the White House: Presidents and the Vietnam War 1945–1975.* Lawrence, Kansas: University of Kansas 1993.

Arnold, James R. *The First Domino: Eisenhower, the Military and America's Intervention in Vietnam.* New York: William Morrow 1991.

Arnold, William A. *Back When It All Began: The Early Nixon Years.* New York: Vantage Press 1975.

Ball, George. Oral History. Lyndon B. Johnson Library, Austin, Texas.

– *The Past Has Another Pattern.* New York: W.W. Norton 1982.

Barber, James David. *The Presidential Character: Predicting Performance in the White House.* 2nd ed. Englewood Cliffs, N.J.: Prentice-Hall 1977.

Barnet, Richard. "The Game of Nations." *Harper's,* November 1971.

Barrett, David M. "The Mythology Surrounding Lyndon Johnson, His Advisers, and the 1965 Decision to Escalate the Vietnam War." *Political Science Quarterly* 103 (1988): 637–63.

– *Uncertain Warriors: Lyndon Johnson and His Vietnam Advisers.* Lawrence, Kansas: University of Kansas Press 1993.

Barron, John. "Special Report – The Johnson Money – Presidential Family Holdings Estimated at $9 Million." *Washington Evening Star,* 9 June 1964.

Bator, Victor M. *Vietnam: A Diplomatic Tragedy.* Dobbs Ferry, N.Y.: Oceana Publications 1965.

Baudry, Francis. "Character, Character Type, and Character Organization." *American Journal of Psychoanalysis* 37 (1989): 655–86.

Beeson, Sheldon. *Richard M. Nixon Project: Oral History Program.* Interview no. 809. Fullerton, Calif.: California State University 1970.

Berkowitz L. "The Frustration-Aggression Hypothesis Revisited," in *The Roots of Aggression: A Re-Examination of the Frustration-Aggression Hypothesis.* New York: Atherton 1969.

Berman, Larry. *Planning a Tragedy: The Americanization of the War in Vietnam.* New York: W.W. Norton 1982.

– *Lyndon Johnson's War: The Road to Stalemate in Vietnam.* New York: W.W. Norton 1989.

Billings-Yun, Melanie. *Decision Against War: Eisenhower and Dien Bien Phu, 1954.* New York: Columbia University Press 1988.

Birdwell, Sherman. Oral History II. Lyndon B. Johnson Library, Austin, Texas.

Blos, Peter. "Modifications in the Classical Psychoanalytic Model of Adolescence," in *The Adolescent Passage: Developmental Issues.* New York: International Universities Press 1979: 473–97.

– *Father and Son.* New York: The Free Press 1985.

Bradley, Omar N. *A Soldier's Story.* New York: Henry Holt 1951.

Brandon, Dorothy. *Mamie Doud Eisenhower: A Portrait of a First Lady.* New York: Charles Scribner's 1954.

Brinkley, Allan. "Do We Like Ike?" *The Wilson Quarterly,* spring 1990: 110–19.

Brodie, Fawn M. *Fawn Brodie Collection.* Salt Lake City, Utah: University of Utah, Marriott Library, Special Collections.

– *Richard Nixon: The Shaping of His Character.* Cambridge, Mass.: Harvard University Press 1983.

Brown, Bert. "The Effects of Need to Maintain Face on Interpersonal Bargaining." *Journal of Experimental Psychology* 4 (1968): 107–22.

Bundy, McGeorge. Papers of McGeorge Bundy. Lyndon B. Johnson Library, Austin, Texas.

– File of McGeorge Bundy. Miscellaneous Meetings. Lyndon B. Johnson Library, Austin, Texas.

– "Holding on in South Vietnam." National Security Council History – Troop Deployment, 30 June 1965. *The Defense Department History of United States Decision-Making on Vietnam.* Senator Gravel ed., 4 (1971–72): 610.

Bundy, William. Oral History. Lyndon B. Johnson Library, Austin, Texas.

Burke, John P., and Fred I. Greenstein (with the collaboration of Larry Berman and Richard Immerman). *How Presidents Test Reality: Decisions on Vietnam, 1954 and 1965.* New York: Russell Sage Foundation 1989.

Bursten, R. "Some Narcissistic Personality Types." *International Journal of Psychoanalysis* 54 (1973): 294.

Buttinger, Joseph. *Vietnam: A Political History.* New York: Praeger 1968.

Caro, Robert. *The Years of Lyndon Johnson: The Path to Power.* New York: Random House 1982.

– *The Years of Lyndon Johnson: The Means of Ascent.* New York: Alfred A. Knopf 1990.

Clifford, Clark with Richard Holbrooke. *Counsel to the President.* New York: Random House 1991.

Conkin, Paul. *Big Daddy from the Pedernales: Lyndon B. Johnson.* Boston: Twayne Publishers 1986.

Cook, Blanche Wiesen. *The Declassified Eisenhower: A Divided Legacy.* Garden City, New York: Doubleday 1981.

Cooper, Chester L. "Meetings on Vietnam, July 21, 1965," Memorandum for the Record, Meeting Notes File, Lyndon B. Johnson Library, Austin, Texas.

– Oral History Interviews, 1969. Lyndon B. Johnson Library, Austin, Texas.

– *The Lost Crusade: America in Vietnam.* New York: Dodd, Mead 1970.

Costello, William. *The Facts about Nixon: An Unauthorized Biography.* New York: Viking Press 1960.

Dallek, Robert. *Lone Star Rising: Lyndon Johnson and His Times, 1908–1960.* New York: Oxford University Press 1991.

David, Lester. *The Lonely Lady of San Clemente, The Story of Pat Nixon.* New York: Thomas Y. Crowell 1978.

Davis, Kenneth S. *Soldier of Democracy.* Garden City, New York: Doubleday 1945.

Department of State Bulletin, 1954–1975.

De Toledano, Ralph. *One Man Alone: Richard Nixon.* New York: Funk and Wagnalls 1969.

DiLeo, David L. *George Ball, Vietnam, and the Rethinking of Containment.* Chapel Hill, N.C.: The University of North Carolina Press 1991.

Divine, Robert A. *Eisenhower and the Cold War.* New York: Oxford University Press 1981.

Dugger, Ronnie. *Politician: The Drive for Power from the Frontier to Master of the Senate.* New York: W.W. Norton 1982.

Duiker, William J. *The Communist Road to Power in Vietnam.* Boulder, Colo.: Westview Press 1981.

Eden, Anthony. *Full Circle: The Memoirs of Anthony Eden.* Boston: Houghton Mifflin 1960.

Ehrlichman, John. *Witness to Power: The Nixon Years.* New York: Simon and Schuster 1982.

Eisele, Albert. *Almost to the Presidency.* Blue Earth, Minn.: Piper Company 1972.

Eisenhower, Dwight D. *Crusade in Europe.* Garden City, New York: Doubleday 1948.

– *Mandate for Change.* Garden City, New York: Doubleday 1963.

– *At Ease: Stories I Tell to Friends.* Garden City, New York: Doubleday 1967.

– Columbia Oral History Project. New York: Columbia University.

– Post-Presidential Papers, Dwight D. Eisenhower Library, Abilene, Kansas.

Eisenhower, John S.D. *Strictly Personal*. Garden City, New York: Doubleday 1974.

– ed. *Letters to Mamie*. Garden City, New York: Doubleday 1978.

Eisenhower, Julie N. *Pat Nixon: The Untold Story*. New York: Simon and Schuster 1986.

Eisenhower, Milton. *The President Is Calling*. Garden City, New York: Doubleday 1974.

– "Portrait of a Brother," in Kenneth W. Thompson, ed., *The Eisenhower Presidency: Eleven Intimate Perspectives of Dwight D. Eisenhower*. Lanham, Md.: University Press of America 1984: 3–14.

Ellsberg, Daniel. "The Quagmire Myth and the Stalemate Machine." *Public Policy* 19 (1971): 217–74.

Ely, Paul. *L'Indochine Dans La Tourmente*. Paris: Plon 1964.

Erikson, Erik. *Childhood and Society*. New York: W.W. Norton 1963.

Evans, Rowland, and Robert D. Novak. *Lyndon B. Johnson: The Exercise of Power*. New York: New American Library 1966.

– *Nixon in the White House*. New York: Random House 1971.

Fairbairn, W.R.D. *An Object Relations Theory of the Personality*. New York: Basic Books 1982.

Fall, Bernard B. *Hell in a Very Small Place: The Siege of Dien Bien Phu*. Philadelphia: J.B. Lippincott 1966.

Fenichel, Otto. *The Psychoanalytic Theory of Neurosis*. New York: W.W. Norton 1972.

Ferrell, Robert H., ed. *The Eisenhower Diaries*. New York: W.W. Norton 1981.

Finch, Robert. "The Cabinet and the Nixon Presidency," in Kenneth W. Thompson, ed., *Portraits of American Presidents*. Vol. 6: *The Nixon Presidency*. Lanham, Md.: University Press of America 1987: 243–71.

Foreign Relations of the United States, 1952–54. *The Geneva Conference*. Vol. 16. Washington D.C.: United States Government Printing Office 1981.

– *Indochina*. Vol. 13. Washington D.C.: United States Government Printing Office 1982.

Freud, A. "Comments on Aggression." *International Journal of Psychoanalysis* 8 (1953): 167.

– *The Ego and the Mechanisms of Defense*, revised ed. New York: International Universities Press 1966.

Freud, S. *Further Remarks on the Neuropsychoses of Defense*, Standard Edition (SE), 3. London: Hogarth Press 1962.

– (1905). *Three Essays on the Theory of Sexuality*, SE, 7. London: Hogarth Press 1953.

– (1914). *On Narcissism*, SE, 14. London: Hogarth Press 1957.

- (1920). *Beyond the Pleasure Principle*, SE, 18. London: Hogarth Press 1955.
- (1926). *Inhibitions, Symptoms and Anxiety*, SE, 20. London: Hogarth Press 1959.
- (1932 [1933]). *New Introductory Lectures on Psychoanalysis*, S.E, 22. London: Hogarth Press 1964.

Gacek, Christopher. *The Logic of Force: The Dilemma of Limited War in American Foreign Policy*. New York: Columbia University Press 1994.

Gardner, Lloyd C. *Approaching Vietnam*. New York: W.W. Norton 1988.

Glad, Betty and Charles S. Taber. "Images, Learning and the Decision to Use Force: The Domino Theory and the United States," in Betty Glad., ed., *Psychological Dimensions of War*. Newbury Park, Calif.: Sage Publications 1990: 56–82.

Gelb, Leslie H. with Richard K. Betts. *The Irony of Vietnam: The System Worked*. Washington, D.C.: Brookings Institution 1979.

Gibbons, William Conrad. *The U.S. Government and the Vietnam War. Executive and Legislative Roles and Relationships*. Parts 1, 2, and 3. Originally prepared for the committee on foreign relations of the United States Senate. Princeton, N.J.: Princeton University Press 1986 and 1989.

Gilbert, Martin. *Winston S. Churchill*. Vol. 7, *Never Despair, 1945–1965*. Boston: Houghton Mifflin 1988.

Goldwater, Barry. *With No Apologies*. New York: William Morrow 1979.

Goodman, Allan E. *The Lost Peace: American's Search for a Negotiated Settlement of the Vietnam War*. Stanford, Calif.: Hoover Institution Press 1978.

Goodwin, Doris Kearns. *The Fitzgeralds and the Kennedys: An American Saga*. New York: Simon and Schuster 1987.

Goulden, Joseph C. *Truth is the First Casualty: The Gulf of Tonkin Affair – Illusion and Reality*. New York: Rand McNally 1969.

Greenstein, Fred I. *The Hidden-Hand Presidency: Eisenhower as Leader*. New York: Basic Books 1982.

Griffith, Robert. "Dwight D. Eisenhower and the Corporate Commonwealth." *American Historical Review* 87 (1982): 87–122.

Grunberger, Bela. *Narcissism: Psychoanalytic Essays*. New York: International Universities Press 1979.

Guntrip, Harry. *Schizoid Phenomena, Object Relations and the Self*. New York: International Universities Press 1969.

Gurtov, Melvin. *The First Vietnam Crisis*. New York: Columbia University Press 1967.

Guthman, Edwin O., and Jeffrey Shulman, eds. *Robert Kennedy: In His Own Words*. New York: Bantam Books 1988.

Hagerty, James C. James C. Hagerty Papers. Dwight D. Eisenhower Library, Abilene, Texas.

Halberstam, David. *The Best and the Brightest.* New York: Random House
  1972.
– *The Powers That Be.* New York: Alfred A. Knopf 1979.
Haldeman, H.R. with Joseph DiMona. *The Ends of Power.* New York: New
  York Times Books 1978.
Haldeman, H.R. *The Haldeman Diaries: Inside the Nixon White House.* New
  York: G.P. Putnam's Sons 1994.
Hammer, Ellen. *The Struggle for Indochina: 1940–1954.* Stanford, Calif.:
  Stanford University Press 1966.
Harlow, Bryce. Memorandum for the Record, 23 June 1954, Legislative
  Meetings Series, Dwight D. Eisenhower Library, Abilene, Kansas.
– "The Man and the Political Leader," in Kenneth W. Thompson, ed.,
  Portraits of American Presidents. Vol. 7: *The Nixon Presidency.* Lanham, Md.:
  University Press of America 1987: 3–27.
Harris, T. George. "A Policy-Maker's View: Experience vs. Character." *Psy-
  chology Today*, March 1975.
Hartmann, H., E. Kris, and R.M. Loewenstein, "Notes on the Theory of
  Aggression." *Psychoanalytic Study of the Child* 374 (1949): 9–36.
Heimann P. and A.F. Valenstein, "The Psychoanalytic Concept of Aggres-
  sion: An Integrated Summary." *International Journal of Psychoanalysis* 53:
  31–5.
Hendrick, J. "Instinct and the Ego During Infancy." *Psychoanalytic Quarterly*
  11 (1942): 33–58.
– "Work and the Pleasure Principle." *Psychoanalytic Quarterly* 12 (1942):
  311–29.
Herring, George C. *America's Longest War: The United States and Vietnam
  1950–1975.* 2nd. ed. New York: Alfred A. Knopf 1985.
– "The Reluctant Warrior: Lyndon Johnson as Commander in Chief," in
  David L. Anderson, ed., *Shadow on the White House: Presidents and the
  Vietnam War 1945–1975.* Lawrence, Kansas: University of Kansas Press
  1993: 87–112.
– *LBJ and Vietnam: A Different Kind of War.* Austin, Texas: University of
  Texas 1994.
– and Richard Immerman. "Eisenhower, Dulles, and Dien Bien Phu: 'The
  Day We Didn't Go to War' Revisited." *Journal of American History* 71
  (1984): 343–63.
Hersh, Seymour, M. *The Price of Power: Kissinger in the Nixon White House.*
  New York: Summit Books 1983.
Hoopes, Townsend. *The Limits of Intervention: An Inside Account of How the
  Johnson Policy of Escalation Was Reversed.* New York: McKay 1969.
– *The Devil and John Foster Dulles.* Boston: Little, Brown 1973.

Hughes, Emmet, John. *The Ordeal of Power: A Political Memoir of the Eisenhower Years.* New York: Atheneum 1963.

Humphrey, Hubert. *The Education of a Public Man.* Garden City, New York: Doubleday 1976.

Immerman, Richard H. "Eisenhower and Dulles: Who Made the Decisions?" *Political Psychology* 1 (1979): 2, 21–38.

– "Between the Unattainable and the Unacceptable," in Richard A. Melanson and David Mayers, eds., *Reevaluating Eisenhower: American Foreign Policy in the 1950's.* Urbana and Chicago: University of Illinois Press 1987: 120–54.

International Series – Vietnam. Russell Memorial Library, University of Georgia, Athens, Georgia.

Isaacson, Walter. *Kissinger.* New York: Simon and Schuster 1992.

Jacobson, E. *The Self and the Object World.* New York: International University Press 1964.

Janis, Irving, L. "Escalation of the Vietnam War: How Could It Happen?" In *Groupthink: Psychological Studies of of Policy Decisions and Fiascoes.* 2nd. ed. Boston: Houghton Mifflin 1982: 97–130.

– *Groupthink: Psychological Studies of Policy Decisions and Fiascoes.* 2nd ed. Boston: Houghton Mifflin 1982.

Johnson, Lyndon B. Address to Johns Hopkins University, Baltimore, Md., 7 April 1965, *Public Papers of the Presidents: Lyndon B. Johnson, 1965,* 394–5.

– Letter to Mike Mansfield, 28 July 1965, International Series – Vietnam, Subject file 23–31 July 1965, Russell Memorial Library, University of Georgia, Athens, Georgia.

– *The Vantage Point: Perspectives on the Presidency 1963–1969.* New York: Holt, Reinhart and Winston 1971.

– Oral History. Lyndon B. Johnson Library, Austin, Texas.

Johnson, Rebekah Baines. *A Family Album.* New York: McGraw Hill 1965.

Johnson, Sam Houston. *My Brother Lyndon.* New York: Cowles Book 1969.

Jones, Ernest. *The Life and Works of Sigmund Freud* (edited and abridged by Lionel Trilling and Steven Marcus). London: Hogarth Press 1961.

Joseph, E.D. "Aggression Re-defined – Its Adaptational Aspects." *Psychoanalytical Quarterly* 42 (1973): 197–213.

Kahin, George McTurnan. *Intervention: How America Became Involved in Vietnam.* New York: Alfred A. Knopf 1986.

Kalb, Marvin L. and Elie Abel. *The Roots of Involvement: The U.S. in Asia, 1784–1971.* New York: W.W. Norton 1971.

Karnow, Stanley. *Vietnam: A History.* New York: Viking Press 1984.

Kaufman, G. *Shame: The Power of Caring.* 2nd revised ed. Cambridge, Mass.: Schenkman Publishing 1985.

Kearns, Doris. *Lyndon Johnson and the American Dream.* New York: Harper and Row 1976.

Kernberg, Otto. *Borderline Conditions and Pathological Narcissism.* New York: Jason Aronson 1975.

– *Severe Personality Disorders.* New Haven: Yale University Press 1984.

– *Aggression in Personality Disorders and Perversions.* New Haven: Yale University Press 1994.

Khong, Yuen Foong. "Credibility and the Trauma of Vietnam," in L. Carl Brown, ed., *Centerstage.* New York: Holmes and Meier 1990: 232–54.

– "Korea and the Vietnam Decisions of 1965," in George W. Breslauer and Philip E. Tetlock, eds., *Learning in U. S. and Soviet Foreign Policy.* Boulder, Colo.: Westview Press, 1991: 302–49.

– *Analogies at War: Korea, Munich, Dien Bien Phu and the Vietnam Decisions of 1965.* Princeton: Princeton University Press 1992.

Kimball, Jeffrey P. "Peace with Honor": Richard Nixon and the Diplomacy of Threat and Symbolism," in David L. Anderson, ed., *Shadow on the White House: Presidents and the Vietnam War 1945–1975.* Lawrence, Kansas: University of Kansas Press 1993: 152–183.

Kissinger, Henry. *White House Years.* Boston: Little, Brown 1979.

Klare, Michael, T. *War Without End: American Planning for the Next Vietnams.* New York: Alfred A. Knopf 1972.

Klein, Melanie. "Envy and Gratitude" (1957). In *Envy and Gratitude and Other Works 1946–1963.* London: Hogarth Press 1980: 176-235.

– "Notes on Some Schizoid Mechanisms" (1946). In *Envy and Gratitude and Other Works 1946–1963.* London: Hogarth Press 1980: 1–27.

– "On the Theory of Anxiety and Guilt" (1948). In *Envy and Gratitude and Other Works 1946–1963.* London: Hogarth Press 1980: 25–42.

Kohut, Heinz. "The Psychoanalytic Treatment of Narcissistic Personality Disorders." *Psychoanalytic Study of the Child* 23 (1968): 86–113.

– *The Analysis of the Self.* New York: International Universities Press 1971.

– "Thoughts on Narcissism and Narcissistic Rage." *Psychoanalytic Study of the Child* 27 (1972): 360–400.

– *The Restoration of the Self.* New York: International Universities Press 1977.

Kolko, Gabriel. *The Roots of American Foreign Policy: An Analysis of Power and Purpose.* Boston: Beacon Press 1969.

– *Anatomy of a War.* New York: Pantheon Press 1985.

Kornitzer, Bela. *The Great American Heritage: The Story of the Five Eisenhower Brothers.* New York: Farrar, Straus 1955.

– "My Son: Two Exclusive and Candid Interviews with Mothers of the Presidential Candidates." *Los Angeles Times,* 18 September 1960.

– *The Real Nixon: An Intimate Biography.* Chicago: Rand McNally 1960.

Kris, A.O. "Helping Patients by Analyzing Self-Criticism." *Journal of the American Psychoanalytic Association* 38 (1990): 605–20.

Lacouture, Jean and Philippe Devillers. *End of a War: Indochina 1954.* Trans. Alexander Lieven and Adam Roberts. New York: Praeger 1969. Trans. of *La Fin D'une Guerre-Indochine, 1954.* Paris: Seuil 1960.

Laplanche J. and J.B. Pontalis. *The Language of Psychoanalysis.* New York: W.W. Norton 1973.

Latimer, Gene. Oral History, 17 August 1971. Lyndon B. Johnson Library, Austin, Texas.

Lee, R. Alton. *Dwight D. Eisenhower: Soldier and Statesman.* Chicago: Nelson-Hall 1981.

Levin, S. "Some Metapsychological Considerations on the Differentiation between Shame and Guilt." *International Journal of Psychoanalysis* 48 (1967): 267–76.

– "The Psychology of Shame." *International Journal of Psychoanalysis* 52 (1971): 355–62.

Lewis, H.B. *Shame and Guilt in Neurosis.* New York: International Universities Press 1971.

Lichtenberg, Joseph. *Psychoanalysis and Infant Research.* Hillsdale, N.J.: Analytic Press 1983.

Lynd, H.M. *On Shame and the Search for Identity.* New York: Harcourt, Brace and World Publishing 1958.

Lyon, Peter. *Eisenhower: Portrait of the Hero.* Boston: Little, Brown 1974.

Macmillan, Harold. *The Blast of War 1939–1945.* New York: Harper and Row 1968.

Mansfield, Mike. Letter to the President, 27 July 1965, National Security File, Name File: Mansfield, box 6, Lyndon B. Johnson Library, Austin, Texas.

Mazlish, Bruce. *In Search of Richard Nixon: A Psychohistorical Inquiry.* New York: Basic Books 1972.

Mazo, Earl. *Richard Nixon: A Political and Personal Portrait.* New York: Harper and Brothers 1959.

– and Stephen Hess. *Nixon: A Political Portrait.* New York: Harper and Row 1968.

McCain Smith, Helen, as told to Elizabeth Pope Frank. "Ordeal! Pat Nixon's final days in the White House." *Good Housekeeping,* July 1976: 127–130.

McCann, Kevin. *Man from Abilene.* Garden City, New York: Doubleday 1952.

McNamara, Robert with Brian VanDeMark. *In Retrospect.* New York: Random House 1995.

Melanson, Richard A. "The Foundations of Eisenhower's Foreign Policy," in Richard A. Melanson and David Mayers, eds., *Reevaluating Eisenhower: American Foreign Policy in the 1950's.* Urbana and Chicago: University of Illinois Press 1987: 13–30.

Milburn, Thomas W. and Daniel J. Christie, "Effort Justification as a Motive for Continuing War: The Vietnam Case," in Betty Glad, ed., *Psychological Dimensions of War.* Newbury Park, Calif.: Sage Publications 1990: 236–51.

Miller, Francis Trevelyan. *Eisenhower: Man and Soldier.* Philadelphia: John C. Winston 1944.

Miller, Merle. *Plain Speaking: An Oral Biography of Harry S. Truman.* New York: Berkley 1973.

– *Lyndon: An Oral Biography.* New York: G.P. Putnam's Sons 1980.

Mitchell, S.A. *Relational Concepts in Psychoanalysis: An Integration.* Cambridge, Mass: Harvard University Press 1988.

– "Aggression and the Endangered Self." *The Psychoanalytic Quarterly* 62 (1993): 351–82.

– *Hope and Dread in Psychoanalysis.* New York: Basic Books 1993.

Mitscherlich, A. "Psychoanalysis and the Aggression of Large Groups." *International Journal of Psychoanalysis of Large Groups* 52 (1971): 161–7.

Montgomery, Bernard Law. *The Memoirs of Field Marshal the Viscount Montgomery of Alamein.* Cleveland: World Publishing 1958.

Morgan, Lael. "Whittier '34: Most Likely to Succeed." *Los Angeles Times,* 10 May 1970.

Morris, Roger. *Uncertain Greatness: Henry Kissinger and American Foreign Policy.* New York: Harper and Row 1977.

– *Richard Milhous Nixon: The Rise of an American Politician.* New York: Henry Holt 1990.

Morrison, A. "Working with Shame in Psychoanalytic Treatment." *Journal of the American Psychoanalytic Association* 32 (1984): 479–505.

Muslin, Hyman L. and Thomas H. Jobe. *Lyndon Johnson: The Tragic Self – A Psychohistorical Portrait.* New York: Plenum Press 1991.

Nathanson, D.L. *The Many Faces of Shame,* New York: Guilford 1987.

National Security Council History, Deployment of Forces. Lyndon B. Johnson Library, Austin, Texas.

National Security Council Meeting File, Deployment of Forces. Lyndon B. Johnson Library, Austin, Texas.

National Security File: Mansfield, box 6, 1965. Lyndon B. Johnson Library, Austin, Texas.

Neal, Steve. *The Eisenhowers.* Garden City, New York: Doubleday 1984.

Neustadt, Richard and Earnest May. *Thinking in Time: The Uses of History for Decision-Makers*. New York: Free Press 1986.

Newman, John. *JFK and Vietnam: Deception, Intrigue and the Struggle for Power*. New York: Warner Books 1992.

Nixon, Hannah, as told to Flora Rheta Schreiber. "Richard Nixon, a Mother's Story." *Good Housekeeping*, June 1960.

Nixon, Richard M. *Six Crises*. Garden City, New York: Doubleday 1962.

– *RN: The Memoirs of Richard Nixon*. New York: Grosset and Dunlap 1978.

– *In the Arena*. New York: Simon and Schuster 1990.

O'Donnell, Kenneth P. and David J. Powers. *Johnny We Hardly Knew Ye: Memories of John Fitzgerald Kennedy*. Boston: Little Brown 1970.

Parens, Henry. *The Development of Aggression in Early Childhood*. New York: Jason Aronson 1979.

Parmet, Herbert S. *Eisenhower and the American Crusades*. New York: Macmillan 1972.

Parsons, Lucille. *Richard M. Nixon Project: Oral History Program*. Interview no. 928. Fullerton, Calif.: California State University 1970.

The Pentagon Papers. The Defense Department History of United States Decision-Making on Vietnam. The Senator Gravel Edition. Vols. 1–4. Boston: Beacon Press 1971–72.

The Pentagon Papers. New York Times edition. New York: Bantam Books 1971.

Pickering, Cecil. *Richard M. Nixon Project: Oral History Program*. Interview no. 933. Fullerton, Calif.: California State University 1970.

Piers, G. and M.B. Singer. *Shame and Guilt*. New York: W.W. Norton 1953.

Porter, Gareth. *A Peace Denied: The United States, Vietnam, and the Paris Agreements*. Bloomington, Ind.: Indiana University Press 1975.

– ed. *Vietnam: A History in Documents*. New York: New American Library 1981.

Post, Jerrold M. "Current Concepts of the Narcissistic Personality: Implications for Political Psychology." *Political Psychology* 14, no. 1 (March 1993): 99–122.

Price, Raymond. *With Nixon*. New York: Viking Press 1977.

Public Broadcasting Service. "LBJ Goes to War: 1964–1965." PBS Documentary on Vietnam: A Television History. Part 4. Undated.

Pruitt, Dean. "Aggressive Behavior in Interpersonal and International Relations," in P. Stern, R. Axelrod, R. Jervis, and R. Radner, eds., *Perspectives on Deterrence*. New York: Oxford University Press 1989: 287–93.

Public Papers of the Presidents: Dwight D. Eisenhower 1954. Washington: Office of the Federal Register, National Archives and Records Service, General Services Administration 1954.

Public Papers of the Presidents: Lyndon B. Johnson 1964. Washington: Office of the Federal Register, National Archives and Records Service, General Services Administration 1964.

Public Papers of the Presidents: Lyndon B. Johnson 1965. Washington: Office of the Federal Register, National Archives and Records Service, General Services Administration 1965.

Public Papers of the Presidents: Richard N. Nixon 1969. Washington: Office of the Federal Register, National Archives and Records Service, General Services Administration 1969.

Public Papers of the Presidents: Richard N. Nixon 1970. Washington: Office of the Federal Register, National Archives and Records Service, General Services Administration 1970.

Pusey, Merlo J. *Eisenhower the President.* New York: Macmillan 1956.

Radford, Arthur W., and Stephen Jurika Jr. (ed.). *From Pearl Harbor to Vietnam: The Memoirs of Admiral Arthur W. Radford.* Stanford, Calif.: Hoover Institute Press 1980.

Ramsey, Don, with an introduction by Mamie Doud Eisenhower. *Ike: A Great American.* Kansas City: Hallmark Cards 1972.

Randall, Forrest. *Richard M. Nixon Project: Oral History Program.* Interview no. 934. Fullerton, Calif.: California State University 1970.

Rangell, L. "Aggression, Oedipus, and Historical Perspective." *International Journal of Psychoanalysis* 58 (1972): 3–11.

Rank, Otto. "Emotion and Denial." *Journal of the Otto Rank Association* 3 (1968): 9–25.

Reedy, George. *Lyndon B. Johnson: A Memoir.* New York: Andrews and McMeel 1982.

Reich, Annie. "Pathogenic Forms of Self-Esteem Regulation." *Psychoanalytic Study of the Child* 15 (1960): 215–31.

Reston, James. "Dulles Returning to Face Criticism on Asiatic Policy." *New York Times,* 4 May 1954.

Ridgway, Matthew B. *Soldier: The Memoirs of Matthew B. Ridgway.* New York: Curtis 1956.

Roberts, Chalmers M. "The Day We Didn't Go to War." *Reporter,* 11 September 1954: 14.

Rochlin, G. *Man's Aggression: The Defense of the Self.* Boston: Gambit 1973.

Roosevelt, Franklin, D. *Roosevelt Presidential Press Conferences.* 1 July 1941, vol. 18: 6–7. Franklin D. Roosevelt Library, Hyde Park, New York.

Rostow, Walt W. *The United States in the World Arena: An Essay in Recent History.* New York: Harper 1960.

Rothstein, Arnold. *The Narcissistic Pursuit of Perfection.* New York: International Universities Press 1984.

Rovere, Richard H. "Letter From Washington, September 29, 1955." *The Eisenhower Years.* New York: Farrar, Straus 1956. Orig. publ. in the *New Yorker,* 17 April 1954: 71–2.

Rowe Jr, James H. Oral History, 1969. Lyndon B. Johnson Library, Austin, Texas.

– Rowe Papers. Franklin D. Roosevelt Library, Hyde Park, New York.

Russell, Richard. Letter to L. Wolfson, 4 January 1966. General File, International Series-Vietnam, Russell Memorial Library, University of Georgia, Athens, Georgia.

Rust, William J. *Kennedy in Vietnam.* New York: Scribners 1985.

Safire, William. *Before the Fall: An Insider's View of the Pre-Watergate White House.* New York: Da Capo Press 1975.

Sandler, J., A. Holder and D. Meers, "The Ego Ideal and the Ideal Self." *The Psychoanalytic Study of the Child* 18 (1963): 139–58.

Sandler, J. "Panel Discussion on 'Aggression.'" *International Journal of Psychoanalysis* 53 (1972): 13–19.

Saunders, Richard M. "Military Force in the Foreign Policy of the Eisenhower Presidency." *Political Science Quarterly* 100 (1985–86): 97–116.

Schell, Jonathan. *The Time of Illusion.* New York: Vintage 1976.

Schlesinger, Jr, Arthur. *A Thousand Days: John F. Kennedy in the White House.* Boston: Houghton Mifflin 1965.

– *The Bitter Heritage: Vietnam and American Democracy, 1941–1966.* Boston: Houghton Mifflin 1967.

– Book review of *JFK and Vietnam: Deception, Intrigue, and the Struggle for Power,* by John M. Newman. *New York Times,* 29 March 1992: 3, 31.

Senate Papers, October 1960. Lyndon B. Johnson Library, Austin, Texas.

Shapley, Deborah. *Promise and Power: The Life and Times of Robert McNamara.* Boston: Little, Brown 1993.

Shawcross, William. *Sideshow: Kissinger, Nixon and the Destruction of Cambodia.* New York: Andre Deutsch 1979.

Shearer, Lloyd. "Richard Nixon and Ola-Florence Welch: 'Everyone Expected Them to Get Married.'" *Parade,* 28 June 1970.

Sidey, Hugh. "The Man and Foreign Policy," in Kenneth W. Thompson, ed., *Portraits of American Presidents. Vol. 6: The Nixon Presidency.* Lanham, Md.: University Press of America 1987: 299–314.

Slater, Ellis. *The Ike I Knew.* Privately printed (1980).

Smith, Paul S. *Richard M. Nixon Project: Oral History Program.* Interview no. 814. Fullerton, Calif.: California State University 1977.

Snyder, Orin. Oral History, 1964. Dwight D. Eisenhower Library, Abilene, Kansas.

Solberg, Carl. *Hubert Humphrey.* New York: W.W. Norton 1984.

Spalding, Henry, D. *The Nixon Nobody Knows*. Middle Village, N.Y.: Jonathan David 1972.

Special Report on American Opinion, 22 July 1954, box 42, File: Southeast Asia, 1953–1961. Washington, D.C.: National Archives.

Spero, M.H. "Shame: An Object-Relational Formulation." *Psychoanalytic Study of the Child* 39 (1984): 259–82.

Stamm, J.L., "The Meaning of Humiliation and Its Relationship to Fluctuations in Self-Esteem." *International Review of Psychoanalysis*, 5 (1978): 425–33.

Steinberg, Alfred. *Sam Johnson's Boy*. New York: Macmillan 1968.

Steinberg, Blema S. "Shame and Humiliation in the Cuban Missile Crisis: A Psychoanalytic Perspective." *Political Psychology* 12 (1991): 653–90.

Stone, L. "Reflections on the Psychoanalytic Concept of Aggression." *Journal of the American Psychoanalytic Society* 27 (1979): 195–243.

Storr, Anthony. *Human Aggression*. New York: Atheneum 1968.

Sullivan, Harry S. *The Interpersonal Theory of Psychiatry*. New York: W.W. Norton 1953.

Szulc, Tad. *The Illusion of Peace: Foreign Policy in the Nixon Years*. New York: Viking Press 1978.

Tang, Truong Nhu with David Chanoff and Doan Van Toai. *A Viet Cong Memoir*. New York: Vintage Press 1985.

Teger, Allen I., Mary Cary, Aaron Katcher, and Jay Hills. *Too Much Invested to Quit*. Elmsford, N.Y.: Pergamon Press 1980.

Thomson, Jr, James C. "How Could Vietnam Happen? An Autopsy." *The Atlantic Monthly*, April 1968: 47–53.

Timberlake, Edith M. *Richard M. Nixon Project: Oral History Program*. Interview no. 969. Fullerton, Calif.: California State University 1970.

Turley, William. *The Second Indochina War: A Short Political and Military History, 1954–1975*. New York: New American Library 1987.

Valenti, Jack. *A Very Human President*. New York: W.W. Norton, 1975.

Vertzberger, Yaacov Y. *The World in Their Minds: Information Processing, Cognition and Perception in Foreign Policy Decisionmaking*. Stanford, Calif.: Stanford University Press 1990.

Volkan, Vamik. *Primitive Internalized Object Relations: A Clinical Study of Schizophrenic, Borderline and Narcissistic Patients*. New York: International Universities Press 1976.

– "Narcissistic Personality Disorder," in J. Cavenor, J.O. and H.K. Brodie, eds., *Critical Problems Psychiatry*. Philadelphia: J.B. Lippincott 1982: 332–50.

Volkan, Vamik and Norman Itzkowitz. *The Immortal Ataturk* Chicago: University of Chicago Press 1984.

– Norman Itzkowitz, and Andrew Dod. *Richard Milhous Nixon: A Psychobiographical Portrait.* Unpublished manuscript (1991).

Waelder, Robert. "Critical Discussion of the Concept of an Instinct of Destruction." *Bulletin of the Philadelphia Association for Psychoanalysis* 6 (1956): 97–109.

West, Merle. *Richard M. Nixon Project: Oral History Program.* Interview no. 981. Fullerton, Calif.: California State University 1970.

Westen, Drew. "Psychoanalytic Approaches to Personality," in Lawrence A. Pervin, ed., *Handbook of Personality.* New York: Guilford Press 1990: 21–65.

Westmoreland, William C. "Vietnam in Perspective." *The Retired Officer,* October 1978: 21–4.

Weymouth, Lally. "The Word from Mamma Buff." *Esquire,* November 1977: 154–7, 200–12.

Whalen, Richard. *Catch the Falling Flag: A Republican's Challenge to His Party.* Boston: Houghton Mifflin 1972.

Wheeler, Keith and William Lambert. "The Man Who is the President – How LBJ's Family Amassed Its Fortune." *Life,* 21 August 1964.

White, Theodore H. *The Making of the President 1964.* New York: Atheneum 1965.

– *The Making of the President 1968.* London: Jonathan Cape 1969.

Wicker, Tom. *LBJ and JFK: The Influence of Personality upon Politics.* New York: William Morrow 1968.

– *One of Us: Richard Nixon and the American Dream.* New York: Random House 1990.

Wildermuth, Floyd. *Richard M. Nixon Project: Oral History Program.* Interview no. 983. Fullerton, Calif.: California State University 1970.

Wills, Garry. *Nixon Agonistes: The Crisis of the Self Made Man.* Boston: Houghton Mifflin 1969.

– *The Kennedy Imprisonment: A Meditation on Power.* Boston: Little, Brown 1981.

Winnicott, D.W. "Aggression in Relation to Emotional Development," in *Collected Papers.* New York: Basic Books 1975: 204–18.

Witcover, Jules. *The Resurrection of Richard Nixon.* New York: G.P. Putnam's Sons 1970.

Wurmser, Leon. *The Mask of Shame.* Baltimore, Md.: Johns Hopkins Press 1981.

– "Shame, the Veiled Companion of Narcissism," in D.L. Nathanson, ed., *The Many Faces of Shame.* New York: Guilford 1987: 64–92.

Zagoria, D.S. *Vietnam Triangle: Moscow, Peking, Hanoi.* New York: Pegasus 1968.

Index*

ABC-TV, 176
Abilene (Kansas), 209, 215, 219, 238
Abraham, Karl, 10
Abrams, Creighton, 173, 179, 187, 194, 198, 303, 335n10
Acheson, Dean, 98, 303, 322n10, 349n4, 360n22
Adams, Duque, and Hazeltine (law firm), 166, 167
Adams, Earl, 166
Adams, Sherman, 151, 247, 270, 276, 289; *First Hand Report* (memoirs), 289
aggression, 11, 15, 360n6; Berkowitz on, 360n6; Bowlby on, 21; destructive (defined), 18; Fairbairn on, 20; and foreign-policy decision making, 5, 23–4, 308; Freud (A.) on, 19, 20; Freud (S.) on, 18, 20; and grandiosity, 20; Guntrip on, 20; Hartmann on, 21; identification with the aggressor, 14, 20, 143, 314n33; Kagan on, 21; Kernberg on, 19–20; Klein on, 19; Kohut on, 22, 316n79; and leader-

ship, 23–4, 308; Mitchell on, 20–1; and narcissism, 8, 12, 18–24, 334n156; non-destructive (defined), 18, 315n59; oral, 16, 19, 126; Parens on, 22–3; Rochlin on, 23; Sandler on, 20; Stern on, 21; Sullivan on, 20, 21; theories of, 18–23; Waelder on, 22; Winnicott on, 21. *See also under* DDE(5), LBJ(5), RN(5)
Agnew, Spiro, 184, 189, 193
Aiken, George, 120
Air Force One, 37, 83, 174
Albert (Texas), 33
Alexander, Harold, 234
Alice (Texas), 58
Alsop, Joseph, 76, 89, 90–2, 94, 324n57
Alsop, Stewart, 147–8
Ambrose, Stephen, 163
American Bar Association, 181
American Friends of Vietnam, 96
American Psychiatric Association, 313n28
Americans for Democratic Action (ADA), 74

---

* This index uses the abbreviations DDE (Dwight David Eisenhower), LBJ (Lyndon Baines Johnson), and RN (Richard Nixon). The entries for DDE, LBJ, and RN are divided into numbered sections, which are identified in *See under* and *See also under* cross-references in the following manner: DDE(1).

Resor, Stanley, 328n144
Reston, James, 161, 306
Restoration of the Self, The (Kohut), 22
Reuther, Walter, 66
Revolutionary League for the Indepen-
dence of Vietnam. *See* Viet Minh
Rhee, Syngman, 251, 307
Rhodes, James, 205
Richards, Horace, 43
Richardson, Elliot, 177, 187
Richardson, Ralph, 70
Ridgway, Matthew B., 261, 266
River Brethren (Mennonite group),
208, 209
Rives, Lloyd, 189
RN: The Memoirs of Richard Nixon
(Nixon). *See under* RN(1)
Robertson, Walter, 251
Rochlin, G., 23
Rock Crusher, Operation, 196
Rockefeller Foundation, 80
Rockefeller, Nelson, 196
Rogers, William, 150, 175, 176, 177,
180, 187, 188, 190, 192, 193–4, 195–
6, 198
Rolling Thunder, Operation, 25, 99–
100, 103
Roosevelt, Eleanor, 141
Roosevelt, Franklin Delano (FDR), 48–
9, 51, 55, 155, 231, 233, 246
Roosevelt, James, 233
Roosevelt, Theodore (Teddy), 205
Rose, Alex, 66
Ross, E.P., 37
Ross, Kitty Clyde, 36–8, 49
Rostow, W.W., 303
Rowan, Carl, 327n133
Rowe, Jim, 54, 67, 68
Rusk, Dean, 72–3, 76, 87, 88, 93; back-
ground, 80; as LBJ adviser, 78, 79–81,
89, 92, 96, 98, 99, 100, 106, 108–9,
293, 295, 303, 327n133
Russell, Richard, 60, 79, 80, 81, 120,
301
Russia. *See* Union of Soviet Socialist Re-
publics
Ryan, Thelma Catherine. *See* Nixon, Pat

Safire, William, 197
Saigon, 91, 93, 175, 350n19
St Johns, Mac, 141

Salas, Luis, 59
Sam Houston High School (Houston),
46
Sam Rayburn Library, 54
Sandler, Joseph, 20
San Juan Hill, 205
San Marcos (Texas), 38, 445
Saxbe, William, 182–3
Schee, Marie, 144–5
Schell, Jonathan, 198
Schlesinger, Arthur, Jr, 65, 74
Seat, Fred, 151
SEATO. *See* Southeast Asia Treaty Organization
Securities and Exchange Commission,
56
self-esteem: and foreign-policy decision
making, 4, 307–8; and humiliation,
9–10, 11–14; and leadership, 4, 307–
8; and narcissism, 5, 12, 14, 17, 21–2,
23, 136, 300, 334n156; Rochlin on,
23; and shame, 8, 9, 11–14. *See also
under* DDE(5); LBJ(5); RN(5)
Senate (United States), 60–2, 68–9, 86,
120, 179, 196, 201, 258- 9, 263, 273,
300, 301, 305; armed services committee, 258; foreign relations committee, 184–5, 186, 194, 199, 258.
See also Congress *and under* LBJ(2);
RN(2)
separation (psychological concept),
11, 12, 21
17th parallel (Vietnam), 287, 305, 307
Seward, William, 69
shame, 7, 23, 335n10; Abraham on, 10;
Bursten on, 12; defined, 8–9; Erikson
on, 11; Fenichel on, 10; and foreign-
policy decision making, 4–5, 23–4,
307–9; Freud (S.) on, 10, 11; humiliation as a variant of, 8–10, 313n9; Jacobson on, 10; Kohut on, 312n7; Kris
on, 9; and leadership, 4–5, 23–4,
307–9; and narcissism, 4, 5, 8, 9, 10,
11–14, 23–4, 300, 312n7, 313n28,
336n36; psychoanalytic explanations
of, 10–14; Rank on, 11; and self-esteem, 8, 9, 11–14; Wurmser on, 12.
See also under DDE(5); LBJ(5); RN(5)
Sharp, Ulysses G., 326n100
Sheppard, Morris, 50
Sherwood, Georgia, 141